OFF COLOR

OFF COLOR

The Violent History of Detroit's Notorious Purple Gang

DANIEL WAUGH

Photographs
As credited and used with permission. Front cover: Members of the Purple Gang
under arrest at the Detroit Police Department's Thirteenth Precinct in May 1929,
(author's collection) and mug shots (from left) Louis Fleisher *(author's collection)*,
Harry Sutton *(NARA),* and Raymond Burnstein *(State of Michigan archives).* Back
cover: Joe Burnstein, *(Wayne State Collection),* superimposed over a photograph of
Ben Bronston's body in the street in front of 3318 Sturtevant Street in Detroit after
being killed by the Purple Gang on June 21, 1931 *(author's collection).*

Published
In the United States of America by In-Depth Editions, 2014
www.in-deptheditions.com
18 17 16 15 14   5 4 3 2 1
First Edition

Publisher Cataloging-in-Publication Data
Waugh, Daniel
Off color: The violent history of Detroit's notorious purple gang
336 p. : 55 ill., map
Includes bibliographical references and endnotes (296-330)
ISBN 978-09889772-2-8 (pbk: alk paper)
1. The Purple Gang 2. Burnstein, Abe
3. Gangsters—Michigan—Detroit—Biography 4. Fleisher, Harry
5. Organized crime—Michigan—Detroit—History.
6. United States History—20th Century.
7. Michigan—History.
I. Title. II. Author.

2014
364.1 Wau   2014940473

For Cookie

ABOUT THE AUTHOR

Daniel Waugh grew up in Northwest Detroit. After hearing stories of the Purple Gang as a teen, curiosity got the better of him. In the two decades since, Waugh accrued a vast knowledge of this country's Prohibition-era mobsters and has spoken both in person and on radio about this topic. He is also the author of *Egan's Rats* and *Gangs of St. Louis*.

CONTENTS

If you're part of a crew, nobody ever tells you that
they're going to kill you. It doesn't happen that way.
There aren't any arguments or curses like in the movies.
Your murderers come with smiles. They come as your
friends, the people who have cared for you all your life,
and they always come at a time when you are at your
weakest and most in need of their help.

- Henry Hill

AUTHOR NOTES

I remember the day I first discovered the Purple Gang very clearly. I was a mere sixteen years old and sitting down in the kitchen of my Northwest Detroit house to thumb through the morning's edition of the *Free Press*. It was another bleak day, with the sky the color of gunmetal and heavy clumps of March snow on the ground. In the "Other Voices" section, a brief story by Editor Neal Shine caught his eye. Entitled "Distilled Memories," it was about the Purple Gang. I had vaguely heard of them before, the biggest Prohibition-era gang in Detroit and a staple of local folklore for years. As Shine wrote, "Part of their success can be traced to the uncommonly low survival rate of their competitors."

I was fascinated. My attention was particularly drawn to the line-up picture of some of the Purples that accompanied the story. Originally taken almost exactly sixty-six years before, the picture showed a few of the gang's main members under arrest during the "Cleaners and Dyers War." Like other youths my age, I had seen my share of gangster movies, such as *The Untouchables, The Godfather*, and *GoodFellas*. I especially liked the tales of Prohibition, with its illegal booze, Tommy Guns, and blood feuds.

Most other kids I knew preferred Al Pacino's Tony Montana character from *Scarface* to the old-school gangsters. Besides, my side of Detroit had more than it's fair share of tough guys in the early 1990s. The Bloods and Crips were well represented, with a few Folk sets thrown into the mix. There were immeasurable gangs named after streets and neighborhoods (SNS, Linwood Boyz, etc.). There was even a crew that dubbed themselves the "Nautica Boyz," after their preferred line of clothing. Just a few days before, one kid I knew had proudly displayed a brand-new AK-47 assault rifle that he had just acquired.

Farther up Detroit's criminal food chain from the street gangs were the big time drug dealers, like the Chambers Brothers, Butch Jones and the Y.B.I. (Young Boys, Inc.). There were the leaders of Best Friends, Demetrious Holloway and Maserati Rick Carter. After the latter's 1988 assassination, he was interred in a custom-made $16,500 silver casket that was shaped like a Mercedes Benz (complete with gold rims and a license plate.) In the face of such modern gangsterism, the Purple Gang just didn't seem relevant. The Purples and the Best Friends had about as much in common with each other as a harquebus does with an UZI. Both criminally and culturally, they could not have been more different.

But I couldn't stop thinking of the picture; the line-up photo that went with Neal Shine's article that featured Detroit's original "Bad Boys" G'ed up in suits, overcoats, spats, flat caps and fedoras. Some, such as Harry Fleisher, blinked from the flash when the camera clicked, but others glared back in defiance. One of the boys, hit man Abe Axler, sat on a chair in front of the group, a large diamond ring on his finger and a what-the-hell-you-looking-at sneer on his hollow face. Looking into the eyes of the long dead Axler, I saw there *was* something he had in common with Maserati Rick; that look in the eyes of determination, toughness, resiliency, and street-smarts. The look that basically said, "*The only way to stop me is to kill me.*" Perhaps they were not so different after all.

Since I hadn't heard of the Internet yet, I stuck my nose in a few books to learn more about the Purples. Most sources had brief, contradictory notes about the gang; mostly that they dominated the city of Detroit during Prohibition and committed over 500 murders (more than Al Capone's mob in Chicago, the books trumpeted). Crime historian Herbert Asbury called them, "…the most efficiently organized gang of killers in the United States." They were suspected of participating in the St. Valentine's Day Massacre and the Lindbergh baby kidnapping. The stories usually ended with a line about them peacefully disbanding and joining a national gambling syndicate led by New York gangster Meyer Lansky.

Local anecdotes about the Purples abounded. That was one thing all Detroiters had, old or young, rich or poor, black or white, everyone had a story about the Purple Gang;

Five hundred murders, hell, the Purps offed a THOUSAND, if anything, kid.

Capone had nothing to do with the Valentine's Day Massacre, the Purples did it own their own because Bugs Moran was hijacking their booze shipments.

The Purples used a dance hall up on Gratiot Avenue as a meeting place.

The Purples spent their summers along Lake St. Clair.

Or at St. Joseph.

Or at Cheboygan.

The Purples knocked off radio muckraker Jerry Buckley when he was getting too close.

The Purple Gang planted drugs in the soil of Bay City parks.

The Purples ran illegal gambling on Hastings Street with the help of a one-legged black gangster.

The Purple Gang found the axe-murderer that chopped up the Evangelista family and put him in a cement overcoat before they dumped him in the river.

The Purples ran booze out of Flint and robbed banks in Albion.

The Purple Gang gave the Mafia their marching orders and made Capone and Luciano shit shotgun shells.

The stories continued rising to the surface like bubbles in a case of Faygo, some more crazy than others. The Purple Gang had mushroomed from a Detroit street gang into a regional menace. It seemed that every time someone in the state of Michigan reminisced about some shady characters doing shady things back in the day, it was invariably said to be the work of the Purple Gang.

Was any of it true? It was impossible to tell the difference between fact and folklore. And, because there were no printed answers to my questions, I went looking for them on my own. On an off day I jumped in my sky-blue Oldsmobile Cutlass and went down to the main library on Woodward Avenue, where I found that facility's newspaper microfilm projectors were out of order.

Disappointed but not really surprised, I got back behind the wheel of my hoopdie (bashed-in front end, slushy brakes, gleaming chrome rims) and aimed it west on the Jeffries Freeway, trading the potholes and white pine houses of the city for the sterile halls of Ann Arbor academia. At the University of Michigan's undergraduate library, scanning old newspapers of the 1920s and 1930s, the real Purple Gang began slowly to emerge. I was mesmerized as the pieces began to audibly fall into place. Without even realizing it, I had begun to write the book you are about to read.

OF COURSE, I hadn't set out to write *anything* that day. I had no idea that a mild curiosity about the Purple Gang would lead to a two-decade long obsession with early 20th century organized crime. As time passed, my knowledge of the Purples and other early Detroit gangsters increased.

While driving a taxicab around the city of Detroit during the winter of 2000-01, I began weaving the story of its early gangster history together in my first attempt at a book. I plugged away feverishly in my off hours (imagine if Travis Bickle spent his free time writing about long-dead mobsters instead of stamping crosses into the tips of bullets.) It grew to be a sprawling history that not only covered the Purple Gang, but the early years of the city's Mafia family and other Prohibition bootleggers. I detailed the Giannola-Vitale gang war of 1919-21, a disturbingly violent conflict that I had *never even heard of before*. The book covered the equally bloody "Crosstown War" of 1930-31 and eventually ended the narrative after the 1945 assassination of Michigan State Senator Warren Hooper. After finishing on St. Patrick's Day, 2001, I christened it *Misplaced Wiseguys: The Forgotten Gangsters of Early 20th Century Detroit*. Not the snappiest title in the world, but it was from the heart.

I realized two things right off the bat; that this work was enormous (430 pages) and completely unpublishable. Despite my good intentions, my skills as a writer and researcher left something to be desired. Not long after I finished, I discovered that Detroit-area engineer/historian Paul R. Kavieff had published his own groundbreaking book about the Purple Gang. Needless to say, I felt as if the wind had gone out of my sails. Anything I had to say on the Purples seemed superfluous at that point. Thus, my manuscript went into the fabled "trunk," or in my case, a series of computer hard drives. I did nothing, and nothing did me back.

I continued to drive my cab, but I was still bitten by the bug. As if being pulled by some unseen magnet, I spent most of my time picking up fares on the Purple Gang's old North End turf. Oakland Avenue, Brush, Woodward, 12th Street, Clairmount, Linwood, Dexter, Chicago…I soon knew the neighborhood like the back of my hand. While many of the physical landmarks associated with the Purples were long gone, I knew the addresses by rote. For example, I couldn't help but think of the night Irving Shapiro was killed every time I cruised through the 2400 block of Taylor Street.

As the years passed, my ability as a writer and researcher gradually improved, and I was fortunate enough to have my first book published in 2007 about the St. Louis-based Egan's Rats gang, and followed it up three years later with *Gangs of St. Louis: Men of Respect*. A month or so after my second work was published, I found myself idly perusing my long-languishing Detroit manuscript one lazy Sunday afternoon. For reasons I can't fully explain, I spent the next half-hour or so splitting the original work into two files; one for the Mafia/Partnership and one for the Purples. It turned out to be a fateful decision.

In the winter of 2012, one of my trusted colleagues, Chicago-based author/historian Jeffrey Gusfield, asked to take a look at my Purple Gang manuscript. Now neatly condensed into one crisp document, it was easy to read. To my surprise, he loved it. Suddenly, I felt a reinvigorated sense of purpose regarding my early work. Perhaps there *was* something I could add to the Purple Gang's story, after all. After a rewrite and editing session, this work is the product of my twenty-year fascination with the Purple Gang.

Nowadays in the 21st century, it's easy to view the gangsters of Prohibition as mythological, almost quaint figures. Their exploits are now far enough in the past that the only living Americans that have even a vague memory of them were only children at the time, and unlikely to have any real knowledge of what was really going down on the street. Films like *Miller's Crossing* and *Road to Perdition*, as well as the HBO series *Boardwalk Empire*, present Chesterfield-clad mobsters that seem as distant to us now as the grubby gunslingers that inhabited the epic Sergio Leone spaghetti westerns of the 1960s. The tools of their trade, like six-shot .38 revolvers, the M1911 Colt .45 automatic, and even the world-famous Thompson submachine gun (Tommy Gun) seem woefully inadequate next to modern ordinance like helicopter-mounted mini-guns, laser-sighted machine pistols, and satellite-guided drone strikes.

Despite the vast chasm of time that has elapsed (a minimum of three-quarters of a century), there are still a handful of people alive today who remember when booze was illegal in Detroit, who remember the Purple Gang, who remember running errands for the Purples, and who spent the vast duration of their long lives without their fathers specifically because of the Purples.

With that said, it is not my intention in this book to condemn these men; many of whom were fathers, sons, brothers, uncles, and cousins. Not every man named in this work had cloven hooves and a pointed tail, so to speak, and a few of them did manage to live productive lives after they finished their association with the Purple Gang. Nothing can be served by me getting on a soapbox, preaching about law-and-order, morality, and other such righteous topics that seem to be all the rage in 21st century true-crime books.

On the other hand, it is also not my intention to lionize these men, either. Many of the crimes committed by the Purple Gang ruined livelihoods, families, and lives. Whenever possible, the Purples murdered their victims when they were unarmed and unable to resist; one of whom was a seventeen-year old ice peddler who had the audacity to *not* be intimidated by them. Lest anyone think that Detroit's Prohibition-era gangsters were somehow more "honorable" or "noble" than Detroit's present-day inner-city gangsters, keep in mind that on one *Psycho*-like occasion, a member of the Purple Gang rammed an ice pick into the brain of a helpless man and then proceeded to break off the blade in his skull as the victim's bowels voided.

I WOULD LIKE TO HUMBLY extend my thanks to my family for their continuous support. Thanks to Elizabeth Murray Clemens at Wayne State University's Walter Reuther Library, as well as Steve Spence at the Kansas City branch of the National Archives. Special thanks to Bill Helmer, Jeffery Gusfield, and the late Rick "Mad Dog" Mattix. Thanks to Mario Gomes, who runs the best Al Capone site on the web at www.myalcaponemuseum.com. Special thanks to Chriss Lyon and Valerie van Heest for helping to facilitate this work. Thanks to Rose Keefe for reviewing the book. Thanks to Judge Neill and Tim O'Neil of the St. Louis Post-Dispatch. Thanks to Griff, Vince, and Uncle Mickey for being themselves. Thank you to St. Louis-based freelance artist J. Rickman for recreating four drawings from horrible newspaper microfilm photocopies. Thank you to the team at In-Depth Editions for doing what it took to get this in print.

IN CLOSING, I've tried to create as complete and impartial a version of the Purple Gang's story as I can muster. The reader may notice that I have written my book in strict chronological order, and that I do not actually refer to the Purple Gang as the "Purple Gang" in print until early 1928; the reason for this is that they did not become known as such to the Detroit public until this point in the narrative. Before this, I refer to them by their original name of "Sugar House Gang." If you, the reader, are curious as to how I reached a conclusion on a particular fact, please check my endnotes. Despite my best Virgo-inspired efforts to ensure that this work would be perfect, I'd never dream to say that it actually is. Any mistakes in this book are mine and mine alone. Thank you for taking the time to read this, and I hope you enjoy *Off Color* at least *half* as much as I enjoyed producing it.

- Daniel Waugh

This cropped group shot of Purple Gang mobsters shows Abe Axler sitting in the chair front and center. *Walter Reuther Library.*

SOBRIQUET

I t is uncertain exactly where the name came from. The Detroit media didn't start using the term until the winter of 1928. The most popular story says it originated in 1918 with two Jewish pushcart merchants on Hastings Street that had been victimized by delinquent boys from the neighborhood. After one such raid, the peddlers muttered to each other, "Those boys are tainted, off-color!"

"Yeah, purple. That's what they are," the other replied. "Purple, they're a purple gang."[1]

Another account had that same group of rambunctious kids skipping out of school to spend warm spring days at a cottage on Lake St. Clair, where they would don purple swimming trunks and go for a dip. Some claim it originated in the so-called Cleaners and Dyers War, when gangsters looking to terrorize recalcitrant cleaning plant employees would ruin expensive bundles of clothing by dousing them with purple paint. Others say it came from Eddie Fletcher, a featherweight boxer and one of its most dangerous members: During his fights he and his seconds wore bright purple jerseys. Another account has it coming from an early crew member, Sammy Purple.[2]

Detroit gambler Lou Wertheimer told the FBI in the 1930s that the moniker originated during a violent trade war between rival taxi companies. The hired thugs who secured victory for the Purple Line Company appropriated their name for themselves.[3]

Detroit News reporter John "Jack" Carlisle, who covered the city's crime beat during Prohibition, said the name was coined by an inventive police inspector.[4] Yet another version was told by a David Levitt in 1990, "I was at the warehouse on Oakland Avenue where the boys hung out. It was a sugar warehouse. The boys called themselves the Sugar House Boys.

"We were sitting around and the boys discussed changing their name. One of the members, whose name was Silverstein, had a purple sweater on. Someone suggested Purple Gang. It stuck."[5]

Abe Burnstein was the long-term leader of the former Hastings Street gang that became known as the Purple Gang. *Walter Reuther Library.*

INCEPTION

Late 19th Century – Spring 1918

2

he vast majority of them came from peaceful, law-abiding homes, which made their violent evolution all the more shocking. They and their families had fled anti-Semitic persecution in Eastern Europe for a better life in America. First known as the Burnstein Boys, then as the Sugar House Gang, they would finally make their name under the catchy banner of Purple Gang. Their story begins not on the mean streets of Detroit, but in the hardscrabble countryside of western Russia.

THE RUSSIAN EMPIRE of the late nineteenth century was a vast realm that spread over nine million square miles and stretched from the forests of Poland to the icy waters of the Bering Strait. One hundred twenty-five million subjects who spoke nearly a dozen different languages peopled a monarchy that was rivaled only by the British Empire in terms of sheer size. For all its might, however, Imperial Russia had been largely bypassed by the Industrial Revolution due to its continued dependence on the antiquated practice of serf-based labor.

The emancipation reform of 1861 infused Russian industry like never before and resulted in impressive economic growth. Nevertheless, there still remained large gaps between the classes. Newly freed peasants had to pay exorbitant taxes to the government in order to cultivate what was often substandard land. Poor working conditions and periodic famine took their toll on the populace and eventually gave birth to radical political organizations that sought to break down the empire's rigid social order. No one typified that caste system more than the tsar and his family, who lived an opulent lifestyle largely detached from the bulk of Russian society in Moscow's White Palace.

Whether poor peasants, middle-class workers, or wealthy aristocrats, Russians of the late 19th century were a generally positive yet increasingly restless lot. There was no doubt, however, that the Jewish residents of "The

Pale" were considered by most Russians to be at the bottom of the empire's intricate social totem pole.

WHILE ANTI-SEMITISM had been present in Russia for hundreds of years, nowhere else in the empire was it more prevalent in the existence of the Pale of Settlement. Created in 1791 by Catherine the Great, this swath of land in western Russia was designated as the only place where Jews could legally reside while in the country. At its largest, the Pale took up about 20% of the empire's total land mass and included parts of the present day nations of Belarus, Lithuania, Moldova, Poland, and Ukraine.

Various decrees from a succession of Russian rulers forbid Jews for owning their own land, or attending schools, or heavily censored Hebrew and Yiddish texts. Most Jews were prohibited from even traveling outside the Pale into Russia proper. Jewish children were frequently conscripted into the Russian military at extremely young ages, and often gave their lives in faraway lands for a Gentile empire that considered them a nuisance (at best) or an aberration from God (at worst.)[1]

The reign of Nicolas I, from 1825 to 1861, had been especially frightful. Six hundred anti-Jewish decrees were passed during that time period and the tsar himself had said, "The purpose in educating Jews is to bring about their gradual merging with the Christian nationalities and to uproot those superstitious and harmful prejudices which are instilled by the teachings of the Talmud." It was also under Nicolas's reign that the dreaded *pogrom* made its first insidious appearance. Essentially a violent mob attack by Gentiles against Jews, these riots claimed the lives of countless Jewish citizens and caused the residents of the Pale to live under the perpetual threat of destruction. The *New York Times* described one such *pogrom* thusly:

The anti-Jewish riots in Kishinev, Bessarabia, are worse than the censor will permit to publish. There was a well laid-out plan for the general massacre of Jews on the day following the Russian Easter. The mob was led by priests, and the general cry, "Kill the Jews," was taken- up all over the city. The Jews were taken wholly unaware and were slaughtered like sheep. The dead number 120 and the injured about 500. The scenes of horror attending this massacre are beyond description. Babes were literally torn to pieces by the frenzied and bloodthirsty mob. The local police made no attempt to check the reign of terror. At sunset the streets were piled with corpses and wounded. Those who could make their escape fled in terror, and the city is now practically deserted of Jews.[2]

THE GOVERNANCE OF Nicolas's successor, Alexander II, brought a welcome relief to Russian Jews. Under his watch, the conscription time for Jews in the Russian military was reduced from twenty-five years to five; the doors of Russian universities were opened to some Jews, and select Jewish businessmen were allowed to travel throughout the empire, among other things. However, most of Alexander's liberal reforms died upon his assassination by bomb in March 1881. While the fatal bomb thrower was revealed to be a Russian Gentile, it came out that a Jewish seamstress had rented the apartment that the conspirators used as a headquarters. As a result, violent anti-Semitism broke out afresh in Russia. The murder of the tsar and the *pogroms* that came along with its aftermath sparked the great Diaspora of over two million Jewish citizens to the points around the globe.

Those Jews that remained behind in the Pale continued their harsh, segregated lifestyle. Denied the opportunity to own and cultivate land by law, many Jews embraced artisan trades such as those of merchants, shopkeepers, bakers, blacksmiths, tailors, and jewelers. Most Jews lived in small towns known as *shtetls* while others gravitated to cluttered neighborhoods (*ghettoes*) in large cities. Some towns specifically barred Jews from residing within their limits.[3]

The *shtetl* itself was usually a small town that perhaps sported cobblestone rather than dirt streets and maybe a handful of imposing structures. The amenities usually ended there, however. One chronicler of the day provided this unflattering view of the average *shtetl*:

...a jumble of wooden houses clustered higgledy-piggledy about a market-place...as crowded as a slum...The streets...are as tortuous as a Talmudic argument. They are bent into question marks and folded into parentheses. They run into culs-de-sac like a theory arrested by a fact; they ooze off into lanes, alleys, back yards...[At the center is] the market-place, with its shops, booths, tables, stands, butchers' blocks. Hither come daily, except during the winter, the peasants and peasant women from many miles around, bringing their livestock and vegetables, their fish and hides, their wagonloads of grain, melons, parsley, radishes, and garlic. They buy, in exchange, the city produce which Jews import, dry goods, hats, shoes, boots, lamps, oil, spades, mattocks, and shirts. The tumult of the market-place...is one of the wonders of the world.[4]

In addition to the holy language of Hebrew, most Jews of the Pale conversed daily in Yiddish, a High German language that originated as a fusion of Hebrew and Aramaic in the first centuries of the previous millennium. They worshiped in *shul* (synagogue) and sent their children to *cheder* (school), where the *melamed* (teacher) instructed them on the Torah, reading and writing, and other worldly skills.

Whether in a small-town *shtetl* or a big-city *ghetto*, the Jews of the Pale lived a very confined existence. Shunned by the vast majority of their Gentile neighbors, they depended on themselves and on one another (the first Russian *yeshiva* programs were founded during the late 19th century.) As a result, they mostly regarded the world outside the Pale with fear and trepidation. There was always the constant threat that government soldiers and/or bloodthirsty Gentiles would descend upon their self-contained environment and destroy it. Some regarded such hazards with grim resignation, as if the *pogroms* were punishment from a vengeful God.

However, not all denizens of the Pale lived in perpetual fear. Indeed, some wanted to fight back. Jewish-American gangster Meyer Lansky remembered one such individual when recounting his Russian childhood to Israeli journalist Uri Dan:

"One man – I don't remember his name, but I wish I did – held a meeting at my grandfather's house. 'Jews', he shouted. 'Why do you just stand around like stupid sheep and let them come and kill you, steal your money, kill your sons, and rape your daughters? Aren't you ashamed? You must stand up and fight. You are men like other men. A Jew can fight. We have no arms, but it doesn't matter. We can use sticks and stones. Fight back! Don't be frightened. Hit them and they'll run. If you're going to die, then die fighting.'

"This speech is burned into my memory…I carried the words with me when I finally traveled with my mother to America and the Lower East Side. I remembered those words when I fought back at the Irish as a boy on the East Side. They were like flaming arrows in my head."[5]

Not only were there people who were prepared to resist persecution, there were also those who chose to live outside the law. Like the rest of the civilized world, social banditry had been present in Russia for nearly as long as anyone remembered. Toward the end of the 19th century, many cities and towns were plagued by clans of criminals who belonged to what was known as the *Vorovskoy Mir* (Thieves' World), a secret yet loosely organized brotherhood that featured its own cryptic slang (*fenya*) and adhered to a strict code of conduct that emphasized loyalty to one another as well as opposition to the Russian government. These men were noted primarily as smugglers, extortionists, and bandits. Very often they would plunder from the Gentile government and redistribute the wealth to their Jewish brethren Robin Hood-style. These men often included some of the wealthiest and strongest individuals of their community. In idle moments, the *vory* (thieves) would often repair to a local *beder* (bath house) to have a *shvitz* (sweat) and discuss the business.[6]

Renowned Russian-Jewish author Isaak Babel touched on these hoodlums in *The Odessa Tales*, his excellent collection of short stories that depict a group of Jewish gangsters led by a *vor* (thief) named Benya Krik, better known to the cognoscenti as "The King." These fictional yet colorful mobsters are perhaps best described by this poetic passage from *How Things Were Done In Odessa*: "Tartakovsky has the soul of a murderer, but he's one of us. He sprang forth from us. He is our blood. He is our flesh, as if one mama had given birth to us. Half of Odessa works in his stores."[7]

Those lines could easily apply to the men on whom this chronicle is based.

TOWARD THE END OF THE 1890s, economic hardship once again hit Russia, and the Pale felt its fair share of the pinch. The migrations that had begun with the *pogroms* of 1881 continued on, with Jews traveling to points west throughout Europe and, increasingly, America. Indeed, the Land of the Free was on the lips and minds of many Jews. Children would often pantomime immigration in the streets of the *shtetl* and adults frequently discussed those who had left for the United States or one that was leaving. Rare was the Jew who did not know someone who had made the arduous journey to what they hoped was a better life. Some saved all their resources for the trip while others sneered at the idea of going to such a foreign place. One said, "You are heading for a corrupt and sinful land where the Sabbath is no Sabbath. Even on Yom Kippur they don't fast. And for what purpose are you going there? So you can eat meat every day?…But their meat is *treyf* (non-Kosher.) No good Jew would touch such meat."[8] There were also elderly Jews who were in no physical condition to make such a lengthy, demanding trip.

It was right around the time of the first thaw of the late winter of 1902 that Sarah Burnstein received the letter she had been eagerly waiting for. Her husband Harry had departed for America three long years earlier in order to earn enough money for their whole family to finally escape the drudgery of the Pale. Harry was a cobbler by trade, and had been working very hard on the Lower East Side of New York City since his arrival in the spring of 1899.

Like most Russian Jews of the period, Harry Burnstein could not afford to take his entire family to America with him. He would have had to go first and earn enough money to bring the rest over. The strain of being separated must have been considerable for the Burnsteins. Would they be able to reunite as one family? More than a few Jews left for the United States over the years only to never be heard from again. Would a *pogrom* tear through their hometown in his absence? Would Sarah and/or the children be carried off by one of the lethal diseases that plagued the Russian countryside? Now, three years later, constant worry had given way to a cautious optimism. Thus in the spring of 1902, twenty-seven year old Sarah Burnstein prepared to leave the Pale forever with her five children (Eva, 12; Aberham, 11;[9] Jennie, 5; Ida, 4; and 2-year old Joseph.[10])

The trip the Burnsteins were proposing was no small enterprise. The going rate for a *single* steerage ticket to New York from European ports such as Hamburg, Bremen, or Antwerp was around $32 in 1902. Such a sum was a veritable fortune to some of the poorer Jewish denizens of the Pale; some hard luck travelers sold their final remaining belongings to make the voyage and arrived at Ellis Island completely destitute.

As western Russia was mostly landlocked, Jews leaving the Pale often had to make a long, circuitous trip across Eastern Europe to get to a suitable overseas port. Many America-bound immigrants crossed illegally into Austria-Hungary, where they would catch a train to Berlin or Vienna, from which they would proceed to Hamburg, Bremen, Amsterdam, or Antwerp, among other places. Some could choose a longer route through southwestern Russia and depart from Trieste, Italy. Other Jewish migrants from outside the Pale in the neighboring regions of Poland, Romania, or Austria-Hungary faced similar tribulations.

Although history did not record exactly how the Burnsteins began their trip to America, they almost certainly bid a sad farewell to their friends and any remaining family. After promising to write, the Burnsteins slipped across the border out of Russia en route to one of the various European ports that handled immigration to the states. Along the way, Sarah and the children would have had to contend with various military and law enforcement units of the countries they were passing through; thieves and con artists who were looking to fleece gullible indigents; sexual predators who would be ready to victimize a lone woman traveling with five small children; depending on how much money was available to them, the Burnsteins may have had to battle hunger and malnutrition, as well. Upon arrival upon the port city, customs officials would have subjected the family to a rigorous medical inspection before they would be allowed to board.

Their journey in steerage across the North Atlantic would have been no easier. The Burnsteins most probably spent the trip crammed into crowded compartments on the lower decks of an ocean liner, sharing their meager space with hundreds of fellow immigrants. If food was provided to the passengers, it was often substandard, and on some ships there was little to no cleanliness or hygiene. The vast majority of Jewish immigrants had never been to sea before, and any storms the group encountered on the capricious ocean must have been terrifying. As one man recalled some years later: [11]

"On board the ship we became utterly dejected. We were all herded together in a dark, filthy compartment in the steerage…Wooden bunks had been put up in two tiers…Seasickness broke out among us. Hundreds of people had vomiting fits, throwing up even their mother's milk…As all were crossing the ocean for the first time, they thought their end had come. The confusion of cries became unbearable…I wanted to escape from that inferno but no sooner had I thrust my head forward from the lower bunk than someone above me vomited straight onto my head. I wiped the vomit away, dragged myself onto the deck, leaned against the railing and vomited my share into the sea, and lay down half-dead upon the deck."

Despite the usually miserable conditions, there were those in good spirits. There may have been music, card playing; laughter; others eagerly discussing what awaited them in America. Some may have even been perusing Russian-English dictionaries to learn a few words of their new land's mother tongue. Regardless of their morale, the newcomers undoubtedly brightened when the gaudy structures of Coney Island came into view, representing their first glimpse of America. Within minutes, they would get their first glance at a legendary object they had merely heard of at that point; the Statue of Liberty.

After their ship docked at Ellis Island, Sarah and the children joined the teeming masses in order to gather their luggage and be herded like cattle into the large red-brick hall where new immigrants were processed. Inside the huge building, the bewildered Burnsteins lingered in line while their ears rang with the din of hundreds of people loudly babbling in various languages as Bureau of Immigration officials strained to hear the words of the interpreters designated to translate for the newcomers.

United States Public Health Service medical inspections loomed next as harried military physicians and nurses examined the immigrants for diseases and deformities. In order to save time, doctors often observed the newcomers as they trudged up the stairs of the Great Hall. Those who were discovered to have maladies were marked with white chalk and quarantined until their suitability for admittance could be determined. Some managed to slip into America by wiping off their chalk marks on the sly.

After enduring this grueling and often humiliating process, Sarah Burnstein and her five children were discharged into America in order to reunite with patriarch Harry. It was then that the newly arrived Burnsteins learned that their destiny lay not in New York City, but seven hundred miles to the west.

After an undoubtedly joyous reunion with Harry Burnstein, Sarah and the children were probably surprised to learn that they would be moving west as soon as possible. Harry had found the Lower East Side to be overcrowded and quite dangerous. Thousands of immigrants lived crammed into tenements that were often lacking in basic amenities. Roving street gangs made life a hazardous venture for those who stayed, as did the various diseases that jumped effortlessly from person-to-person in the densely populated district. Harry found his solution in the city of Detroit, Michigan, where the city's Jewish neighborhood reportedly had separate houses instead of cramped apartment blocks. The opportunity of owning their own home was too good for the Burnsteins to pass up.

Little could Harry and Sarah Burnstein have imagined that day in 1902 that they would be remembered primarily because of the affect this new city would have on their young boys.[12]

DÉTROIT. THE FRENCH WORD for "strait," it was how the new European settlers referred to both the fort and the river that connected Lake St. Clair and Lake Erie. In 1670, two French Sulpician missionaries named François Dollier de Casson and René Bréhant de Galinée landed on the flat riverside land while on their way north to Sault Ste. Marie. The two and their small party found a stone idol that was apparently worshiped by local Indians. The Frenchmen hacked the monument to pieces and tossed the detritus into the river before proceeding on their way.

A more permanent settlement came in 1701 at the behest of brilliant French explorer and adventurer Antoine Laumet de La Mothe, sieur de Cadillac. On July 24th of that year, Cadillac (as he is usually referred to) and his party dedicated Fort Pontchartrain du Détroit and the Jesuit parish of Sainte Anne. The new fort, dubbed Le Détroit for short, served as a fur-trading outpost for Cadillac and his small group of pioneers. The enterprising Frenchman soon earned the enmity of both the French monarchy and the Jesuit clergy by illegally selling alcohol to local Indians. It is one of the small ironies of this chronicle that Detroit's founding father was also its first bootlegger.

Sixty years after its incorporation, Le Détroit sported over 800 inhabitants; many of whom had been attracted by the French government's promise of free land. The bustling outpost was noted as the largest city between Montreal and New Orleans. The French period of prosperity came to a crashing halt with the onset of the French and Indian War. Victorious British troops took control of the fort and its environs on November 29, 1760. The settlement's formal name was then shortened to Detroit.

Fort Detroit's strategic location on the well-traveled waterways of the Great Lakes made it a handsome target during the ensuing American Revolution. Detroit and the surrounding territory west of the river were ceded to the newly created United States of America with the Treaty of Paris in 1783. Twenty years later, Detroit was attached to the Indiana territory while Ohio became a state. The fledgling burg was virtually destroyed by a brutal fire on June 11, 1805. Two weeks after this, the Michigan Territory was established and Detroit's official incorporation as a city followed the next year.

In the aftermath of the fire, Judge Augustus B. Woodward created the new street plan in the model of that of Washington, D.C. The judge's vision called for a city with wide avenues and traffic circles that fanned north from the river like spokes in a wheel. The recovering town was briefly in the possession of the British once again due to the War of 1812, but the city continued to grow. Detroit now functioned as in important trade hub on what has now become known as the St. Lawrence Seaway, with the city serving as a port of call for many ships that traveled the Great Lakes. New rail hubs also linked the town to other areas of the Midwest and East. Detroit's close proximity to Canada made it an ideal stop on the Underground Railroad, and many escaped slaves plotted their final trip across the border to safety from the city. As a result of this multitude of citizens, workers, sailors, and travelers, individuals of all colors and nationalities brushed elbows with each other in a city that epitomized the melting pot of America.

Detroit's first government body was known as the Common Council; it initially included the mayor, five ward aldermen, and the recorder. As the 19th century progressed, Detroit added five more wards and the population swelled to over 45,000 people by the start of the Civil War. Many of the city's males joined the Army and served with distinction in the war. A major black mark for Detroit occurred on March 6, 1863, when the city suffered through its first race riot. The disturbance was aggravated by racism and fury over the military draft. At least two people were killed and dozens of others in injured.

Into the late 19th century, Detroit grew in different directions from its downtown base. Upscale neighborhoods like Brush Park, Indian Village, and Boston-Edison gave the city a very cosmopolitan feel as the Gilded Age progressed. Newfangled "skyscrapers" began rising downtown. Detroit was soon given the nickname of the "Paris of the Midwest." Immigrants flocked to the city, lured by the prospect of a home of their own and a job in one of

Detroit's manufacturing plants. Indeed, carriage maker Henry Ford and his popularization of the automobile made the city ground-zero of an industry that would revolutionize the entire world. The year after the Burnsteins first set foot in Detroit; Ford officially incorporated his Ford Motor Company.[13]

Irish, German, Greek, Polish, Slavic, and Italian immigrants had arrived in Detroit in successive waves over the years. Jews had been present in Detroit as far back as 1762, and the late 19th century Diaspora from Eastern Europe had seen many settle in Detroit.

Like most immigrants, Detroit's Jewish population tended to live in the same neighborhoods as their countrymen. Irish settlers lived in west of downtown in Corktown while Greektown flourished east of Campus Martius. New migrants from Southern Italy and Sicily primarily settled east of downtown in "Little Italy." Just north of them was the quarter where the newly arrived Burnstein family would settle.

Unlike Harry Burnstein's former home on Manhattan's Lower East Side, his new Detroit neighborhood consisted primarily of one and two-family houses. The district was bounded roughly between Gratiot Avenue, Brush Street, Willis Avenue, and Russell Street. Hastings Street ran through the heart of the neighborhood and served as its main drag. On it were, "Hebrew stores of every description: butchers, bakers, clothiers, shoemakers, printing shops, and restaurants." While the quarter was variously called "New Jerusalem," "Little Jerusalem," and "The Ghetto" by the Detroit media, other ethnicities were spread amongst the large Jewish population. One former resident joked as to how you could tell the groups apart, "The non-Jews grew flowers in front of their houses," he said. "The Jews grew dirt."[14]

While "Little Jerusalem" didn't quite approach the sardine can-style crowding of the Lower East Side, it was still a very densely populated district. When the Burnsteins arrived in 1902, the area lagged behind the rest of Detroit in basic amenities. Indoor plumbing and sewers were still luxuries rather than the norm; nearby factories belched smoke into the sky around the clock, covering the streets with a thin layer of black soot; rents, disease rates, and premature deaths were much higher than the city's average. The *Jewish American* stated that Little Jerusalem contained, "…tenement houses that are actually unfit to live in: old, decrepit, polluted and infected hovels, where human beings endeavor to exist and where a young generation is reared."[15]

It was into this new environment that the Burnsteins settled during their first full year in America. Harry opened a shoe repair shop at 401 Gratiot Avenue, a major thoroughfare that formed the southern boundary of Little Jerusalem.[16] He and the family settled into the small apartment above the shop. Harry worked tirelessly to provide for his brood, and while money was frequently scarce, the Burnsteins began to assimilate into the melting pot of America. Slowly but surely, Harry began putting some money away; the family began learning the English language; and the children began attending school. While the Burnsteins were not Orthodox Jews, they did observe holidays such as Rosh Hashanah, Yom Kippur, Purim, and the Passover festival. Most probably, they attended one of the local synagogues with varying degrees of regularity.

As it always does, time passed for the Burnstein family. Sarah gave birth to two boys during their stay on Gratiot; Raymond in 1903 and Isadore in 1909.[17] Within months of the latter's birth, the family moved into larger digs at 346 Winder Street. Their new home was right down the block from the Bishop Union School, which the children attended. Twenty-year old Eva was working as a saleslady at a local dry goods store while nineteen-year old Aberham toiled as a machinist in a Ford Motor Company plant. Even ten-year old Joey kicked back money he made by selling newspapers in the street. The elder Burnsteins supplemented their income even further by renting out space to a young boarder who called himself Harry Hart.[18] By this point in time, however, Harry Burnstein had almost certainly realized that he was in danger of losing his two eldest sons to the streets.

WHILE ABERHAM (Abe) Burnstein had always been an intelligent child, he showed little interest in academics. Not long after he first arrived in Detroit, Abe dropped out of school and began selling newspapers on the street. Hawking papers on the streets of America's cities was a dangerous business in the early 20th century. Most often, newsboys were from poverty-stricken families (if they even they had a family to begin with) and had to contend with rival kids, bullying policemen, or adult predators. The danger of violence hovered over each day. On the streets of Little Jerusalem, it was take or get taken. In no time, Abe became very skilled with his fists. While he stood at medium height with a slightly stout build, Burnstein gained a reputation as a street-fighter. His younger brother was even wilder.[19]

Like his older brother, Joe Burnstein showed no inclination for book learning and quickly found his way into the streets. While Abe moved up into the factory, Joe took his place on the corner aggressively selling papers. Despite his slight build, "Little Joey" was tremendously strong and possessed a hair-trigger temper. While Abe was somewhat quiet and reserved like his father, Joey was peppy and ebullient. Due to his rambunctious nature, Joey was kicked out of regular classes at the Bishop Union School and sent to the ungraded trade school next door. His outgoing personality attracted other children in his new classes. Before long, Joey and his younger brother Raymond were palling around with several other boys from Little Jerusalem. Street gangs were a fact of life in Detroit's Jewish ghetto, and kids often banded together not only out of friendship and camaraderie, but for sheer survival.[20]

Joe and Ray Burnstein most likely first met Harry Fleish on the streets of Little Jerusalem, where he occasionally sold newspapers when he wasn't screwing around up in the ungraded classes at Bishop Union. Born 1903 in the Pale, Fleish was brought to America around the age of four. Although Harry was a quiet and slightly pudgy youth, he was a fierce fighter who would savagely attack after lulling his potential victim with peaceful words. In no time at all, Harry and the two Burnsteins became close friends.[21]

Another good pal of Joey's was Sam Garfield, whose family brought him to Little Jerusalem from his native Rhode Island when he was very young. The same age as Burnstein, the pair would eventually grow to be best friends. Mike Gelfand was known as "One-Arm Mike" because he had lost one of his limbs to a childhood accident. His disability didn't prevent him from holding his own on the streets.[22]

Another boy named Sam Burnstein (no relation) was, if anything, even bigger than Harry Fleish. While he sported the unwitting nickname of "Fats", Sam was a tough street fighter and welcome addition to Joey's crew, as was "Little" Morris Raider. Standing at medium height with a muscular build, Sam Purple also found a home in the youthful street gang.[23] The two Dalitz brothers, Lou and Moe, also joined the boys in their various adventures.[24]

After daily classes finished at the ungraded section of the Bishop Union School, these boys would gather in the schoolyard and shoot craps. When they weren't in class, they hung out in the neighborhood, weaving a mischievous path through the teaming masses of Hastings Street. At this point in time, few of the things the boys did were really dangerous; their antics seem almost tame by modern standards. The boys would swipe fruits and vegetables off of pushcarts; break windows of shops and houses in the neighborhood; shoot dice in the shadow of a synagogue; pull the beards of older male Orthodox Jews; bully and gang up on weaker kids; or shoplift from the stores along Hastings.

Fighting was their primary activity during these formative years. The boys fought for enjoyment as well as for survival. In this era of hyper-conscious ethnic division, Joey Burnstein's gang usually brawled with rival *goyim* of all different stripes, whether Irish, Italian, Polish, or Black, to name a few. The boys learned the rudiments of gambling through card games, their schoolyard crap shooting, and betting on just about anything. By the time of Joe Burnstein's December 1912 Bar Mitzvah, he and his youthful crew had gained a tough reputation in Little Jerusalem, much to the consternation of their parents.[25]

AROUND 1913 OR SO, twenty-two year old Abe Burnstein decided that he had had enough of toiling for Ford Motor Company and began his criminal apprenticeship in the Dresden Café on Monroe Street in downtown Detroit. The Dresden wasn't your usual restaurant, as its rear room housed one of the most profitable illegal gambling dens in the city. The place was run by a one-time Detroit alderman named Eddie Barnett, who introduced Abe to what would become his life-long passion; gambling. Ostensibly employed as a waiter, Burnstein quickly became skilled with cards and dice and soon began his real work as a card dealer in a variety of games, including poker, blackjack, faro, stuss, and three-card monte. Unlike the usual image of the posh illegal gaming casino, the Dresden was an exceedingly tough dive known as "The Black Hole." Burnstein's skills with his fists came in handy when dealing with the hardcases who frequented the joint.[26]

While Abe Burnstein began making the transition into a more refined criminal, his younger brother Joey was growing into his teens and more serious offenses. The exuberant pranks that defined Joey's early gang career had given way to arson, extortion, rolling drunks, pick pocketing, automobile theft, and armed robbery. He and the boys began carrying various weapons, including brass knuckles, blackjacks, and knives.

To the dismay of Harry and Sarah Burnstein, young Raymond seemed intent on following in the footsteps of his older brothers and acted as a tough second-in-command to Joey. Even the baby boy, Isadore, was showing signs of straying down the wrong path. Other kids from ungraded Bishop Union, most of them younger than Joey, ached to join up with his gang.

America entered World War I in April 1917, and many of Detroit's young men prepared to enter the armed forces before making the long trip "over there" to show the Kaiser "what fer." Neither Abe nor Joe Burnstein served in the military, and most others in the gang were too young (besides, there was plenty of fighting to be had on the streets of Little Jerusalem.) Abe had left the Dresden Café by now and made the move to a more profitable gambling game a bit closer to home. Located in the heart of Little Jerusalem at the corner of Alfred and Hastings streets, the Workingman's Café was known as a "high-roller" joint. Joe Murphy and Max Rosenstein, two Jewish gamblers who saw much potential in Abe Burnstein, ran the place.

The leader of the operation was Murphy (his Hebraic name either forgotten or unknown by the chroniclers of the day) while Rosenstein was known as "Max the Blink" because of his chronic blepharitis, which made him blink constantly. Abe made good money working as a dealer and stickman at the Workingman's Café, and also acting as a chauffeur for the dapper Joe Murphy. During his employment, Abe came into frequent contact with the movers-and-shakers of Detroit, ranging from gamblers, politicians, policemen, and gangsters. Unlike the cut-ups who frequented the Dresden Café, the refined clientele at the Workingman's presented far more lucrative business potential for the up-and-coming gangster.[27]

Meanwhile, seventeen-year old Joey Burnstein was brimming with virulent energy and swaggering at the head of an increasingly large band of troublemakers. Known in Little Jerusalem as a *shtarker* (a Yiddish word for strong-arm man,) Burnstein headed a gang that featured several new, younger faces. As another generation of tough kids passed through the ungraded Bishop Union School, the ranks of Joey's gang swelled.

Now in the mix was Harry Fleish's kid brother Louis. Two years younger than his older sibling, Louis was a tall, ropily muscled youth who possessed a dangerous sense of mischievousness. Harry and Louis Fleish's father (Louis, Sr.) ran a Hastings Street junkyard that served as something of a headquarters for the gang.[28] Another recent addition was a shy, dark-haired kid named Abraham Zussman. Recently arrived in Detroit from his native Romania, Zussman was soon dubbed "Abie the Agent" after a then-popular *Detroit Times* comic strip. Skilled with knives, he became known as one the more dangerous members of the crew.[29]

Jacob "Scotty" Silverstein and Jack Budd were also now running with Joey Burnstein. The latter youth, a recent Russian émigré, eventually became the inseparable sidekick of Joey's older brother Abe. Scotty Silverstein was one of the few members of the gang who bothered to attend school on a somewhat regular basis. An intelligent student with a somewhat nerdy exterior, Scotty was nevertheless able to hold his own in a fight.

Not long after he signed on at the Workingman's Café, Abe Burnstein introduced his brother Joey to Joe Murphy and Max the Blink, who admired the spunk of the youthful Burnstein gang. Abe and Joe Burnstein also were soon introduced to Samuel Abramson, a Russian Jew who had recently arrived in Detroit from New York City. Abramson opened up a Hastings Street saloon/eating house called the Circle Restaurant that served as a hangout for a group of older Jewish mobsters that often made the journey up to Old Bishop to watch the kids shoot craps in the schoolyard after class. It would prove to be a dangerous mix.[30]

The Bishop Union crew looked at their own parents (ceaselessly working hard yet still poor) and compared them to the gamblers and gangsters, who never seemed to work hard but had plenty of money, nice clothes and jewelry, beautiful women, and shiny new automobiles (which were still rare enough then to be novelties.) What excitement did a shoe repair store owner have? While their parents derided the older gangsters as *trombeniks* (a Yiddish term for a no-good bum,) the rampaging youths of Hastings Street soon succumbed to the lure of easy money and menacing power.[31]

While the pace of the Bishop Union gang's transgressions gradually quickened, so did the response from the police. Most often, if they wound up in the hands of the cops, they were swatted and told to go home to their mothers. Others were hauled off to the Thirteenth Precinct station at Canfield and Woodward for formal charges. Soon enough, Abe Burnstein was arrested for speeding while Joey Burnstein was held for grand larceny.[32] Morris Raider was convicted of stealing an automobile and sentenced to a brief term in the Michigan State Prison at Jackson.[33] Ray Burnstein was nailed for armed robbery not long after his 14th birthday and served ninety days in jail.[34] If anything, these early busts served only to harden the boys and further marry them to the vocation of crime.

Meanwhile, practically a world away from the tough streets of Little Jerusalem, events were taking place in the Michigan state capitol of Lansing that would forever alter the lives of the Burnstein brothers and their friends.

Mostly of Russian-Jewish descent, the Purple Gang shown here as adults got their start as a juvenile street gang along Hastings Street in Detroit's Little Jerusalem. They are pictured here under arrest at the Detroit Police Department's Thirteenth Precinct in May 1929 under suspicion of violating the Volstead Act. *Author's Collection.*

ENRICHMENT

Spring 1918 – Spring 1923

America's anti-alcohol movement had its origins in the 1840s, when preachers across the country began to gradually spread the word about the evils of "John Barleycorn." The temperance movement didn't really pick up a good head of steam until the turn of the century, when more and more states began to outlaw alcohol consumption. Hatchet-wielding women such as Carry Nation began smashing bottles and the popular evangelist Reverend Billy Sunday spearheaded the growing anti-alcohol movement.

A former major league baseball player, Sunday crisscrossed the country preaching about how alcohol was "the bloodsucker of humanity; it's God's worst enemy and hell's best friend." He also preached about the largely foreign proprietors of taverns and beer gardens; "They are no less than the handmaidens of hell." Michigan church leaders echoed his words. More and more counties went dry in the state, and by 1917 an amendment was on the ballot to outlaw the sale and consumption of alcoholic beverages in the state of Michigan. A main stance was that the hundreds of thousands of bushels of grain should be used to provide food for the troops in Europe, not whiskey.

On November 6, 1917, Michiganders voted to outlaw booze; the new law was due to take effect on the following May 1. Many people, however, did not want alcohol banned and started up protest groups in response. The real benefit of Prohibition, however, was to crime. The six-month grace period sent many otherwise law-abiding folks into the bootlegging business. From stockpiling whiskey, to brewing beer, to distilling moonshine, the windfall would be enormous.

Detroit was a particular hotbed of pro-alcohol, or "wet", sentiment. A city whose economy was built almost entirely on manufactured goods, Detroit's numerous factory laborers frequently depended on a large bucket of beer to ease the strain of their daily workday. Neighborhood children often learned to listen for the five o'clock factory whistle every afternoon that signified the end of their father's shift. They would then grab Dad's beer bucket, a ten-cent piece, and run down to the corner tavern for a fill-up. The local saloon keeper knew each kid's bucket by sight, so he would hurriedly snatch up their dimes, top off the growlers, and send the youths on their way. Woe to the child that didn't have their exhausted father's suds on the table by the time he got home from work...

A visitor who entered the city on April 30, 1918 unaware of local current events may have thought that Detroit was on the verge of Armageddon. Patriotic bunting hung from building's awnings while fliers and billboards exhorted locals to buy war bonds. A handful of agitators lined the downtown streets, loudly exhorting passerby to vote "wet" in the next election as a form of protest. Meanwhile, lines of people were seen hoarding all types of alcohol in anticipation of the coming statewide ban on booze. Men were maneuvering wheelbarrows crammed with liquor bottles down the street while others exited grocery stores with bags filled with beer and liquor. Others swarmed inside saloons to "kiss John Barleycorn" one final time.

The overall atmosphere in the city that day was one of depressed trepidation. A cold spring downpour began falling around dusk, driving the booze hoarders indoors and scaring away customers from scheduled galas at such upscale places as the Hotel Pontchartrain, Hotel Statler, and the Detroit Athletic Club. Rain was still falling on Detroit's mostly deserted streets at one minute after midnight when the state of Michigan officially went "dry." All that was missing was a poncho-clad bugler mournfully blowing "Taps" in the middle of Campus Martius.

Little could the residents of the Motor City have imagined that night that this new "noble experiment" would both enrich and kill untold numbers of men before it was all said and done.

THERE WERE TWO main types of illegal alcohol sold in Detroit during Prohibition; genuine and homemade. The former consisted on authentic beer and liquor smuggled across state lines (until 1920) or the Detroit River from Canada. The best quality stuff around, it was highly prized and sold for exorbitant prices. While the Ontario Temperance Act wouldn't be officially repealed until 1927, some distilleries were still operational. Profit-minded Canadian bootleggers like Harry Low and Blaise Diesbourg quickly found a way to tap this windfall and find wealthy distributors on the American side of the river.

With the passage of Prohibition, Detroit's breweries were now allowed to produce only a "near-beer" that contained 0.5% alcohol. They accomplished this by continuing to brew the real deal only to "bleed off" the alcohol content to the level mandated by law. Essentially, this meant that breweries such the Stroh Brewery Company were swimming in real beer throughout Prohibition, a product that could be diverted to the masses by any brewer willing to break the law. Julius Stroh was not one of those individuals, as he downsized his company and began marketing ginger ale, soft drinks, and ice cream. Other Detroit brewers didn't have the financial resources to ride out Prohibition and went bust; their old buildings becoming warehouses, cold-storage facilities, etc. Nevertheless, millions of barrels of real beer were consumed in Detroit during Prohibition. Some of it came from unscrupulous Detroit brewers or from across the river in Ontario, such as from the Riverside Brewing Company in Riverside or the Walkerville Brewery in Walkerville.

Home-distilling whiskey, or "alky cooking", involved a still that ranged in size from a small unit in a tenement flat to huge devices that took up entire buildings. Otherwise law-abiding citizens would often earn extra money by tending to a still at the behest of criminals. The gangsters would supply everything Joe Public needed; the still itself, distilling supplies, and instruction on how to operate their charges. A grain-based raw mash mixture was spread around with yeast in order to begin the distillation process. The mash ultimately had to react with the yeast and convert to sugar in order to ferment into alcohol. The introduction of genuine sugar into the mixture sped up this process considerably. Corn sugar was the preferred additive; it converted much easier than cane or brown sugar. The still tenders then had to keep a careful eye on the still as the whiskey cooked, as a moment's inattention could result in a potentially fatal explosion.

Smart distillers learned how to tap into local water and gas lines, not only to keep costs down but to keep the powers-that-be from zeroing in on their operations *via* utility bills. Since the acrid fumes emanating from the stills could be smelt all over the neighborhood, enough money was spread around with local beat cops to operate in peace. In one typical instance, the Genna brothers of Chicago had the roster of badge numbers of their local police precinct and paid them off accordingly. The roster also helped to keep outsider cops from mooching on the action.

The end result in alky cooking usually ranged from quaffable to potentially deadly. In order to maximize profits, non-toxic materials would frequently be used to "cut" the product and increase quantity. Hot water would be added to the newly fermented booze. Pure alcohol was then mixed in to level off the proof and caramel was introduced for color. Rye oil and glycerin were added next, and the process was complete. One bottle of whiskey could become 2 ½ bottles, creating a profit of 150% for the bootlegger. Liquor that cost a mere fifty cents per gallon to produce by still could be sold for three to four dollars on the local market.

Some unscrupulous distillers would use bathtubs and automobile radiators to ferment their product. Others went so far as to procure licenses to distribute industrial alcohol, which was used in such diverse compounds as toilet water and paint thinner during Prohibition. They would then cut their raw product with the traditional dyes and flavorings in order to simulate whiskey, gin or rum. These often lethal concoctions were then bottled *en masse* and served to the parched populace. While these actions did wonders for the gangster's wallet, they would often sicken or kill an unsuspecting consumer.

Homemade beer, popularly referred to as "homebrew" during Prohibition, was produced in a similar manner to hard liquor. Like the stronger liquor, homebrew covered a vast spectrum of taste and quality. The gangsters dealt heavily in beer-making ingredients such as malt, hops, and yeast while brew kettles were set up in warehouses or private residences. While ostensibly obeying the laws of the land, the Stroh Brewery Company did market in tip-a-wink fashion a "Hopped Malt Syrup" during this era. Its label read: "Baking, Confections, Beverages" with a "Rich Bohemian Hop Flavor, Light or Dark." As author Philip Parker Mason wrote, "Most Detroiters knew that the syrup wasn't produced to help consumers bake cakes."[1]

Indeed, some lower-income drinkers sought to bypass the gangsters and create their own beer, liquor, and/or wine at home using raw ingredients or commercially sold "kits." Citizens avidly perused old *Farmers' Bulletins* to learn how to distill liquors from various fruits, grains, sugar beets, even potato peelings. As humorist Will Rogers commented, "The worst crime a child can commit is to eat up the raisins that Dad brought home for fermenting purposes."

One simple technique for making booze, known as "steam cooking", required only a little corn sugar mash, a tea kettle, and a cloth towel. One had to heat the mash inside the kettle over a slow stove flame. Alcohol volatilizes between the temperatures of 180 and 200 degrees Fahrenheit. Once this happened, the cooker draped the towel over the spout to absorb the resultant steam fumes. After the towel was sufficiently dampened, he merely had to cool it and wring it out over a glass to produce a small amount of horrible-tasting yet powerful liquor. With enough patience and time, the cooker could conceivably squeeze out enough hooch to get his whole family schnookered. Another crude yet effective method of booze production involved mixing alcohol, water, glycerin, and juniper oil together in a bathtub in order to create the eponymous "bathtub gin."

While these dedicated amateurs got an A+ for creativity, their lack of skill often resulted in a substandard product. What Average Joe hoped would be a decent whiskey often turned out to be a muddy, sour-smelling potion that tasted vaguely of detergent. One such individual said after sampling his wares, "After I've had a couple glasses I'm terribly sleepy. Sometimes my eyes don't seem to focus and my head aches. I'm not intoxicated, understand, merely feel as if I've been drawn through a knothole."[2]

For those Detroit imbibers who didn't want to roll the dice with home-brewing, speakeasies became a normal fact of life during Prohibition; though they were more commonly referred to as "blind pigs" in the Michigan metropolis. Usually fronted by what appeared to be a legitimate business, the blind pig would often have some kind of a barred entrance and a goon who stood watch while the customer said a password. Inside, patrons were served with beer and liquor. Customers who bought one or more drinks would sometimes be offered "free lunch" that may have ranged from cold-cut sandwiches, sardines, boiled eggs, peanuts, or fish and chips. There may have been a piano player and/or singer, or perhaps a couple of slot machines to keep them entertained while they drank. The blind pig operator usually paid off neighborhood beat cops so they could remain in business. Every now and then, just to maintain the appearance of law-and-order, the occasional bust was made. The victims were usually those who had fallen behind in their payoffs, or had sold bad booze that had sickened customers (a frequent risk of drinking the homemade alcohol common during Prohibition.)[3]

FOR THE BOYS in Little Jerusalem, the new booze laws meant little. Besides not being old enough to drink, few of them had a taste for the stuff as it was. Their older crime mentors, however, were ecstatic about the news. The owner of the Circle Restaurant, Sam Abramson, soon got in touch with his friends who had remained in New York City and told them of the great riches to be had by selling illegal booze in Michigan. By early 1919, Jacob Trager and his brother William, accompanied by Benny Glast, had arrived in Detroit.

Jake Trager, somewhere in his late thirties, had migrated to Michigan with little but the know-how to distill good whiskey. Trager and his pals set up secret stills in various locations throughout Little Jerusalem. Over the course of time, they became known around town as the "Saw Still Gang." At their optimum output, Trager's cookers produced around 40 to 50 gallons of whiskey a day per still. Once finished, the boys would slap a phony label on the now-bottled booze and distribute it amongst a select group of trustworthy individuals for sale.

One such merchant was Jack Selbin, who peddled Trager's whiskey out of the back of a fake storefront on Hastings Street. Legend had it that Selbin would place his infant son Max in a highchair facing the front window. When a uniformed cop would pass by, the baby instantly began crying, alerting the boys to cover up their back-room illegalities.[4] Incidentally, Selbin's hyperactive stepson Ziggie had recently found a home in the notorious Bishop Union gang.

While a far cry for the major bootlegging operations of the future in quantity and quality, the Saw Still Gang's whiskey did wonders to slake the thirsts of Little Jerusalem's residents. A steady supply of corn sugar was essential to Jake Trager's booze-cooking operation, and he found what he needed in an Oakland Avenue sugar dealership run by Isadore Cantor and George Goldberg.[5]

OAKLAND AVENUE runs north-south through Detroit's North End for approximately four miles between East Davison Road and East Grand Boulevard. By the late 1910s, the avenue had its own streetcar route and acted as a main artery for new residential subdivisions that were coming into existence at the time. The vast majority of these new homes housed Jewish families who were looking to escape their increasingly run-down Little Jerusalem abodes. Along Oakland were many Jewish-owned businesses such as tailor shops, markets, restaurants, delicatessens and candy stores that served "two cents plain" seltzer water up front and bootleg booze out of the back. There were also a good deal of car-oriented endeavors, such as garages, filling stations, and tire salons. At No. 9415, on the west side of Oakland between Kenilworth and Westminster streets, was the corn sugar warehouse owned by Isadore Cantor and George Goldberg.[6]

Born 1892 in the Pale, Isidor Kantrowitz came to America around the age of fourteen and settled in New York City, where he trained to work as a plumber. By 1919, he had tired of unclogging drains and moved west to Detroit. Upon arriving in his new city, Kantrowitz "Americanized" his name to Isadore Cantor. While it is unknown if Cantor knew Jake Trager and Sam Abramson before arriving in Michigan, "Izzy" soon became fast friends with them.[7]

Cantor's store supplied all the corn sugar used by Jake Trager's Saw Still Gang (as well as other independent bootleggers.) Izzy was a large man who stood six feet tall and weighed more than 200 pounds. With his massive bulk, hard face and New York accent, Detroiters probably figured Cantor for some kind of outlaw muscle at first, but he was well known as an easy-going guy. Izzy always saw himself as a legitimate merchant who just sold sacks of sugar. What people did with it after he sold it to them was *their* business. Cantor's partner, twenty-three year old George Goldberg, felt the same way. The business not only dealt in sugar but all other manner of whiskey and beer making supplies such as mash, yeast, hops, and malt.

While Goldberg was physically smaller than his partner, George was known to be temperamental. During the early years of Prohibition, Goldberg would notch arrests for assault and battery as well as obstructing justice. George at one point would be convicted for the theft of 300 cases of oleo from a downtown shipping company. He would get the conviction downgraded to a civil case and settle out of court.[8]

Their top two employees were Charles Leiter and Henry Shorr, who were best friends and partners in crime. Born on December 25, 1893 in Kovne, Russia (present-day Kaunas, Lithuania), Leiter immigrated to America with his family as an adolescent. As a young man, he worked as a vegetable peddler along Hastings Street. It is a small irony that as a vendor on Hastings, Leiter may well have been victimized by the very same young delinquents he would later hire as a wealthy racketeer. It was most probably during his pushcart days in the 1910s that Charlie first met Henry Shorr.[9]

About five years younger than Leiter, Shorr was born in Kiev and brought to America as a boy. Henry got his start working for a produce wholesaler at Detroit's Eastern Market, where Charlie Leiter would refill his pushcart in the pre-dawn hours before every workday. While both men stood around 5'9", there the physical similarities ended. Leiter was a rotund man with dark hair and eyes, generally looking as if he belonged behind a desk instead of in the street. By contrast, Shorr had rugged facial features that were highlighted by fair hair and blue eyes. Unlike Leiter, Shorr sported a muscular physique that had been honed by many hours of hefting heavy bags of potatoes in Eastern Market.[10]

Despite their differences, both men were brilliant and ambitious individuals who saw the new law of Prohibition as their ticket to great riches. By the end of the decade, both Leiter and Shorr had given up their old careers for full-time employment at what was now known as the Oakland Sugar House.

PROHIBITION QUICKLY began to make the racketeers who frequented Workingman's Café and the Circle Restaurant rich men. Up-and-coming gangsters such as the Burnstein brothers were increasingly cognizant of the potential wealth to be had from bootlegging. In such a high-profit illegal business, however, the threat of violence was always lurking below the surface of even a peaceful operation such as the Workingman's Café. The boys' first major exposure to this was not through Joe Murphy or Max Rosenstein, but through an unwanted silent partner.

The secret Sicilian criminal society known to its members as *L'Onorata Società* (the Honored Society) and to outsiders as the Mafia had arrived in Detroit with immigrating criminals as early as 1900. Over the course of that decade, a distinct *cosca* (family) had developed in the city. Local businessman/politician Pietro Mirabile was the *capofamiglia*, or boss. The family consisted of several distinct *regimes*, or crews; these small subsections were run by *caporegimes*. The *caporegime* of the strongest crew, Antonio Giannola, engaged Mirabile in a particularly nasty feud for leadership of the family from 1913-14. A mail-order bomb that killed two men, wounded several more, and completely missed target Tony Giannola climaxed this war. Upon its completion, Giannola was dubbed the new boss of the family. As time went on, more and more Sicilian criminals were sworn into the local Mafia. One of the Giannola family's new recruits was Cesare LaMare.[11]

Born 1884 in Italy's Basilicata region, LaMare was brought to America as a young boy. After growing up on a Louisiana farm, Chester (as he was called by English-speakers) eventually cut his teeth in the underworlds of both New Orleans and Chicago. Despite the fact that he wasn't Sicilian, he appears to have been accepted into the Mafia. By 1915, he was in Detroit working for John Vitale, a high-ranking member of the local Mafia family. After the Giannola-ordered murder of a well-respected *caporegime* named Peter Bosco in the fall of 1918, Vitale led several key members away from the Giannola family and prepared for war. One of these men was Chester LaMare.[12]

The fighting began in earnest after mob boss Tony Giannola was gunned down in January 1919 while visiting a Rivard Street wake (after a murder that had been committed specifically to draw him into the open.)[13] Tony's brother Sam and Pasquale D'Anna were attacked a month later in Wyandotte. D'Anna died of his wounds and Sam Giannola was reported to have led a military-style raid on the Wayne County Jail on February 26, which resulted in one Vitale henchman shot dead and two others wounded.[14]

In the midst of his Mafia tribulations, LaMare had approached Joe Murphy and Max "The Blink" Rosenstein at the Workingman's Café. Flanked by his menacing bodyguards, Louis Ricciardi and Tony Ruggirello, LaMare made it clear to the pair that it would be best for their health if they let him come in as a partner and share in a healthy portion of their gambling profits. There was nothing they could do; LaMare was strong and Murphy was weak.

Thus, Joe and Max the Blink began turning over a good chunk of their house earnings to Chester LaMare. Other than this extortion, the two Jewish gamblers were about as far removed from the raging Mafia war as possible; that was, until the war came to their front door.

At seven-fifteen on Thursday evening, March 6, 1919, Chester LaMare was on the premises of the Workingman's Café when two Detroit Police Department detectives, Phil Ellenstein and Clifford Price, arrived to interview LaMare, possibly about the ongoing gang war. Across Hastings Street, the Circle Theater was just letting out and dozens of people milled about. After just a few minutes of conversation, a young boy walked inside and told LaMare that there were some men who wished to see him outside. Chester bid the cops farewell and began to step outside. The youthful messenger quickly darted into the crowd, never to be seen again. Partially obscured by the mass of people, a curtained sedan was parked at the opposite curb.

As LaMare exited the front door, two men aimed sawed-off shotguns out the sedan's curtains and opened fire. The ear splitting sounds of the blasts sent people (many of them children) running and screaming. Chester immediately dashed back inside the café, nearly knocking Detective Price over in his zeal to find cover. Buckshot pellets peppered the façade of the café and the adjacent building. Passerby dropped here and there, howling with pain. Once their weapons were empty, the gunmen sped south on Hastings.

While the main target was unharmed, five people had been injured during the attack. Thirty-eight year old Samuel Selz was severely wounded in the head while thirty-seven year old Charles Krinsky was hit in the leg. Three teenaged theatergoers (Anna Green, Alexander Hillman, and Oliver Paris) had been hit with varying degrees of severity by shotgun pellets. Amazingly, no one was killed. Police immediately chalked up the attack to the rival Giannola mob; it was later discovered that one of the shooters was a former friend of LaMare's named Angelo Meli.[15]

Whether or not Abe and Joe Burnstein were on the scene of the attack, the shooting undoubtedly made a great impression on them, as well as the rest of their fledgling gang. The resulting police pressure forced Joe Murphy to close down the gambling rooms that made them rich. Chester LaMare, shaken by the attempt on his life, temporarily left Detroit for a safer clime while the resentful Murphy struggled to rebuild.

WHEN PROHIBITION became the law of America in 1920, Detroit was a city of 993,678 residents of just about every nationality and creed. Known as the undisputed capital of the budding automobile industry, migrants from all over the world flocked to the city with hopes of landing a job in one of the factories. Detroit's population would only continue to surge upwards during the coming decade.

Unlike other metropolitan areas, the neighborhoods of Detroit were covered primarily with one and two family houses; many of them constructed with the plentiful supply of Michigan white pine lumber found in the northern part of the state. The prospect of a well-paying factory job and a home of their own was a tempting prospect for those who settled in the city. Even those in Little Jerusalem who could afford to leave were looking toward the more spacious dwellings that were sprouting in new subdivisions being built north of Grand Boulevard, both east and west of Woodward Avenue. The steady northern migration of Jewish families would continue throughout the following decade.

By this year, Detroit's political ward system had been abolished and a nine-member city council that was elected at large and the current mayor, former street railway and police commissioner James Couzens, governed the metropolis. While the economy was still in a post-WWI recession, times were generally good for the city's denizens. More citizens owned automobiles than at any other time in the town's history. Those that did not rode Detroit's extensive streetcar system. Sports fans journeyed to Navin Field at Michigan and Trumbull to watch Ty Cobb and the Tigers do battle against the rest of the American League while filmgoers crowded theaters to watch silent classics like *The Mark of Zorro*, *Dr. Jekyll and Mr. Hyde*, and *Way Down East*.

The second-largest industry in Detroit, behind automobile production, was the illegal alcohol business. The city's close proximity to Canada provided the perfect portal for sneaking booze into the country. Although the Canadian government still officially prohibited alcohol in the province of Ontario, wineries were allowed to remain open. Select breweries and distilleries were still in operation as well. Smuggling methods ranged from the Average Joe hiding a few bottles of hooch in the trunk of his car as he caught the ferry back to Detroit to professional rum-runners transporting large shipments of booze across the Detroit River by speedboat in the dead of night. As time went on, these methods for bringing liquor across the border became increasingly innovative. At one point, a thin hose was run along the floor of the river and whiskey piped through it from the Canadian side.

The newly created Bureau of Prohibition was tasked with stopping that flood of booze. Nicknamed "prohis," the outmanned and often overwhelmed agents did their best to enforce a law that few respected or wanted. Given the enormous amount of alcohol coming across the river from Canada, these early days of Prohibition law enforcement were the equivalent of throwing a few sandbags in the way of a Biblical flood.

Another large illegal market in Detroit was for gambling. The downtown area featured many well-known gambling halls that, like the blind pigs, were made possible by police and political payoffs. Most of these underground casinos were open twenty-four hours a day and featured all manner of games. Blue-collar workmen who could ill-afford to lose their paltry wages could be seen tossing dice and cards next to the Dapper Dans of the underworld. Two of the more popular joints were run by Ms. Hattie Miller on West Congress and Charles "Doc" Brady at 326 Grand River Avenue. Merton "Mert" Wertheimer ran a popular casino on the fifth floor of 113 State Street. William Bischoff was known around town as Lefty Clark, and his place at 2228 Woodward Avenue was yet another popular gambling spot. The dapper Clark was one of the city's more colorful gamblers and could often be sighted walking down the street with a small monkey perched on his shoulder. Yet another famous gambling joint was the Greektown hall of the aptly nicknamed Jimmy "The Greek" Thompson at 445 Monroe Street.

By the start of the new decade, Joe Murphy had transferred his operation from Little Jerusalem to a swankier spot downtown at 20 West Columbia Avenue. Twenty-nine year old Abe Burnstein had by now made his own name as a successful gambler while working in partnership with Murphy. Despite the Hastings Street drive-by shooting a year earlier, Murphy's operation was peaceful. Inheriting the traits of his criminal mentor, Abe sought to treat crime as a business while maximizing profits and minimizing strong-arm work. Even twenty-year old Joe Burnstein got in on the respectably profitable action by opening a small barbershop just down from Murphy's joint at 10 West Columbia. The back room of Joey's shop frequently hosted high-stakes card games. It wasn't long, however, before the Burnsteins got their hands dirty.

Twenty-three year old Marty Steele was a hard case through and through. Born Martin S. Levey, he grew up tough on the streets of Chicago and drifted east to Detroit during World War I. After time spent as a cab driver and lightweight boxer, Marty eventually found his true calling as a lowly stick-up artist. After beating a 1918 rap for armed robbery, he was found guilty two years later of the same offense. Steele was out on an appeal bond on the night of November 11, 1920 when he stepped to the rear of Joey Burnstein's barbershop and sat down to play cards with several men, including the elder Burnstein brothers.

Shortly before 10 o'clock, Patrolman Arthur Shemansky was walking his beat along West Columbia when he saw a group of men stampede out of the barbershop, leaving the street door wide open in their haste to flee. The officer investigated further and found Marty Steele lying face down on the shop's floor, a small trickle of blood running from a bullet wound to his right temple. A small, unfired automatic pistol lay on the floor next to him and $400 cash was untouched in his pocket. Steele died of his wound an hour later in Receiving Hospital.

The investigation quickly centered on Joe Murphy and the elder Burnsteins. Indeed, the next morning, Abe Burnstein telephoned police and said he would surrender at the Hotel Tuller at 4 o'clock that afternoon. At the appointed time and place, the dapper, visibly relaxed gambler greeted Detective George Wilson with, "I knew you'd find me sooner or later, George." According to Abe's statement,

"We had just finished a game of 'Black Anne.' I owed Steele $2.50 but he claimed I owed him $25. There was a little argument, but I didn't think it was anything serious. Then when I started to go out, Steele put his hand on my shoulder and pulled me back. I saw he had a gun half-drawn from his overcoat pocket. I pulled out mine and shot. If I hadn't he would have killed me."

Due to the fact that no witnesses in the shop had seen a gun in Marty Steele's hand, the authorities believed that Burnstein was lying and that the pistol found at the scene had been planted. Despite these doubts, a jury would later acquit Abe on the grounds of self-defense.[16]

While Abe Burnstein would make a name for himself with non-violent operations such as bootlegging and gambling, he had shown that he was capable of personally taking a human life. In the unforgiving Detroit underworld, it was a near prerequisite for prolonged success.

AFTER BEATING THE murder charges, Abe Burnstein's reputation on the street soared even higher. During his criminal career, he had seldom been arrested and never convicted. With the exception of pleading guilty to a July 1919 robbery charge (he was given probation), Joe Burnstein managed to beat most raps as well. Both men now dressed in expensive suits and drove flashy automobiles. Their younger brother Raymond had followed them out of the street and was now working as a card dealer in Joe Murphy's downtown joint.

The Bishop Union crew continued marching on as a sort of existential criminal farm team. New faces in the gang included the youngest Burnstein brother, Isadore (Izzy.) Also tagging along was the youngest Fleish brother,

Sam.[17] These two troublemakers wanted nothing more than to follow in the footsteps of their older siblings. It was around this time that Sam Fleish's eighteen-year old brother Harry notched his first arrest for receiving stolen property. The booking sergeant mistakenly tacked an "er" onto his last name of Fleish, and it was thus destined that Harry would become infamous under the alias of Fleisher (as Harry and his two brothers shall be referred to from here on.)[18]

Harry Altman, seventeen years old in 1921, was one of the older members of the gang. Altman was nicknamed "The Indian" because of his swarthy skin, jet-black hair, and facial features that resembled those of a Native American. Harry was a rough-looking customer who was known as a "debt collector."[19]

Sam Davis was alternately known as "The Gorilla" for his ape-like features and "Stinky" for his ubiquitous body odor. He also often mispronounced basic words. When somebody got shot, Davis would say they got "shooted." When talking about a wall or partition, he would say "pishmission." Although Sam stood barely 5'2", he had a compact, muscular build and was known as a lethal fighter. Decades later, one of Sam's pals described him thusly; "… (*Davis*) was a pretty tough guy. They called him The Gorilla. He was built like a gorilla. If they wanted a job done on the second floor of an apartment or something, they'd send him over there and he'd climb up the side of the building. He never went up through a house, he went up the side. Up the mortar."[20]

Two other new recruits were Philip and Harry Keywell, two brothers whose mild-mannered father operated a Hastings Street junkyard across the street from that of Louis Fleish, Sr.[21]

Fifteen-year old Irving Shapiro had already been kicked out of Garfield Elementary School for fighting when he arrived at ungraded Bishop Union. Irving had a short, slight build, which along with his smooth face and bow-legged gait made him a prime target for neighborhood bullies, who quickly dubbed him "Bowlegged Charlie." At first glance, the Burnstein crew probably thought they would make short work of Shapiro. The boys couldn't have been more wrong.

From some dark well deep inside of him, Shapiro would draw vicious juices and lash out constantly, going out of his way to pick a fight with someone, *anyone*, and always winning. Years later, one of Irving's classmates recalled his fearsome reputation, "He was a little runt, a tough guy. He was always fighting. He went out of his way looking for trouble. If there wasn't any he made it." Finally, even Bishop Union had enough of Shapiro and expelled him. Although he occasionally helped his father out at his Alexandrine Avenue tailor shop, Shapiro spent most of his time selling newspapers or running the streets with his new friends.[22]

As for the younger generation of ungraded Bishop Union ruffians, the boys screwed around in school and committed petty crimes. More and more in the early 1920s they found themselves in contact with older, more experienced mobsters. Jake Trager and his Saw Still Gang often dropped by the schoolyard crap games to shoot the breeze with the boys and fill their ears with grand tales of the riches to be had in the liquor racket. Trager, in particular, turned heads with an ostentatious Stevens-Duryea E series touring car that reputedly cost an astronomical $9500.[23] To the mostly poor, rambunctious kids, Trager and the older Burnstein brothers probably seemed like rock stars. Also present during these bull sessions were Oakland Sugar House owners Isadore Cantor and George Goldberg.

The Sugar House owners hit it off quite well with the Bishop Union boys and gave many of them jobs at their business. Even Joey Burnstein pitched in on Oakland Avenue when he wasn't preoccupied with his gambling ventures. Because the Saw Still Gang's network was spread out across the neighborhood, the centrally located Sugar House quickly became the gang's primary hangout outside of their sporadic school attendance. The money to be earned slinging sugar sacks far outweighed whatever kiddie games they were playing in the street. Soon enough, the Bishop Union crew dubbed themselves "The Sugar House Boys" or just "The Boys" for short.

Under the auspices of the Oakland Sugar House crew, the old Bishop Union gang made the transition into more serious criminality. The youngsters were frequently tutored by a group of older mobsters who worked for Cantor and Goldberg.

One of the older mentors was Isadore "Izzy" Schwartz, a huge, fearsome man who not only had the strength of a lion but the brain of a fox.[24]

Another was Abe Kaminsky, a Russian-born *shtarker* who had drifted into Detroit from the Pittsburgh area around 1919. Nicknamed "Angel Face" because of his perpetual scowl, Kaminsky was a violent man who specialized in extorting large sums of money from area blind pigs.[25]

Jack Wolfe was a large, wide-eyed man who handled the accounting chores for the Oakland Sugar House. Wolfe was specifically tasked with maintaining *two* transaction ledgers; one for Federal inspectors/Prohibition agents and another with the gang's *real* business matters.[26]

Although his delicate eyeglasses contrasted with the dangerous company he kept, Jacob Levites was a clerk and stock agent for the Sugar House. He was also charged with performing maintenance on the business's delivery trucks.[27]

William Laks was a tall, Eurasian-looking hoodlum who had served prison time in Russia before immigrating to America. A close-mouthed man, Laks specialized in selling narcotics, specifically opium.[28]

BY THE EARLY 1920s, the up-and-coming Sugar House Gang had formed alliances with two well-known out-of-town Jewish gangsters. The first was Chicago mobster Samuel J. Morton, better known as "Nails." As tough as his nickname implied, Morton controlled rackets in Chicago's Maxwell Street ghetto. At the beginning of World War I, Morton enlisted in the Army and went overseas with the 131st Infantry Regiment. During ferocious combat on the Western Front, Morton was wounded multiple times, awarded the Croix de Guerre for valor, and received a battlefield commission to First Lieutenant. Despite that fact that he was a criminal, Nails Morton was seen as a guiding light in his neighborhood, personally protecting elderly Jews from hordes of Gentile hooligans ('Jew-baiters') who attempted accost and assault them. By the beginning of national Prohibition, Nails Morton was buying shipments of genuine Canadian whiskey from the Sugar House Boys as well as operating a "stolen car exchange" racket with them.[29]

Born Irving Wexler on New York's Lower East Side, Waxey Gordon had gotten his start picking pockets in his neighborhood in an era when gang boss Monk Eastman was still brawling with his rivals bare-knuckled in the street. Thirty-two years old when national Prohibition began in 1920, Gordon had served jail time for larceny and assault. He worked as a labor slugger for Lower East Side crime boss Dopey Benny Fein in the years leading up to Prohibition, and most probably made the acquaintance of future Detroit mobsters like Joe Murphy, Jake Trager, and Sam Abramson during this time period. In the early 1920s, Gordon's dealings with the Sugar House mob seem to have involved drugs more than illegal liquor. It was while dealing opium and heroin that Gordon partnered up with rogue St. Louis gangster Max Greenberg. As the decade and his influence progressed, Waxey Gordon would be one of Sugar House crew's closest allies.[30]

WITH THE BUSINESS of bootlegging booming in the North End of Detroit, the youthful members of the Sugar House soon found themselves either loading trucks with sacks of corn sugar in addition to other home distilling and brewing supplies, or driving said trucks to their delivery stops. The boys also moonlighted by doing errands for Jake Trager's Saw Still Gang. For the most part, the old Bishop Union crew's new work was not all that violent.

Profits were climbing ever higher as Prohibition progressed, until a cloud appeared on the horizon in the form of their old nemesis.

BY THE SUMMER of 1921, Detroit's Little Italy (located just south of Little Jerusalem) had finally returned to some semblance of normalcy. The blood-stained Giannola-Vitale feud had been finished for almost three months now. The near-gothic gang war had claimed between thirty and fifty lives; included amongst the dead were two of the three Giannola brothers and John Vitale himself. The survivors had met in late April of that year to formulate a peace treaty and re-draw the map lines. The mediators were Ignazio Caruso and Salvatore "Sam" Catalanotte, who had taken over the Giannola and Vitale factions, respectively, after their titular heads had been murdered.

Detroit's shattered Mafia *regimes* (crews) were re-organized into a single large organization that would control different parts of the city. Joe Tocco would boss the Downriver suburbs while Joseph DeStefano became the head of the East Side crew. Chester LaMare (former nemesis of Joe Murphy) was given exclusive rights to the rackets in Hamtramck. Caruso was dubbed the Detroit family's new boss, with Catalanotte himself in place as his *sotto capo*, or underboss. All disputes and problems would be brought to them and decided upon.[31]

At first, the new deal seemed sweet to LaMare. The blatantly corrupt mayor Peter C. Jezewski led Hamtramck, which was almost completely surrounded by the city of Detroit. The town had been flooded with Polish immigrants who were eager to get jobs in the nearby Dodge assembly plant. Said workers would definitely need a place to have a drink and blow off steam at the end of their shift. Chester soon opened the Venice Café at 11411-11415 Joseph Campau Avenue in downtown Hamtramck. The Venice quickly became known as the most popular cabaret in the city, and sizeable profits began flowing in for the mob.

Trouble sounded when Hamtramck was officially incorporated as a city in 1922 to protect itself from being absorbed by Detroit. Michigan Governor Alex Groesbeck's corruption probes began sniffing for dirt on Mayor Jezewski, and the Venice Café began being raided by police with increasing frequency. LaMare's attempts to bribe the local police were met with indifference. At one point, Chester got a restraining order against the Hamtramck Police Department, on the grounds that they were unduly harassing him.

In November 1922, LaMare closed the Venice Café for three weeks and completely remodeled it with the intention of reopening on the 30th. The doors were open only two hours that night when a task force of Hamtramck and Detroit police, along with the assistant Wayne County prosecutor, barged in and raided the place. They confiscated three cases of liquor and arrested several people, including gangster Leo Cellura and Chester LaMare himself. The Hamtramck mobster was charged with violating the Federal Prohibition Law.[32] Chester posted his $1,000 bail and waited for his April court date. To add insult to injury, mob boss Ignazio Caruso continued to bust LaMare's chops for his percentage.

By the winter of 1923, LaMare had decided to make up this deficit at the expense of bootlegger Jake Trager. Chester had dealt with Jewish mobsters during his Workingman's Café days and probably thought them people that could be easily intimidated. One of Trager's rival distillers, Joseph Rothman, was friendly with LaMare and ran down the rudiments of the Saw Still Gang's operation for the Hamtramck gangster.

In a face-to-face sitdown, Chester explained to Trager that he was coming in as his "partner." LaMare said he wanted a weekly tribute of $100 for each still that Jake and his crew operated. In return, Chester would keep the cops at bay and "protect" him from rival mobsters looking to rip him off. Jake was incensed at the thought of an outsider cutting in to take his hard-earned money but played it cool, telling LaMare that he would need to discuss it with his partners.

Trager and his boys vigorously debated the merits of paying protection money to Chester LaMare. The Italian mobster was roundly cursed, and his extortion of Joe Murphy was probably duly recalled. Some of the alky cookers recited some gruesome stories of the Giannola-Vitale feud and said that it would be best for everyone to pay the money, while others vehemently spoke against giving LaMare one cent. Ultimately, Trager got word to Chester that he would not pay.[33] Undeterred by this, the Hamtramck mobster plotted his target's demise with a touch that was equal parts Machiavelli and Shakespeare.

Since he began making big money in the alky cooking business, William Trager had been gambling more frequently. Unfortunately, he was also losing more frequently. According to his great-nephew Frank Bari, "Willie couldn't pick the winner in a two-horse match race." Trager's markers began piling up and he started embezzling from the Saw Still Gang's coffers to cover his staggering losses. By the time Chester LaMare came calling, the relationship between the two brothers had become severely strained. While the exact mechanics are uncertain, it is plausible that LaMare offered to erase Willie's debts if he would put his own brother "on the spot."[34]

At 12:30 on the afternoon of March 11, 1923, Jake Trager arrived at the corner of Hastings and Wilkins streets for a meeting with what he thought was one of his brother's gambling creditors. Willie himself was on the scene, as was Jack Ekelman and Benny Glast. After waiting about fifteen minutes, the quartet saw a curtained sedan pull to the curb. Jake walked over to the car alone and quickly realized that Willie had tricked him into a meeting with LaMare and/or his men. Jake was seen by witnesses briefly talking with the occupants. A voice clearly asked, "Are you going to pay?" Jake gave the extortionists that same answer he gave them before. Suddenly a revolver thrust out of the curtains and barked three times. Trager fell mortally wounded as the sedan accelerated north on Hastings. William and Ekelman rushed forward to aid their dying comrade while Benny Glast melted into the crowd without a word.

As angry as the boys were at Jake's murder, their rage doubled when they learned that he been sold out by his own brother. Benny Glast was also discovered to have been in on the plot. During his police interview, Glast smugly declared that Jake Trager distilled horrible whiskey that he sold at high prices. Police traced the murder car's license plate to LaMare henchman Louis Ricciardi. Despite his well-known reputation as a Mafia assassin, Ricciardi beat the rap.[35]

Chester LaMare ended up with a handful of air in his grab for Jake Trager's whiskey business, as Willie Trager quickly liquidated his brother's estate and hightailed it back to New York.[36] Sam Abramson, meanwhile, ordered the remaining stills to be dismantled and relocated away from Little Jerusalem. Thus, when LaMare's men came around again after the heat had died down, they could not find one trace of the Saw Still Gang's operation. The frustrated mob boss eventually set his sights on Jake Trager's corn sugar supplier.

Despite the dismantling of the stills, tensions remained high amongst the Sugar House crew. Such hostility even spread into the Burnsteins' downtown gambling operations. Two weeks after Trager's murder, on the night of March 25, one of the boys got into an argument with a small-time gambler known as "Stovepipe Jake" Mensky over a card game at Joe Murphy's place. The argument ended when Mensky was shot dead in the front doorway in full view of numerous witnesses, who naturally saw nothing.[37] A little over a month later, the boys got even more bad news when they found out that one of their biggest customers, Chicago gangster Samuel "Nails" Morton, had met his end in a bizarre, violent horseback riding accident.[38]

And this was only the beginning.

Jake Trager was a New York gangster who came west to Detroit to cook and smuggle illegal whiskey. His small yet highly efficient Saw Still Gang laid the foundation for the then-embryonic Purple Gang's lucrative bootlegging business. Trager was shot dead along Hastings Street in March 1923 by extortionists working for Hamtramck gangster Chester LaMare. *Re-created by J. Rickman from a lost newspaper photograph.*

Sam Abramson journeyed from New York's Lower East Side to open the Circle Restaurant on Hastings Street in the mid-1910s. After Prohibition began, Abramson became a wealthy bootlegger and restaurant owner who served as a mentor to the young members of the Purple Gang. Sammy Trombenik, as he was known, also acted as a bail-bondsman for the gang. *Re-created by J. Rickman from a lost newspaper photograph.*

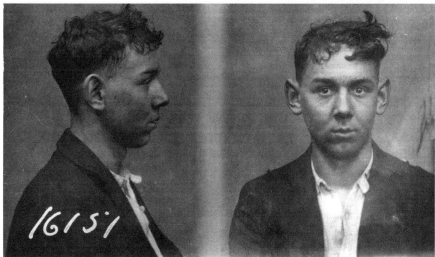

Harry Fleisher was a childhood friend of the Burnstein brothers and a member of the juvenile Purple Gang from the start. This June 1921 mug shot shows Fleisher at the age of 18 after being arrested for receiving stolen property. *Author's collection.*

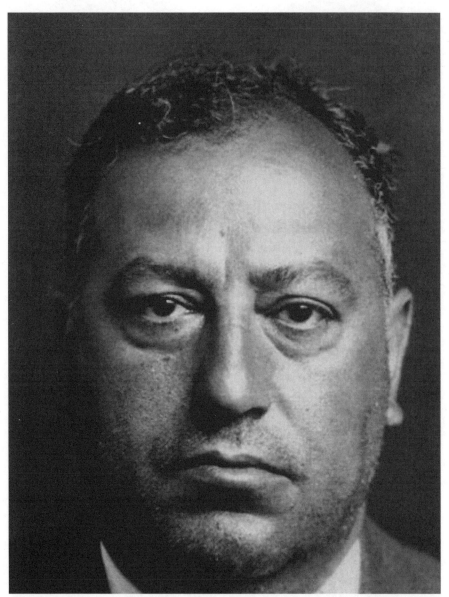

New York gangster Waxey Gordon was a wealthy bootlegger and narcotics peddler during Prohibition. A long-term ally of Abe Burnstein, Gordon and his men would frequently be linked to the Sugar House Gang aka Purple Gang over the years. Gordon's emissary, Henry Sherman, was involved in a nightclub brawl and shootout in November 1924 while partying with some members of the future Purple Gang. *Author's collection.*

CONFRONTATION

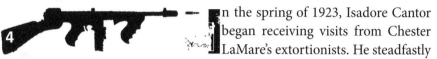

In the spring of 1923, Isadore Cantor began receiving visits from Chester LaMare's extortionists. He steadfastly refused them as Jake Trager had done. The harassment came to a head on July 8 of that year, when four of LaMare's men approached Cantor as he parked his car behind the Sugar House. On point was twenty-eight year old Frank Speed, an Italian gangster who originally hailed from New York and had served three years in the penitentiary at Jackson for armed robbery. The dangerous Speed was known to be quick with a pistol. Backing him up that day were Louis Ricciardi, Benny Glast, and an underworld character known as "Jimmy the Dog."

The quartet's employer, Hamtramck mobster LaMare, had a controlling interest in the Michigan Greyhound Racing Club at Gratiot and Eight Mile Roads. One of LaMare's classic extortion schemes was to coerce local businessmen into buying copious amounts of betting tickets for exorbitant prices. If the victim refused, he was intimidated into line or killed. On this July day, Speed handed Cantor 250 betting tickets to the dog races. He specifically said he wanted $275 in return. Cantor said he could not pay that amount. Speed growled that he would "get what Jake Trager got" if he didn't bring the money to the Venice Café by 9 o'clock the next morning. Izzy still refused, and the four extortionists retreated. As they did, Speed muttered that he would shoot Cantor in the mouth as soon as he saw him again.[1]

Cantor and his partner George Goldberg discussed their options. There was no way Izzy was going into the Venice Café, as he knew all about the Mafia's fondness of mixing linguine and lead. The two had already complained to the police, but they were doing nothing. Frank Speed's deadline passed and both Oakland Sugar House bosses tensely awaited LaMare's next move. Unlike Jake Trager, both Cantor and Goldberg would carry guns, and at the first sight of anything wrong they would blast away.

On July 11, just three days after his tense stand-off with Chester LaMare's goons, Izzy Cantor was up and about handling business in Little Jerusalem. The .38 caliber revolver resting heavily in his pocket provided some reassurance. After a humid morning, large purple clouds began rolling in from the west with the intention of drenching the North End with a summer rainstorm. Thunder rumbled in the distance and the sharp smell of ozone hung in the air as Cantor walked toward the intersection of Hendrie and Hastings streets. As he turned the corner into Hastings, Izzy happened to see none other than Frank Speed pull to the curb in his roadster. Speed got out, walked to the curb, and then stopped dead in his tracks as he saw Izzy Cantor. The two glared at each other for several long moments, their hands creeping toward their pockets. Suddenly Speed took a step back and went for his gun. Cantor clawed the .38 out of his pocket and fired all six shots as fast as he could. Only one bullet missed its mark as Speed toppled to the sidewalk, his unfired revolver dropping from his hand.

Passerby screamed in terror and fled in all directions as Izzy ran north, his sweaty fist still clutching the now empty pistol. He arrived, panting, at the DPD's Ninth Precinct, located at Bethune and John R streets, just as the heavens broke loose with rain. His tie was askew and his eyes were wild with excitement and shock as he explained what had just happened.[2]

Isadore Cantor detailed the LaMare crew's attempts to extort him and their identities as well. The sugar merchant later claimed that several detectives privately congratulated him for killing Speed. A week later, on Friday, July 20, Judge Pliny W. Marsh acquitted Cantor on the grounds that he acted in self-defense. Immediately after the judge announced the verdict, George Goldberg received a telegram saying that he and Cantor would not survive the weekend. After showing the telegram to police, both Cantor and Goldberg were granted permits to carry concealed weapons. The police placed a 24-hour guard around the Oakland Sugar House. That Saturday, a *Detroit News* reporter made note of about a dozen youths working in the Sugar House (the old Bishop Union crew, no doubt) as well as three detectives and two patrolmen guarding the warehouse.

George Goldberg felt quite talkative (a revolver was visibly dangling from his pocket) and had some strong words for his Hamtramck adversary. "Let him come. He has threatened to kill me before Sunday night, but I have no fear of the man personally as he does not fight his battles alone. He is too yellow. He has a gang to drive up in automobiles and shoot through curtains. If he kills me he will be killed sure, but if he doesn't come by Sunday night I will go to him and settle once and for all."[3]

A small crowd had gathered around the Sugar House to wait and see if the Venice Café Gang (as the LaMare crew was referred to by Detroit police and media) would attack. But Sunday night came and went, and all was quiet.

Throughout the rest of July and August, the police maintained a guard on the Oakland Sugar House. Both Cantor and Goldberg carried pistols everywhere they went. Many of the boys also began packing as well. Decades later, gangster Izzy Schwartz would reminisce about these tense days, "All of us started carrying guns back in 1923 in the old Sugar House days. One of our Jewish boys killed a Dago named Speed on Hastings Street. Then all hell broke loose."[4]

It was perhaps the biggest understatement Schwartz would ever make.

THE EVENING of Wednesday, September 5 was warm and pleasant in Detroit, foretelling the possibility that summer would hang on just a bit longer. Nearly seven weeks had gone by since Isadore Cantor was exonerated of killing Frank Speed at Hastings and Hendrie streets. Despite numerous threats from the Venice Café Gang by post and telephone, they had done nothing. As a result, vigilance around the Oakland Sugar House had relaxed somewhat; the police department's guard on the building had shrunk to a single man.

Around 10 o'clock that night, Isadore Cantor was enjoying a cool drink while reclining in a chair on the sidewalk outside of Abe Finkelstein's restaurant. The café was located one door north of the Sugar House and was a popular hangout for the boys. Sitting with Cantor that night was Finkelstein himself and his wife Goldie, George Goldberg, and one of the Sugar House boys, Solomon Conrad. Also with them were two young women, Lilly Parkiet and Fannie Jacobs. The surrounding sidewalks were moderately crowded with people enjoying the balmy evening.

Despite the carefree atmosphere in the neighborhood that night, the Sugar House boys had not forgotten the matter at hand; all the men sitting in front of Finkelstein's carried pistols. The lone remaining DPD sentry, Patrolman William Ward, loitered across the street fighting boredom.

A little after ten o'clock, Goldberg excused himself from the group in order to walk to the nearby Levine Tobacco Shop and purchase a cigar. Shortly after he left, a maroon touring car containing four men approached from the north and slowed to a crawl in front of Finkelstein's. Bullets spewed from the vehicle and raked the party sitting in the line of chairs in front of the restaurant. The fusillade of lead was so loud and rapid that multiple witnesses compared it to the chatter of a machine gun. Slugs stitched the windows and walls of the storefront.

Isadore Cantor, the main target, was shot through the left thigh even as he got his own pistol clear. The young gangster, Sol Conrad, was hit in his leg and torso. The women sitting with them screamed in terror while they were struck with varying degrees of severity. While husky restaurateur Abe Finkelstein was completely unsuited for gangland warfare, he did manage to return fire at his assailants. Cantor clutched his wounded leg with one hand and emptied his revolver at the slow moving touring car with the other. Patrolman Ward dashed across the street, firing his .38 as fast as his finger could work the trigger. A scream of pain sounded from the maroon vehicle. With three guns now pouring bullets at them, the shooters accelerated south on Oakland and disappeared from sight. As they did, a wild-eyed George Goldberg sprinted up the block with a pistol in his hand, safe from harm but too late to help his friends.

Pandemonium reigned on the sidewalk outside of Finkelstein's. Gunsmoke wafted through the air and screams filled the night. Bloodstains and broken glass were everywhere. Izzy Cantor now lay on the sidewalk, weak from blood loss and shock. "There's only one way. Beat em' to it. That's it. Beat em' to it," he kept murmuring. Sam Kornheiser, proprietor of a nearby candy store, attempted to call the police only discover that his phone was dead. It was later determined that the telephone lines for the block had been deliberately cut just before the shooting.

Goldberg and other bystanders took quick stock of the damage. Cantor was hit bad but seemed like he would pull through. Young Sol Conrad was severely wounded; one of the bullets had severed his femoral artery. He would bleed to death within a short time. Abe Finkelstein was quite shaken but otherwise unharmed. His wife Goldie had been struck in her right shoulder and elbow while three bullets had grazed Fannie Jacobs. Lilly Parkiet was struck through the left leg and cut by flying glass; she and the other two ladies would survive their wounds.

Detroit police and paramedics arrived soon after, as did a large crowd of traffic-blocking gawkers who crowded around the restaurant. The attack was so overwhelming and unexpected that no one knew what to make of it. Cantor said there were three automobiles, and that the killers used shotguns. Police declared only one car and automatic pistols as the weapons of choice.[5]

There were neat lines of bullet holes along the entire storefront, as high as a man's chest and waist, which could have been made by a Thompson submachine gun or a Browning Automatic Rifle (BAR.) Since many police had not even heard of the "Tommy Gun" yet, they guessed that the bullet holes came from a tremendous volley of automatic pistol fire, which is how they officially recorded it. Police determined that the killers had fired between 50 and 100 bullets in their efforts to wipe out the upper echelon of the Sugar House Gang.

Though the accounts from all parties involved were horribly confused and the evidence is far from definitive, it's possible that the Venice Cafe crew used an automatic weapon in their attack on the Sugar House. If they did indeed use a Thompson or BAR, it was an exceptional incident, for the first *recorded* of a machine gun in Detroit would not be for another four years.

At 10:30 the next morning, while curious crowds were gathered to view the carnage of the previous night, a coupe containing three Italian men pulled to a stop in front of the Sugar House. A young-looking kid in the driver's seat called out in a sarcastic tone, "How do you like that, Goldberg?" The kid then roared with laughter. One of his companions in the back slapped him on the shoulder and growled, "Cut that out! Get out of here!" The car then accelerated away.

At Harper Hospital, local newspapermen crowded around Isadore Cantor's bed and listened intently as the resting sugar merchant eagerly detailed his struggle; "That gang has been operating for months. They go to bootleggers and blindpiggers most, but sometimes to legitimate businessmen and levy blackmail. The liquor dealers pay them a stated sum weekly. Nowadays the blind pig, instead of paying a license fee, pays blackmail to gangsters who sneer at the civil authorities. The police know this. They know the fellows who are levying the blackmail. Everybody knows about it. Most of those approached pay the blackmail."

Cantor went on to describe the extortion attempts and his quick-draw contest with Frank Speed on Hastings Street. He then propped himself up on an elbow. "It's a dirty shame and a disgrace to this city to have this sort of thing going on. Who runs this city, anyway? Are we who are law abiding citizens going to be dictated by a bunch of outlaws? Are these thugs going to bluff the police forever?

"I'll answer that question, as far as I'm concerned. They aren't going to run me. I'll be out of this hospital before long. If they thought they could scare me by this gunplay, they are going to find they were fooled. They laugh at the police. Frank Spede isn't laughing any more. I can trust my partner, George Goldberg. He feels the way I do about it. Those fellows will never bluff me. They may run the rest of Detroit, but not me."[6]

Clearly Isadore Cantor did not care about any gangster code of silence. Izzy identified the two shooters as Charles Barone and Dominic Ferro; their accomplices as George Cordell and John Bush. Cordell and Bush eluded the authorities, but Barone and Ferro were arrested and charged with the murder of Sol Conrad. Cantor gladly agreed to testify as the state's star witness.[7]

The police took Chester LaMare into custody immediately following the Oakland Sugar House drive-by. He was released soon after on a writ of *habeas corpus*.[8] LaMare had seen this whole situation snowball out of control. Not only had he missed Cantor, two of his best men were in jail awaiting trial. LaMare decided that a bribe would be the best way to silence Cantor, as there was too much publicity on him to actually take his life.[9]

WHILE ON THE SURFACE, Isadore Cantor and George Goldberg seemed to be holding their own against Chester LaMare and his crew, the September 5 attack had badly rattled them. The time for tough talk was through and the two sugar merchants (as well as their young acolytes) seemed dangerously out of their element in going toe-to-toe with the seasoned Mafiosi from the Venice Café. The only possible solution was to bring in killers to face killers.

Shortly after Cantor left the hospital in late September 1923, a series of phone calls were made from the Oakland Sugar House to New York City. Within a short period of time, a few Jewish hoodlums were on the way west to assist the boys in their fight against the Venice Café crew. One was twenty-seven year old Jake Weinberg, who in addition to being an ace bootlegger was a known triggerman. Another was a twenty-year old tough guy from Brooklyn named Irving Milberg who, despite his youth, was a crack shot with a pistol.[10] Yet another was Edward Shaw aka Little Abie, whose undersized build concealed a ferocious temper and eagerness to use revolvers to solve his problems.

JOSEPH ROTHMAN had lived in Brooklyn after his immigration to America and, like Jake Trager, had come out to Detroit in the late 1910s to cash in on Michigan's new Prohibition laws. Ultimately, he had not joined Trager's consortium and developed his own network of illegal stills. Like so many others of his ilk, Rothman ran his business out of an ostensibly legitimate front, the Michigan Advertising Soap Company at 1544 St. Aubin Avenue. Rothman was a longtime friend and ally of Venice Café chief Chester LaMare, but he was also friendly with Trager and the rest of his alky cookers. Joe even bought his corn sugar from Isadore Cantor and George Goldberg, who lived just a block away from him on Holbrook Avenue.

Although Rothman and the Sugar House Boys were business rivals, they were all Eastern European Jews who were successful in their chosen vocation. Then LaMare's greed tore those friendships to pieces. Now Rothman found himself in the awkward position of offering Cantor $5,000 not to testify against his assailants. "You do not even have to recant, Izzy," Rothman said on Cantor's front porch at 534 Holbrook, "just wait until you go to court and then say you cannot identify them." When Izzy appeared nonplussed, Joe *unsweetened* the deal by hinting that he just might "meet with an accident" if he decided to testify. Cantor then slammed the door in Joe Rothman's face.

Rothman and his family lived in a large red house at 445 King Avenue. After his tense confrontation with Izzy Cantor, Joe began taking safety precautions of his own, as he began sleeping with a loaded shotgun and pistol within his reach. The moonshiner had also rigged an elaborate alarm system in his home. Each door and window of Joe's house was covered with thin wires that, if tripped, would activate a large bell next to his upstairs bed.

On Thursday evening, November 8, Rothman relaxed somewhat when Benny Glast and Tony Ruggirello came to visit. The three men repaired to the living room, where they talked and sipped whiskey while listening to Joe's brand-new radio set. After a short time, Rothman got up to answer the doorbell. When he opened the door, Joe promptly received a bullet in his forehead. Glast and Ruggirello dashed up toward the door, firing five rapid shots at two men who hopped into a touring car and sped away. Rothman's wife rushed into the room screaming while the two gangsters, not wanting to wait for the police, fled out the back.

Incidentally, the Detroit Police Department's Chief of Detectives, Edward H. Fox, lived a block away and heard the gunfire. Fox pulled his service revolver and ran over to the Rothman home bareheaded; alas, the inspector was too late to catch the shooters. Despite the bullet in his head, Joe Rothman was still conscious when taken to Receiving Hospital. He sang out in his delirium that he knew damn well who shot him but that but he would never tell. Rothman died at 5 o'clock the next evening, never telling.[11]

THE SUGAR HOUSE BOYS had struck their first blow in the war, and it was only a matter of days before they were linked to yet another murder.

Forty-year old Vito Bullaro was ostensibly a fruit peddler and known to be linked to local Mafiosi, namely Chester LaMare. He lived at 1563 E. Fort Street with his family. One of Bullaro's seven children had passed away the fall of 1923, devastating him and his family. Just a few weeks later, on the rainy evening of December 4, Bullaro attended the wake of a friend's dead child. It had been almost a month since Joe Rothman was killed up in the North End. On this mournful night, Vito did not know that four men were stalking him in a curtained taxicab. The quartet spotted Bullaro leaving his friend's house around midnight and discreetly followed him as he made his way to his Fort Street house.

Distracted by the driving rain, Vito did not seem to pay much attention to what was going on around him. As he began to turn into his yard, the taxi coasted to a stop and a short, stocky man clad in a gray overcoat hopped out onto the running board. Bullaro wheeled around in time to see this man aim a sawed-off, double-barreled shotgun and utter an Italian curse. Vito's resultant scream of terror was quickly cut off by a double blast that blew off most of his head. One of the taxi's passengers let out a cackle at the gruesome sight. "Come on, get in the car," another growled. As the shotgun killer slid back inside as one of his accomplices drew a pistol and pumped five shots into Bullaro's body. The cab then sped south on Orleans Street to a clean getaway.

At first glance, the murder of Vito Bullaro did not seem to be related to the "Oakland Sugar House War", until the taxicab used in the murder was located at the corner of Richton Street and Oakman Boulevard in the North End. The vehicle turned out to be owned by twenty-year old Sugar House gangster Harry Fleisher. The cab had been reported stolen several hours before the murder, but despite this clue, the police were unable to pin Bullaro's murder on the Sugar House Boys.[12]

Just a couple of days after the Bullaro murder, on the night of December 7, Wayne County sheriff's deputies raided several popular area cabarets. Heading the list was Chester LaMare's Venice Café in Hamtramck. Several arrests were made and nearly $1,000 worth of booze was confiscated. LaMare himself was said to be out of town at the time.[13]

AS 1924 BEGAN, Chester LaMare remained out of Detroit, lying low while his lawyer prepared for his trial on violation of the Volstead Act. LaMare ultimately never appeared for his court date, and the judge forfeited his bond. With the month of January rather calm, business as usual went on at the Oakland Sugar House. Isadore Cantor was still dead set on testifying against Charles Barone and Dominic Ferro, and looked forward to the February 15 trial.

Two weeks before the trial was set to begin, Izzy Cantor left for New York on a business trip and also to visit relatives. Cantor made the journey in his own car, arriving in the Big Apple around the third of February. The Sugar House boss handled his business (the shipping of a damaged automobile from Brooklyn to Detroit) uneventfully and repaired to the home of his cousin Meyer Mordetzky at 22 Pike Street on the Lower East Side. Cantor said the "Detroit mob" was after him, but laughed at the notion that they would follow him all the way to New York, let alone find him. He carelessly drove around in his ostentatious luxury sedan, still affixed with a Michigan license plate.

Four days after Cantor's arrival, a rough-looking man appeared at his brother Sam's house in the Bronx and demanded to know where Izzy was.

After being informed of this, the hunted sugar merchant packed up and said he was going to Brooklyn in order to hide out with "Sonny, my best friend." After noting that a strange man whom they did not know accompanied him, the Mordetzkys bid Izzy Cantor farewell and watched him walk out their door into the chilly winter night.[14] They never heard from him again.

IN THE COLD DAWN twilight of February 8, George Goldberg was asleep in his home at 554 Holbrook Avenue when the telephone bell awakened him. After fumbling for the receiver and microphone, the operator informed Goldberg that he had a long distance call from New York. George listened in as a tough voice he vaguely recognized told him, "We got Cantor at last. We plugged him last night with five bullets and threw him in the river. We're saving the sixth bullet for you." A loud *click* sounded as the line went dead. A suddenly numb Goldberg hung the receiver up and slumped back into his bed.[15]

CHARLES BARONE went on trial for the murder of Solomon Conrad in the Recorder's Court on Friday, February 15. In the courtroom, Isadore Cantor was called to the stand as the state of Michigan's star witness. He was nowhere to be found. Judge Edward J. Jeffries asked, "Is he dead or alive?" Detective Lieutenant Edward Mitte explained how Cantor said a couple weeks before that he was going to New York and that none of his friends had heard from him in 12 days. The case was granted a continuance until March 21.[16]

Three days later, an anguished George Goldberg spoke to a *News* reporter about his missing partner, "They got him, that's what happened." Goldberg spoke in a barely audible whisper, his eyes burning with hatred and determination. "Cantor went to New York two weeks ago to arrange for the shipping of an automobile which had been in an accident. The car arrived all right but…" Goldberg then gritted his teeth and clenched his fists. "His mother and brother live in New York, and they are just wild wondering what has happened to him. I know what happened…those dirty gunmen!"[17]

The police pooh-poohed Goldberg's statements and claimed they had it on good authority that Cantor had accepted the $5,000 bribe and was living in Europe until the trial was completed.[18] February came and went, and so did March, with no sign of Isadore Cantor. Louis Ricciardi, held on a concealed weapons charge, was quizzed as to the whereabouts of his enemy. The Italian gangster merely grinned and shrugged his shoulders. When Cantor still failed to resurface, the case against Charles Barone and Dominic Ferro was dismissed.

ON THE EVENING of Saturday, April 12, George Goldberg spent a pleasant night on the town with his fiancée Sadye Jacobs. Her seventeen-year old brother Samuel, a student at Cass Tech High School, drove them to Goldberg's Holbrook Avenue home. As they pulled up in front of the house, a sedan passed them going the opposite way, and a fusillade of .25 caliber bullets engulfed the car. Samuel Jacobs slumped dead in his seat while Goldberg drew his revolver and fired three shots at the passing automobile. Both he and Sadye Jacobs were unhurt.

After Jacobs' body was removed to the morgue, Goldberg disappeared. At the boy's funeral two days later, Goldberg suddenly telephoned police, saying he wanted an armed guard while he attended the burial. Two detectives were sent to the Jacobs home at 314 Owen Avenue. They stayed with Goldberg until the service was over. While in the company of the detectives, George told them that Tony Ruggirello had fired the shots the killed Sam Jacobs, while Louis Ricciardi drove the murder car. Afterwards, the frightened sugar merchant went back into hiding.[19]

Four days later, on the morning of April 18, a body washed ashore at Manhattan's 20th Street. The bloated corpse, which had been in the East River for some time, was fully clothed with the exception of a hat. No identification was found, except for the initials I.K., three stars, and the year 1908, which had been tattooed onto the right forearm. The medical examiner determined the victim had been shot once in the back of the head with a .38 caliber handgun before receiving four more bullets in the back and torso from the same weapon. The body was shortly thereafter identified as Isadore Cantor.[20]

No suspects were ever arrested in Cantor's murder. It was generally assumed the strange man sighted by Izzy's family had lured him to Brooklyn and then either performed the execution himself or let others do it, most probably Mafiosi from Detroit.

WITH THE MURDER of Isadore Cantor and George Goldberg now hiding out in Michigan's Upper Peninsula, Charles Leiter and Henry Shorr assumed full ownership of the Oakland Sugar House in the spring of 1924. Despite (or perhaps *because* of) the notoriety of the gang war with the Venice Café crew, business had been booming. As a result of the drastically increased volume, Leiter and Shorr sold the Sugar House at 9415 Oakland Avenue in May 1924 and transferred the operation to a larger building a few blocks to the south at No. 8634.

Leiter and Shorr proved to be far more effective racketeers than their predecessors. Instead of going out of their way to pick a fight with the Mafia, Charlie and Henry sought to work *with* the Sicilians instead of against them.

The pair believed that there was plenty of money to be had and petty ethnic-based gang wars were pointless. Indeed, Detroit's Mafia leadership responded favorably to the change in leadership. Even the revenge-minded Chester LaMare was brought to heel. After all, Frank Speed's killer was now dead. Through the efforts of Leiter and Shorr, LaMare was eventually convinced to give George Goldberg "a pass."

Learning from the publicity-drenched exploits of Cantor and Goldberg, both Leiter and Shorr sought to avoid the limelight; neither would have been caught dead saying anything of substance to a cop or a newsman. In fact, it was Henry Shorr who famously quipped to a detective, "Do you know the eleventh commandment? It is thou shalt not squeal. I have nothing to say." As a result, the duo would put the Oakland Sugar House in the name of an ostensibly legitimate front man while they secretly pulled all the strings free of scrutiny.[21]

Their first front man was a New Yorker named William Weiss. A close friend of the late Isadore Cantor, Weiss had turned up in town a month after his body washed ashore. A slight, slender man with a reputation as a nervy trigger-puller, he was widely believed to have been the stranger last seen with Cantor before he disappeared. Upon his arrival in Detroit, Weiss introduced himself to the boys. He went on to tell them how sorry he was about Izzy and how blameless he was, as well. Leiter and Shorr appeared impressed and installed the newly arrived New Yorker at the Oakland Sugar House.[22]

THE END OF THE Oakland Sugar House War could not have come at a better time for Hamtramck mobster Chester LaMare. Into the summer of 1924, his legal problems from both the war and his Prohibition cases continued to snowball. After failing to appear at his April trial, LaMare was also charged with operating a large beer distribution ring in Hamtramck. On July 17, LaMare finally surrendered with his attorney Leonard Coyne. Formally arraigned on the beer ring case, His bail was set at $10,000 and the bail from his previous 1922 case was doubled to $3,000. After spending a few hours in a jail cell, LaMare had no trouble producing the money and was quickly freed. Detroit city cops and Department of Justice officials were unaware of these new developments and continued to hunt the gangster.

On Sunday afternoon, July 27, three DPD detectives sighted LaMare being chauffeured up Hastings Street by two of his top men, Louis Ricciardi and Tony Ruggirello. The "dicks" ordered the men to halt while Ricciardi, who was driving, immediately hit the gas and turned right down a side street. A high speed chase ensued as both the gangsters and cops zoomed down the narrow avenue. LaMare's car was halted by a downed railroad crossing at

Dequindre Avenue and all three men were taken into custody. As a result of the still-missing George Goldberg's statement, Ruggirello was charged with the murder of Sam Jacobs.[23]

Now the Detroit police began searching in earnest for Goldberg, without whose testimony they had no case. Goldberg finally turned up on September 5, the first anniversary of the Oakland Sugar House drive-by shooting. He had returned to the city for a quick visit with his fiancée Sadye Jacobs, and detectives staking out her house moved in and served him with a subpoena. Deposited on the witness stand at Ruggirello's trial, Goldberg steadfastly declined to identify the mobster. Despite the prosecution's reading of his police testimony in which he said Ruggirello killed Sam Jacobs, George remained firm, "I refuse to testify in this case!" The state dismissed its indictment against Antonino Ruggirello.[24]

ALTHOUGH THE LATE Jake Trager's Saw Still Gang no longer technically existed, Sam Abramson continued to successfully operate his old alky cooking network. Known affectionately to his associates as "Sammy Trombenik," Abramson was a stocky, happy-go-lucky type who stood medium height with a large mop of bushy hair. By the mid-1920s, Abramson was earning even greater profits by smuggling rum up from Florida. In addition, Abramson still ran the old Circle Restaurant at 2631 Hastings Street, which remained a well-known hangout for the Sugar House Boys.

One of his long time partners in the joint was thirty-four Arthur Whitman, a former understudy of Burnstein mentor Max the Blink and a large-scale bootlegger in his own right. Abramson and Whitman got into a beef in the late summer of 1924 over the books at the restaurant. The dispute continued until Whitman ran Abramson from the Circle at the point of a gun. Abramson immediately went to the Oakland Sugar House looking for vengeance.

While the precise details of the conspiracy were never discovered, this is what most likely happened; Charlie Leiter and Henry Shorr, who had decidedly *not* forgiven front man William Weiss for his role in Izzy Cantor's murder, chose to kill two birds with one stone. They assigned Sammy Trombenik's murder request to Weiss who, eager to get in good with his employers, accepted the job.

Around 6 o'clock on Sunday morning, September 14, Arthur Whitman received a telephone call from an unknown party. Soon after, his semi-conscious wife Bessie heard him get ready to depart their elegant new flat at 3262 Clairmount Avenue. Whitman had just released the parking brake of his car when William Weiss jumped out of the overgrown weeds of the vacant lot next door and opened fire. While Weiss certainly wasn't lacking in the balls department, the forensic reconstruction proved him to be an atrocious marksman. Whitman's would-be killer fired five rapid shots while closing a distance of six feet to the car and missed with each one. Only the sixth and final bullet, fired from mere inches away, hit its mark and proved fatal. The not-so-sharpshooting gangster was accompanied by one or two accomplices as he dashed to a waiting getaway car while the dying bootlegger's vehicle slowly rolled out of control down his driveway and into the street.[25]

The very next day, Weiss fled back to New York City to hide out until the heat cooled down. The Sugar House bosses didn't wait long to avenge Isadore Cantor's murder. On October 9, William Weiss's dead body was pulled from the East River not far from where "Izzy" had been found six months earlier. Two weeks after Weiss's body was found, a close friend of his named Jacob "Shorty" Miller was found murdered outside of what is now Hempstead, New York. Authorities believed the Weiss/Miller homicides were related; both cases went unsolved.[26]

ONE POSSIBLE CANDIDATE for the mantle of avenging angel was twenty-six year old New York gangster Henry Sherman who, along with his older brother Charles (aka Chink), was a top member of the Waxey Gordon mob.[27] Whether or not the Sherman brothers were responsible for the Weiss/Miller rubouts, Henry boarded a Detroit-bound train right around the time that Shorty Miller's corpse turned up in the Long Island weeds. Sherman's mission is uncertain; he may have been accepting payment for the double homicides, or perhaps negotiating a new narcotics deal with the Sugar House Boys. What is known is that on Halloween night, Henry Sherman went out carousing with two unidentified upper-echelon members of the Oakland Avenue bunch. The partying continued well into the early hours of November 1. Around 6 o'clock in the morning, Sherman and his hosts staggered into a nightclub located at 2909 Woodward Avenue.

The criminal career of "Hard Luck Bill" Horrocks had been just as unsuccessful as his moniker suggests. A gambler and armed robber, Horrocks was drinking heavily in the Woodward Avenue cabaret with a Chicago cardsharp named Thomas Cuser when the Sugar House party took a seat at a table next to them. Horrocks made a sarcastic remark about a hat worn by a red-headed woman who accompanied the Sherman party. One of Sherman's Detroit hosts snarled a nasty retort. The dispute quickly spiraled into a full-blown argument; their profane shouting match was clearly audible over the music of the band performing on the stage. At one point Horrocks and one of the

Sugar House boys jerked their pistols and opened fire, sending the customers diving for cover. No one was injured, but the club's owner and his well-armed bouncers evicted both parties from the premises.

Just as the skies over Detroit were just beginning to brighten with the navy-blue twilight of dawn, Horrocks and Cuser continued arguing with the Sugar House party. Both men began to cross Woodward into order to catch a jitney, hurling colorful metaphors over their shoulders all the while. When they were in the center of the avenue, all five men at the center of the dispute suddenly pulled guns and began blazing away. Pedestrians ran for cover while bullets crashed into storefront windows and car bodies. The red-headed female companion of the Sherman party went down screaming, blood gushing from a leg wound. Fifty-three year old Cornelius Van Driel was standing across the street at the jitney stop boggling at the action when a stray slug slammed into his head; he would soon die from his wound. Hard Luck Bill Horrocks' luck ran out for good when a bullet sliced through his brain and sent him down for the count. Thomas Cuser collapsed near him, hit badly but not fatally.

After the fifteen-second melee stopped, the two Sugar House boys ran into Woodward and stopped a passing taxicab by aiming their pistols at the driver. The gangsters helped the wounded red-headed woman into the vehicle, which then sped off. The Detroiters ran to retrieve their own car, never to be positively identified. Henry Sherman, meanwhile, sprinted west on Temple Street in the direction of his nearby hotel. A passing foot patrolman had heard the shots and got the drop on Sherman a block away from the scene. A still-warm .38 revolver with four empty shells in the cylinder was found in his pocket. Despite two potential murder charges hanging over his head, Sherman was cut loose when witnesses failed to identify him. Waxey Gordon's emissary then caught the next train home to New York.[28]

BY THE END OF 1924, the Burnstein crew had completed their transition from gangster pupils to murderers. Their lives had been steadily leading in this direction since their days of wild delinquency on Hastings Street some years earlier. For the most part, nothing in their backgrounds suggested they would turn into brutal criminals. The vast majority of them came from law-abiding Jewish immigrant families. While the Fleisher brothers' father, Louis, Sr., was not above shady dealings in his scrap business, there was nothing to indicate that his boys would turn to violent crime.

Six decades after the Oakland Sugar House War, sociologist Lonnie Athens published his groundbreaking work *The Creation of Violent Dangerous*

Criminals. In it, Athens lays out a theory he describes as "The Process of Violentization," which is a graphic description of how violent criminals come into being. It is probably as good an explanation as any as to how the rambunctious kids from Bishop Union School became known as "...the most efficiently organized gang of killers in the United States."

The first stage of the process, *brutalization*, the subject is violently belittled and subjugated under the pressure of committing violent acts of his own. In essence, the individual is under a ferocious form of peer pressure, as his stronger contemporaries forcibly ridicule and intimidate him into proving himself worthy of their company. The subject begins to reject social and religious norms of civil behavior.

In the second stage, *belligerency*, the subject makes a personal effort to stop the brutalization and begins committing violent acts. He responds to slights, real or imagined, with force. Perhaps the subject makes an aggressive attempt to retaliate against those who brutalized him in the first place. After completing this successful violent reaction, the subject feels increased self-confidence and is greeted with approval from his peers.

The third (and most difficult) stage, *violent performances*, sees the budding criminal commit a dehumanizing and frightening act. The subject pushes through a psychological barrier and inflicts grave bodily harm upon another human being. This violent reaction has resulted in the subject, who was himself subjugated, now brutalizing others.

With the fourth and final stage, *virulency*, the subject revels in the success of his violent performance. His criminal cohorts now admire and respect him while others fear him. The now-emboldened individual who was subjected to withering abuse in the first stage is now a powerful figure that responds with crushing force to the smallest slight. After seeing the apparently positive after-effects of his actions, it becomes easier for the subject to commit additional violent performances in the future.[29]

As time progressed, more and more of the Sugar House Boys would take human lives. Sometimes they would kill for pay, or for revenge, or for sport. In a sense, their criminal education was finally complete. Perhaps it was not easy for them at first; perhaps they hesitated to pull the trigger, grappling with waves of nausea and nervous energy as the moment of truth approached. Regardless, as the Athens hypothesis indicates, the repetition of slaughter soon made it routine. Far from the mischievous delinquents that they had been just a few years earlier, the Burnstein brothers and their friends now belonged to a lethal underworld subculture where a man had to commit murder in order to earn respect.

Chester LaMare is pictured here with his wife Anna. A caporegime in the Detroit Mafia, LaMare controlled the rackets in Hamtramck and ignited the so-called "Oakland Sugar House War" by attempting to extort Isadore Cantor and George Goldberg. *Author's collection.*

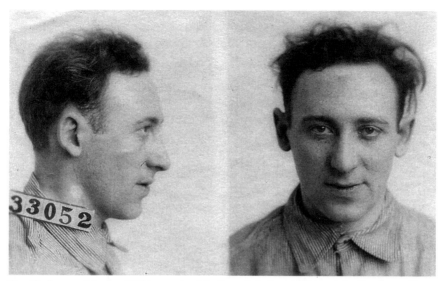

New York gunsel Irving Milberg arrived in Detroit in late 1923 to assist the Sugar House Boys in their fight against Chester LaMare's Venice Café crew. Milberg was known as a crack shot, and would become notorious as one of the Purple Gang's top triggermen. This July 1929 mug shot was taken after Milberg's conviction for violating the Volstead Act. *NARA*

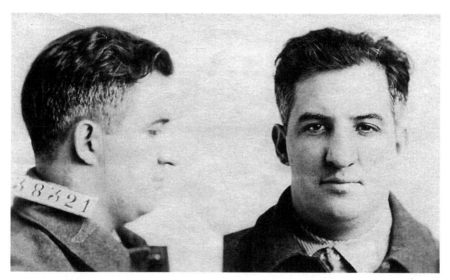

George Cordell was accused by Oakland Sugar House boss Isadore Cantor of participating in a violent September 1923 drive-by shooting that killed Sol Conrad and wounded four others, including Cantor himself. Ironically, Cordell would later be indicted with the Purples during the Cleaners and Dyers War extortion investigation. Cordell is pictured here after his arrival at Leavenworth Federal Penitentiary in February 1931. *NARA*

Charles Leiter, pictured here, and his partner Henry Shorr took over control of the Oakland Sugar House in the spring of 1924 after the murder of Isadore Cantor and the attempted murder of George Goldberg. *Walter Reuther Library.*

MALFEASANCE

By the middle of nineteen-twenties, Detroit was one of the wettest cities in the nation. Most people agreed that Prohibition was *not* working, if only because of the little fact that there seemed to be *more* booze on the streets now than back when it was legal. Detroit Police Superintendent William P. Rutledge stated that there were at least 15,000 blind pigs and saloons in Detroit, ten times the amount before 1918. Adding the number of city police officers, it broke down that blind pigs outnumbered the police nearly seven to one.[1]

News crime reporter Jack Carlisle remembered the era fondly in a 1983 interview, "The town, nobody could understand it, the way it is now. The town was completely wide open…the blind pigs were wide open. The peepholes were just to give them local color, you know…You see, if you could just see a town where anything went, anything. Wide open, nobody thought anything of it. Everybody was drinking themselves goofy."[2]

The Motor City housed a diverse cross-section of criminals in the 1920s, some bigger than others. For the most part, there was no overall criminal combination in place, unlike cities such as New York and Chicago. Average Joes who were otherwise law-abiding citizens sought to supplement their income by smuggling beer and liquor across the river. Add the fact that the Prohibition squads that patrolled the river were tragically inept at this point in time, and that at least half of the police department seemed to be corrupt, that made it all better. But the novices often found themselves working side by side beside vicious men like the Sugar House Boys and the Mafia, and things often turned violent.

Most of the city was divvied up like a large butcher's chart. Downtown was, for the most part, neutral territory. Greektown however, which spread for a few blocks in each direction from the intersection of Beaubien and Monroe streets, housed a surprisingly violent consortium of Greek gamblers headed by Jimmy "The Greek" Thompson and John Kollipoulis that controlled their territory with an iron fist. Corktown, located a mile west of downtown and north of Michigan Avenue, was the home of an Irish gang headed by Bernard Doherty that specialized in bootlegging as well as the occasional payroll robbery.

East of Corktown and centered around the intersection of Third Avenue and Porter Street, Chinatown provided restaurants and curio shops for locals and tourists. Those with vice in mind repaired to the neighborhood's gambling dens and brothels, all of which were controlled by the local branch of the On Leong Tong. More than a few folks, including some of the city's leading gangsters, were drawn to the plentiful opium dens in the district. They would enter the dimly lit rooms, slip off their shoes, and toke themselves into euphoria. Although members of the On Leong's archrival tong, the Hip Sing, would show up periodically and make everyone nervous, Chinatown remained mostly trouble-free.

The Midtown area of Detroit was home to the Tallman Gang. Their namesake and leader, Joseph Tallman, was a throwback to the 19th century when gang bosses battled bare-knuckled in the street. Standing well over six feet tall with a muscular build, Tallman was a fearsome street fighter who was reputed to have beaten at least one man to death with his bare hands. Tallman and his men, mostly of Anglo-American descent, were headquartered out of a blind pig on Third Avenue in the West Canfield district. While Tallman occasionally smuggled beer and rum up from the Florida Gulf Coast, he spent most of his time sparring with the East Side Mafia factions over Detroit River booze landing spots.[3]

The Southwest Side was primarily the domain of bootlegger August Nykiel. The son of Polish immigrants, Nykiel was a handsome, well-built man who looked more like a pro football quarterback than a criminal. Indeed, at one point he had been one of the owners of the short-lived NFL franchise Detroit Tigers. Gus Nykiel supplied whiskey for the thirsty Delray residents who manned the local steel mills.[4] The Southwest Side's beer action was handled by two brothers, Cloyd and Roy Beck, who not only made homebrew but smuggled in large quantities of the real deal from Canada.[5]

Bound roughly by East Vernor Highway, Lafayette Boulevard, Brush Street, and John R, Paradise Valley was home to the city's African-American community. The district was thought to have gotten its name from the Asian "Paradise" trees that grew so easily in the neighborhood. The Valley was home to many thriving businesses, as well as to raucous nightclubs that featured some of the country's biggest up-and-coming jazz musicians. While illegal booze was easy to come by, the name of the Paradise Valley crime game was policy, or illegal lottery.

Migrating Blacks brought with them from the Deep South the custom of betting on a number daily, which was chosen from a wheel spun in the neighborhood. A winning number could often put food on the table for a poor family; bets could be placed for a little as one cent. After a wager was made with a bookie, the runner carried the "slips" to the policy "bank." Often the odds ran as high as 1,000 to 1, creating the potential for enormous profits for whoever controlled the game. The undisputed head of the Valley's policy games was John Roxborough, the wealthiest African-American man in Detroit. An insurance executive and publisher of the weekly *Detroit Owl* newspaper, Roxborough and his family lived in a luxurious house in the North End. The street end of Roxborough's numbers racket was run by Frank Loftis out of a clearing house called The Idle Hour at 2905 St. Antoine Street. A large, powerful man who spoke with a heavy "geechee" accent, Loftis was perhaps the most visible Black gangster in Detroit by the mid-1920s.[6]

The rest of the East Side was almost exclusively the territory of the mostly Sicilian Mafia family. Ignazio Caruso led with an effective, low-key style that contrasted sharply with the blood-soaked years of the 1910s. The family's businesses included large-scale liquor manufacture and smuggling, protection racketeering, counterfeiting, prostitution, illegal gambling, and narcotics peddling. Opiates such as morphine and heroin were the drugs of choice. In addition to being connected to other Mafia families in America and Sicily, the Detroit family now belonged to an effective local crime conglomerate known to law enforcement as the "Pascuzzi Combine." Named for Ontario bootlegger Roy Pascuzzi, this group was responsible for controlling rackets on both sides of the border. Both American and Canadian mob leaders mediated all decisions.

Easily the most powerful criminal force in Detroit during Prohibition, the family's crews controlled large blocs of the city and dealt harshly with those who defied them. They controlled booze running on the upper Detroit River and Lake St. Clair; independents who wished to smuggle in peace were forced to pay staggering tributes (as high as sixty and seventy percent of their profits) to the Sicilians. The family also put a similar squeeze on Downriver smugglers in Ecorse, Wyandotte, and Grosse Ile. By 1925, Sam Catalanotte had replaced Ignazio Caruso as boss of the Detroit family. Angelo Meli inherited leadership of the East Side crew after its previous leader, Joe DeStefano, was afflicted with a fatal case of lead poisoning while sitting in a car on Chene Street. Catalanotte named as his underboss a respected mobster named Gaspare Milazzo. Chester LaMare still ruled the roost in Hamtramck, and now had a lucrative fruit concession with the Ford Motor Company in addition to his gambling, bootlegging, and extortion rackets.

Most of the Detroit Mafia family's liquor smuggling was handled by the newly formed Licavoli crew. Dubbed the "River Gang" by the papers, this crew of young energetic mobsters was headed by Pete and Thomas "Yonnie" Licavoli. While growing up in St. Louis's Little Italy, the Licavoli brothers got their start in the lower rungs of the infamous Egan's Rats mob. After furthering their criminal education with the Sicilian-American Russo Gang, the brothers and many of their associates migrated to Detroit. Sam Catalanotte accepted them into the family and was known to trust them implicitly. Most of the Licavolis' men were former St. Louisans as well. They included amongst their ranks many cousins, such as Peter "Horseface" Licavoli and James "Jack" Licavoli.[7]

Headquartered in the Islandview neighborhood that surrounded the entrance to the Belle Isle Bridge, the Licavolis used the island as an ideal landing spot for smuggled booze. *News* crime reporter Jack Carlisle knew the Licavoli boys well. Although he was technically an outsider, Pete Licavoli liked Carlisle enough to actually invite him along on a rum-running expedition, and Jack would later vividly describe the machine-like efficiency with which the Licavolis worked;[8]

"Over at Riverside they signed manifests and they took the cases of Canadian whisky and labeled them for the Bahamas, Bimini, Nassau. I don't know how they (the Canadian authorities) figured anyone could take a speedboat from Riverside, Ontario to Nassau…What they used to do in those days, the Licavoli Mob, they had gigantic flashlights, great big things in two colors, red and green. They had lookouts on Belle Isle. They put them up in the air in trees. Red meant the federal patrol was out, green meant they were docked, go ahead. And then you dash across the river; nothing to it. They had better speedboats than the federal patrol anyway."

Second cousins to the Licavoli brothers, the Moceri boys handled liquor smuggling north of the city limits, moving alcohol across the river into the Grosse Pointe suburbs and throughout Macomb County. Known to police and the Detroit media as the "Lake St. Clair Gang," this Mafia crew was headed by Joseph Moceri and included his brothers James and Leo, cousins, and close friends. When Lake St. Clair would freeze over in the dead of the Michigan winter, the Moceris would often drive the truckloads of Canadian booze directly across the ice.[9]

The North End of the city was strictly the domain of the up-and-coming

Sugar House Boys. Due to the increasing volume of beer and liquor they were handling, their territory had by now expanded greatly. The Sugar House area of operations was roughly defined by Dequindre Avenue to the east, Mack Avenue on the south, with their western boundary following Woodward Avenue north until Grand Boulevard, where it jogged west to Grand River Avenue. The gang's territory snaked northwest to the then-outskirts of the city around Livernois Avenue and back along Davison until Highland Park city limits. While no underworld observer had actually expected them to win the gang war with the Venice Café Gang, the kids from Oakland Avenue had handled themselves well and gained newfound respect. Abe and Joe Burnstein's power and influence continued to surge upwards. A familiar sight at the city's gaming tables and high-end nightclubs, the Burnsteins enjoyed all the trappings of successful racketeers; tons of cash, expensive automobiles; flashy suits and jewelry.

The Burnsteins' biggest coup during the mid-1920s was to establish a racing wire service. Fronted by the ostensibly legitimate Motor City Filling Pad Company at 7310 Woodward Avenue, this wire service provided the city's betting parlors with race results/information for horse and dog races all over the world. Many of Detroit's betting parlors (usually referred to as handbooks) were forced to pay a handsome fee to use the Burnsteins' wire service.[10]

The Burnstein brothers also traveled to other cities to gamble and set up business deals. They rubbed elbows with such individuals as New York mob figures Arnold Rothstein, Jacob "Little Augie" Orgen, Louis "Lepke" Buchalter, Waxey Gordon and the Sherman brothers, Henry and Charles aka Chink; Philadelphia mob boss Max "Boo Boo" Hoff; Boston gangster Charles "King" Solomon; Atlantic City crime czar Enoch "Nucky" Johnson, and Chicago overlord Al Capone. Abe and Joe frequently journeyed to Miami and Havana, Cuba, both of which were appealing destinations for those looking to escape Detroit's frigid winters.

Both Charlie Leiter and Henry Shorr saw themselves awash in money and prestige as well. Leiter handled the administrative side of the business while Shorr functioned as a bagman and emissary to other gangsters. Both men were vital in the mob's "alley brewery" racket. Leiter and Shorr would set up large-scale whiskey stills or beer brewing operations in barns and/or buildings. Most often these structures were located behind otherwise legitimate homes or businesses, hence the term "alley breweries." Naturally, the operators of these alley breweries bought all their supplies from the Oakland Sugar House. These covert operations proved highly lucrative.[11]

Twenty-two year old Ray Burnstein controlled the street end of the Sugar

House crew's action. Ray could not only effectively give orders but also relay those from his brothers as well as Charlie Leiter and Henry Shorr. Although somewhat small by modern standards (5'7" and 140 lbs.), Ray was strong as an ox and known to have a hair-trigger temper. Ray could be generous with his friends and ruthless with his enemies. A handsome dude with gray-blue eyes and wavy dark hair, Burnstein was known as a ladies man. One associate remembered his appealing personality well, "Ray Bernstein (*sic*) was a very nice, charming guy. I remember my first wife, a young thing. Bernstein and Yonnie Licavoli were supposed to be the two toughest guys in town. My wife said, 'Oh, Mr. Bernstein, I always thought you were a tough gangster. You're such a nice fellow.' Christ, I could have killed her..."[12]

Burnstein's second-in-command, Harry Fleisher, had seen his star rise as well. In addition to acting as Charles Leiter's personal bodyguard, Harry had recently married Bella Burnstein, sister of fellow gangster Sam "Fats" Burnstein. Standing at a modest 5'6", with a stout build and a chubby-cheeked visage that looked as if it belonged to a choir boy rather than a mobster, Fleisher did not evoke fear in any sensible person. Such appearances were deceiving, however, as he was now known in the underworld as a dangerous killer. When a job of murder arose, Harry often handled the "hit" himself rather than delegating it out. Although now widely referred to amongst police by the clerical error-induced name of Fleisher, Harry's gangster pals usually called him "H.F.".

While delivering truckloads of corn sugar and other booze making goodies, Fleisher paid close attention to see if a brewer/distiller guarded his charges. If not, Harry would return later to steal all the jugs of alcohol on the site. Fleisher, backed up by some of his pals, would simply draw his gat and kick in the door. If the booze was well-hidden on the premises, H.F. would dispatch agile gangster Sam "The Gorilla" Davis, whose small height allowed him access to the cramped places where liquor was often stashed. After the booze was found, Fleisher would sometimes offer a nearby derelict a few bucks to load their truck for them. After completing his task, the bum would ask for his reward and invariably be told to get lost. If he persisted, the poor man was paid off in the form of a bullet in the head. The violent avariciousness of Harry Fleisher's methods proved very effective.[13]

Indeed, hijacking became a staple of the Sugar House Gang. While their alley breweries and alky cooking brought in oodles of dreck, most of the alcohol "The Boys" handled was smuggled across the river by someone else. They would often ambush a load as it came off the river and shoot anyone who resisted them. The hijackers were extremely violent, regularly pistol-whipping their victims. Men and women were subjected to equal treatment. Guys like Louis Achtman, the Fleisher brothers; Little Morris Raider, Abe Zussman, Jack Redfern, and the Keywell brothers were all efficient at stealing loads of liquor.

In retrospect, the Sugar House crew's devotion to hijacking beer and booze seems extraordinarily ballsy *and* dangerous. Basing a liquor racket on stolen merchandise was inherently hazardous, as the victims of such raids (especially other bootleggers) tended to be equally violent and armed, to boot. In addition, the criminal penalties of such thefts were far greater than the mere sale. Finally, the potential profits from said thefts were dependent on what the victims could make or smuggle across the river. These risks aside, the boys managed to obtain large financial rewards from stealing from others.

Throughout Prohibition, the younger members of the Sugar House Gang preferred taking their illegal alcohol by force while older, mature members favored wholesale production or smuggling. However it was obtained, the high-test booze was then diluted and re-bottled to create even greater profits. The cut whiskey was distributed through "The Two Sammies," Sam Cohen and Sam Kert. Cohen and Kert had grown up in Little Jerusalem with the Burnsteins and handled the non-violent end of liquor distribution.

Those blind pig owners who refused to buy Sugar House beer and liquor were beaten severely (or worse) and had their businesses trashed. After agreeing to whatever exorbitant sales plan the gangsters worked out, the hapless saloon owners discovered that their troubles were just beginning, for other members of the mob were not far behind. These new guys would coerce the blind pigger into turning over a healthy share of his overall profits to the gang. Never mind that he was already buying booze from the Sugar House Boys. Never mind that goons from *other gangs* were already shaking him down. The choice was simple; pay or die. Sugar House gangsters such as Angel Face Kaminsky, Irving Shapiro, and Ziggie Selbin were exceptionally proficient in blind pig extortion.

Despite their dedication to hijacking, some of the North End boys began smuggling whiskey across the river from Canada, which they usually landed at the railroad yards in between Third and Fourth streets. The dingy motorboats they used to transport their product across the water were jokingly referred to as the "Third Street Navy." The two heads of this crew were Sam Solomon and Jack Selbin; the latter's delicatessen served as a headquarters for the "Navy."[14]

Another key liquor supply route for the Burnstein crew was a rum-smuggling network set up by Sam "Trombenik" Abramson. This large-scale bootlegging outfit by now dwarfed the original alky-cooking operation set up by Jake Trager. Abramson had rum smuggled in from the Caribbean to waiting trucks in southern Florida, which would then transport the booze north. Youthful members of the Sugar House Gang would often drive trucks north along a route parallel with today's Interstate 75. They always went heavily armed in order to protect against hijackers.

By the mid-1920s, Sammy Trombenik was said to be worth nearly a half-million dollars. While living at his lavish West Grand Boulevard apartment, Sam threw wild parties that were so lively that the noise kept his neighbors awake for weeks. When they finally complained to police, Sam sought to placate their injured feelings by buying the entire building out from under them for a substantial sum. In addition to the Circle Restaurant on Hastings Street, Abramson owned a number of profitable blind pigs in and around Little Jerusalem. Sam also ran a popular Division Street chophouse called the Oriental Rest, which was known for rib steaks broiled over a large charcoal fire and served on wooden platters.

Abramson did not usually get personally involved in his rum-running operation. On the one occasion where Sam did, it cost him two years of his life. In late 1925, Abramson himself was driving a truck when US Customs agents pulled him to the side of the road. Sam was dressed in dirty overalls and a cap, but his immaculately manicured hands, along with his snappy bow tie and shiny shoes, gave him away. His truck, disguised as an oil carrier, had only one spigot. Oil trucks usually had three. As a result, Sammy Trombenik was convicted for violating the Volstead Act. After a lengthy appeal process that kept him free for nearly a year, Sam went off to serve a two-year sentence in federal prison. While he was away his Circle Restaurant finally closed, signaling the end of an era.[15]

In addition to the various illegal alcohol endeavors, the Sugar House Boys also entered the narcotics business, specifically specializing in morphine, heroin, and opium. The Burnstein mob not only sold dope but also took sizeable cuts from others in their Detroit territory that did (one heroin ring was reported to have coughed up $20,000 in 'protection' payments to the Sugar House crew.) This "cartelization" of the drug business served as good insulation from the Federal Narcotics Bureau, a notoriously persistent foe of Prohibition gangsters.[16]

More than a few of the North End hoods sampled these products. Sugar House bootlegger Jake Weinberg was a known opium smoker, as were Jack Stein and Willie Laks. Jazz legend Milton "Mezz" Mezzrow knew the Sugar House crew well and vividly recalled in his autobiography when Jake Weinberg and a few other gangsters introduced him to opium during a card game at the

Charlotte Hotel. After several hands, a few of the boys disappeared into an adjoining bedroom without explanation. An experienced user and dealer of marijuana, Mezzrow was intrigued by the strange, pungent smell wafting from the room. Curiosity got the better of him and Mezz was invited inside; [17]

"That was one walk I sure wish I had never taken. It took me five seconds to get into that room and, later on, damn near five years to crawl all the way out again, on my hands and knees.

"The smell in that room was enough to knock you out. It was sort of sweet, with a punch in it, heavy as an insomniac's eyelids, so thick and solid it was like a brick wall built all around you. It made my smeller tingle, got me scared and excited me too, put me on edge – it promised a rare, jam-up kick, some once-in-a-life-time thrill. The three guys were stretched out crossways on the bed, one of them facing the other two, and between them was a round brass tray filled full of funny little gadgets, with a small lamp burning right in the center of it. There was a bowl of fruit laying on the bed too. It looked like a scene straight out of the Arabian Nights, with the thieves and princes disguised in pinchback sports jackets. I was looking for the carpet to flap and take off any minute now and sail out of the window, bed and all, with the four of us sprawled out on it."

After some hesitation, Mezzrow gave in to the gangsters' wooing and lay down on the bed. Weinberg came inside and instructed the young musician how to smoke his first "pill:"

"...a heatwave heaved up out of my stomach and spread all through me, right down to my toes, the most intense and pleasant sensation I have ever felt in all my life. At first it tipped easy-like through my main line, then it surged and galloped down all my sidestreets; and every atom in my body began to shimmy in delight. That fiery little pill was dancing up and down every single strand of my nervous system, plucking each one until it hummed a merry song, lighting up a million bulbs in my body that I never knew were there – I didn't even know there were any sockets for them. I glowed all over, like the sun was planted in my breadbasket. Man, I was sent, and I didn't want to come back."

The Sugar House gangsters also began acting as guards for local gamblers. While exiting one of the city's posh casinos with a boatload of cash, the gambler could frequently be targeted by amateur cowboys who thought the soft-handed cardsharps would be easy marks for a heist. No doubt on the recommendation of Abe and Joey Burnstein, Detroit's high-rollers would pay for one or two of the Sugar House Boys to accompany them on their gaming ventures. Some Detroit gamblers that enjoyed protection from the crew were Danny Sullivan, Ruby Mathias, Cassius "Cash" McDonald, Lincoln Fitzgerald, and the Wertheimer brothers, Mert, Al, Lionel, and Lou.[18]

In addition to extorting blind pig owners and drug dealers, the North End gangsters began shaking down legitimate businesses, including local movie theaters. The theater owners were forced to pay high fees to play prizefight films that the Sugar House Boys had provided. A group of the owners eventually wrote a complaining letter to J. Edgar Hoover, the head of the burgeoning FBI (Federal Bureau of Investigation), "We think that this is an outrage and you should investigate this matter right now and not let these gangsters make thousands every year at this racket and pay no income tax and get away with it. Can't we have some protection please?" They asked that their names not be made public, "because we don't want no stink bombs put in our theaters or else the back blown up, or worse."[19]

Another man wrote the FBI, "Several years ago this mob came to my office and announced that they would take charge and if I didn't like it my body would be found floating in the Detroit River...I was compelled to let these parasites run my business and take the biggest cut of the profits or face death."[20]

The Sugar House crew also dabbled in insurance fraud. One prime example involved one of the cofounders of the Sugar House, George Goldberg. Although no longer the owner of the Oakland Avenue depot, Goldberg continued to rake in thousands of dollars with his pals in bootlegging and other businesses. One of the latter was an auto parts store known as Credit Sam's, Inc. at 14034 Woodward Avenue. After maxing out his profits here, Goldberg watched as Credit Sam's was destroyed by a large fire late one February night. George was not distressed, however, as he pocketed a healthy insurance claim from the blaze, which was suspected by police to have been deliberately set.[21]

Hijacking. Bootlegging. Robbery. Burglary. Extortion. Arson. Fraud. There was not a felony that the Sugar House Boys would not commit; including, increasingly, murder.

One prime example of this was when Lou Fleisher took out William Glanzrock, who was on the run from a Bronx jewel heist when he turned up in Detroit in the spring of 1926, where he immediately hit it off with the Sugar House Gang. The New York jewel thief was occasionally called "Two-Gun Willie" because he carried two pistols in matching shoulder holsters. The flamboyant Glanzrock quickly wore out his welcome by acting the part of a bully; he often demanded money to help fight his extradition to New York for the robbery. One night in a Hamtramck nightclub, "Two-Gun Willie" got into a beef with local Mafia chieftain Chester LaMare. The latter, without his customary bodyguards, went for his gun only to have Glanzrock beat him to the draw and fire several shots that sent the mobster running for his life. LaMare publicly declared that he forgave Glanzrock for his boozy hot-headedness.

At midnight on July 20, 1926, Two-Gun Willie Glanzrock was drinking with his friend Charlie Goodman in the Exchange Café at 9136 Oakland Avenue. This speakeasy was an especially popular roost for the Sugar House Boys, who would spend endless hours on the premises drinking, playing cards, shooting dice, plotting crimes, and bullshitting. Many of the boys were on hand that evening, including Louis Fleisher. Later testimony revealed that he and Glanzrock had an intense private discussion, possibly amount a liquor deal. A few minutes before 1 o'clock, Fleisher got up and left in silence.

Around 1:30, Charlie Goodman went to get his car as Glanzrock staggered out the door and into the humid night. Goodman waited in the car across the street from the Exchange at the corner of Leicester and Oakland. As Glanzrock got within a few feet of the vehicle, a burst of pistol shots came from the dark areaway between the two houses closest to the corner. Two-Gun Willie went down with bullets in his head and neck. A stray round hit a woman named Dora Sarfatti as she stepped off a streetcar that had just stopped across from the Exchange. Louis Fleisher dashed out from between the two houses, smoking gun in hand, and sprinted south toward his home at 631 Chandler Street.

Glanzrock had ingested so much alcohol in the Exchange that he was far from dead. Willie amazingly got to his feet and staggered after Fleisher on rubbery legs, only to collapse on the corner. Glanzrock then managed to sit up and get both of his pistols out before sinking back onto the sidewalk. Goodman ran forward, grabbed the guns, and sped off in his car. William Glanzrock would later die at the hospital. Fleisher and Goodman both eventually ended up in police hands. After giving the usual litany of gangland epithets to the police, Lou Fleisher apparently confessed to the killing, pleading self-defense. The police apparently bought Fleisher's story and declined to prosecute.[22]

OF COURSE, the Sugar House Gang and their various counterparts could not have gotten away with all this for as long as they did without at least tacit approval from the powers-that-be, meaning local law enforcement and politicians. While little evidence of specific corruption during the 1920s survives, members of the Detroit Police Department were known to receive payoffs to look the other way when concerned with "acceptable" vices such as bootlegging, gambling, and prostitution. They were seen as "acceptable" because they provided a high-demand service to the community and seemingly harmed no one. While narcotics didn't fall into this category, as long as they were sold strictly in lower-income and/or minority neighborhoods, no fuss was raised. Many police officers, regardless of rank, saw no harm in augmenting their meager salaries with a regular bribe in order to help facilitate these vices.

The odd slack-jawed corpse that turned up in the gutter with his toes curled up was mostly seen as an occupational hazard. As long as the victim was a fellow criminal and not an honest citizen, the cops were willing to look the other way, for the most part. This was part of the mythical underworld maxim later made famous by New York gangster Bugsy Siegel, "We only kill each other." Public gangland hits, however (especially those in broad daylight), were bad for business. They tended to have multiple witnesses and endanger innocent bystanders. With these gaudy bloodbaths came the attendant raids and anti-crime platitudes, but they tended to fade once the newspaper headlines did.

Some DPD precincts were reportedly so corrupt that they operated literally as mini-crime families in their respective neighborhoods, taking their cut from every hootch peddler, blind pig owner, pimp, dope pusher, and bookie. While there were good cops on the force, they seemed to be ever-decreasing in number, and one could never be quite sure who they were.

The Detroit underworld's geyser of graft also gushed up into City Hall, as many of the town's politicians agreed that acceptable vices were necessary for a metropolis of Detroit's stature, and knew full well that the councilman, judge, clerk, or mayor who even *tried* to overtly enforce Prohibition could find himself voted out of office as soon as the next election rolled around.

Federal law enforcement wasn't much better off. The Bureau of Prohibition, in addition to being hopelessly outnumbered, was plagued with corruption. The average salary of a "prohi" ranged from $1200 to $2000 per year. Detroit's bootleggers could (and did) offer up to seven times that amount in order to convince them to turn a blind eye to their smuggling and/or cooking. The bureau often failed to run adequate background checks on their prospective agents, resulting in some Detroit prohis who were little better than the gangsters they were hired to catch. Young J. Edgar Hoover and his FBI (still officially named the Bureau of Investigation in the mid-1920s) had little jurisdiction and even less skill in combating Detroit's underworld. While the Federal Narcotics Bureau (FBN) made the occasional large bust, the illegal drug racket had yet to become the megabucks business that it is today.

Thus stacked up against an avalanche of illegal booze and its resultant multi-million dollar profits, those few honest civil servants who managed to bob their heads above the waves of corruption often found that their attempts to enforce the law had the collective impact of a fart in a hurricane. The end result was a city that was, as Jack Carlisle so eloquently put it, "completely wide open."

WHEN THEY WERE not perpetrating any of the previously listed offenses, the Sugar House Boys loitered in Abe Finkelstein's Oakland Avenue restaurant or the Exchange Café. For a change of pace, they would take a *shvitz* at one of the neighborhood bath houses. Invisible in the steam like gravelly-voiced ghosts, the boys would lounge back and discuss criminal business, just as their *Vorovskoy Mir* predecessors did back in Russia a generation before. They also hung out in a strip of pool halls and blind pigs along Woodward Avenue, from Sibley Street up to about Alexandrine Avenue. Located dead center on this strip, at Woodward and Charlotte, was the Addison Hotel, where many of the boys lived. The boys frequented the many illegal gambling parlors in the city; trying their luck at cards, dice, roulette, and countless other games of chance. The Tom Thumb miniature golf course at Woodward and Temple was a particular attraction to the gangsters.

While there was often confusion, then and now, about the nature of these different factions (such as the Sugar House Gang and the Third Street Navy), they essentially consisted of the same individuals. The boys usually drifted from one group to another without even thinking about it. By the virtue of their shared ethnicity and the fact that most of them had grown up together, the boys operated as a cohesive unit. Unlike their crime counterparts in the Mafia, there was no rigid chain-of-command in place in the Sugar House mob, which was a much more elastic, loosely organized criminal consortium.

As the Sugar House Boys rose to the top of Detroit's underworld food chain, more and more crooks were recruited into their ranks. Many of them, like the gang war reinforcements, came from New York City. Their Detroit-raised brethren called these Big Apple transplants "Yorkies." Four new faces in the mid-twenties would make an especially big impact on the crew;

The first was thirty-two year old Harry Kirschenbaum, a native of the Pale who grew up on the Lower East Side of Manhattan. Harry proved to be an unruly type early on and notched his first arrest at the age of fifteen in 1908.

Before he moved to Detroit in late 1924, Kirschenbaum had served one term in the Elmira Reformatory and two more in Sing Sing Prison. Although small physically (5-foot 4-inches and 145 pounds) and missing the first joint of his left index finger, Harry was a very tough customer whose numerous bullet and knife scars suggested he could be a scrapper if pressed. Kirschenbaum's first job in Detroit was as the armed guard of Mert Wertheimer's State Street casino. Harry became a good friend of Joey Burnstein's and found a home in the burgeoning Sugar House Gang. Usually referred to by his gangland associates as "Tim" or "Timmy", Kirschenbaum would eventually be entrusted with management of the gang's lucrative racing wire service at the Motor City Filling Pad Company.[23]

Twenty-six year old Giuseppe Miragliotta was born in Sicily and brought to America as a young boy. Growing up in Cleveland's Big Italy, he apparently fell in with criminal types and was eventually implicated in the murder of a Kent, Ohio police officer. Fleeing across state lines to Michigan, Miragliotta adopted the name of Joseph Miller. After a short time with the Sugar House Boys, Miller picked up the nickname "Honey." One of the few Gentile criminals to catch on with the crew, Honey Miller stood 5'8" and weighed a solid 185 pounds. An extremely capable muscle artist and assassin, Miller was nevertheless known amongst his pals as a "bug," or a mentally unstable criminal. Sporting baby blue eyes, a mouthful of gold teeth, and a lexicon of picturesque slang, Honey proved to be a most colorful add to the Sugar House ranks.[24]

Johnny Reid was born on January 4, 1891 in Manhattan's Hell Kitchen. Brought to St. Louis as a toddler, Reid fell in with local street gangs and became a member of the notorious Egan's Rats mob. He relocated to Toledo, Ohio in 1917 after getting indicted along with his pal Fred Burke for forgery. After a number of pick pocketing arrests, Reid moved across the state line and began running illegal booze north from Toledo. Detroit Police arrested him in February 1919 for the murder of James "Umpty" Devlin, a recently returned soldier who had reportedly stolen two bottles of whiskey from Reid. But Johnny ended up being discharged for that perennial favorite, lack of evidence.

Reid then returned to his native New York City and became a gambler and bootlegger who operated out of Hell's Kitchen. Johnny also began a relationship with Hazel Warner, a beautiful, wealthy socialite who also happened to be seeing the notorious gambler and con man Robert Tourbillion, better known to history as Dapper Don Collins. Collins barged into Warner's home at 1892 University Avenue in the Bronx on the morning of May 16, 1921. He dashed into the upstairs bedroom, .25 caliber automatic in hand,

and found Reid combing his hair in front of a mirror. Collins opened fire on him at point blank range. The first bullet struck Johnny in the forehead, a second crashed into his face just below the left eye, a third entered his open mouth, another struck the right side of his neck and a fifth buried itself in his right thigh. Dapper Don Collins, who had every reason to think that Reid was dead, retreated downstairs past the screaming Warner.

Incredibly, Johnny was still breathing when police arrived and managed to gargle that he had shot himself before passing out. The reason Johnny lived to tell of this was at the instant of the first shot, he had instinctively twisted to his right, which caused the bullet bound for his forehead to traverse the skull rather than penetrate it. While Reid survived, he did lose his left eye due to the severe trauma of his second bullet wound.

Police opinion was about evenly divided as to the motive, whether Don Collins was jealous of Reid's relations with Hazel Warner or acting on orders from gambler Nicky Arnstein. After several months of recuperation, Johnny returned to Detroit with a reputation of leading a "charmed life." Soon after his return he opened a blind pig at the corner of Third and Peterboro. Despite his small, almost frail build, his bullet-scarred face and glass eye marked Johnny Reid as a tough customer, someone never to cross.[25]

Reid became one of the key liquor distributors for the Sugar House mob. Harkening back to his St. Louis roots, Johnny drew recruits for his operation from a surprisingly large pool of Missouri State Prison alumni that thrived in the city. These Show-Me-State ex-cons, drawn like moths to the flame of Detroit's illegal liquor business, often bunked at flophouses in the Cass Corridor area and checked in at Reid's new blind pig to see if there was any "heavy work" available. They included amongst their number Robert Carey, Raymond "Crane-Neck" Nugent, James Ellis, Leroy "Doggy" Snyder, Tony Ortell, Charles "Tennessee Slim" Hurley, John "Pudgy" Dunn, and Joseph "Red" O'Riordan (Carey's brother-in-law.) The most important member of Reid's crew was his old buddy Fred "Killer" Burke.

Born in May 1893, Burke was a one-time Kansas farm boy who had briefly studied veterinary medicine before embarking on life of crime after garnering a forgery indictment as the result of a land fraud scheme that he had been roped into. After serving as a Tank Corps sergeant on the Western Front, Burke was arrested and convicted of forgery in Detroit in 1919. Burke ultimately served a year in Jackson and another fourteen months in Missouri's notoriously tough Jefferson City penitentiary. Burke became known in the St. Louis underworld as a closed-mouthed yet industrious gangster who was noted for both his marksmanship with machine guns and for donning a police uniform in order to fool potential victims. Burke initially arrived back in Detroit during the winter of 1924. He and his pals pulled off a disappointing jewelry robbery in downtown Detroit's Book Building on March 10 of that year, which resulted in one of their number, Isadore Londe, getting a lengthy sentence in the penitentiary up in Marquette.

By the beginning of 1925, the St. Louisans had reassembled in Detroit to plan another caper. Their impending job was interrupted by a January 1925 intergang rift when Pudgy Dunn drunkenly accused Tennessee Slim Hurley of being in on the 1916 murder of his brother Harry and shot him as a result. Hurley survived his wounds and Dunn got a long stretch in prison. If possible, their upcoming crime was even sloppier.

In the early morning hours of January 10, 1925, the Rats sought to rob a gambling den located at 2439 Milwaukee Avenue. Thirty-year old Raymond Bishop, a former stick man for Lefty Clark, had recently opened up the joint. Joe Burnstein himself was on the scene when three men entered the place through a second-story skylight and hid in the bathroom until the owner retired to his office to count the night's take. Unbeknownst to the Rats, owner Ray Bishop possessed an anti-robbery device in the form of a Colt .45 automatic pistol. During the fast and furious gun battle that ensued, both Bishop and gangster Arthur Wilson were fatally wounded while the other heisters fled empty-handed.[26]

The Burnstein brothers sought to keep Reid and the St. Louis boys in their fold by telling them that their Jesse James tactics just wouldn't be tolerated in Detroit; that they should join them in the lucrative booze business instead of doing penny-ante stick-ups. This view was only reinforced when one of the Rats, Tennessee Slim Hurley, tied on a good one in a Hamtramck speakeasy and ran into (of all people) Chester LaMare. Hurley had been drunk and abusive at the bar, boasting of how much money he would make in Detroit. LaMare called the St. Louisan over to his table. The place got pin-drop quiet as the mobster softly introduced himself and then slapped Slim in the face, the noise sounding like a rifle shot in the stillness. Despite the .45 in his shoulder holster, Tennessee Slim returned to the bar, bought the house a round, and quietly left.

Fred Burke and his crew, more bandits than racketeers, established an autonomous relationship with the Sugar House Boys and agreed to keep their noses clean. What the Burnsteins didn't know was that the Rats had already begun a lucrative racket that would eventually help tear the newfound alliance apart.

Burke and his pals had perfected what was called the "Snatch Racket," meaning that the St. Louis boys would kidnap a wealthy businessman or gambler and drive him south into Toledo to get beyond the reach of Michigan authorities. Burke usually chose those who operated either in or on the fringes of the underworld, as such people were less likely to go to the police. While in Ohio, the mark's family and/or associates were contacted and told to pay a sizeable ransom or else. Once the money was obtained, the victim was released unharmed. The so-called "St. Louis Gang" eventually snatched many well-heeled gamblers and rumrunners. Over a three year period, the Detroit Police estimated that the Burke crew would collect over $334,000 in various ransoms. In addition, their closeness to the Sugar House Gang gave the St. Louis boys a unique edge in determining when their targets would not be guarded and be vulnerable for a snatch.[27]

PERHAPS THE MOST important new recruit for the Sugar House mob had started out, incidentally, on the right side of the law. This man proved to be the first half of the most deadly murder team known to Prohibition-era Detroit.

Local police and media would refer to the pair by many terms, including "The Siamese Twins," "sawed-off Napoleons," or "Public Enemy No. 1 and 2." History has recorded their names as Abe Axler and Eddie Fletcher.

Samuel Edward Fleischacker was born in 1900 in Stanislau, Austria-Hungary (present-day Ivano-Frankivsk, Ukraine) to Tobias and Celia Fleischacker. Brought to America at the age of six, Samuel proved to be ambitious and outgoing from an early age. Samuel's family initially settled in the ghetto of Manhattan's Lower East Side in a cramped apartment at 117 Norfolk Street. Not long after Samuel's tenth birthday, the Fleischackers had moved into a different tenement a few blocks away at 61 Clinton Street. Like most other neighborhood boys, Samuel (he most often went by his middle name of Eddie) fell in with the other local Jewish youths, hanging out in the streets and getting into trouble. Fleischacker struck up a friendship with a boy who lived in his building named Samuel Axler.[28] As they were nearly the same age and had the same first name, they immediately hit it off. Axler soon introduced Fleischacker to his cousin who lived next door at No. 63, and the die was cast.[29]

Abraham Axler was born in 1901 in the *shtetl* of Złoczów, Austria-Hungary (present-day Zolochiv, Ukraine) to Bernard and Anna Axler. Brought to America with his family at the age of six, Axler had been a product of the Lower East Side through and through. The youngest boy in his family, Abe was also the roughest. While his cousin Samuel (who most often went by his middle name of Simon) was known to occasionally show positive traits, Abe was a problem from the start.[30]

Just how Abe Axler and Fleischacker hit it off is unknown, as they were completely opposite personalities; Eddie was a year older and outgoing, while Abe was quiet and morose. Eddie showed pugilistic talent and yearned to be a prizefighter while Abe was picking pockets and stealing from an early age. Nevertheless, the two became best friends and inseparable companions.

Fleischacker and his two new friends passed through adolescence in the teeming underbelly of the Lower East Side, hearing stories of powerful Jewish gangsters such as Big Jack Zelig, Dopey Benny Fein, and Charlie Auerbach. Much as Joe Murphy and Jake Trager had served as role models for the Bishop Union crew in Detroit, this trio of *shtarkers* did for Fleischacker and the Axlers.[31]

While the Axler cousins were continuing to get into trouble, Eddie Fleischacker had set his sights on boxing. While relatively undersized (as an adult, he never stood taller than 5'3" and weighed more than 130 pounds), Eddie was rock-hard with muscle and a feared street fighter; his left hook was especially powerful. After Tobias Fleischacker passed away in the summer of 1915, his family was thrown into crisis with the loss of the bread-winner.

As the eldest remaining male in his family's home, Eddie recognized the need to provide an income for his mother and younger siblings and set his sights on the boxing ring. The fifteen-year old boy padded his age by two years and began training hard at the Military Athletic Club across the river in Brooklyn; Eddie was eventually set in the featherweight class. Like many ethnic boxers of the early 20th century, Eddie Fleischacker gave himself a more Irish-sounding ring name; and thus, Eddie Fletcher was born. The young fighter's first bout was a preliminary match on October 13, 1915 at the City Athletic Club in Manhattan against Johnny Taylor. While Fletcher held his own against his opponent, he ended up losing on a newspaper decision. On March 24 of the following spring, Fletcher battled a free-swinging goon named "Smiling Willie" to a draw at the New Polo Athletic Club. After losing to George Maas by TKO a month later, Eddie went back to training. Fletcher spent countless hours in the gym doing rigorous calisthenics, sparring, and skipping rope to build up his wind.

In between their usual delinquent street action, Abe and Simon Axler often appeared at the gym to help and/or watch Fletcher train. At first, Eddie's success in the ring didn't improve. After journeying up to Poughkeepsie, New York to fight a no-name boxer named Joey Leonard (this was his only pro fight) on February 21, 1917, Fletcher went the distance but lost on a newspaper decision. Eddie Fletcher suffered a fourth-round knockout by Abe Friedman on his home turf (Brooklyn's Military Athletic Club) exactly three months later.

While Eddie worked menial jobs and trained at the Military Athletic Club in his spare time, Abe and Simon Axler had graduated into more serious street crimes, such as assault and armed robbery. Their specialty was burglary, and the cousins began increasing their depredation as they gained more experience and confidence. During the war years, Fletcher's luck in the ring gradually began to improve and he caught the eye of someone who could maximize his talent. As trainer Silvey Burns later said, "I took the kid under my wing because he's willing to fight four times a week if you'd let him, and when he gets paid off he brings the dough home to his mother."

On the blustery winter day of January 29, 1920, Eddie took on Terry Davis at Griffith's Hall in Kingston, New York and gained a solid victory by newspaper decision. A month later, Eddie journeyed west to Reading, Pennsylvania and lost a newspaper decision to Billy Bevan. Over the coming spring and summer, Fletcher fought a series of preliminary bouts in New Jersey. Eddie always went the distance but finished 2-2 on this Garden State tour. Fletcher finally hit the big time on September 28, when he faced Bud Dempsey in an undercard match at Madison Square Garden. Once again, Eddie went the distance but ended up losing on points.

This bout seemed to give Fletcher a modicum of respect, and Eddie went the distance in a brutal bout against Sammy Nable on October 20 at the Star Athletic Club in Manhattan. Eddie won the match on points, but lost a similar rematch a month later in the same fashion.[32] On Christmas Day, up in Poughkeepsie, everything went right, as Eddie used his fabled left hook to knock out no-name Johnny Wallace in the first round. It was Fletcher's first (and only) win by knockout.

By this time, Eddie Fletcher had gained a reputation on the Lower East Side as a boxer who, while modestly skilled, always gave his all in the ring. Throughout the first half of 1921, Fletcher fought a series of bouts across the Tri-State area, losing about as often as he won. Perhaps the most noteworthy fight was when he battled Bud Ridley for twelve rounds at the Palace of Joy in Coney Island. Unfortunately, he lost on points.

Abe and Simon Axler continued their crime spree and increasingly began to press their luck. One such caper, on the evening of March 8, 1921, saw Abe stride into a night class at Public School 168 and impersonate a substitute teacher. While he kept the students busy, an accomplice (almost certainly Simon) swiped a dozen of their coats. Abe was eventually busted when a student saw through his ruse and hailed a passing beat cop. Axler managed to beat the rap.[33]

More trouble sounded that September when Simon Axler was nailed on a burglary charge (Abe had barely managed to get away.) What Eddie thought about all this is unknown at this late date, but the Axlers were undeterred. After Simon made bail, they went right back out to the street. During the autumn of 1921, Eddie outpointed Johnny Llewellyn in Brooklyn and lost to Johnny Monroe up in Yonkers. Disaster struck on December 16, when Abe and Simon Axler were caught in the act of burglarizing a house. Both men were convicted of burglary and grand larceny. The Axlers drew consecutive sentences of 2½ to 5 years at Sing Sing Prison in Ossining.[34]

Regardless of the loss of his best friends, Eddie Fletcher was now at the height of his modest fame as a Lower East Side boxer. Denizens of his neighborhood would occasionally congratulate him on a job well done or ask for an autograph. A local thoroughbred horse trainer named Fred Musante offered Fletcher a job as his main jockey; Eddie thanked the trainer but decided to stick with his first love of boxing.[35] In late June 1922, Fletcher made his most momentous journey yet when he traveled far beyond the Tri-State area to fight a Fort Worth featherweight named "Dandy Dick" Griffin in Ciudad Juarez, Mexico. The fight was suddenly canceled when one of the fighters became seriously ill.[36]

While virtually no other details survive about Eddie's Mexican sojourn, something during the trip must have provoked a change in the young fighter. Upon his return to New York that July, Eddie's fight career gradually began to go downhill. Perhaps he felt the lure of the mob for the first time. Fletcher's final pro fight occurred on April 22, 1923 in Portland, Maine, when Lou Paluso knocked him out in the eighth round. After this bout, twenty-three year old Eddie decided he needed to make some more serious coin. His final record tallied at thirteen wins, fourteen losses, and two draws.[37] After spending a brief period as a cab driver, Fletcher tried to cash on his modest boxing reputation by running for alderman in the 1924 city election.[38] Like his boxing career, politics proved to be a bust.

Just how Eddie knew of the boys in Detroit's Little Jerusalem is unknown. What is known is that by the beginning of 1925, Fletcher was a full-time associate of the Sugar House Gang, whose members immediately gravitated to the gregarious ex-boxer from New York. Not long after his arrival in Detroit, the boys soon talked Eddie into one more match so they could see him in action. Fletcher donned his gloves a final time in the Fairview Club, located at Fairview and Mack avenues. Going up against a young bruiser named Don Burchard, Fletcher was outpointed in eight rounds.

Before the fight, Fletcher and his seconds had followed a custom then prevalent in New York City by wearing colored jerseys as they entered the ring. On this prophetic occasion, Eddie's jersey was colored purple.[39]

Booze gushes after a "prohi" raid along Brush Street. It was later estimated that $215 million worth of illegal alcohol moved through Detroit each year of Prohibition, rivaling only the automobile industry in terms of sheer revenue. *Walter Reuther Library.*

Downtown Detroit in a photograph taken from a rooftop in Windsor, Ontario, by William A. Kuenzel, head photographer for the *Detroit News*, in May 1928. *Walter Reuther Library.*

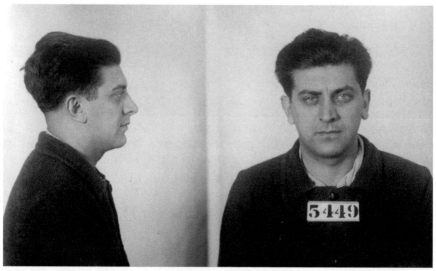

Raymond Burnstein was one of the leaders of what eventually became known as the Purple Gang. Handsome, charming, and dangerous when provoked, Burnstein became one of the most powerful gangsters in Detroit during Prohibition. This mug shot was taken on November 19, 1931 after his arrival at Marquette Penitentiary after being convicted of first-degree murder in the Collingwood Manor Massacre case. *State of Michigan Archives.*

Eddie Fletcher standing at right was a featherweight boxer from Manhattan's Lower East Side who turned to crime when his fighting career didn't pan out. After joining the future Purple Gang in 1925, Fletcher became known as one of its most lethal assassins. *NARA.*

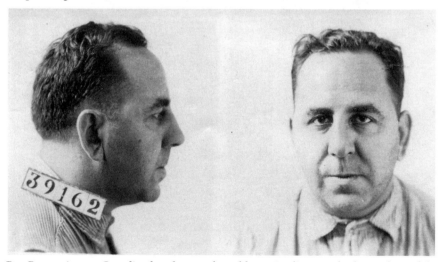

Roy Pascuzzi was a Canadian bootlegger who sold genuine liquor to both members of the Detroit Mafia and the Sugar House Mob aka Purple Gang. He is pictured here in 1929 upon his arrival at Leavenworth for violation of America's Volstead Act. *NARA.*

Gang boss Joe Burnstein, right, chats with Joe "Honey" Miller during a courtroom break. Burnstein was one of four brothers who led the Purple Gang during Prohibition. The Sicilian-born Miller was one of the few non-Jewish members of the crew. *Walter Reuther Library.*

TERROR

he Cleaners and Dyers War originated with a group of greedy yet naive cleaners. Back in the days before washing machines were popularized, most people's clothes could only be laundered through cleaning shops. Detroit's cleaning and dyeing industry consisted of several different elements that were all dependent on one another. There were the wholesale cleaners, owners of the plants where the actual cleaning and dyeing of garments was conducted. There were the retailers, who were the tailors and small shop owners who dealt directly with the general public. The third element was the so-called "commission men," who were essentially independent drivers who picked up the clothes, transported them to the laundering plants and then returned them to the cleaning shops. They were paid an impressive average wage of $300 a week for this work by the wholesalers who employed them. Finally, there were the "inside" workers of the cleaning and dyeing businesses, who represented the bulk of the industry's labor force.

An intense price war between wholesale cleaners sprouted in 1924. Many of them were losing money, so they began offering cut rates and discounts to tailors to keep the business coming in. The tailors themselves exacerbated the unrest by switching from one wholesaler to another in order to avoid paying their bills. In this chaotic breach came Chicago labor racketeer Ben Abrams, who looked to capitalize on the uneasiness in Detroit's cleaning and dyeing industry. Abrams was very good at what he did, but he had been linked to labor-related terrorism and homicides in Chicago. Not long after he arrived in town, Abrams and an associate were arrested for carrying concealed weapons. Abrams blithely admitted that he was in Detroit to make money off the labor racket and even offered to cut the arresting officers in on the action. At the request of Frank Xavier Martel, the president of the Detroit Federation of Labor, Abrams called the larger wholesale cleaners to a meeting at the Hotel Tuller to pitch his unionization plans. At first, things didn't go over as well as Abrams expected.

The Chicago union organizer finally hit pay dirt in the spring of 1925 when he convinced Detroit's cleaning and dyeing wholesalers to create their own union, which they could then use to manipulate the industry's profits. What followed was a "collusive agreement," which is what happens when the greed of ostensibly legitimate businessmen brings them into collusion with criminals. From this meeting was born the Detroit Cleaners and Dyers, the formal name for the wholesalers' association. The other elements of the industry followed suit. Ben Abrams laid down the rules, namely that the cleaners and tailors could not switch plants unless they showed just cause, and a newly formed review board would handle such cases. On the surface, things seemed to have improved drastically for the city's cleaning and dyeing industry. Trouble was lurking just beneath the surface, however.

Frank Martel filled the wholesalers' ears with lurid tales about what would happen to those who didn't fall into line with the new program. Beatings, bombings, and brick throwing were routine. This view was reinforced when the new inside workers union attempted to improve their meager work conditions. Martel stonewalled them into inaction and received a $700 reward from the wholesalers' association.

In the summer of 1925, Ben Abrams phased himself out of the union and picked as his representative Harry Klor, head of the driver's union. Before he returned to Chicago, Abrams was presented with a $1500 reward from the wholesalers' association for "organizing" the Detroit cleaning industry. The new president of the Detroit Cleaners and Dyers was Charles Jacoby, vice-president of French's Cleaners and Dyers, the largest cleaning and dyeing organization in the state of Michigan. Jacoby just happened to be married to the former Ida Burnstein, sister to the notorious Burnstein brothers. It was at this point that the Sugar House Gang clandestinely entered the fray. While the wholesalers' union dues were originally $25 a week, Jacoby upped it to 2% of the cleaners' gross, which ostensibly was to take care of "advertising and other things." In reality, the money went directly into the Sugar House Gang's pockets.

The wholesalers set a uniform price of $1.50 for the cleaning and pressing of a suit of clothes. This was the price that the general public was obligated to pay through the retailers such as tailors and low-level cleaning shop owners. In the past, the price had ranged from 75 cents to $1.50, leaving room for the tailors to cut the price if they so desired in order to increase their own profits. Nowadays, any price-cutting would be dealt with severely by the disciplinary board. When word of the high set price reached the retail tailors' union, they angrily called a meeting at the Labor Temple, located at

274 E. Vernor Highway. Frank Martel chaired the meeting with a dictatorial flair; he even fondled a brick as he spoke to the delegates. When one tailor got obstreperous, Martel slammed the brick on the table and shouted, "You better shut up if you know what's good for you!"

Due to the high set price, the organized tailors began losing business to non-union tailors at an alarming rate. As a form of protest, a group of the retail tailors switched their business to two independent plants, The Empire Cleaners and Dyers Company and The Novelty Cleaners and Dyers Company. Many retail cleaners decided to work in conjunction with the two non-union groups, as well. As a result, in the third week of October 1925, ten of these recalcitrant cleaning shops were stink-bombed.

Around 4:30 on the morning of October 26, 1925, the main plant of the Novelty Cleaners and Dyers Company at 8737 Grand River Avenue was vaporized by a huge explosion that rattled the surrounding neighborhood. Police later determined that homemade nitroglycerin bombs were the culprit. Before the smoke had cleared from the ruins of the Novelty, the Empire Cleaners and Dyers Company plant was destroyed in a similar manner. The dozen or so bombings shocked the cleaning business from top to bottom.[1]

With the entire industry groaning under the high set price by December 1925, even some of the wholesalers themselves began losing money. They discussed quitting the union in order to lower the prices and save their businesses. When word of this reached Frank Martel, he introduced the upstart wholesalers to the Sugar House Boys at the next union meeting. Ray Burnstein, Eddie Fletcher, Irving Milberg, and Joe "Honey" Miller lectured the men about what would happen if they tried to pull out and lower the prices, all the while brandishing pistols at the frightened businessmen. Martel also announced that the dues had just gone up to 10% of their overall gross, ostensibly for a buy-out fund for non-union plants.

By now the wholesalers clearly realized the folly of their ways. Criminals had completely taken over the industry, and anyone who dared to buck them had a brick tossed through the window of his shop, or worse. Perhaps a fire would break out in the middle of the night, destroying years of hard work. Beatings and even death were all a possibility. After all, the Sugar House Gang had been terrorizing other crooks for nearly three years. They would not have much trouble strong-arming a group of mild-mannered cleaners.

Having been pushed to the breaking point by January 1926, William Krispenz, head of the Tailors Union, organized a boycott of the unionized wholesale cleaners in response to the exorbitant set price. One of the new companies formed in this boycott was the Perfect Cleaners and Dyers, which was headquartered in a new $1,000,000 plant in Hamtramck. Krispenz's boycott did make the wholesalers blink a bit, as the set price was lowered ten cents a garment.

By the beginning of spring, Charles Jacoby and his gangster cohorts had virtually throttled the city's cleaning and dyeing industry to death. Jacoby left the wholesalers association. Others followed his lead. Almost immediately, the Perfect Cleaners and Dyers and those that patronized it became targets for the Sugar House Boys. The gangsters attempted to blow up the factory, but succeeded in only destroying a corner of the plant.

Terrorist tactics used by the gangsters included the hijacking of trucks of clothes. Another, when warning a plant operator, was to leave a stick of dynamite with a half-burnt fuse on his doorstep. Something more interesting involved spraying an overcoat with highly flammable solvents and sending it to a targeted cleaning plant. When the dry-cleaning process began at said plant, the high temperatures would cause the coat to burst into flames, which immediately spread to other garments on the rack and started a large fire.

These incidents multiplied over the rest of the year. Things grew so dire by the summer of 1926 that a Wayne County grand jury was convened to look into a mysterious rash of labor-related bombings. Potential witnesses had been scared into silence, however, and the four-month investigation turned up nothing. Each day, the now-independent cleaners and tailors went to work cautiously, always wondering if this was the day someone finally tossed a bomb into their shop, or they were killed.[2]

WHILE THE CLEANERS AND DYERS WAR progressed throughout 1926, Sugar House Gang liquor distributor Johnny Reid and his St. Louis crew showed they were geographically diverse by committing crimes throughout the Midwest. Indeed, they spent most of the spring and summer of 1926 in St. Louis, where they were suspected in at least one bank robbery and the stick-up of a bank messenger. By August, they were compelled to return once Reid found himself in a dangerous feud with a rogue Sicilian gangster.[3]

Michele (Mike) Dipisa was born in Sicily and immigrated to America in 1913 at the age of seventeen. As a young man on the streets of Chicago's Little Italy, he quickly got himself into trouble. By the age of twenty-one, he was sent to Indiana's Pendleton Reformatory on a charge of criminal conspiracy. Dipisa was pardoned two years later and first appeared in Detroit around 1923, when he caught on as a doorman at Lefty Clark's Grand River Avenue gambling house.

A short, squat hoodlum, Dipisa was a physically powerful man who (in the parlance of the era) had a pronounced "yellow streak." As a result, Mike hadn't advanced farther than hijacking booze and guarding criminals more powerful than himself. Dipisa most probably would have been regarded as a joke except for his willingness to kill. One 1924 incident particularly illustrates the contrasts of his personality; after being accused of gunning down independent bootlegger Andrew Walk in broad daylight on a busy East Side street corner, Dipisa then complained to newspapermen that the police had given him an especially rough beating while trying to get him to confess to the murder. Mike eventually did admit to killing Earl Maher in March 1925 while he was guarding two gamblers in Cadillac Square. Dipisa claimed that he only shot Maher when he had tried to stick them up and was, after two trials, acquitted.[4]

The Sugar House Boys had originally crossed paths with Mike Dipisa in the late spring of 1925, while he was fighting the Earl Maher murder case. Dipisa and a couple of his friends began staking out bookmaker Jacob "Big Jake" Fricker's handbook at 113 Cadillac Square. Fricker's handbook (betting parlor) was a hidden room where bets could be placed on horse-races, ball games, and boxing matches. These sports results were provided via the racing wire service controlled by the Burnstein brothers. Nevertheless, Mike Dipisa was undeterred.

On June 7, 1925, he and two of his crew stuck up Big Jake Fricker at his office, getting $3,000 worth of diamonds and a fancy ring. Dipisa had used his *own* car in the robbery, and did not even bother to report it stolen. Police immediately questioned him and Mike disingenuously claimed two strange men had stuck him up, forced him to drive, and then tossed him out onto the street. To add injury to insult, Big Jake immediately called the Burnstein brothers, who in turn passed the job down to the Sugar House Boys. A few days after the heist, Dipisa was driving his car when another vehicle pulled alongside and let go with a flurry of shots. Although unharmed, the combination of police heat and Sugar House bullets proved too much, and Dipisa dispatched a messenger to return all of Fricker's stolen jewels back to him.[5]

And so went the criminal career of Mike Dipisa, a brutal yet hopeless thug who was not even respected by those that feared him. Despite his ineptitude, Dipisa did enjoy a good friendship with Hamtramck mobster Chester LaMare. By the summer of 1926, Mike was looking to advance his poor standing in the underworld by extorting independent blind pig owners around the city. Dipisa probably figured strong-arming a known tough guy like Johnny Reid would improve his meager résumé. With the Egan's Rats back in St. Louis, Dipisa moved in for what he thought would be easy pickings.

Around the first of August 1926, Johnny Reid was serving a small evening crowd in his blind pig at Third and Peterboro. The only other gangster on the premises was Tennessee Slim Hurley. Three young men strode inside and told Reid that they were with Mike Dipisa. Johnny would later learn their names were Clarence "Bud" Gilboe, Paul Clark, and the enigmatic "Jimmy the Dog." The trio then aggressively demanded a cut of the profits. Johnny and Slim both responded by pulling out pistols and opening fire, which sent the extortionists running out the door. There were no casualties, save for a customer who was grazed by a bullet.[6]

Reid immediately got on the phone to St. Louis and, within a few days, Fred Burke and all his pals were back in Detroit and loaded for bear. On August 10, Reid's crew visited several East Side blind pigs in an effort to find Mike Dipisa, who in turn took the streets with a couple of henchmen looking for his enemies. The two groups stumbled upon each other in downtown Detroit several hours later and furiously traded shots while racing up Broadway toward Grand Circus Park. Despite all the bad intentions, no one was killed.[7]

Such was not the case about twenty-four hours later, when the Rats invaded a Brush Street restaurant that was a known hangout of Dipisa's. Five men, including Reid himself, walked into the joint and shot anything that moved. Two people were killed and three others wounded in the gunplay.[8] Alas, the intended target was not on the premises. These two very public, violent attempts on his life had badly frightened Dipisa and he called for a truce meeting.

In a sit-down with Johnny Reid, Dipisa claimed that Bud Gilboe and Paul Clark had used his name without his knowledge and that he had not sent them. Reid said he was willing to agree to peace if the three extortionists were turned over to him. Dipisa, eager to save his own life, readily agreed to betray his helpers. While Jimmy the Dog had fled the city after the Brush Street murders, Bud Gilboe and Paul Clark were lured to Reid's speakeasy on the evening of August 25. As Gilboe himself explained later in the hospital, "I was framed into a meeting with Reid, and when they came in and put the rod on me I knew it was all up. I should have broke then but I thought I could talk them out of it..."

Reid and Tennessee Slim Hurley forced the pair at gunpoint into Reid's Lincoln and then they took off. Reid kept the two covered in the back seat as Tennessee Slim drove north out of the city. Near the intersection of Southfield and 11 Mile Roads, Reid suddenly shot Clark squarely between the eyes. The feisty blind-pigger then emptied his five remaining shots into the terrified Gilboe. Reid, slight and slender, quickly scrambled into the back seat and unceremoniously shoved the bodies out the door. Bud Gilboe was still alive when found, and on his deathbed gave detailed statements to the police and prosecutor. He expired from his wounds about twenty-four hours after being shot.

Johnny Reid voluntarily came to the police headquarters at 1300 Beaubien Street and offered up his alibi. Despite being identified by Gilboe as one of the killers, Reid was released. The shooting war was over, and Reid's reputation flourished bigger than ever while Mike Dipisa slunk away in defeat.[9]

WHILE THE SUGAR HOUSE GANG had no part in the Reid/Dipisa fight, they were most pleased to see their reliable liquor distributor succeed. In fact, just after the war's conclusion, the Sugar House crew got some formidable reinforcement from New York when the so-called Siamese Twins became formally conjoined.

In August of 1925, Abe and Simon Axler had been released on parole from Clinton and Sing Sing, respectively. The two burglars came out of prison hardened criminals, having learned violence and depravity that could not be found anywhere else, not even on the mean streets of the Lower East Side. Abe was arrested not long after his release for attempting to rape a woman, but was discharged when his victim did not file a complaint. After a year spent ostensibly driving taxicabs around the city, both Abe and Simon were released from parole in October of 1926 and headed west to join Eddie Fletcher. The Axlers initially moved into Fletcher's apartment building at 434 Peterboro Street, just a block away from Johnny Reid's pig.[10]

The new arrivals threw themselves into the Cleaners and Dyers War, and there wasn't a job of intimidation or violence that the New York burglars would shy away from. The seemingly inseparable Abe Axler and Eddie Fletcher cut a distinctive path through the Detroit underworld. Both men were relatively small physically (Abe stood two inches taller than Eddie, bringing him up to a modest 5'5" in height), but there the similarities ended. Fletcher was a loquacious wisecracker with the broken nose, cauliflowered ears, lumpy knuckles, and missing teeth common to boxers.

By contrast, Axler was a quiet man who usually let Fletcher do most of the talking. Despite a slim build and a case of chronic tonsillitis, Abe was a surprisingly strong man who attacked with the ferocity of a wolverine. Axler was seldom without a cigarette or a chew of tobacco in his mouth; when something stronger was desired, he proceeded to destroy whatever remained of his lung tissue by smoking copious amounts of opium. With razor-sharp features, dark shadows under his lifeless eyes, and hollow cheeks that gave his face a skeletal appearance, Axler could have passed for the Angel of Death. While the muscular Fletcher was a feared brawler, Axler was widely regarded as the most dangerous of the pair. *News* crime reporter Jack Carlisle knew Abe personally and described him as "saturnine, moody, and quick on the trigger of a machine gun."[11]

By the time the Axlers heeded Horace Greeley's advice and went west, the relationship between the Sugar House Boys and the St. Louis crew had begun to fray a bit. Like most of their colleagues back home, the Egan's Rats refugees were hard-drinking partygoers who loved to commit pranks and goof off. The vast majority of the Sugar House boys were not heavy drinkers (opium was their drug of choice.)

At one such party in the early morning hours of September 20, Tennessee Slim Hurley and a group of Rats were power-drinking in a cabaret at 4107 Cass Avenue. At 6:45 a.m., Slim made clumsy advances toward 24-year old Melba Rhodes. When Miss Rhodes resisted, Slim pulled a gun and began spraying bullets in her general direction. One shot fatally wounded Melba and two slugs winged a lounge singer named Lee Lawson. Hurley and the rest of his buddies beat it from the club before the police arrived. Rhodes' sister May happened to be Eddie Fletcher's live-in girlfriend, and after Melba's murder she went into an emotional tailspin, rarely eating or going outdoors.[12]

A month later on October 30, while Eddie was out of their Peterboro Street apartment, May Rhodes attempted suicide by shooting herself near the heart with one of his pistols. She survived, but police arrested Fletcher and Abe Axler on the suspicion that they might have actually shot her.

The entire episode left a bad taste in the Sugar House Gang's mouth. Nevertheless, the Burnstein brothers sought to keep the capable Johnny Reid in their fold by telling him to keep the drunken antics under control. Reid attempted to make amends by banishing Tennessee Slim Hurley from his inner circle. For the moment, things seemed to have been smoothed over.[13]

BY THE FALL OF 1926, the upstart Perfect Cleaners and Dyers Company had been enduring months of Sugar House Gang-administrated terrorism. After the failed bombing of their plant, their delivery trucks had been hijacked and/or stolen with regularity. Their outspoken treasurer, twenty-eight year old Samuel Sigman, was a specific target. Sigman complained to the police so frequently that they granted him a permit to carry a concealed weapon.

The last straw came on November 9, 1926, when a truckload of Perfect clothes was hijacked in front of 2831 St. Antoine Street. Sam Sigman once again called the police and claimed that he knew who was responsible. Ray Burnstein, Irving Milberg, Abe Axler, and Eddie Fletcher were indeed arrested and questioned as a result of his complaint, but they were discharged.[14]

Abe Burnstein sent word to Sam Sigman that they should meet and talk. Hopefully, they could reach a mutually beneficent agreement. Burnstein instructed Sigman to meet George Cordell in the lobby of the Addison Hotel at 8:30 p.m. on Thursday, December 9. George would then take Sam to the meeting place. Ironically, Cordell had been on the opposing side of the Sugar House Gang during the 1923-24 war and was even named by Izzy Cantor as a participant in the drive-by shooting that killed Sol Conrad. Over time, both he and the Burnsteins had been able to put aside their differences in order to reap riches by extorting thousands of dollars from the cleaning and dyeing business.[15]

Sam Sigman was understandably nervous going into the enemy's main hotel to meet them, but he was probably reassured by the presence of the .32 caliber pistol in his overcoat pocket. Sigman made a point of telling his friend Louis Smith that he was going to meet Cordell at the Addison and shortly thereafter called his wife to tell her he would be home by 10 o'clock. Sigman arrived at the hotel on time for his meet. Cordell was there, but so were three of the Sugar House crew. Two of the boys grabbed Sigman and shoved him in the backseat of a car, while the third got behind the wheel. They quickly disarmed the now terrified treasurer as the vehicle got moving.

During the ride, Sigman's abductors beat him viciously, inflicting multiple contusions and abrasions, as well as broken ribs and a dislocated vertebra in his neck. They eventually shot Sam three times and dumped his body into a snow bank near the intersection of West Chicago Street and Coolidge Highway (present-day Schaefer Highway.) Although he was still breathing when found just before midnight, Samuel Sigman died in the ambulance while en route to Highland Park General Hospital. He left behind a wife and 8-month old son.[16]

Fear swept throughout the cleaning industry as the holdouts' situation became increasingly desperate. Some were wondering if it would be safer to just submit to the gangsters and re-unionize.

CHRISTMAS NIGHT, 1926 found Johnny Reid drinking at the Log Cabin Inn, located in downtown Detroit on East Adams Avenue. For a short time that evening, Abe Axler and Eddie Fletcher sat in with him. They were long gone by the time an unsteady Reid got up to leave at 4 o'clock in the morning.

Johnny got behind the wheel of his car and headed north for his apartment building at 3025 E. Grand Boulevard. Reid had just parked his vehicle in the darkened alley behind his building when someone emerged from the shadows and blew off half his head with a shotgun blast.

While Reid's murder was destined to remain officially unsolved, there was little mystery in the underworld as to who was responsible. A little over a month earlier, Mike Dipisa's older brother Leo was shot and killed by armed robbers at the Fair Haven roadhouse they both ran. Before he died, Leo Dipisa was able to shoot and kill one of his assailants (Mike was not on the premises at the time.) While the dead hijacker was revealed to be a Canadian hoodlum named William Dehire, Mike automatically assumed that his old nemesis, Johnny Reid, was responsible. According to this theory, Dipisa hired a recently arrived Chicago crook named Frank Wright to kill Reid.[17]

The twenty-six year old Wright was known as a dangerous character as well as a successful thief. Chicago police suspected him of pulling a jewel heist that netted nearly $100,000, and "Frankie" had once escaped from a Utah prison detail after throwing red pepper in the eyes of his guard. Arriving in Detroit in October 1926, Wright had befriended Meyer "Fish" Blumfield, who was the "stick-man" at Doc Brady's profitable gambling operation. A tuxedo-clad Wright soon became a common fixture at the Grand River Avenue casino, cold-eyeing anyone who looked as if they may make trouble and bouncing out those that did. About two months after his arrival, Frank Wright was commissioned by a vengeful Mike Dipisa to kill Johnny Reid.

After the Christmas night homicide, Wright decided to stay in Detroit, apparently oblivious to any revenge-minded friends that Reid may have had. Frankie began throwing money around and making the rounds at the city's gambling spots. Wright even became a partner in Molly Day's blind pig at 2503 Park Avenue. Along with two ex-New York burglars, Joseph Bloom and George Cohen, Frank decided to crash Fred Burke's infamous "snatch racket." Unfortunately for Wright, Johnny Reid's friends were soon back in town and out for blood.[18]

Once Reid was underground, Fred Burke and his crew began their own investigation into who killed him and came to the same conclusion as the Sugar House Boys. While the string-pulling Mike Dipisa made a logical target for revenge, taking him out ran the risk of starting a shooting war with Chester LaMare and the rest of the Mafia. The trigger-pulling Frank Wright got no such immunity. Through sheer luck, Wright managed to avoid Burke's wrath for several weeks. The ex-Egan gunman went straight to the Burnstein brothers for help in trapping Wright. Abe and Joey balked at first but soon agreed wholeheartedly once they got the word about Jake Weinberg.

BY THE BEGINNING OF 1927, Weinberg operated what was left of the old alky cooking network formerly run by Jake Trager and Sam Abramson. Jake oversaw about fifty hidden whiskey stills, and he paid their keepers $75 a week. Having dabbled in bootlegging while still living in New York, Weinberg had become a student in the chemical process of distilling whiskey and went out of his way to make sure his customers got the best product possible. Jake had managed to avoid being arrested since he moved to Detroit, and he lived in a well-furnished apartment at 355 Leicester Court.[19] At the end of 1926, Weinberg began to experience problems with an unseen foe.

Sometime that fall (the incident was never reported to police) two masked men attempted to kidnap Weinberg. The bootlegger saw them coming and opened fire, grazing the two would-be kidnappers. Not too long after this incident, Jake was successfully snatched; his captors drove him down to Toledo and demanded $25,000. Weinberg said he was unable to raise that much, offering $10,000 instead. The kidnappers had no choice but to agree. As Weinberg himself related, "It was dark when they put the sack over my head and I was in darkness until after I was released. I think I was driven about 60 miles before we reached the place where the money was demanded. The sack was not removed and I couldn't see anything but I could hear many voices."

In the wake of his return, Weinberg and his pals swore they would find out who was responsible. When word of this reached the street, the kidnappers apparently decided to beat Jake to the punch. At 10:40 on the evening of February 3, 1927, Jake was grabbed once again and driven to 89 Belmont Street, where another man was waiting on the sidewalk. Weinberg fought for his life, receiving several bruises. Jake managed to get his pistol out, but his attackers blew his brains out before he could use it.[20]

Within just a day or so, the gangland grapevine indicated that none other than Frank Wright and his two pals, Joseph Bloom and George Cohen, were responsible.[21] Thus, the Sugar House Boys had a double reason to kill Wright; avenging not only Johnny Reid but Jake Weinberg as well. Despite his high-profile way of operating, Wright proved impossible to trap. Finally, it was decided to give him a little taste of his own medicine.

IN LATE MARCH 1927, Meyer "Fish" Blumfield was kidnapped by unknown parties and held for a $25,000 ransom. Frank Wright let it be known he would do whatever was necessary to reacquire his friend. After paying the ransom, Wright soon got a cryptic telephone call telling him he could find Fish in Apartment 308 at the Miraflores Apartments, located at 106 E. Alexandrine Avenue.[22]

At 4:30 on the morning of March 28, Frank Wright pulled his expensive sedan to a stop in front of the Miraflores and scanned the street for anything that seemed even remotely suspicious. Both the apartment building and the Alexandrine block it was located on at were completely quiet in the dark stillness. A cold wind thumped against the glass as Wright, backed up by Joe Bloom and George Cohen, stepped out of the car and made his way inside the Miraflores. Number 308 was located at the end of the hallway on the third floor, and Frank rapped loudly on the door. He got no answer. Wright caressed the handle of the pistol in his pocket and pounded a few more times for emphasis. Frank listened in and was unable to discern any sounds behind the door.

Something was definitely wrong.

The three men had just turned to leave when Wright heard the creaking of a door being opened, and then the deafening chatter of a submachine gun drowned out everything else. Bullets ripped into the three gangsters and caused them to jerk like blood-bursting marionettes before tumbling to the floor in a tangle of arms and legs. As his life leaked into the cheap carpeting, Frank thought he heard one of his partners moan. Then a strong voice barked, "Get him! Get him again!" Another roar of gunfire followed, along with the horrid sensation of more hot lead tearing into his flesh. The last thing Wright heard before he passed out was the sound of footsteps charging down a stairway.

Detroit police and paramedics were on the scene within minutes and found the butchered bodies of Frank Wright, Joe Bloom, and George Cohen lying near the door to Apartment 308. Slugs had flown so thick that they had punched dozens of holes in the walls of the hallway, and a thin cloud of plaster dust and gunsmoke created a surreal setting as they went to work. Bloom and Cohen were dead at the scene; the two men were so riddled with bullets the coroner would be unable to tell how many times they had been shot. The main target, despite being wounded fourteen times, was still breathing when arrived at the hospital.

It was determined that the killers had hid behind a nearby fire door and fired on the men from there. A total of fifty-eight .45 caliber shell casings were found strewn across the floor, with fifty having come from a Thompson submachine gun and the other eight from an automatic pistol. There was also evidence of two other revolvers being used as well. This shooting was unprecedented in the history of the Detroit underworld. The three gangsters had been lured to a neutral location and mowed down without warning by a virtual firing squad.

Inside Apartment 308, police found three shotguns, a dozen pistols, several hundred rounds of ammunition, and other assorted gangster paraphernalia. Other items implicating Sugar House gangsters Abe and Simon Axler, Joe "Honey" Miller, Eddie Fletcher, and John Tolzdorf were found.

None of that mattered to Frank Wright, who was barely clinging to life in the hospital. Detective Sergeant Frank Holland questioned the dying gangster;

"Why did you go to the apartment?"

Wright replied in a low voice, "A friend of mine got kidnapped. 'Fish', one of the stickmen at Doc Brady's. A friend of mine called me up at the hotel and said that 'Fish' had been kidnapped. So Joe Bloom and George Cohen and I went up there."

"Did you find 'Fish' when you got there?" Holland asked.

Wright gave what turned out to be his valediction, "No, the machine gun worked. That's all I remember." He died about twenty-seven hours after being shot.

The next evening, Abe Axler and Fred Burke were pulled over at the corner of Woodward and Atkinson streets. Loaded pistols were found in their car and both gangsters were taken into custody. A national fingerprint check revealed that Burke was wanted on suspicion of robbing a Louisville bank. After being "vigorously" questioned, Axler was cut loose while Burke found himself extradited to Kentucky. While the "Miraflores Massacre" would remain officially unsolved, Detroit police had no doubt that both Axler and Burke were involved. Other suspects included Eddie Fletcher, Simon Axler, and Honey Miller.[23]

While the Sugar House Boys still remained a bunch of faceless Jewish thugs to the majority of Detroit's population, criminals around the city took notice of the lethal gangsters from the North End and the cold-blooded way they had avenged their colleagues. The massacre also had an unintended historical significance, as it made the Sugar House crew the first hoodlums to use a Thompson submachine gun in the commission of a crime in Detroit. While Hollywood would later exaggerate this weapon's popularity with gangsters, the revolutionary submachine gun was indeed the "gun that made the Twenties Roar."[24]

AFTER HIS RETIREMENT from the U.S. Army, Brigadier General John T. Thompson founded the Auto-Ordnance Corporation in 1916 in order to develop a "one-man, hand held machine gun." Like most others, Thompson had read of the staggering casualty figures being produced by World War I's brutal trench warfare and sought to create a "trench broom" that would sweep the Germans away.

The basic operation of any machine gun involves using the recoil power of one cartridge's explosion to propel the bolt rearward and eject the empty shell casing while simultaneously chambering a fresh round by the time the bolt strikes the breech. As long as the user keeps the trigger depressed, the sear will not catch the bolt and this back-and-forth process will rapidly repeat itself until all ammunition is expended and/or the trigger is released. General Thompson desired a weapon that did not rely on a gas-operated or recoil reloading mechanism, as most machine guns of the era used. He found a solution in the revolutionary Blish lock, which produced a friction-delayed blowback operating system.

Working deep in the bowels of a nondescript Cleveland machine shop, Thompson and his team began to painstakingly create their weapon. By September 1917, they had discovered through trial-and-error that the .45 ACP was the largest caliber round that the Blish lock could accept without frequent mechanical failures and near-constant lubrication. This news was discouraging at first, as General Thompson had originally envisioned a "machine rifle" that American troops would fire from the hip and spray trenches with. As a result, Thompson now set out to create a then-unheard of smaller-sized machine gun to accommodate the lower caliber cartridge.

The Auto-Ordnance crew had worked out the bugs and completed a prototype entitled the "Annihilator I" by the autumn of 1918. The first batch of Annihilators had just arrived in New York for overseas shipment when news of the Armistice broke. Now that the Western Front's trenches no longer needed to be swept, General Thompson's brooms were modified just a bit more and prepared for commercial sale. The marketing department considered names such as the "Autogun" or "Machine Pistol," but the new weapon was ultimately christened the "Submachine Gun."

In the spring of 1921, the weapon was first made available to the public. While such a thing may seem inconceivable by modern standards, in those days any civilian who had the money could purchase a submachine gun from hardware stores, sporting goods firms, or by mail order. Its original retail price was a somewhat pricey $225 (a brand-new Ford sedan cost around $400, by comparison.) The sticker-shock notwithstanding, there was no doubt that the Thompson was quite a firearm. It could fire single shots or fully automatic bursts (the M1921 had a rate of fire of 860 rounds per minute) from a variety of magazines, ranging from straight twenty-round clips to circular drums that held either fifty or one hundred rounds. Completely stripped, the weapon weighed only eight and a half pounds; re-assembled with the wooden butt stock and a loaded 100-round drum, the weight rose to a tad over twenty pounds. The Thompson's ability to spray powerful bullets in such mass quantities made it a most potent weapon. The gun could stop a moving automobile, reducing both it and its occupants to Swiss cheese-style ruin in mere seconds.

Despite an inventive marketing campaign (one infamous ad featured a cowboy mowing down Mexican *banditos* with his trusty Thompson), the submachine gun was slow to catch on with the American public. This consumer apathy seems to have been stemmed from the weapon's expensive cost, a lack of post-war publicity, and the fact that the innovative Thompson was simply ahead of its time. Even after Auto-Ordnance dropped its price to $175 in 1923, sales continued to stagnate. By the third anniversary of the submachine gun's release, only around two and a half thousand units had been sold, and the sales rate was declining.

General Thompson's masterpiece may well have remained an obscure ordnance novelty were it not for Chicago gang boss Dean O'Banion, who purchased three of the "baby machine guns" while vacationing in Colorado in the late summer of 1924. While O'Banion was murdered before he had a chance to use his new Thompsons, members of his crew eventually loaned one of the submachine guns to vicious South Side triggerman Frank McErlane, who used it in an unsuccessful attempt to kill one of his rivals in the autumn of 1925. Soon after this incident, the rest of the Windy City's gangs caught on. Other Illinois bootlegging mobs, such as the Birger Gang and the Shelton Gang, also used the weapon with lethal effectiveness.

By the time of the Miraflores Massacre in the spring of 1927, the use of submachine guns was just beginning to spread amongst the country's criminals (much to the dismay of General Thompson.) As such, the Miraflores shootings ensured that the Sugar House Boys would be forever remembered for introducing the "Tommy Gun" to the Detroit underworld.[25]

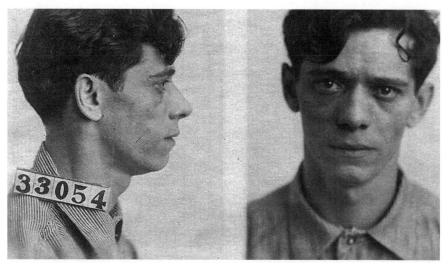

Abe Axler was a burglar from Manhattan's Lower East Side. Heading west in 1926 to join his best friend Eddie Fletcher in the Sugar House Gang, Abe and Fletcher became inseparable partners in crime, known as the "Siamese Twins." Axler is pictured here upon his 1929 arrival at Leavenworth for violation of the Volstead Act. *NARA.*

The Sugar House Gang aka Purple Gang was believed to have introduced both Thompson submachine guns and bulletproof vests to the Detroit underworld. This catalog page from Chicago sporting goods dealer Peter von Frantzius offers both. *Neal Trickel Collection.*

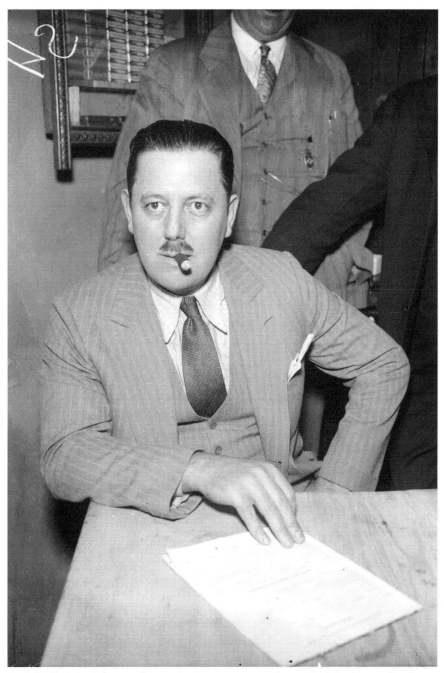

Fred "Killer" Burke was a former St. Louis gangster who worked for liquor distributor Johnny Reid during the mid-1920s. Known for his skill with the Thompson submachine gun and for using police uniforms to fool his victims, Burke was a prime suspect in Detroit's Miraflores Massacre. *Walter Reuther Library.*

MIRAFLORES

Chicago gangster Frank Wright and two of his friends were mowed down with submachine gun fire in the so-called "Miraflores Massacre" of March 1927. The three had been lured to Apartment 308 of the Miraflores Apartments after the kidnapping of Meyer "Fish" Blumfield. Several members of the Sugar House Gang were questioned, but no one was convicted. *Drawn by J. Rickman.*

NOTORIETY

The aftermath of the Miraflores Massacre saw the Sugar House Gang's reputation in Detroit's underworld soar to new heights. While they had gained modest respect for holding their own in the Oakland Sugar House War, the act of mowing down three of their foes with the newfangled submachine gun sent waves of fear through those who would think of crossing the Burnsteins or their men.

The crew now had hundreds of thousands of dollars coming in from their various rackets, and beginning in the spring of 1927, the Sugar House boys went on an extended crime spree. Indeed, after the massacre they began swaggering even more than usual. Many of their crimes in the coming months seemed public and chancy, as if they were letting their recent success go to their heads.

While Abe and Joe Burnstein were the Sugar House Gang's titular heads, they spent a good deal of their time doing high-stakes gambling. During one of his gaming junkets to New Orleans, Joe Burnstein struck up a good friendship with a gambler named Theodore Werner. Both men had great success at the local gambling houses. Werner was not only formerly from St. Louis, but a good friend of Fred Burke and Gus Winkeler. Burnstein and his new friend soon opened up the Victory Inn on the outskirts of New Orleans. While the exact causes were never discovered, Joe and Ted Werner soon got into a dispute and the latter wound up being shot dead in his Crescent City apartment by two unidentified men on April 16, 1927, just three weeks after the Miraflores Massacre up in Detroit.

While New Orleans police questioned Joey Burnstein thoroughly, he was not charged. While Fred Burke and his friends were scattered around the country at that moment, they were greatly perturbed by the murder of Ted Werner. The Burnsteins, who had their hands full with the Cleaners and Dyers War and other matters, paid little attention. Johnny Reid was quickly fading from memory, and the Sugar House Boys had gotten powerful enough to the point where they didn't really need the ex-Egan's Rats anymore. Such a cavalier attitude would prove to have its consequences.[1]

WHILE LOUIS FLEISHER did not rank quite as high on the Sugar House totem pole as his older brother Harry, he was still a dangerous character. Just shy of twenty-two years old in the summer of 1927, Lou stood almost 5'11" inches tall and was tremendously strong. His large size made him an excellent strong-arm artist and Lou had shown in the William Glanzrock killing that he had no compunction about using firearms. Fleisher also had a rather bizarre sense of humor; if he spotted a friend while driving down the street, Lou would often gun his car's engine and chase his buddy down the sidewalk as a joke.

Fleisher stirred contradictory emotions in those that knew him. One said, "I was always glad to see Lou walk into a place. Things livened up every place he went." Another had a less laudatory view, saying that he "…would always get out of a joint when Lou walked in. You never knew what would happen." Despite being somewhat rough around the edges, Lou actually continued to work part time at his father's junkyard during Prohibition and had little contact with his brother Harry. Nevertheless, he rounded up a few of the boys for a caper in July 1927.[2]

On Sunday evening, July 10, Fleisher led four of his pals into action outside the village of Flat Rock, twenty-four miles south of the city. Their target was a truck en route from Akron, Ohio that was loaded down with $4,000 worth of tires and other rubber goods. Lou's intimate knowledge of the auto and scrap business would make fencing the loot no problem. As the truck pulled over at a roadhouse, the boys moved in to waylay the two drivers. Two of the Sugar House boys got behind the wheel of the truck and sped north toward Detroit while Fleisher, Henry Kaplan, and Morris "Butch" Sandler herded the two hostages into a green Studebaker sedan.

Unfortunately for the boys, one of the truckers had the observation skills of a trained detective. He noticed that hijackers conversed in both perfect English and a foreign language (probably Yiddish.) The trucker memorized the number of miles on the car's odometer. He also noted that one of the Studebaker's door panels was torn and made a point of discreetly dousing the rear window with tobacco juice, lest he be able to identify it later. The man even saw that the Studebaker sported disk wheels, and that all of its tires were Millers. The gangsters took a roundabout way into the city and sped through the darkened Wayne County roads with no discernible pattern.

About six hours after they were taken hostage, the two truckers were let go on the Southwest Side.

Two days later, Detroit police found the abandoned truck and the now-empty trailer. Four hundred tires from the truck were soon uncovered at a rented garage in the North End. The green Studebaker sedan was discovered as well. All the details the trucker remembered (even the tobacco juice stain) were confirmed. The car was revealed to be registered to Lou Fleisher and cops immediately began looking for him.[3]

Fleisher showed little concern for the police dragnet, as he continued to carouse in the neighborhood. On the night of July 21, Lou made the rounds along Oakland Avenue with fellow hijacker Henry Kaplan. Drinking with them were two youthful members of the Sugar House mob, Edward Fecter and Sam Drapkin. Around 10:30 they exited the Exchange Café and stood next to their parked car talking in the warm summer evening. As they were, a northbound sedan cruised by and sprayed them with gunfire. Fleisher went down with a round in his side while Kaplan was fatally wounded. Drapkin was hit five times and toppled to the pavement. Fecter amazingly had a bullet glance off his forehead. Both of them, as well as Fleisher, would survive their wounds.

Police speculated that friends of the late New York gangster William Glanzrock had attempted to take Lou Fleisher out in revenge, as the attack took place almost on the first anniversary of Glanzrock's murder. Later events would suggest that the Sugar House Gang's so-called allies, the Egan's Rats refugees, conducted the attack in retribution for the murdered Ted Werner. The hospitalized Fleisher now claimed that he had indeed killed Glanzrock by "beating him to the draw" after the New Yorker had tried to hijack a load of liquor he was watching. The cops even went so far as to exhume Glanzrock's body during their investigation.[4]

Fleisher was eventually ruled to have killed "Two-Gun Willie" in self-defense, but the feds came right after Lou for violating the Interstate Shipment Act *via* the tire truck hijacking. Unable to post his $25,000 bond, Fleisher was grilled relentlessly about that night. When his trial came around several months later, Louis Fleisher changed his plea to guilty and received a ten-year sentence in Leavenworth Federal Penitentiary.

IF THE FRED BURKE crew did indeed randomly attack the Sugar House Boys on the night of July 21, the boys certainly went on high alert because of it. The vast majority of them began going everywhere armed. Two of the gang's top gunmen, Abe Axler and Irving Milberg, sought to ease this pressure by doing some club hopping on the evening of Friday, August 12. Accompanied by their respective girlfriends, Evelyn Burkley and Madeline Wolfe, the boys made the rounds of the city's nightclubs throughout the night. Around 5 o'clock on Saturday morning, the quartet entered a "black and tan" cabaret at 1708 St. Antoine Street in Paradise Valley.

After the gangsters ordered drinks, Miss Wolfe got into an argument with a woman sitting another table with two Black men, Godfrey Qualls and Hobart Harris. The squabbling grew worse and was climaxed by Wolfe hurling her glass at the woman. Qualls and Harris immediately jumped up to respond to the menace the Purples presented. Insults flew back and forth as the two Sugar House hoods got up in their opponents' faces and shoved them. The boyfriends hit back, and then the gangsters pulled guns. Milberg quickly opened fire, killing both Qualls and Harris. Axler and Milberg dashed out of the club, with Evelyn Burkley being dragged by her boyfriend. The irate patrons of the cabaret grabbed Madeline Wolfe and held her. Many others in the club swarmed out the doors and gave chase to the gunmen.

The fleeing trio jumped into a parked taxicab and told driver Leroy Butler to step on it. When Butler began to dawdle, one of the gangsters whacked the cabbie over the head with a pistol and dumped him into the street. He then got behind the wheel of the taxi and sped north on St. Antoine, leaving Miss Wolfe to her fate. She broke away from her captors and attempted to outrun almost fifty people. Wolfe was easily re-captured and held in the cabaret amid relentless threats until the police arrived.

Both Axler and Milberg surrendered with their attorney within a day or so and admitted to the murders. Since he did the shooting, it was Irving Milberg who eventually went in the dock. A year and two trials later, he would be found not guilty on the grounds of self-defense.[5]

BY THE END OF THE SUMMER of 1927, the Sugar House leadership seemed to have finally put it together that the St. Louis crew had been kidnapping and ransoming their gambler associates for the better part of three years. This unpleasant truth was especially rammed home when Gus Winkeler, Bob Carey, and "Crane Neck" Nugent snatched one of the Wertheimer brothers earlier in May. Not only did they earn the ire of the Burnsteins but Chicago gang boss Al Capone. The latter managed to persuade the trio to release Wertheimer unharmed. Fred Burke, meanwhile, was still bent on avenging his friend Ted Werner. To make matters worse, a mob led by Joseph "Legs" Laman had set out to imitate Burke's snatch racket by kidnapping gamblers. The Sugar House Gang's hurt prestige demanded violent retribution.[6]

In early September, Abe Burnstein contacted Fred Burke and his crew and proposed a peace meeting where they could settle their differences. Burke was instructed to report to the Carlton-Plaza Hotel at 2931 John R Street. Eddie Fletcher would be waiting for him there to escort him to the room where the Burnsteins would be. Burke was naturally suspicious, as the Miraflores Massacre had been set up in the same manner.[7]

After careful consideration, Burke sent Raymond Shocker in his place. Born Charles Maginness, Shocker was a bootlegger from St. Louis who had joined the Johnny Reid crew in Detroit. He would go there, check things out, and if everything was kosher he would telephone Burke. If it wasn't, Shocker was to escape by any means necessary.

Shocker arrived at the Carlton-Plaza on the afternoon of September 6. After being greeted in the lobby by Eddie Fletcher, the bootlegger made his way up to the third floor suite, where Sugar House gangster Abe Axler stood waiting. A submachine gun was stashed in the closet, and Axler was to use the Thompson on Burke and whoever else was with him. When Shocker stepped into the room and saw no one but Axler, he immediately realized that it was a trap and instinctively rushed the Purple killer. During the fierce scuffle that ensued, the Siamese Twins beat the St. Louis bootlegger so severely they fractured his skull and shot him twice. The Twins left him for dead, retrieved the submachine gun, and made their escape. Shocker miraculously survived the assault and predictably gave the police nothing to work with.[8]

With this vicious attack on Raymond Shocker, the three-year alliance between the Sugar House Boys and the former Egan's Rats was officially at an end.

IN THE WAKE OF the wave of gang violence that engulfed Detroit in the summer of 1927, the Detroit Police Department created the Crime and Bomb Squad. The Crime and Bomb Squad was a descendant of the old Black Hand Squad and its head was Inspector Henry J. Garvin.

Garvin was the youngest Detroit Police inspector in its history, and he was widely hailed as a future Chief of Police. He had joined the force in June 1914, and began a meteoric rise to power. Garvin had a reputation as an energetic, dedicated officer who racked up an impressive list of arrests and citations for bravery. He made Detective after less than three years, and by 1923 was a Detective Lieutenant, en route to Inspector. Garvin was fond of speaking to newspaper reporters and he detailed his plans to clean up the crime problem in the city, starting with a rash of kidnappings that had occurred throughout the summer.

Garvin was not as on the straight and narrow as he appeared, however. He was rumored to take payoffs from the Sugar House Gang and he would later be suspected of extorting members of the Licavoli crew. Two detectives in his squad, Adolph Van Coppenolle and Max Waldfogel, also had allegations of corruption.

Detective Lieutenant John Hoffman was a dedicated officer who did his duty the best he could, when corrupt police and judges didn't hamper him. Inspector John Navarre, who was beaten out for head of the Crime and Bomb Squad by the younger Garvin, was noted by observers as unquestionably being on the level. Two other detectives in the squad, William DeLisle and Roy Pendergrass, were also renowned for their incorruptibility.[9]

Immediately after its official inception on September 1, 1927, the Crime and Bomb Squad made a series of lightning raids on the gangland elements of the city, determined to put an end to the crime spree. After Raymond Shocker's near murder in the Carlton-Plaza Hotel, Garvin declared that he had been attacked by group of gangsters hired by gamblers to ensure no more kidnappings. Sugar House mobsters were hauled in left and right. Charles Leiter and Henry Shorr found themselves submitting to a rare arrest. Angel Face Kaminsky went to post bail for Shorr and found himself put in a cell right along with him.[10] As dedicated as the new investigative unit may have been, it wasn't long before the Sugar House Boys resumed business as usual.

During this ultra-active criminal period, the Sugar House Gang continued hijacking against various bootleggers and cleaning industry terrorism unabated. On December 7, 1927, Irving Shapiro and Jack Budd were lurking near the intersection of Hastings and Wilkins streets, the same corner where Jake Trager had been murdered four years before. While Budd waited behind the wheel of a high-powered sedan, Shapiro stepped out and waited for the opportune moment to throw a stink bomb through the plate glass window of a nearby cleaning shop. Stink bombs did considerable damage to cleaning shops because the stench produced from such devices never washed out of the clothes it infected. The smell would even permeate the walls and cement floor of a store, forcing it to close down.

At that moment, Patrolmen John Lookridge, Joe Schmuck, and Hobart Mainard cruised slowly through the intersection in a DPD squad car and spotted the two known Sugar House gangsters acting in a suspicious manner. Shapiro was unnerved by the sudden presence of the cops and sought to quickly get away. He leapt into the passenger seat while Budd sped north on Hastings Street, followed closely by the squad car. Just north of Erskine Street, Shapiro threw the stink bomb out of the passenger window of their car in an attempt to destroy evidence of their crime. The bomb hit the pavement and exploded into a wall of flame several feet high. The police were undeterred by this and drove straight through the conflagration. The gangsters were finally overtaken at East Grand Boulevard and Brush Street. Budd and Shapiro faced several charges, and they eventually received three years probation for the stolen automobile in which they were riding.[11]

One curious incident during this time period illustrated the extent of the Sugar House Gang's clout amongst Detroit's authorities. On the evening of December 16, Crime and Bomb Squad Detectives William DeLisle and Roy Pendergrass were staking out the gang's Woodward Avenue roost, the Addison Hotel. The two detectives observed Joe, Izzy, and Ray Burnstein, Honey Miller, and Jules Joffa getting into a brand-new Cadillac sedan at the curb. They quickly overtook the Sugar House boys and discovered that they were all carrying concealed weapons. DeLisle and Pendergrass were ecstatic as they booked the men and wrote their reports.

Upon arriving home at two o'clock in the morning, DeLisle got a phone call from Inspector Henry Garvin, who stated that Mayor John Smith had declared that no arrest warrants were to be issued for the five men. DeLisle, who probably knew full well that Garvin was on the take, informed him that they were already planning to file a report the next morning. Three hours later, Garvin called Pendergrass and repeated the mayor's directive. Garvin stated they already had a second report typed up which said the pistols were found on the ground and not on the gangsters themselves. After assuring him that he had destroyed the original reports, Garvin told Pendergrass to ask the prosecutor for an arrest warrant based on the bogus second report.

Meanwhile, Chief of Detectives Edward Fox had gotten hold of the detectives' original reports and wanted them to explain the differences between the two. DeLisle and Pendergrass went to Garvin, who said that Mayor Smith's orders must be carried out and that he himself would explain away the discrepancies in the reports. That ended the case. The Burnsteins and their two associates were released. Detectives DeLisle and Pendergrass continued to go about their jobs, even though the Mayor of Detroit had sandbagged them.[12]

Less than a week later, in the early morning hours of December 21, two Ecorse rumrunners named Jake LaZeno and John Thorman were driving an empty truck through the Southwest Side on their way to pick up a load of booze when they were victimized by Sugar House hijackers. Ray Burnstein, Harry Fleisher, and Phil Keywell (who didn't know the truck was empty) quickly overtook them and demanded their truck at gunpoint. One of the smugglers drew a pistol and got off a few shots, one of which clipped Fleisher's left thumb. Burnstein and Keywell promptly opened fire in retaliation, hitting LaZeno in the left thigh and grazing Thorman's head.

Despite their injuries, the Ecorse smugglers quickly got their truck in gear and sped off. After a high-speed chase up Oakwood Boulevard, both parties were stopped by police and arrested at the corner of West Fort and Reisner. The gritty liquor guards survived their wounds and, probably not wanting to exacerbate the damage already done, refused to file a complaint. As a result, Fleisher, Burnstein, and Keywell were released from custody.[13]

BY THE END OF 1927, the Sugar House Boys faced a challenge on their North End turf not from the cleaners and dyers or rival bootleggers, but from two Detroit police officers who decided to cut themselves in on the crew's rackets.

Vivian Welch had arrived in the city from Montgomery County, Mississippi in 1923 at the mere age of seventeen. Like many other Southerners, he came to Detroit in search of a better life and prosperity. After working for two years on the assembly line of a Chevrolet plant, Welch joined the police force and was assigned to the Ninth Precinct, which encompassed the North End where the Sugar House Boys ruled. In three years of service, Welch had racked up as spotless record as a dedicated officer of the law. Unfortunately his friend and partner, Max Whisman, drew him into bad things.

The two cops sought to supplement their income by shaking down blind pig owners on their beat by selling them "protection service" against the gangsters. Whisman was caught and fired off the job in June 1926. Eventually reinstated, he and Welch resumed their extortion activities with little regard to the hornet's nest they were disturbing. In March 1927, Whisman was caught once again and voluntarily resigned after charges of extortion were threatened against him.

Patrolman Welch totally escaped detection during Whisman's troubles, and he continued to make the rounds, splitting the profits with his now silent partner Max Whisman. They knew many of their victims paid protection money to the Sugar House Gang, but they smugly figured that because they were cops, they would not be harmed. What they did not realize was that this new breed of gangster didn't adhere to any protocol whatsoever. Anyone who got in their way was punished severely.

The last straw apparently occurred just after the New Year of 1928 began, when Welch and Whisman deviated from their usual MO and shook down the operator of one of the gang's alley breweries, located to the rear of 980 Melbourne Avenue. The enraged brewery boss, Benny Weiss, immediately called the Oakland Sugar House to report this latest incursion. After a week or two and an intimidating visit from a few gangsters, both cops seemed to realize that they had finally gone too far.

On the morning of January 31, 1928, Vivian Welch was visibly nervous. He had taken the day off and was in civilian clothes. The officer had drawn fifteen days of his pay in advance. A little before noon, Welch purchased a brand new .38 Colt revolver at a Woodward Avenue hardware store. At 1 p.m. a green Chevrolet sedan picked him up somewhere in the North End. Its occupants quickly put the rod on Welch, who never even had a chance to reach for his gun. They cruised north on St. Aubin Street. One of the gangsters roughly reached into Welch's pocket and confiscated the wad of cash that was the patrolman's paycheck.

Just over the Hamtramck city line, near the corner of Faber and St. Aubin streets, the Chevy's driver hit the brakes. The keyed-up cop broke out of the right rear passenger door and ran up St. Aubin, wildly zigzagging back and forth in a desperate attempt to dodge the bullets he knew would come. Two triggermen got out and gave chase, pistols blazing all the while. A shot caught Welch in the leg and drove him forward onto the pavement. The two shooters ran up to the wounded patrolman, who rolled over on his back and raised his hand in a final defensive gesture that failed to stop the eight bullets that tore into his head and torso.

The killers ran back and jumped inside the sedan, which peeled rubber north on St. Aubin and ran directly over the dead body of Patrolman Welch. The car was later found abandoned near the corner of Woodward and Melbourne. Just a short time after the murder, gang boss Ray Burnstein called police and said that the darndest thing had happened; two men had stolen his Chevrolet sedan at gunpoint the previous evening.[14]

Stunned residents of the St. Aubin block where the murder took place related events as they saw them, and provided police with the murder car's license plate number. The tag number matched that of Ray Burnstein's Chevy sedan. The gang boss soon surrendered with his attorney, Edward H. Kennedy, Jr. and gave his alibi. The next morning's *Detroit Times* article on the murder turned out to have unintended historical significance. It began;

"A 'hijacker,' alleged by police to be a known member of the notorious 'Purple' gang and a passenger in the car from which came the hail of bullets which killed Patrolman Vivian Welch was on his way to headquarters to give himself up, a tipster informed the police homicide squad today."

It turned out to be the first time that the name "Purple Gang" was mentioned in print. Wherever the name had come from, it was now a matter of public record.[15]

The murder of one of their own sent the Detroit Police Department into an investigative frenzy. Within a few days, nearly every member of the "Purple Gang" was in police custody. Many of them were photographed in "show-up" pictures.[16] Poolrooms and houses across the North End were raided. Often men who just happened to be hanging around the poolrooms when the cops came calling were subsequently labeled as members of the Purple Gang by the police and press. As a result, harmless delinquents often had their names listed in the "Rogue's Gallery" right alongside vicious killers. In order to keep the suspects in custody as long as they could, the police transferred them from precinct to precinct before their lawyers could secure their release. The process was known as giving the gangsters "the loop."

Police questioned Ray Burnstein extensively but released him when no other corroborating evidence presented itself. It was rumored that the Purples forced Welch's partner Max Whisman to set up a meeting between Welch and Burnstein. The murder was the result. Abe Burnstein himself was grilled, but to no avail. The cops found Eddie Fletcher in his flat at 136 Clairmount Avenue along with Willie Laks and another thug who had recently arrived from New York. In his apartment, among other things, police confiscated a bulletproof vest often worn by Fletcher during sensitive times.[17]

Despite the flurry of arrests and the exposure of the Purple Gang, no one was ever convicted of Patrolman Vivian Welch's murder. As notorious as they were, the Purples were about to be rudely introduced to the whole region.

THE CLEANERS AND DYERS WAR was now in its third year, and thousands of dollars in extortion money flowed into the Purple Gang's coffers. Sam Sigman's violent December 1926 homicide had badly frightened the independent holdout cleaners. A month later, DFL leader Frank Martel called the wholesale cleaners to a downtown meeting in order to re-stabilize the industry. The thoroughly terrorized wholesalers felt that they had no choice to re-unionize. Their new reconstituted union was dubbed the Associated Cleaners and Dyers. Burnstein brother-in-law Charles Jacoby was installed as the union president. The prices were once again raised on the tailors. Most, if not all, Detroit cleaners fell into line; even the formerly recalcitrant Perfect Cleaners and Dyers came aboard.

In the summer of 1927, a series of events had combined to push the Purple Gang-related labor terrorism to a whole new level. Harry Rosman, business rival of Charles Jacoby and president of Famous Cleaners and

Dyers, suggested at a wholesalers' meeting with doing away with the laundry drivers' high commissions and putting them on a straight salary. The retail tailors were hurting under the high set price, and Rosman proposed lowering the drivers' 30% commission down to 15% in order to help alleviate this. In response, Jacoby began to "line up" the commission drivers and sent word to his fellow wholesalers that the drivers would agree to the commission cuts if the tailors' set price would remain unchanged. It later turned out that several of the Purples had barged into a meeting of the laundry drivers and snarled "We don't what will happen to you!" if they refused to work for Jacoby. A vote was then taken and, not surprisingly, the drivers agreed to his terms.

Jacoby then sent an emissary to Harry Rosman offering to eliminate the commission drivers for $1,000. At the very next meeting of the drivers union, Charles Jacoby appeared as a "representative" of the national drivers' union, and oversaw a successful vote to eliminate the commissions. Those cleaning shops that used Rosman-allied drivers were promptly fire-bombed and/or stink-bombed. Then, in a move seemingly unrelated to the commission driver dispute, Jacoby resigned his position as head of the wholesalers' union. He had been suspected of embezzling union checks and ultimately resigned his position rather than account for the money.

With Charles Jacoby no longer head of the wholesalers' union, none other than Purple Gang boss Abe Burnstein stepped in to replace him. Officially on the payroll as an "arbitrator," Burnstein didn't bother with kid gloves and announced to the wholesalers that he "would run the parade from now on and it would be too bad for anyone who dropped out of line." The gang boss bluntly declared that he wanted $1,000 a week to keep everything "hotsy-totsy." The cleaners understood full well that they were paying the Purple Gang to keep them from trashing their businesses and/or killing them. Charles Jacoby made a speech saying he would not rejoin the union unless Burnstein was the "boss."

Harry Rosman courageously decided not to pay the dues. Abe Burnstein told him they'd go up to AFL President Frank Martel's office and hash the whole deal out. Surprisingly, Martel told *both* men that they had to make their agreements elsewhere. Emboldened by seeing someone openly defy the Purple Gang boss, Rosman continued to refuse to pay the money. Just a few nights later, two of Burnstein's men showed up at his plant. The gangsters proceeded to beat up the night watchman, douse the main office with gasoline, and set it ablaze. Any other wholesalers who tried to buck the Purples met with similar fates. Thereafter, at each wholesalers meeting, Burnstein would oversee the proceedings and collect his money while several of his strong-arms waited in an adjacent room. The $1,000 weekly tithe was divided amongst the wholesalers in payments ranging from $50 to $175 apiece.[18]

At Charles Jacoby's cleaning plant, the gangsters would hang out and take target practice on an indoor range set up there. Abe and Simon Axler, Eddie Fletcher, Honey Miller, and Irving Milberg could be seen in there on any given day laughing, joking, blasting holes in targets, and spinning pistols around on their fingers Johnny Ringo-style. One worker saw two of the Purples wearing rubber gloves and carrying glass jars filled with what he assumed to be chemical bombs of some sort. The Purples even went so far as to invade the wholesalers' stag party at the Armenian Club, located at 307 E. Ferry Avenue. The gangsters stuck up the cleaners at gunpoint and relieved them of $800 in cash and about $4,000 worth of jewelry. Such an incident occurred not because the Purples needed some chump change, but was done to send an intimidating message to the wholesalers.[19]

The business representative of the wholesalers union was thirty-seven year old Samuel Polakoff. The vice-president of the Union Cleaners and Dyers, it was Polakoff's job to act as a conduit between the various wholesalers and the Purples. Essentially an ombudsman, Polakoff was charged with fielding complaints from those in the union and also assigning drivers and tailors to various wholesalers. Already thoroughly afraid of the gangsters, Sam now found himself the unenviable position of ferrying messages between his rebellious colleagues and an increasingly hostile Abe Burnstein. Several wholesalers complained to Polakoff about the high weekly dues, who said that with Burnstein and Jacoby setting the amount, there was nothing that could be done. At a secret meeting on January 7, 1928, the wholesalers in the union voted to take Burnstein off the payroll. A visibly apprehensive Polakoff hesitantly agreed. After three years of terrorism, the cleaners officially cut the gangsters loose.[20]

A furious Abe Burnstein confronted Sam Polakoff face-to-face and demanded that both he and the $1,000 weekly payments be immediately reinstated. The union rep bravely stood his ground. As a result, an intense wave of bombings struck Detroit-area cleaning shops and plants. Mysterious fires, attributed to chemical-tainted garments, broke out in the plants and caused thousands of dollars worth of damage.

At 8 p.m. on March 21, 1928, Sam Polakoff left the Union Cleaners and Dyers plant at 8737 Grand River Avenue, telling his partners he had to keep an appointment with a friend whom he did not name. About forty-five minutes after Polakoff left the plant, a man standing on Hazelwood Street near LaSalle Boulevard saw a small Nash sedan being chased down the street by a larger LaSalle sedan. As he watched transfixed, the LaSalle crowded the Nash to the curb and both vehicles loudly skidded to a violent stop. Two men leapt out of the LaSalle and into the smaller car. The LaSalle then sped off down Hazelwood, followed a few seconds later by the Nash. Early the next morning, passerby found Polakoff's dead body slumped inside his Nash sedan at the intersection of Dexter and West Grand boulevards. He had been brutally beaten and then shot four times.[21]

Sam Polakoff's partners, upon hearing of his murder, finally broke over three years of silence and went to the police. They detailed the long history of Purple Gang extortion which had driven more than a few of them to the brink of both bankruptcy and madness. Abe Burnstein got wind of the impending arrests and left town, but they got virtually everyone else. When taken into custody on March 29, Abe Axler and Eddie Fletcher were both armed and wearing bulletproof vests as if they were expecting trouble.

Charged with extortion were Abe and Ray Burnstein, their brother-in-law Charles Jacoby, Joe "Honey" Miller, Abe Miller (Honey's cousin), Irving Milberg, Abe and Simon Axler, Eddie Fletcher, Abe "Angel Face" Kaminsky, George Cordell and Irving Shapiro. Newspapers splashed the names and exploits of the Purple Gang onto their front pages. The *Detroit News* ran mug shots of practically all of them, along with their criminal records and a written account of their story. Most remaining members of the gang began lying low, while a handful of others exercised no such caution.[22]

TWENTY-YEAR OLD Zygmund "Ziggie" Selbin was not named in the extortion warrants. A Russian-born Polish Jew, he was a stepson of Third Street Navy smuggler Jack Selbin. The youthful Selbin didn't rank very high in the Purple Gang; he was known a brutal extortionist who frequently worked with Irving Shapiro. A snazzy dresser, he favored silk suits, silk shirts, and even silk underwear. Ziggie was also a cold-blooded psychopath that would kill without hesitation either on command or on a whim.

According to one graphic anecdote, one night while Selbin was on a toot in a local blind pig, he noticed a large diamond ring on the finger of a patron. The gangster then drunkenly swayed over to the man and demanded the ring. When the guy refused, Ziggie introduced his skull to a set of brass knuckles. Unable to pry the ring from the now unconscious man's hand, Selbin drew a large switchblade from his pocket and sliced off the ring finger itself. Ziggie took the ring and absently tossed the victim's finger aside while appraising the jewel. The gangster then left, sporting a brand new diamond ring and leaving behind a blind pig clientele that had been shocked into utter silence by the gratuitous display of brutality they had just witnessed.

Almost three weeks after the Cleaners and Dyers extortion raids, on April 17, Selbin and his mother Anna were visiting his sister Bessie and her husband at their home at 660 E. Alexandrine Avenue. It was the first birthday of Ziggie's nephew George. Around 6 p.m. on this ostensibly happy occasion, Bessie and her husband, Joseph Sykes, got into a fierce argument. Ziggie quickly came to his sister's defense. After precious few words, Selbin whipped out a pistol and fatally shot Sykes through the heart in full view of his family. The Selbins kept quiet about the matter, because Ziggie had threatened to kill them all if they told what happened. Eventually he would surrender and beat the rap on a self-defense plea.[23]

FORTY-EIGHT HOURS after Ziggie Selbin killed his brother-in-law, Inspector Henry Garvin and his Crime and Bomb Squad raided the Oakland Sugar House at 8634 Oakland Avenue. Among those arrested were Charles Leiter, Henry Shorr, and Joe Burnstein. During the raid, Shorr decided to play it rough with the arresting officers and got beaten senseless in the melee. In court shortly thereafter, he sported a swollen right eye and multi-colored bruises all over his face. The police claimed that the Sugar House bosses had imposed a tax of fifty cents per pound of corn sugar they sold in an effort to raise money for the Purple Gang's defense fund. Henry Shorr was discharged when Lieutenant Arthur Ryckman announced to the court, "We are all through with this man," a remark that brought laughter to the courtroom because of Shorr's battered visage.[24]

Harry Fleisher, Isadore "Uncle Issie" Kaminsky, Sam "The Gorilla" Davis, and John Wolfe were charged in a separate warrant of extortion. This warrant was later expanded to include Charles Leiter, Phil Keywell, and two unknown men (John Doe and Richard Roe.) The chief complainant was Samuel Lerner, president of the Michigan Millwork and Lumber Company, who alleged that the Purples had extorted him out of $25 a week for three weeks. Why the Purples targeted Lerner for extortion is unclear to this day; one source says that he may have been operating a 30-gallon whiskey still at his lumberyard. If so, Lerner was almost certainly buying his distilling supplies from the Oakland Sugar House. At any rate, Sam Lerner provided police with a graphic description of a prime example of the classic extortion schemes that allow organized crime to thrive.

Here is his account of the incident, which took place along Oakland Avenue a week earlier on Wednesday, April 11;

"When I finished my business with (Irving) Seligman, I went across the street to a tire store. There I saw Sam Davis. A gun was sticking out of his pocket. The tire store men told me that they had heard Davis say he was 'going to give Lerner plenty'."

While Lerner did not speak to Davis, he watched the diminutive gangster walk outside and enter a car that then drove a few blocks north to the Oakland Sugar House. Lerner followed the vehicle to the sugar warehouse and walked inside the main office to see bookkeeper John Wolfe sitting at his desk. He wanted to know why Davis wanted to kill him, his confidence bolstered by a pistol he had borrowed from Irving Seligman, one of his customers.

"Harry Fleisher and Sam Davis were at the sugar house when I got there. I asked them where Henry Shorr and Charlie Leiter were. They told me Leiter was in a restaurant nearby. I went to the restaurant, and the first thing Leiter asked me was whether I had a gun. When I told him I had one, he asked me why I didn't kill them. I replied that I would if there had been only two or three of them, but that I was afraid of the whole gang."

Leiter told Lerner to give him his gun and the businessman refused. Sam then accompanied the crime boss across the street. Once they got there, Charlie Leiter called Harry Fleisher into his office for a private *tête-à-tête*. Harry quickly exited the office and got right to the point;

"I went back to the sugar house, and when I came in Fleisher shoved an automatic pistol against my chest and demanded my gun. When I refused, he pulled the trigger, but the gun didn't go off, and only clicked. Then I gave him my gun.

"(Philip) Keywell came in then and they said they would all go over to the tire store. I went to a friend's house. Later William Bernstein came in and took me back to the sugar house. Fleisher and Keywell were there. They said they needed money. I agreed to meet them the next day at the sugar house. When I went to the sugar house the next day, Keywell and Wolff (sic) were there. Wolff told me to give Keywell $25 then and $25 the next week...I gave him $10 cash and a $15 check. The next day I met (Isadore) Kaminsky at the sugar house. I told him I was ashamed of being a lodge brother of his. He said it was too late, that I'd have to straighten things out with the boys."

Exactly who William Bernstein remains unknown; he may have been one of the Burnstein brothers using an alias. Either way, as author Paul Kavieff would write decades later, "This incident represented a very similar scenario to the way that Italian and Sicilian Black Handers extorted money from the businessmen in their community—first a death threat, then a mysterious mediator appears to straighten out the problem—the mediator all along being a member of the extortion gang himself."[25]

The following Saturday, April 14, Sam Lerner went back to the Sugar House. Henry Shorr had returned from a trip to New York and Lerner hoped he would call his dogs off. Shorr gave him a choice; they could call up Phil Keywell and "work something out" or Henry would personally accompany Lerner to the downtown police headquarters to file a complaint. Shorr then got on the telephone and called who Lerner thought was someone at the police station. Whomever the Oakland Sugar House boss spoke to suggested they talk to none other than Crime and Bomb Squad head Inspector Henry J. Garvin.

Shorr picked up Sam Lerner at Irving Seligman's house. Two large men who identified themselves as detectives accompanied the gang boss. Downtown at 1300 Beaubien, Inspector Garvin's office was found to be empty. Disturbed by the whole incident, Lerner then went to the police. One of the crew, Sam Potasnik, was charged with obstruction of justice while trying to intimidate Sam Lerner into silence. Harry Fleisher, Sam Davis, Isadore Kaminsky, and John Wolfe were eventually convicted of attempted extortion and received probation, a peculiarly light sentence which indicated the level of the boys' clout with the Detroit court system.[26]

THE PURPLES WERE CHARGED with extortion in the Cleaners and Dyers case and bound over for trial on May 17, 1928. Defense attorney Edward H. Kennedy, Jr. argued for a continuance in order to prepare his defense. Judge Charles Bowles agreed, and the trial was pushed back to Monday, June 4.

On the second day of the trial, Irving Shapiro was not present in court along with the rest of the defendants when the court convened. Judge Bowles asked where he was, and Simon Axler volunteered to search for the missing Purple. Axler found Shapiro still in bed at his home at 355 Owen Street. Simon dressed Irving and then got him back to the Recorder's Court. Shapiro was barely able to sit up; slumping to the side occasionally as Angel Face Kaminsky roughly elbowed him up back into position. Judge Bowles deemed Shapiro too "ill" to sit in court and adjourned until 9 a.m. the next day.[27]

Throughout the month of June, the Purples watched from the defense table as a parade of cleaners and dyers took the stand to describe their various terrorism tactics. One star witness for the prosecution was Harry Rosman, president of the Famous Cleaners and Dyers. DFL president Frank Martel had flown the coop when their original raids began and testimony stalled as police searched for him. The gangsters' main line of defense was that Harry Rosman and Frank Martel had done the all extorting, and that the "Purple Gang" was merely a figment of Rosman's imagination.[28]

The North End boys got a small measure of satisfaction when they opened the morning papers on June 28 and discovered that after years of trying, Mike Dipisa had succeeded in getting himself killed. The night before, River Rouge Constable Edward A. McPherson had gunned down Dipisa just seconds after the gangster and his henchman murdered Delray bootlegger Gus Nykiel who, like Johnny Reid before him, had stubbornly rejected Mike's extortion demands.[29]

The Purples began smiling even more when word came that someone had broken into the Cleaners and Dyers' Union headquarters on the evening of June 28. The office, located at 274 E. Vernor Highway, contained union records that were vital to the prosecution's case. The burglars had taken a filing cabinet and five ledgers (as well as $30 cash for good measure.) The ledgers contained financial accounts of the union as well the minutes for all the union meetings that had taken place over the last three years. While the Purples claimed that they had no knowledge of the thefts, the prosecution hinted that the gangsters had arranged for the files to disappear.[30] With their absence, the state's case suddenly got a lot more difficult. On July 11, the trial was halted nearly two months to the sudden and grave illness of Judge Charles Bowles.

The closing arguments in the Cleaners and Dyers trial were finally delivered in the first week of September 1928. Judge Bowles dismissed the charge against Angel Face Kaminsky before the case went to the jury, stating that no evidence in the trial had linked him to the crimes. Prosecutors reminded the jurors that Detroit's cleaning and dyeing industry had been peaceful until it was "organized" by Chicago labor racketeer Ben Abrams; that Charles Jacoby had brought the Purple Gang into the union to extract exorbitant dues and/ or terrorize those who didn't fall into line. They also noted that once the dues were paid to Abe Burnstein, the bombings and fires ceased abruptly.

On September 13, the jury took only one hour to deliver its verdict. Not Guilty.[31] Frank Martel was brought up on extortion charges as a result of the trial testimony (he was eventually acquitted as well), but Abe Burnstein and the rest of the Purples were free as birds. The gang threw a huge party to celebrate their victory. The Purple Gang felt invincible. Their reputation soared to unfathomable heights after the trial, and they soon established an alliance with the most famous gangster in this country's history.

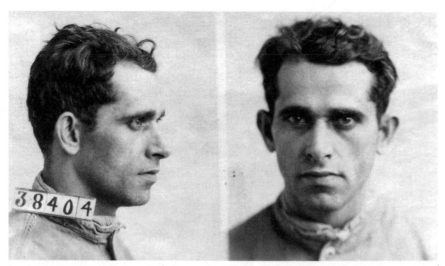

Joe Saxer was a strongarm artist who worked for the Sugar House Gang aka Purple Gang during their 1920s heyday. He's pictured here upon his arrival at Leavenworth in the early 1930s. *NARA.*

Members of the Purple Gang in custody after an April 19, 1928 raid on the Oakland Sugar House. Standing from left to right are Jack Redfern, Harry Fleisher, Charles Leiter, Henry Shorr, Alfred Russell, Ben Marcus, Isadore "Uncle Issie" Kaminsky, and Louis Achtman. *Walter Reuther Library.*

The group shot of Purple Gang mobsters was taken on March 30, 1928 after the end of the Cleaners and Dyers War. Standing from left to right are Simon Axler, Eddie Fletcher, Sam Goldfarb, Phil Keywell, Abe Zussman, Willie Laks, Harry Fleisher, and Jack Stein. Sitting in the chair in front of the group is Abe Axler. *Walter Reuther Library.*

Purple Gang mobster Abe "Angel Face" Kaminsky has a smoke and a smirk after hearing the Cleaners and Dyers War-related extortion charges against him dismissed in September 1928. *Walter Reuther Collection.*

PINNACLE

Al Capone had arrived in Chicago in late 1919 from Brooklyn and quickly rose through the ranks of Windy City's underworld at the knee of crime boss Johnny Torrio. After the Torrio/Capone mob engineered the 1924 killing of the rival leader of the North Side Gang, Dean O'Banion, Chicago was swept with a war that would make the Tommy Gun, as well as the city itself, world famous. Torrio was shot and severely wounded by the North Siders two months after O'Banion's assassination, and he turned over an estimated $200 million dollar-a-year business to Capone, who was but twenty-six years old at the time.

Gradually Al consolidated his empire, eliminating his rivals and getting to the point where he was considered the *de facto* mayor of Chicago. Capone got his booze from many different places, but his primary source was imported Scotch whiskey trucked in from New York. His first crime mentor and longtime friend, celebrated gangster Frankie Yale, oversaw security for these shipments. But Yale started double-crossing Capone by hijacking his trucks, and as a result, was shot to death while driving his car in Brooklyn on July 1, 1928.

After Yale's murder, Capone started looking for an additional supplier of liquor, something much closer than New York. The Chicago crime czar set his sights on Detroit, America's prime entry point for smuggled booze. Dating back to the summer of 1926, Capone had been in town more than once to inquire about the acquisition of Canadian-produced alcohol. *News* crime reporter Jack Carlisle remembered his 1928 Detroit visit well;[1]

We heard that he had a suite of rooms at the top floor of the Fort Shelby Hotel. So we took his picture around. We didn't have any trouble finding out this nice, quiet gentleman that everyone thought was from Battle Creek, Michigan was Al Capone of Chicago. And he apparently stayed here three days and apparently he had a series of conferences with very notorious gangsters of Italian extraction, about five different bootleg gangs, not only in Detroit but from Ecorse and River Rouge and from Hamtramck. He had found a market for uncut whiskey and it didn't make any difference what the price was; the problem he had was getting it out of Michigan and he would bring his truck and he would bring in his bodyguards – because if you recall those days, they were very violent days where a lot of money was concerned.

BECAUSE AL WAS OF Campanian descent and at odds with Sicilian Mafia leadership in his hometown, Detroit Mafia boss Sam Catalanotte declined to do business with him. Since a good deal of the liquor that came across the Detroit River went through the hands of the Purple Gang at some point, Capone reached an agreement with the Burnstein brothers to buy large shipments of Canadian whiskey. The Purples were able to meet Chicago's demand for thousands of cases of booze by smuggling genuine Old Log Cabin whiskey (an American bourbon that was distilled in Montreal during Prohibition) across the river and sending it west on U.S. 12 (present-day Michigan Avenue) via truck.

Ultimately, the Purple Gang's new business deal with Al Capone would ensnare them in the most notorious gangster mass murder in America's history.[2]

THOSE WHO WERE within earshot of the S.M.C. Cartage Company at 2122 North Clark Street for those fateful seconds at 10:30 on the morning of February 14, 1929 thought they heard the clattering of air hammers, or a pair of pneumatic drills. This muffled chatter sounded for several long seconds and was interspersed with at least two loud blasts, similar to automobile backfires. In less than ten seconds, the noise abruptly stopped. Then there was a brief resumption of the drilling sound and all was quiet again.

Witnesses then saw two men in overcoats and fedoras emerge from the garage's front door; at least one of them had his hands up as if he was under arrest. Two uniformed policemen were herding them into a Cadillac detective sedan parked at the curb. This vehicle then sped away from the garage, sounding its siren as it moved out into traffic. Most passerbies assumed some kind of police raid had taken place. Jeanette Landesman, who lived next door, convinced one of her neighbors to investigate the strange noises she had heard. Clair McAllister entered the front door and was shocked to discover six butchered corpses and a dying gangster still trying to painfully make his escape. Chicago, Illinois, a city known worldwide for gangster violence, now had the granddaddy hit of them all.

The St. Valentine's Day Massacre has tantalized Americans since its occurrence. The precise identities of the killers and the reason for the mass slaughter are disputed to this day. The massacre has been thoroughly examined in other works, and the author feels no need to rehash the entire case within these pages. It is noteworthy for mention in this chronicle because of the long-held suspicion that Detroit's Purple Gang was somehow involved. A landlady in the brownstone across the street from the S.M.C. Cartage garage tentatively identified Philip and Harry Keywell as those who rented a third-floor room from her. This theory says that the Keywell brothers were watching for the arrival of the main target, North Side Gang leader George "Bugs" Moran, from this perch. Once the man they thought was Moran arrived, the Keywells supposedly telephoned the signal to the actual killers. Another long-held belief was that the seven victims of the massacre were lured there by the promise of a shipment of Purple Gang-distributed Old Log Cabin whiskey. Some stories even say that Abe Burnstein made the decoy phone call himself. Were the Purples really involved?

The roots of the massacre lay in the long-term bootleg feud between the Al Capone mob and the rival North Side Gang. The original leader of the latter crew, Dean O'Banion, had been shot and killed in his State Street flower shop on November 10, 1924. O'Banion's successor was Earl "Hymie" Weiss, a vicious Polish Catholic who was reputed to be the only man Al Capone was ever truly afraid of. Weiss made many attempts to kill Capone, even leading several automobiles full of machine-gunners past Scarface's headquarters at the Hawthorne Hotel in Cicero. The cavalcade of killers riddled an entire city block with lead trying to kill him in what was probably the most spectacular drive-by shooting in American history; to this day, it's said that Weiss was the only man Capone was ever truly afraid of. On October 11, 1926, three weeks after the Cicero attempt, Weiss himself was machine-gunned in front of the Holy Name Cathedral by two Capone gunmen. For five months after Weiss's murder, Vincent "The Schemer" Drucci shared leadership of the gang with George "Bugs" Moran, but a detective killed him while he resisted arrest on April 4, 1927.

That left Bugs Moran in sole charge of the North Siders. Moran was a short, stocky fellow who is often inaccurately portrayed as a slow-thinking, temperamental dolt. In reality, Moran was a shrewd, tough gang boss who successfully sparred with his arch-rival Capone throughout the late 1920s. The oft-told version of events says that despite their rivalry, Moran bought much of his whiskey through Capone, the Old Log Cabin that was distributed by the Purple Gang. Bugs supposedly became irritated by the high price he paid Capone, and eventually found a cheaper supplier. Moran's customers rejected the new booze and began demanding Old Log Cabin. When the North Side boss tried to buy from Big Al once again, he was turned away. Moran found a way around this by simply hijacking the trucks coming in from Detroit. Both Capone and Abe Burnstein were said to be infuriated. The North Side Gang also allegedly had a hand in the murders of several of Al's friends, including Pasqualino Lolordo, president of Chicago's *Unione Siciliana*. Capone began to plot the death of Bugs Moran.[3]

By ten o'clock on the morning in question, six men were congregating inside Moran's garage depot at 2122 N. Clark Street. They were;

Frank and Pete Gusenberg; two brothers who were the crew's main killers.
Adam Heyer, the gang's bookkeeper and dog racing track manager.
James Clark, a Moran gang extortionist and gunman.
John May, a mechanic who maintained the North Side gang's vehicles.
Reinhart Schwimmer, an optician and gangster "groupie."

The half-dozen North Siders were crouched around a pot of coffee and box of crackers, awaiting the arrival of their boss. Unbeknownst to them, two men were watching the front door of the garage from a rented room across the street. According to Bugs Moran's descendant G.J., the gang chief was running late that morning due to an overly long barbershop appointment.[4] As Moran dallied, Albert Weinshank arrived at the garage; a North Side labor racketeer and speakeasy operator, his general physical appearance and winter wardrobe resembled Moran's from a distance. The lookouts, mistakenly thinking that the target had arrived, phoned the signal to the shooters.

Within just a few minutes of their call, a Cadillac sedan outfitted to look like a detective sedan made a sharp left turn onto Clark Street from Webster Avenue and struck a delivery truck that was plodding through the intersection. The truck driver, Elmer Lewis, pulled over and got out of his cab in time to a man dressed in a blue suit and chinchilla overcoat emerge from the Cadillac. According to the official CPD report, Lewis glimpsed three other men sitting inside the Cadillac wearing what appeared to be police uniforms. Regardless of fault, Lewis was nervous over having hit what seemed to be a police car; thus, he was relieved when the man in chinchilla looked at the minor damage and just waved it off. Lewis watched as he climbed back behind the wheel of the Cadillac and drove a bit farther down Clark, only to stop in front of the S.M.C. Cartage garage less than a block away.

At this same time, at least two witnesses saw a *second* detective squad car drive through the alley behind the garage. From this vehicle three armed men, two dressed in police uniforms and the other in civilian clothes, barged inside the garage's rear doors and began yelling about a raid. The "police" aimed pistols and ordered the men to face the north wall of the garage and put their hands up against it. The gangsters grudgingly complied, thinking it was nothing more than a routine bust. One of the "officers" quickly went down the line and frisked the gangsters for weapons.[5]

Once the North Siders were subdued, one of the intruders unlocked the garage's front office door and let in two more men, dressed in civilian clothes, from the Cadillac. The "cops" readied their primary weapons; two Thompson submachine guns and a sawed-off .12 gauge pump shotgun. Whether or not the killers realized that Bugs Moran was not there will never be known. At any rate, one of the machine gunners suddenly emptied a fifty-round capacity drum in a left/right center mass sweep at the backs of the North Siders, who (unaware of the impending danger) still had their hands in the air at the moment of the first shot. At the thunderous eruption of this initial volley, one of the other killers instinctively opened fire with his shotgun, sending a load of buckshot into Reinhart Schwimmer's lower back. This firestorm ripped the Moran gangsters literally to pieces, sending them sprawling onto the garage floor. The second machine gunner then stepped toward the fallen men, squatted, and sprayed a twenty-round stick mag in a right/left sweep at the tops of the victims' heads; one of these shots blew away the left side of mechanic John May's skull and another tore an obscene-looking hole in the seat of Pete Gusenberg's pants.[6]

After this grisly work was completed, two men in civilian clothing were marched out of the garage by two uniformed "patrolmen", a charade to convince any onlookers who heard the shots that a police raid had just taken place. According to one witness, one of the "arrestees" slid behind the wheel of the phony squad car and gunned it down Clark Street.

These mass killings, initially dubbed "The North Clark Street Massacre," generated international headlines. In the hours after the massacre, the deputy Chicago Prohibition administrator, Major Frederick D. Silloway, caused quite a storm of controversy by alleging that the killers actually *were* police, rather than gangsters in disguise. When asked to clarify, Major Silloway immediately began backpedaling; he only meant to say he believed that the massacre was "an outgrowth of a hijacking job on Indianapolis Boulevard" a few weeks earlier. The major's basic premise was that five hundred cases of whiskey had been hijacked from Bugs Moran and he had suspended all his payoffs to police, which resulted in the massacre. While most thought

Major Silloway's theory was off-the-wall, the Chicago Police Department ordered 255 of its detectives to account for their whereabouts at the time of the killings. Major Silloway was transferred away, and then eventually fired.

Some days later, Major Silloway's hypothesis was resurrected by a *Chicago Tribune* reporter, who claimed that the North Siders had met at the Clark Street garage to drive empty trucks to Detroit to pick up a liquor shipment. Phone records revealed that Bugs Moran had indeed received a long distance call from Detroit the day before the massacre (there's no evidence that Abe Burnstein or anyone else in the Purple Gang made the call.) Over the years, this story evolved into the widely accepted notion that the North Side Gang was waiting to receive a load of the Purples' Old Log Cabin when the machine gun killers came calling. A freelance hijacker who insisted that Bugs Moran appear personally to take delivery supposedly offered this whiskey to them. Afterwards, the boys would drive to Detroit and pick up more booze.

The trouble with this was that none of the victims (with the exception of coverall-clad mechanic John May) were dressed for the physical labor of unloading eighty cases of whiskey in the relatively small garage; nor were they clad for what was in those days a long, uncomfortable ride to Detroit. The North Siders killed that day all wore fine suits, overcoats, and diamond jewelry (one even wore a carnation as his *boutonnière*.) Recent research, including testimony from G.J. Moran, indicates that the North Side Gang boss himself called the meeting with his men on Valentine's Day. The reasons were twofold; Moran mustered his troops to discuss a recent attempt on his life and a growing suspicion that there was a Capone spy in his inner circle (Bugs was proven right soon after the massacre when high-ranking Moran gangster Ted Newberry defected to the Capone mob.) It appears that the story that the North Side Gang was waiting for a shipment of Purple Gang booze is just that, a story.

The Chicago police did follow up on Major Silloway's booze hijacking theory and looked into the possibility that the Purple Gang had been involved. Mrs. Michael Doody, who owned rooms across the street from the S.M.C. Cartage at 2119 North Clark Street, told police that her third-floor front room had been rented out in late December to a man who identified himself as a cab driver. Two other men accompanied him on most days until she last saw them in late January. She described them as; 1.) 30 years old, 5-9 or 10, 160, dark complexion, wore puttees and a khaki shirt, looked like an Italian. 2.) 28-30 years old, 5-9 in height, 175 pounds, stout, light complexion and hair, gold hose and knicker pants, long dark overcoat, and gray cap. 3.) 35 years old, 5-6 or 7 in height, 140 pounds, medium build and complexion, shell-rimmed glasses, black derby hat and dark clothes and overcoat.

With suspicion of the Purple Gang in their minds, Chicago police showed Mrs. Doody sixteen mug shots of its members. She "partly" identified Philip and Harry Keywell as two of the men who occupied her room. Another landlady nearby, Mrs. Minnie Arvidson at 2051 North Clark, allegedly identified a picture of Eddie Fletcher as a mysterious roomer in her building who disappeared on the day of the massacre.

On the morning of February 16, forty-eight hours after the shootings, Detroit newspapers trumpeted the Purple Gang's connection to the machine gun murders. The *Detroit Times* printed in large blocks letters, "NAME 3 PURPLES IN GANG MASSACRE." While the news media seemed to have already convicted the gangsters, Detroit police were less convinced. Inspector John Donovan had known most of the Purples for years. When asked about the massacre, he said, "I don't believe they are quite hard enough for that. And as for the three identified by the pictures, well, of all the gang those are the three who would be least likely to take part in such a nervy affair." For whatever it was worth, Inspector Henry Garvin said he didn't buy their involvement either. Garvin stated that he had seen Eddie Fletcher watching a prizefight at the Olympia just the night before.[7]

In fact, the case against the three Purples began unraveling almost from the start. Mrs. Doody took another look at the pictures and claimed that she now wasn't sure if the Keywells were the men she saw. She described her roomers as being in their early to mid thirties, and the Keywell brothers were quite a bit younger (Phil was twenty at the time of the massacre, while Harry was only eighteen.) Mrs. Arvidson told police three days later that she could not identify anyone. According to the official CPD report, "Mrs. Arvidson said that when the newspapers are quoting her as identifying pictures of her roomers, they're wrong." Just to cover their bets, the Chicago police requested the arrest of the three suspects.

Early on February 21, Phil Keywell and Eddie Fletcher were arrested and held at the Thirteenth Precinct to await questioning by the Assistant Illinois State's Attorney and a CPD detective lieutenant. Also taken into custody was an underworld character named George A. Lewis. Often incorrectly labeled as a member of the Purple Gang, Lewis had recently arrived in Detroit from Chicago and had boasted to a woman that he "bumped off a party" in that city. Fletcher satisfactorily proved to Chicago authorities that he had been ill with jaundice most of the winter, and had been released from the hospital only on February 12 (Minnie Arvidson's roomer rented the room on January 27.) Keywell had an unshakable alibi as well, and George Lewis came off as an attention-seeking goofball. All three men were cleared.[8]

Ultimately, the North Clark Street shootings were never officially solved. Police later charged that the lead machine gunner was none other than former Egan's Rats associate Fred "Killer" Burke. Other charged suspects included Capone hit men Jack McGurn and John Scalise. Authorities eventually found the two submachine guns used in the killings in Burke's Stevensville, Michigan house, which they searched after he murdered a local policeman in the wake of an automobile accident. Two years later, Burke drew a life sentence for that crime, and was never tried for the Chicago massacre. While the identity of the killers is still debated, the bulk of hard and circumstantial evidence indicates that they did not come from Detroit. It is the opinion of this author that the Purple Gang had nothing to do with the St. Valentine's Day Massacre.[9]

WHILE THE PURPLES had nothing to do with the Chicago massacre, rumors abounded in Detroit that they indeed had been responsible. Their reputation was soaring to astronomical heights. Indeed, since the end of the Cleaners and Dyers War in the spring of 1928, the Purple Gang had been generating a plethora of newspaper copy. With their catchy nickname, colorful gangsters, and thrilling stories of sinister deeds, the thugs from the North End captivated the entire region. Add to this that the vast majority of the public viewed most bootleggers as providing badly wanted alcohol deprived of them by a law no one supported, a near romantic aura surrounded the Purple Gang.

One member of the crew, one of the most feared enforcers in Detroit, was a gargantuan goon known simply as "Tiny Sam." As one Purple associate said many years later, "...he (*Tiny Sam*) weighed about 350 pounds and he was a muscle man. He had a sister, and they tell me – I never met her – that she was like a bookkeeper for the gang. They tell me she would make Bonnie Parker look like a girl scout. She was a Polish Jew. She wore a butch haircut. She fought with her fists, and if anyone got out of line, she could handle it."[10]

The Purples were big spenders at the city's clubs and cabarets. They dressed in expensive suits, mostly conservative darks or grays, but with occasional striking color combinations that would catch anyone's attention. By this time, Abe Burnstein owned a popular cabaret at 3747 Woodward Avenue named the Club Lido. The Purples were frequently on the premises and otherwise law-abiding citizens loved to show up at the Lido and mingle with the increasingly notorious gangsters. Some other joints frequented by the boys were Ray Burnstein's Kibbutzer Club, located catty-corner from the newly constructed Fox Theatre at Woodward and East Columbia; Luigi's Café, a popular jazz cabaret run by mobster Louis Ricciardi; The Whip, located at

Holbrook and Lumpkin avenues; The Lantern Room, a posh nightclub done up in the motif of Paris's Montmartre district; the exclusive Stork Club on Rowena Street, whose membership cards were decorated with a picture of a large stork; The K&C Club, which was owned by Purple booze distributors Sam Cohen and Sam Kert.

For more exotic entertainment, sometimes the boys would round up some good-looking ladies and head for a remote Oakland County lodge for wild, all-night orgies. Still other Purples would stretch out for seemingly days at a time in the Chinatown opium dens. The boys were frequently seen at sporting contests, particularly at baseball games or at the fights. Ray Burnstein was a noted ice hockey fan, and he regularly occupied choice seating at the Olympia while watching the Detroit Cougars play (they wouldn't become known as the Red Wings until 1932.) Abe Axler and Eddie Fletcher could be often spotted sitting ringside at the Arena Gardens watching one boxing match or another. Their respective wives, Evelyn and Emma, often accompanied them and cheered with even more passion than their husbands.[11]

Stories abounded, both then and now, that the Purples dominated organized crime in Detroit during Prohibition. When Al Capone first arrived in town to investigate about getting whiskey from across the Detroit River, the Purples allegedly told him, "That is our river!"[12]

Nothing could have been further from the truth.

In fact, the Purple Gang controlled only a fraction of the illegal booze that came across the river from Canada. Their main landing spots for booze were south of downtown, specifically in the area around Third Street; hence the colorfully named Third Street Navy. Even this operation was somewhat out of character for the Purples, as they were much more reliant on hijacking. Meanwhile, the Mafia family headed by Sam Catalanotte monopolized all landing slips north of downtown Detroit. The increasingly violent Licavoli crew controlled booze smuggling on the upper Detroit River with an iron fist. Those that didn't work for the Sicilians paid heavy tributes (usually a whopping 60% of their profits) to the bosses to smuggle in peace.

While the Purple Gang was fully capable of busting hell wide open in the North End, they knew better than to hijack a truckload of Mafia whiskey. The Purples had gone up against them in the past (the Oakland Sugar House War) and were lucky to escape with a draw. For the most part, however, relations between the Purples and the Mafia were cordial. The Detroit family's hierarchy held the Burnstein brothers in considerable esteem, and as a result, the two groups never came into conflict. Ultimately, as the events of the next few months would show, the Purple Gang's worst enemy was itself.

BY THE TIME Sam "Trombenik" Abramson was released from federal prison in the late spring of 1928, his sizeable fortune had mostly evaporated. He soon opened up a new chophouse at 12th and Euclid streets that quickly became a rendezvous for the boys. Abe Axler, Eddie Fletcher, Irving Milberg, and Abe Zussman were frequently on the premises. Abramson developed an especially close friendship with Irving Shapiro. It seemed that one of the few people Shapiro showed respect to was Sammy Trombenik, who now functioned as the chief bail bondsman of the Purples.

During the autumn of 1928, a group of freelance hoodlums from Cleveland began hanging around Sam Abramson's 12th Street restaurant. They specialized in hijacking loads of booze from all over southeastern Michigan and selling them to the Purples for a profit. Their MO consisted of waylaying alcohol-laden trucks under the cover of darkness, forcing the driver and his guard to transfer all but a single case of the beer and/or liquor onto their truck, and then sending them on their way with their drastically reduced load. Leaving behind just a bit of the alcohol cargo was crucial to the bonus stage of their plan, which entailed the Clevelanders giving a final "kick in the ass" to their victims in the form of hurrying to a telephone in order to tip off the Michigan State Police to the location of the booze truck they had just robbed. The hapless truck drivers would soon find themselves under arrest for violating the Volstead Act, as a result.

The hijackers were led by forty-one year old Isadore "Izzy" Shiller, who was first busted in Duluth, Minnesota in 1912 while posing as a deaf-mute. He eventually did prison time in both Ohio and Pennsylvania. Shiller centered his activities in Cleveland's tough Woodland district.[13] His right-hand man was a twenty-seven year old ferret-faced *shtarker* named Morris "Skinny" Ferstman. Two hoods named Bruce Morris and Joseph Bronstein rounded out their crew.[14]

On February 23, 1929, a Wayne County farmer named Arthur Lindeman was surprised to find a truckload of liquor in his barn at Inkster and Van Born roads. The State Police soon arrived and removed the truck from Lindeman's property. It matched the description of the same truck that had eluded Border Patrol inspectors in a spirited chase only a few days before. The inspectors had been run into a ditch by a car driven by Izzy Shiller. Shortly after they left, two cars pulled up and the four Clevelanders demanded to know what had happened to the truck. While they were yelling and threatening Lindeman, his wife called the Dearborn Township Police, and the hijackers were busted. The arresting officers found pistols on all four men and a submachine gun in the back seat of Shiller's vehicle.

After he and his pals were charged with carrying concealed weapons, Isadore Shiller called Sam Abramson. The Purple bondsman posted for all four men, and they were released on February 26. The quartet immediately jumped their bonds and high-tailed it back to Ohio. The bonds were forfeited when they failed to appear in court, and Abramson was furious. Over the next month, Sam made several phone calls to Shiller, attempting to get the men to return and make good the bond. The hijackers merely dickered with the Purple Gang bondsman. Abramson, at one point, threatened to go down to Cleveland and bring them back forcibly.[15]

Nearly two months after the jumped bond beef began; Sam Abramson got a call from Isadore Shiller on Wednesday, April 17. The Cleveland hijacker said he and his pals were back in Detroit and ready to surrender. Abramson arrived at the stated rendezvous at 8:30 that evening. Once there, he discovered that the Cleveland crew had no intention of going quietly. Sam fought for his life, but he was battered into unconsciousness and shot three times in the head. The Clevelanders then wrapped Abramson's overcoat around his bleeding head and carried him outside to their vehicle. They dumped the body in a garbage-strewn alley to the rear of 6717 Strong Street. A few hours later, police entered the alley and found forty-two year old Sam "Trombenik" Abramson lying face down in a large puddle of water.[16]

Irving Shapiro was being held on a charge of felonious assault at the Ninth Precinct at the time of Sammy Trombenik's death. Two days earlier, the Purple mobster had been picked up on a routine roust. Most of the others in the holding tank knew enough about Shapiro to leave him alone. Unfortunately one lout, perhaps emboldened by the same diminutive physique that attracted the bullies in grade school, made several wisecracks about Shapiro. Irving lashed out at the larger man and used a sawed-off broom handle to beat the man to a bloody pulp. While grappling with the man on the floor, Shapiro hooked his right thumb into his victim's left eye socket and gouged said eyeball clear out of the skull. With the would-be comedian now shrieking like a woman, the guards were finally attracted and Shapiro had to be dragged off the man, who eventually filed the assault complaint. Irving, of course, denied injuring the prisoner. While cooling his heels on this charge, Shapiro fell into a visible funk when he heard of Abramson's murder. This time, none of his cellmates dared to crack wise. The vicious Purple quickly made bail and dropped from sight.[17]

On the evening of April 23, six nights after Sam Abramson breathed his last, Isadore "Izzy" Shiller and Morris "Skinny" Ferstman were making their usual rounds in Cleveland's Woodland neighborhood. The pair was noted as spending most of the night in a poolroom near the corner of 55th and Woodland avenues. Shiller and Ferstman were last seen eating at a nearby 24-hour restaurant around 2:10 in the morning.

Four and a half hours later, a city garbage man was walking to work along Schaaf Road in the Cleveland suburb of Independence. While passing around the base of Skinner's Hill, the garbage man was shocked to see the bodies of two men lying face down in the mud at the bottom of an embankment next to the West Creek Bridge. As the corpses were still warm, the coroner estimated that the pair hadn't been dead for more than an hour and a half when found. Detectives on the scene identified the victims as Izzy Shiller and Skinny Ferstman.

A medical examination showed the two hijackers had died an especially painful death, or what gangsters refer to as "buckwheats." After being driven to the lonely spot on Schaaf Road, Shiller and Ferstman were dragged from a car and garroted with such force that the vertebrae in their necks were broken. While being strangled to death, both men were brutally beaten about the head, probably with the claw end of a hammer. These blows literally caved their faces in. After this grisly work was completed, both men were stabbed through the brain with an ice pick. As a final *coup de grace*, the blade of the ice pick was broken off in Shiller's skull.

Like many other gangland murders, the dual homicide of Izzy Shiller and Skinny Ferstman would never be solved. Despite this, police were certain that the Purple Gang had killed the pair in retaliation for Sammy Trombenik's murder. Irving Shapiro, in particular, was believed to have been the maestro who conducted the gruesome symphony of death that night on the outskirts of Cleveland.[18]

WITH THEIR APPETITE for vengeance sated, the Purples got back to business in the spring of 1929. By now, they had generated so many headlines that individuals in Washington were beginning to take notice. The net income of illegal liquor and beer smuggled in the Detroit area had reached an estimated 215 million dollars by 1929, second only to the automobile industry among the city's businesses.

During the late winter of 1929, the Increased Penalties Act was signed into law by outgoing President Calvin Coolidge. Colloquially known as the "Jones Law" (after one of its two sponsors, Republican Senator Wesley L. Jones), the act stated that any penalty for illegal manufacture, sale, transportation, importation, or exportation of alcohol as defined under the Volstead Act was subject to a fine not to exceed $10,000 and a prison sentence not to exceed five years. One of the prime champions of the bill was noted Prohibitionist Mabel Walker Willebrandt, who was on record as saying the new act was designed to "wipe out the Purple Gang of Detroit."

As a result, the Purples suddenly began to catch grief from federal authorities, which was attributable to both increased river patrolling and their sloppy bribe habits. While the Purples greased the palms of many local officials, they were either unable or unwilling to buy off the feds. Between March and May 1929, the Purples lost approximately $90,000 in seized booze shipments.[19]

Around 3:45 on the morning of Thursday, May 2, 1929, the Purple Gang was in the process of unloading a large shipment of liquor at the foot of 24th Street, right in the shadow of the still-under construction Ambassador Bridge. Five motorboats waited offshore for the all-clear signal. After receiving it, the first boat quickly cruised up the dock to offload its precious cargo, which was to be loaded onto waiting trucks. Unbeknownst to the Purples, they were being watched by the law.

An anonymous informer had contacted the U.S. Customs Service and tipped them off to the raid. Soon enough, two agents were staking out the dock and watching as the smugglers' motorboats approached the site. The agents clearly recognized Abe Axler and Eddie Fletcher among those present at the landing site. As soon as the first boat docked, the intrepid agents pulled their pistols and moved in.

At the first sight of law, the Purples opened fire without hesitation. Their fusillade of shots drove away the two outgunned agents, who retreated to call for backup. Fifteen minutes later, they returned loaded for bear and accompanied by two squads of reinforcements. The six agents peered through their binoculars and saw that the Purples were still unloading their booze, albeit much quicker than before. The heavily armed agents cruised down 24th Street to make the bust only to be stopped dead in their tracks. Its timing horrible, a slow-moving freight train cruised past them and blocked their path to the riverfront. The gritty feds quickly abandoned their vehicles and hopped between the cars of the train.

The gangsters were on high alert after the earlier skirmish and opened fire as soon as they saw the agents clumsily spilling from between the cars of the somnambulant train. For a couple minutes or so, the Purples and the Customs agents furiously traded bullets in the kind of gunfight seldom seen outside of movies. The remaining motorboats waiting offshore sped off just after the second battle began. The Purples managed to escape by running around the train and reaching three automobiles that had been parked near

West Jefferson Avenue. Axler and Fletcher jumped into an unoccupied sedan belonging to the agents and rocketed backwards to West Jefferson, on which they sped off into the darkness. All told, the two groups had exchanged nearly one hundred shots. The Customs agents seized two trucks and ninety-six cases of whiskey.[20]

Two weeks later, in the early morning hours of May 13, more heat came. Abe "Angel Face" Kaminsky was carousing around town with Mrs. Irene Richardson, whose husband was conveniently out of sight. They ended up at Lefty Wallace's blind pig at 645 Stimson Avenue. After downing drinks at the bar, Kaminsky suddenly declared that he was now a partner in the place, and therefore entitled to half the profits. The husky blind pigger responded by mashing his namesake into Angel Face's nose. Kaminsky staggered back and pulled a .38 caliber revolver. Wallace hit the deck as the gangster emptied all six shots in an unsuccessful attempt to hit the bartender.

As a result of Kaminsky's belligerent behavior, the police had already been called, and he and his date were busted before they could leave the premises. Police had recently questioned Angel Face in the kidnapping of Samuel Gross, an electrical contractor who lived in the same apartment building as him at 355 Leicester Court. Kaminsky was held on a charge of assault with intent to kill as a result of his drunken rampage.[21]

Thirty-six hours later, federal agents of made a series of raids against the Purple Gang and picked up twelve members, including Abe Axler, Eddie Fletcher, Izzy Burnstein, Irving Milberg, Joe "Honey" Miller, and Harry Sutton.[22] The busts were the culmination of a three-month long sting operation, during which the feds had tapped various phone lines of the Purples' businesses and conducted roving surveillance on the suspected bootleggers.[23] The new laws did not exclusively target the Purples; Jack Licavoli was busted (his cousin Pete escaped the feds' grasp) and drew a one-year sentence in Leavenworth. The Purples were held on $100,000 bonds.[24]

On Friday, May 17, a large group of newsmen went to the Wayne County Jail to interview the men of this famous gang. Reporters noted that the gangsters slept quite late, as they were creatures of the night. According to one scribe,

"The majority of the group are in their twenties. Two have just passed 30. They have lived high and well, first-nighters all, with eyes on the Tigers and the horse races at Tia Juana. The cafes and night clubs know them well. Where the lights are bright and the saxophone and gin rickey are sovereigns, entertainers chant their first names. They are spenders.

"Few of them look tough or hard. Their clothes are tailor-made and look expensive. Their trousers have the mark of the pressers' attention. They might be successful salesmen, young business men. The Government says they are not..."

Eight of the Purples were in one ward, listening to a phonograph and playing various card games. Occasionally Harry Sutton would get up and change the record. In another cell nearby, Abe Axler and Eddie Fletcher shot an animated game of craps with two or three others. The dice tumbled endlessly on the cement floor, with the men loudly calling and yelling points. Irving Milberg, Izzy Burnstein, Honey Miller, and Harry Sutton were playing cards. Miller was a particular delight of the newsmen, with his gold teeth and picturesque speech. He would often bark "Change that needle!" or "Deal those cards!" and someone, usually Sutton, would comply.

Honey Miller eventually came out to meet the press, with a cigarette in his mouth and his hands in his pockets. Honey's animated comments underscored his reputation for strange behavior, [25]

"Newspaper guys, eh? Now get this straight - I don't know nothin'. See Abe. See Abe. What do I know? Listen - I don't know nothin'. What am I here for, anyway? I should know!

"This Purple Gang stuff makes me sick. The Purple Gang! The Purple Gang! All the time the Purple Gang! Who got up that name? Everybody's a Purple. I talk to a guy a minute, and the police spot him as a Purple. I have friends. They're Purples - not! Some punker kids, young sheiks, get arrested. 'We're members of the Purple Gang' they pipe up. I have to laugh.

"Same way in St. Louis. Always Egan's Rats. The Rats have been dead for 30 years but the police are still screamin' - Egan's Rats. Now get this straight, there never was no Purple Gang!"

Miller went back inside and was replaced by the youngest Burnstein brother, Izzy, who strolled out while casually puffing on a fat cigar,

"This drives a guy crazy, this sittin' around all day. One more game of hearts and I'll go nutty. Like this shirt? Washed it myself this morning.

"What am I in here for? How should I know? The coppers throw me in the can every now and then on general principle. They hear the Purple Gang stuff so much they believe it themselves. Boys, this Purple Gang stuff is the bunk."

As their voices were heard most frequently on the wiretaps, Abe Axler,

Eddie Fletcher, Irving Milberg, and Harry Sutton were officially charged with a violation of the Jones Law. Their trial was set for late July 1929, and they remained incarcerated in lieu of $100,000 bonds.

Additional heat came for the Purples from the Federal Narcotics Bureau, who charged that the boys were linked to a large opiate ring formerly headed by the recently murdered New York gambler Arnold Rothstein. One of Rothstein's lieutenants, Harry Reiter, had come west to Detroit several months earlier when Jack Stein and Willie Laks were sentenced to brief terms in federal prison for selling drugs. Federal agents visited Leavenworth Prison to question several imprisoned Purples, including Louis Fleisher, about the crew's narcotics racket. While no new indictments resulted, this investigation helped fill in the government's growing file on the Purple Gang.[26]

About this time (specifically May 13-16), Abe Burnstein is believed to have attended a national organized crime conference at the President Hotel in Atlantic City, New Jersey. Both his brother Joey and valet Jack Budd were said to have accompanied him. Most accounts have many other organized crime figures from America attending, including Charles "Lucky" Luciano, Meyer Lansky, Frank Costello, Dutch Schultz, and Johnny Torrio, among others.

Al Capone was supposedly chastised at this meeting for the heat resulting from the St. Valentine's Day Massacre. Another grievance of the Sicilian Mafia bosses resulted from Capone's murder of three of his top Sicilian mobsters; John Scalise, Albert Anselmi, and Joseph Giunta, in the days before the meet (the Chicago mob boss reportedly beat the trio with a baseball bat before he and his men finished them off with a slew of bullets.) Between the national heat brought on by the massacre and Capone's repeated abuse of their countrymen, the Sicilian mob hierarchy was quite disappointed. Perhaps in an effort to appease his colleagues, Capone set up his own concealed weapons arrest in Philadelphia to take the heat off.

Actual evidence as to who exactly attended this conference is sketchy at best. With the exceptions of Al Capone and local crime boss Enoch "Nucky" Johnson (who were prominently photographed together on the boardwalk), there is no evidence that any of the other mobsters so frequently named in true crime accounts were in Atlantic City in May 1929 (a list that varies from author to author.) Whether or not the Burnsteins attended this meet, they were indeed well regarded by mobsters around the country. While America's mob bosses thought highly of the Burnstein brothers, their opinion of their organization was less than favorable. When questioned about the Purple Gang in 1980, Meyer Lansky merely replied, "They were nothing."[27]

ABOUT THIS TIME, Irving Shapiro had gone into the kidnapping business with a group of Purple Gang associates. His partners were the Rappaport brothers, David and Morris (Big Chief), their cousin Louis, and Simon Friedman, a local hood whom Shapiro knew through Harry Fleisher. The kidnappers used a dingy office at 562 Brewster Street as their headquarters. On June 20, the Rappaports kidnapped electrical contractor Max Kogan. Although a $25,000 ransom was demanded, Kogan was only able to produce $4,000. The Rappaports, probably knowing that Shapiro would take the largest cut of the measly four grand, kept the cash and did not give Irv anything. What they failed to realize was that *nobody* took anything from Irving Shapiro. He loudly proclaimed that he would get his fair share of the money.[28]

While Shapiro dickered with his kidnapping partners, Abe Axler, Eddie Fletcher, Irving Milberg and Harry Sutton went on trial for violation of the Jones Law. The government said they transacted booze out of two front businesses in Apartment 205 at 8679 12th Street, the Hart Novelty Company and the Max Gordon Real Estate Company. U.S. Treasury Agents Royal Lease and Samuel McKee introduced transcripts of the wiretaps on the apartment's phone lines. These conversations provide a glimpse into the bootlegger's business day;[29]

One man called Fletcher to ask for some Old Log Cabin whiskey; "Log Cabin? Fifty-eight bucks a case. "Well for ---------, we got it for fifty-seven last time," the irate customer whined. "It's fifty-eight now," replied the business-like Fletcher.

Earl from Wyandotte calls; "Abie there? Who is this? Eddie? Well Eddie when are you going to have those four cases? You haven't got any? Well that's sure tough down here too. The boys can't pull a single load."[30]

A colorful character known as Zookie rings; "Who is it, Eddie? Is Harry there? Send me four cases of Old Teacher. You haven't got it? Yeah, I know it's tough. Well, send some when you're able to pull it across (smuggle across the river)."

A personal call for Axler; "Hello, Abie. Babe got back today." Axler snarled, "I should worry? Let her come back!"

Axler calls the office; "We got a boat load this morning, where's Eddie?" "He's in Toledo."

"Well get him. We got the stuff."

A guy named Hymie calls; "Got a case of bourbon?"

"Yeh, what you want, quarts or pints?"

"Well, I want to cut it."

"Pints best for cutting..."

"Make it pints."

On the second day, court officials made note of a quartet of provocatively-dressed women watching the proceedings. When asked if they were the wives of the defendants, one of the women snarled, "It's none of your damn business who we are." It was Abe Axler who attempted to set the record straight as to if the mystery women were their wives, "No…our wives ain't flappers. They wouldn't be in a dump like this. Our wives are respectable women home taking care of the kids."

On Wednesday, July 24, the jury found the four Purples guilty. The families of the quartet burst into screams at the announcement of the verdict. Judge Charles C. Simons sentenced the four men to the maximum of two years (they were credited with two months served.) In addition, the quartet was fined $5,000 each. Simons seemed unimpressed by the famous North End mobsters; "I don't know if you are the hard-boiled gangsters the police and the newspapers think you are. I don't care. I don't care if you are members of a Purple Gang, a Yellow Gang, or any other gang."[31]

The news came as quite a shock to the Detroit underworld, as the Purple Gang's seemingly invincible aura had been dented. An even bigger shock was coming within the next seventy-two hours.

A LITTLE AFTER ONE O'CLOCK on the morning of July 27, Irving Shapiro awoke in the bedroom of his flat at 355 Owen Street. Irving had recently been suffering through a severe toothache. As a result, he had slept the whole day and most of the evening away. Shapiro woke his wife Mae up and asked her to get him some orange juice. After slaking his thirst, he dressed and bid Mae farewell, saying he was going to Sam "Fats" Burnstein's nearby blind pig at 8983 Goodwin Avenue.

Irving walked inside and saw familiar faces greet him, including Fats himself, Harry Altman, Earl Pasman, "Hunky Sam" Rosenberg, and William Weisberg. The boys noticed that Shapiro's eyes were quite puffy, and he explained them off by saying he had "a long sleep." After a while he prepared to leave, telling a close friend that he was going over to the Rappaports' to get his cut of the Kogan ransom money, or else someone would be hurt. Shapiro then walked out the door and disappeared into the night.

Some two hours later, Albert Rose was asleep next to his wife in the upstairs bedroom of their home at 2464 Taylor Street when he was jerked awake by the loud popping of pistol fire. Rose got to his open front window in time to hear the sounds of shifting gears and a car accelerating away at a high rate of speed. Lying in the street, illuminated by the orange glow of a streetlamp, was the body of a man. Fingerprints would soon identify him as twenty-three year old Purple Gang member Irving Shapiro. He had been shot a total of three times; the fatal bullet entered the back of his head and emerged under the right eye. There was nothing in his pockets other than a single $50 dollar bill and a timepiece. A nearby watchman told of seeing a large gray touring car speed east on Taylor and turn south onto LaSalle Boulevard after the shots were fired.

Shapiro was buried thirty-six hours after his murder, with only a handful of relatives and none of his Purple Gang associates attending. Just after his plain pine coffin was lowered away into Ferndale's Machpelah Cemetery, a torrential downpour struck and turned the new grave into a muddy quagmire.[32]

That same day, Abe Axler, Eddie Fletcher, Irving Milberg, and Harry Sutton boarded a train for the long ride out to Kansas to begin serving their 22 month sentence. They were a bit apprehensive and nervous. Except for Axler, none of them had been to prison before. While changing trains in Chicago, they read a newspaper account of Irving Shapiro's murder and grew even more isolated. Milberg and Sutton anxiously questioned the marshal about their future home. Fletcher had an uneasy look screwed onto his face, as if he was boxing again and about to enter the ring against a fighter he wasn't sure he could take. Only Axler showed no emotion. They eventually arrived and were led into the huge walled gates of Leavenworth Federal Penitentiary.[33]

Almost a week later, on August 2, Detective Lieutenant John Hoffman got a tip from one of his trusted informants within the Purple Gang. He requested the arrests of David, Louis, and Morris "Big Chief" Rappaport, as well as Simon Friedman. David Rappaport, believed by police to have been the actual shooter, had fled to Chicago within hours of Shapiro's murder. The other three were picked up in a drugstore at Hastings and Division streets along with Martin Zucker, a New York hoodlum who had recently joined up with the Purples.

Once they were in custody, Garvin informed all the newspapers that Irving Shapiro's murder had been solved and these men were responsible. The motive given was that the Rappaports had killed Shapiro in a dispute of the Max Kogan kidnapping ransom. However, Lieutenant Hoffman's informant soon got cold feet. A furious Hoffman asked for twenty-four hours to gain evidence against the obviously guilty men.

The gray touring car that Shapiro took his "one-way ride" in was discovered in a nearby used car lot, having been sold three days after the murder. A couple of .32 ACP shell casings were found on the rear floorboards. Suspect Simon Friedman, whose flat at 2242 Blaine Avenue was a short distance from where the murder car was last seen speeding toward after the shooting, had formerly owned the vehicle.

After Abe Burnstein was questioned along with his brother Ray and Angel Face Kaminsky, the evidence against the Rappaports suddenly dried up. As a result, the police were forced to let the men go. Simon Friedman, the suspected driver of the murder car, immediately blew town. Morris Rappaport returned to his apartment at 1740 Collingwood Avenue. Although "Big Chief" could hardly have imagined it, his apartment building would soon play a pivotal role in Detroit gangland history.[34]

The murder of Irving Shapiro and the convictions of Abe Axler, Eddie Fletcher, and Irving Milberg signaled the end of the Purple Gang's untouchable aura in Detroit's underworld. Within one week in the summer of 1929, the crew's four toughest members had been removed from the scene. The gang still wielded considerable influence, and they were still ruthless with anyone who crossed them, but times were changing faster than they thought.

DURING THE LATE SUMMER OF 1929, Abe Burnstein began to put the squeeze on two rival racing wire services to combine into one giant service that he had significant control over. Business had been booming at the Burnstein-controlled service that operated out of the Motor City Filling Pad Company. Harry Lockwood and Harold O'Neill, owners of the rival Lockwood News Service, balked at being intimidated into line by the Purple Gang. As a result, Harry Lockwood's brother Winfield was kidnapped and held for a $10,000 ransom. After paying to get his sibling back, Lockwood was suddenly more receptive.

At a meeting held in Ben Falk's office at the Detroit Opera House, Purple Gang bagman Elmer "Duff" Ryan explained to the two rival wire service operators that Detroit's racing wire service would be reformed as one organization, the Consolidated News Service. In addition, twenty-five percent of the profits were to be paid to Abe Burnstein. By now, whatever fight the independents had gone out. As a result, the Purples now had a sizeable chunk of the racing wire service that supplied over 700 illegal handbooks in the city of Detroit alone.[35]

BY THE FALL OF 1929, federal agents were hitting the river with newfound force, led by a group of incorruptible lawmen headed by Special Agent Dwight E. Avis of the Treasury Department, who probably did more to dry up Detroit than his more publicized counterpart Eliot Ness did in Chicago. This new task force was credited with busting up the lucrative "Pascuzzi Combine" by securing jail sentences for a number of its members, including Roy Pascuzzi himself. In addition, after the end of the summer, the loosely organized Purple Gang had begun to implode on itself. Its new victim was the psychotic Ziggie Selbin, who had spun completely out of control after the murder of his friend Irving Shapiro.

Selbin began shaking down protected blind pig owners, merchants, and shopkeepers in Hamtramck with utter abandon. This greatly angered two prominent local gangsters; Isaac "Forty Grand Ike" Levy and Jacob "Yosher" Kaplan. Both men appealed to Ray Burnstein, who recognized the need to maintain good working relations with the city's other upper-echelon mobsters and agreed to remove Selbin from the land of the living. But Ziggie stayed out of the neighborhood at his mother's house at 3579 Lovett Street, and he was tough to set up for an ambush. In the meantime, police suspected Selbin of murdering Purple associate Jake Isenberg on August 27 and Grand River Avenue butcher John Paul on September 16.[36] While Ziggie managed to avoid his enemies for several weeks, his luck would eventually run out.

The rogue Purple gangster left his mother's house at 8 o'clock on the evening of October 27, and told her he was going to a Halloween party. Where exactly Selbin went that night is unknown, but there is no doubt where he ended up. At fifteen minutes after midnight, Ziggie was seen strolling alone up the largely deserted 8800 block of 12th Street. In a rare occurrence, he was completely unarmed. A witness saw him speak briefly with the occupants of a yellow Checker Cab that had pulled up to the curb. A short, heavyset man then emerged from the back seat with a .38 revolver in his hand. Selbin saw the familiar face of his armed stalker and broke into a quick shamble up 12th Street.

Adrenaline surged through Ziggie's body as he began frantically pulling on locked doors along the storefront in order to make a quick escape. The stocky man stalked calmly but purposely behind the panicking thug, like a shark honing in on a bleeding seal. Selbin appeared to have lucked out when he barged into the doorway of a second-floor apartment at No. 8833, but his pursuer caught up and quickly opened fire. The first shot ripped into Ziggie's back and spun him around. Selbin instinctively raised his right arm in a defensive gesture and took a round through his wrist. A third bullet crashed into his chest just below the heart. Ziggie then crumpled in a heap at the foot of the stairway. The shooter, not caring if anyone was watching, coolly walked back to the waiting taxi and was sped away. Selbin lay semi-conscious in a growing pool of his own blood, gasping for breath as a crowd gathered around him.

Twenty-one year old Ziggie Selbin would die within minutes.[37]

IN THE ENSUING DAYS, the stock market would fall along with the tree leaves. A big change was coming, not only for not only Detroit's underworld... but for the entire country.

Eddie Fletcher, along with Phil Keywell, was questioned by Chicago police about the St. Valentine's Day Massacre. Both men had airtight alibis. Fletcher is pictured here upon his July 29, 1929 arrival at Leavenworth for bootlegging. *NARA.*

Harry Reiter was a New York-based drug dealer with connections to both Arnold Rothstein and Waxey Gordon. Reiter was believed to have come to Detroit and paid the Purple Gang $20,000 for the rights to sell heroin on their turf. *NARA.*

Isadore "Izzy" Shiller left and Morris "Skinny" Ferstman were two Cleveland gangsters who began doing freelance work for the Purple Gang in the autumn of 1928. They are believed to have murdered senior Purple Sam "Trombenik" Abramson in a dispute over a forfeited bail bond. The Purples tracked the pair back to Cleveland and exacted violent retribution. *Drawn from lost newspapers photos by J. Rickman.*

Six of the seven victims of Chicago's St. Valentine's Day Massacre. In the frantic hours after the killings, three members of the Purple Gang were suspected of acting as lookouts for the actual shooters. *Mario Gomes Collection.*

An investigative journalist snapped this picture from atop a coal elevator at the foot of Riopelle Street on April 10, 1929. The car parked sideways is keeping watch while the rum-runners transfer their cargo from the boat to the waiting vehicle. According to the photographer, this entire process took a mere five minutes. *Walter Reuther Library.*

Chicago gang boss Al Capone is shown here relaxing at home with a cigar. In 1928, Capone reached an agreement with the Purple Gang to buy thousands of cases of Old Log Cabin whiskey. The hijacking of one of these shipments has long been said to have led to the St. Valentine's Day Massacre. *Mario Gomes Collection.*

HAPHAZARD

At 7:35 on the morning of January 2, 1930, DPD Inspector Henry J. Garvin left his home at 187 Piper Boulevard in an unmarked Ford sedan. He swung onto Essex and then turned north on Coplin Street, heading for East Jefferson Avenue. Halfway up the block, a black Ford Model A sedan appeared on his tail and began honking its horn. It then crowded Garvin's Ford to the curb and two gunmen opened fire with a .38 automatic and a sawed-off shotgun. A bullet grazed the back of Garvin's neck, and he slumped forward just as a shotgun blast, directed at his head, ripped into his left arm. Four .38 slugs blew wide of the car and struck eleven-year old Lois Bartlett, who was walking to school when the attack began. The shooters, thinking they had killed Garvin, zoomed away while the inspector staggered out of his car to a pay phone to call police. Upon his return the inspector noticed the young girl's screams and, disregarding his own wounds, tended to her until help arrived.[1]

Newspapers thundered headlines about the attempted murder of Inspector Henry J. Garvin. While Garvin and Bartlett hovered near death in the hospital, the inspector's fellow detectives conducted a series of raids across the city, busting gangsters and confiscating caches of booze and weapons. Members of the Licavoli crew were hauled in for questioning; Pete Licavoli voluntarily surrendered with his attorney and professed ignorance of the whole thing. The media spoke of Garvin's exploits and accomplishments. They also intimated that the police knew an attack was imminent on the inspector, but they didn't know when.

Several members of the Crime and Bomb Squad were called before Police Commissioner William P. Rutledge. At this board inquiry, Adolph Van Coppenolle must have buckled under pressure, or thought that Garvin would sacrifice him, for he spilled his guts on his own corruption and that of his superior. Van Coppenolle stated that Inspector Robert McPherson had a hand in the planning of the shooting, and that Garvin was shot for double-crossing a kidnapping mob. His fellow detective Max Waldfogel confirmed his statements, even going so far as to say that Garvin himself was behind many kidnappings in Little Jerusalem.

After realizing that no one was going to support his statements, Van Coppenolle attempted to recant his testimony, but a police trial board was called. The detective faced a charge of "conduct unbecoming an officer." At Detective Van Coppenolle's subsequent trial, the accused detailed his years of corruption at the heel of Inspector Henry Garvin. The detective claimed that he was present along with Inspector McPherson and several gangsters when the murder of Garvin was plotted. Detective Waldfogel corroborated this as well. Among other things, he stated that Inspector Garvin met frequently with Purple Gang bondsman Sam "Trombenik" Abramson over the years. It was through Abramson that Garvin allegedly received his payoffs and marching orders.

In the hallway of the court during a recess Henry Garvin saw Adolph Van Coppenolle talking to some photographers. The inspector, whose left arm was still in a sling due to the assassins' bullets, was overcome with rage at the sight of his former protégé. Garvin cursed and rushed toward Van Coppenolle. The detective sidestepped the furious inspector and watched as his former boss crashed into a wall. Garvin re-broke his left arm in the process and ended up back in Receiving Hospital.[2]

In a surprise note, Morris "Big Chief" Rappaport and his cousin Louis were brought to the stand. They were the two Purple Gang associates connected with the murder of Irving Shapiro. Morris Rappaport testified that Inspector Garvin had seen him win $1400 at pinochle in Johnny Ryan's gaming joint. Two days later, Rappaport claimed, Garvin had him brought in, along with his cousin and two others, and said that for $1400 he could go free. Rappaport refused, and the next thing he knew he and his companions were charged with murder.

Detective Lieutenant John Hoffman, whose house on Coplin Street was grazed by bullets meant for Inspector Garvin, testified next. Hoffman stated that he believed then, and still did now, that the Rappaports had bumped off Shapiro. The lieutenant also said that he alone had requested their arrest.[3]

Toward the end of the trial board, Detectives William DeLisle and Roy Pendergrass came forward with the most damaging allegations yet heard in the examination. The two recounted the December 1927 incident when they nailed the Burnstein brothers outside the Addison Hotel for carrying concealed weapons. DeLisle and Pendergrass testified as to how they were ordered to file a bogus warrant by Garvin, who claimed to be acting on orders from then Mayor John Smith.

Upon hearing these allegations, Smith stormed into court to denounce them as "a black lie." Outgoing Mayor John Lodge and incoming Mayor Charles Bowles also ridiculed the challenges, and it appeared the department was going to bury the whole mess and stick out Detective Adolph Van Coppenolle as the scapegoat. He was convicted of "conduct unbecoming an officer," reduced to a patrolman, and ordered to undergo psychiatric evaluation.[4]

Inspector Henry Garvin recovered from his wounds and returned to active duty, but his reputation was forever scarred and he never handled anything of note again. The new police commissioner, Harold Emmons, dismantled the Crime and Bomb Squad while bringing in new detectives and sending others into retirement.

In late February, Ray Burnstein, Izzy Burnstein, and Honey Miller were finally tried on the concealed weapons charge as a result of the trial board. Joey Burnstein missed the beginning of the trial in order to attend the Sharkey-Scott boxing match in Miami, where he wintered along with brother Abe. Detectives DeLisle and Pendergrass gave very convincing testimony. The two "dicks" even produced the weapons they took off the trio, having stashed them away in the evidence room for three years (against Garvin's orders) in case the case ever came to trial somehow. Nevertheless, the Purples eluded the grasping arms of the law once again.[5]

THE BEGINNING OF THE 1930s had seen the growing economic depression continue to sink its teeth into the manufacturing center of Detroit. More and more people began to lose their jobs as the production demand for manufactured goods steadily decreased. Fewer and fewer people had money to spend in nightclubs and illegal gambling dens as in the past. While most people were content to look the other way as far as institutional corruption went, times were changing. After Chicago's St. Valentine's Day Massacre and other incidents, the American public no longer had such a romanticized view of bootleggers. The Van Coppenolle scandal had swung many Detroit voters over to a "law-and-order" platform. The brazen corruption of newly sworn-in Detroit Mayor Charles Bowles only reinforced their newfound reference for authority.

Bowles had run and lost against incumbent John L. Lodge in 1927, and now he gave up his career as a jurist in order to govern what was the nation's fourth largest city at the time. The former judge wasn't as benign as he appeared, however. Charles Bowles had received support from the criminal underworld as well as the Ku Klux Klan. Bowles' cabinet members were not much better. Some were open members of the KKK while others drank and gambled in City Hall itself. A new era of corruption had reached the city's hierarchy. The new faces downtown were concerned mostly with lining their own pockets instead of alleviating the effects of the ever-worsening Depression on the city. Wiseacres dubbed the new mayor "Wide Open" Bowles.

Despite their understanding new mayor, the gangsters hit hard times in 1930 along with the rest of the city. Many of the ostentatious illegal gambling casinos that had thrived during the Roaring Twenties were forced to permanently close. While the opening of the newly completed Detroit-Windsor Tunnel and Ambassador Bridge made crossing the Detroit River easier than ever, diligent activity by the Border Patrol, U.S. Customs, and Treasury Agent Dwight Avis were finally beginning to tighten up river smuggling. Booze still came across the river, of course, but it was nowhere near the flood it had previously been. As a result, Detroit gangsters turned more to homemade whiskey and beer, produced at a series of breweries and distilleries around the city. In order to maximize this supply, the number of whiskey-cutting plants also increased as well. The new plants helped to supply a city that, with the economy in the toilet, was more inclined than ever to take a drink.

AFTER BEATING THE concealed weapons charges against him in February 1930, Joe Burnstein began looking toward more legitimate enterprises. Along with childhood friend Sam Garfield, the thirty-year old Burnstein began investing heavily in the Mammoth Petroleum Corporation, which would soon grow into the largest oil company east of the Mississippi River.[6] He recently had a huge, luxurious house made to order at 1920 Lincolnshire Drive in the prestigious Palmer Woods neighborhood; the mansion cost a total of $100,000 and sported large golden B's on its awnings. Joey's gorgeous new wife Marguerite gave birth to a son in late April 1930. Things couldn't have been better for the suave Purple Gang leader, but around this time Burnstein began having problems with his friend Harry "Tim" Kirschenbaum.

Since Kirschenbaum's arrival from New York in 1924, he had graduated from a gambling house guard to the boss of the Motor City Filling Pad Company, which served as a front for the Purple Gang's lucrative racing wire service. While Kirschenbaum was very good at his job, his opium habit had gotten progressively worse over the years. The racing wire racket was a delicate business that required close attention, but Kirschenbaum would inexplicably vanish for days at a time. Joe Burnstein always managed to smooth things over for his friend and told him repeatedly to stop smoking opium; Tim finally promised to quit on New Year's Day, 1930.

Kirschenbaum managed to stay clean until late March, when he fell off the wagon and disappeared from his normal haunts. After hearing that Tim had resurfaced at the end of April, Burnstein went to the Kirschenbaum home at 4011 Cortland Avenue to remonstrate his friend. The man of the hour wasn't there, but the gang boss noted the telltale odor of opium wafting through the house. Joey told Tim's wife Kate that he would be back in a few days.

Tuesday, May 6 was a cloudless, eighty-four degree spring day in Detroit. At two o'clock that afternoon, Joe Burnstein caught a cab over to 4011 Cortland. While angry with his friend, Joey had not thought to bring a gun. After all, he and Timmy were pals. Kate Kirschenbaum greeted Joe at the front door and informed the gangster that her husband had been on an extended opium binge and was currently upstairs in the den getting high. Burnstein's temper, which had never been good in the best of times, finally snapped. Joey doffed his coat and flat cap while growling, "I'll take care of that baby!" The gang boss stomped up the stairs in order to knock some sense into his pal. Entering the third-floor room, Burnstein locked the door behind him and turned to face his friend.

Kirschenbaum was sprawled on a cot, dressed in only a gymnasium shirt and shorts, and practically unresponsive. His opium pipe, still warm, was on a stand next to his cot and some smoke still hung in the air as Burnstein lit into him. Tim suddenly reached over and grabbed a Luger P08 automatic. The pistol sported a 32-round detachable drum for a magazine. Burnstein saw the gun and began to slowly back up while Kirschenbaum rose from his cot. Joey then broke through the door so hard he shattered the lock. The first shot struck Burnstein in the back, punched through his spleen, and exited his abdomen. Burnstein nearly fell down the stairs toward the front door. Kirschenbaum followed close behind while pumping bullets after his boss.

Burnstein made it out the door and staggered east on Cortland with the half-dressed Kirschenbaum in hot pursuit. Slugs whizzed by the wounded gang leader as he desperately attempted to find a safe haven. As Joey passed a miniature golf course at Cortland and Dexter Boulevard, he cried out that he had been shot. Burnstein then plunged headlong into oncoming traffic and collapsed onto the sidewalk on the other side of Dexter.

Upon seeing the miniature golf course and the construction workers who were toiling there, Kirschenbaum turned back to his house a block away, tossing the pistol into a vacant lot as he ran. One of the laborers, George Barrett, jogged over and picked up the Luger. Barrett then dashed west toward Kirschenbaum's house in time to see the berserk gangster jump into his car and back quickly out of his driveway. Barrett called for him to stop, but

Kirschenbaum yelled, "I'm not the man you want. I'm going after him!" Barrett wasn't fooled and squeezed the trigger twice, scoring at least one hit on the rear end of the car. Startled by this unexpected resistance, Tim floored the gas pedal and sped away from the scene.

Despite the fact that his Luger had jammed, the gritty Barrett jumped on the running board of a passing auto and told the driver to go after the fleeing gunman. A high-speed chase of several blocks ensued. At Collingwood and Holmur, Kirschenbaum turned over his shoulder and fired through the back window of his car. George Barrett was struck twice near the groin and toppled off the running board into the street. Kirschenbaum drove out of sight; his car was later found abandoned on Buena Vista Avenue, just east of Woodrow Wilson Avenue.

The dangerously wounded Purple Gang boss was rushed to Highland Park General Hospital; his brothers Abe, Izzy, and Ray, as well as Honey Miller, arrived soon after and offered their blood for a transfusion. Meanwhile, police found a shotgun, six pistols, several thousand dollars in cash, and a large quantity of opium in Kirschenbaum's house. The bizarre shooting generated front-page headlines in the city's newspapers. The driver of the car that George Barrett commandeered, eighteen-year old Hyman Lapedus, gave a detailed account of the chase live on the WJR radio program "Today's Best Story."[7]

A day and two blood transfusions later, Joey Burnstein had recovered sufficiently enough to greet police with, "It's a nice day, isn't it?" Detective Lieutenant John Hoffman asked, "What caused all the trouble?" Joey's response set the tone of the inquiry, "What does it matter? Why bring that up?" Burnstein would eventually recover, but Tim Kirschenbaum had disappeared, and neither the police nor the Purples could locate him.[8]

Kirschenbaum didn't turn up until July 1, when he was busted in Los Angeles under the alias of George Davis. Arrested with the Detroit gangster was Frank Foster, a Chicago gunman who was wanted in the sensational killing of *Chicago Tribune* legman Jake Lingle on June 9. Tim nearly escaped the grasp of the LAPD through a clever ruse. Another hood named Frankie Fisher was due to be released on bail. In the crowded line-up, Kirschenbaum deftly switched hats and cards with Fisher. Tim actually made it out of the building, and was about to board a nearby streetcar when the department's ace sleuth, Detective Charlie Edmonds, recognized the Purple and hauled him back inside.

A warrant of assault with intent to kill had been sworn out against Harry "Tim" Kirschenbaum by Recorder's Court Judge Thomas Cotter. The charge stemmed from the shooting of George Barrett, as Joe Burnstein had refused to file a complaint. Local bookmakers laid 1,000-to-1 odds that Burnstein would actually testify against his formal pal. Three other states besides Michigan clamored for custody of Kirschenbaum, including New York, where he faced life imprisonment as a habitual criminal (he had three convictions against him.)[9] By the time Kirschenbaum returned to Detroit, the city was in the throes of its worst gang war since the Giannola-Vitale feud, the violent war that tore the Detroit Mafia apart a decade earlier.

THROUGHOUT THE PURPLE GANG's violent rise to prominence, the city's Mafia family had thrived quietly and effectively. Under Sam Catalanotte's leadership, they branched out into wholesale beer and liquor manufacturing, smuggling, and sales. The family also made thousands of dollars off of narcotics sales, protection racketeering, numbers (illegal lottery) and illegal gambling. Eschewing the publicly messy homicides common to the Giannola-Vitale era, Catalanotte's family handled murders (most of them disciplinary in nature) with discreet efficiency.

Given the nature of their business, however, it was inevitable that some bad blood would develop amongst the Mafiosi. Some of it was rooted in the rackets, some of it was instigated from outside sources, and some of it dated all the way back to the Giannola-Vitale War. All that was needed to ignite this tinderbox situation was a single spark. It came on, of all days, Valentine's Day.

Winter months can be quite fierce in Detroit, and the winter of 1930 was no exception. During this season mob boss Sam Catalanotte caught a bad cold, which eventually developed into pneumonia. Sam lay bedridden and weakening at his posh Grosse Pointe home at 808 Rivard Boulevard. Gang leaders from around the city sent their condolences, including Charles Leiter, Henry Shorr, and Ray Burnstein. On Friday, February 14, Salvatore Catalanotte passed away one day shy of his 37th birthday. He left behind a wife and two daughters. Sam's burial was an extremely elegant affair, with more than one hundred automobiles in the funeral procession and thousands of dollars worth of floral arrangements. As his casket was lowered away into Mt. Olivet Cemetery, a squadron of biplanes buzzed the graveside service.[10]

While underboss Gaspare Milazzo was effortlessly promoted to boss of the Detroit family, trouble was afoot. Chester LaMare made a claim to the mantle of power, as well. Later evidence would also suggest that LaMare was fearful for his life in the days after Catalanotte's death. Chester's old adversary from the Giannola-Vitale War, East Side *caporegime* Angelo Meli, had been promoted to underboss. Always something of an outsider in the Detroit Mafia because of his duplicity in the 1919-21 gang war and his Basilicatese ancestry, LaMare sought the patronage of the most powerful Sicilian Mafia boss in America.

In the winter of 1930, a long brewing conflict between New York Mafia boss Giuseppe "Joe the Boss" Masseria and the Brooklyn-based Castellammaresi family led by Nicola Schiro was coming to fruition. The latter family was recognized as such because most of their members came from the town of Castellammare del Golfo, Sicily. Gaspare Milazzo had been a prominent member of this faction before he arrived in Detroit in the early 1920s. As such, the Schiros were allies of the Catalanotte administration. Indeed, the Castellammaresi (described in the press as 'The Good Killers Society') had played a role in the Detroit-based Giannola-Vitale War a decade earlier.[11]

Since 1928, Masseria had been making a play to take over the New York families. As a result, he sought to increase his power base by making allies in other cities. Unlike other Mafia families across the country who refused to admit non-Sicilians, Masseria accepted new members to his family regardless of where they or their families had originated in Italy or Sicily. LaMare (he and the majority of his crew were from southern Italy) received Masseria's patronage in his effort to seize leadership of the Detroit family.

While Joe Masseria's support of Chester LaMare did not extend to actually sending soldiers west to do his bidding, knowing that such a powerful man had his back seems to have spurred LaMare to action. He was probably correct in assuming that his life was in danger after Catalanotte's death and saw it as a simple case of kill or be killed. The spring of 1930 gradually saw the "West Side" crews under LaMare and Joe Tocco edge into conflict with the "East Side" crews under Guglielmo "Black Bill" Tocco and Pete Licavoli. A few minor figures from both sides were knocked off before Milazzo resolved to stop the sniping and proposed a peace conference between all the *caporegimes* to resolve their bad blood. The meet was set for noon on Saturday, May 31 at Guastella's Fish Market at 2739 E. Vernor Highway.[12]

According to informants, Chester LaMare pointedly planned a slaughter similar to Chicago's St. Valentine's Day Massacre and hoped to trap all of his enemies at once. Gaspare Milazzo and his aide Sasa Parrino arrived on time for the conference and repaired to the back room of the fish market to await the others. New underboss Angelo Meli and the East Side *caporegimes*, Black Bill Tocco and Pete Licavoli, must have smelled a rat because they dallied in making their way to the meeting. Before they got there, two of LaMare's men charged into the fish market and shot both Milazzo and Parrino to death.[13]

Castellammaresi Mafiosi across the country were enraged by Milazzo's murder. An especially high-ranking soldier of the Brooklyn faction named

Salvatore Maranzano would use the Detroit fish market murders as an impetuous to seize control of that family and move to open warfare with the Masseria family.[14] In Detroit, Angelo Meli assumed control of the so-called East Side faction and did not immediately retaliate. Throughout of the month of June, the Sicilian underworld was strangely quiet. The next month however, which would be nicknamed "Bloody July" in Detroit lore, was another story.

Beginning on July 3, when two imported Chicago hoods were gunned down in front of the LaSalle Hotel, the West Side and East Side factions quite literally turned the city of Detroit into a shooting gallery. Nine gangsters were shot to death in eleven days. Far from the discreet murders formerly practiced under the Catalanotte administration, shooters from both sides brazenly attacked each other on crowded streets with sawed-off shotguns and submachine guns while endangering countless bystanders. Elsie Prosky reminisced about these dangerous times years later, "I lived in the middle of the city just off Woodward Avenue, where much of the fighting went on. I recall many times dodging into a store on my way home from school to avoid gunshots."[15]

Detroit's populace was much less tolerant as a whole of organized crime than in the past and they were incensed at the gang war. Their anger at the mob and the incumbent corrupt administration at City Hall had manifested itself in the form of a growing campaign to recall new Mayor Charles Bowles. Charismatic WMBC radio broadcaster Gerald E. Buckley got the pulse of the people down as he used his nightly broadcasts from (of all places) the LaSalle Hotel to rail against Mayor Bowles and the mob. Buckley charged that organized crime had infiltrated the city's government. While "Jerry" had risen to prominence as an anti-crime crusader, he had a reputation for drinking and womanizing. It was also later said that he had dealings with members of the Islandview-based Licavoli crew (who were doing the vast majority of the fighting and killing for the East Side faction.) These tense times, along with a record-setting heat wave, made Detroit quite a "hot town" indeed in July 1930.

While the Purple Gang had no direct role in the internecine Mafia war now terrorizing Detroit, they were not immune from gang violence. Nineteen-year old David Overstein was a lower level member of the so-called "Junior Purple Gang." Most of the members of this group had grown up in the North End looking up to the Sugar House crew and dreaming of the day they emulate their older counterparts. Overstein had served a brief sentence in the Ionia Reformatory for breaking and entering in his mid-teens. For reasons that remained a mystery, Overstein was taken on a "one-way ride" by his Purple cohorts and shot to death in an alley behind 5914 Huber Avenue a little after midnight on July 16.[16]

David Overstein had the dubious distinction of being Detroit's tenth mob-related murder in twelve days. Mayor Charles Bowles was fighting for his political career and staring down an impending recall election. Bowles did not help matters by displaying what some thought a cavalier attitude about the gang war; "...it is just as well to let these gangsters kill each other off, if they are so minded. You know the scientists employ one set of parasites to destroy another. May not that be the plan of Providence in these killings among the bandits?"

Jerry Buckley hit the roof over these comments. While he had been tirelessly slamming corruption and the mob, Buckley had curiously not supported the recall movement. The muckraker stated to the effect that it was unconstitutional. The night before the election, Buckley ignored the numerous death threats he had received and reversed his position live on the air. In an impassioned broadcast, Buckley demanded that Charles Bowles be recalled. Among his comments that night; "We have eleven murders in 12 days – speaking of crime – and Mr. Bowles says, 'Scientists employ parasites to destroy one another. Maybe this is an act of Providence in the killings of these gangsters.' Bullets are not distinctive. Neither is the law when it comes to defining the occupations of those who shall be accused of murder."[17] Later that night after he went off the air, Jerry Buckley reportedly received a telephone call that said simply that if Mayor Bowles was recalled he would die.

Tuesday, July 22 saw severe thunderstorms sweep through Detroit and bring some welcome relief from the brutal heat wave that had been broiling the citizens for most of the month. Detroiters braved the rain and went to the polls to vote on whether or not to recall Mayor Bowles. The day was blessedly quiet on the Mafia front, with most of the city's warring mobsters hiding out due to the intense police pressure brought on by their fight. Early returns late that afternoon showed that Mayor Bowles was almost certainly on his way out of office.

Later that evening, after the rain had stopped and the polls had closed, seventeen-year old ice peddler Arthur Mixon was steadily driving his horse-drawn wagon south on Hastings Street. Born in Conecuh County, Alabama, the African-American Mixon had migrated north to Detroit with his family around 1923. Arthur's father had obtained a decent paying job in one of the city's auto plants and when he grew old enough, Arthur began selling ice from a rented horse-drawn wagon. In the days before electrical refrigeration was widespread, many still depended on ice to preserve their food; the iceman had his daily route, and if people were up on their bill, the iceman would insert fresh slabs under their food boxes. Three of Mixon's friends accompanied him on his route that Tuesday night, William Adams and two brothers, Hessie and Thomas Miller.[18]

As Arthur steadily made his way around the neighborhood serving his customers, the Millers casually tossed a baseball around during idle moments. Around 7:30, the boys had reached the intersection of Hastings and Hendrie streets. Arthur went to service a nearby customer and also to visit a candy store back up the block. While he was gone, his three friends played a spirited game of catch near the wagon. None of them knew at that same corner, inside a barn to the rear of Abraham Jaslove's butcher shop, that the Purple Gang operated one of its biggest whiskey cutting plants.[19]

One especially wild throw got away from one of the boys and he gave chase to the rolling ball. At one point, he looked under the barn's stable door to see if he could find the ball. One of the plant's workers, Eddie Keller, saw the boy and dashed to the office to tell the gangsters. Among the six Purples who set out were Phil Keywell, Little Morris Raider, and the plant's owner Nate Levitt. The sight of the irate gangsters sent the three Black children running, but they were caught before they made it too far and angrily questioned by the Purples.

Arthur Mixon was unaware of the fight brewing and exited the candy store into a confrontation with Keywell and Levitt. Both hoods asked him what he was doing "snooping around" the barn. A well-built teenager who was not easily intimidated, Mixon said he didn't know what they were talking about. When they persisted, Mixon fired off a sarcastic remark and began to climb onto his wagon. Enraged at the boy's cavalier dismissal of them, Levitt turned to Keywell and growled, "Put him on the spot!" Phil pulled a .38 revolver and fired a single shot. The bullet struck the ice peddler in the neck and caused him to topple off of his wagon. While Mixon's friends screamed in terror, the Purples scattered in different directions.

A nearby foot patrolman had heard the gunshot plus the screams and ran toward the scene. The beat cop actually collared Phil Keywell as he made his getaway but let him go after mistakenly hearing from fellow officers that the shooter was a Black man. Nate Levitt's brother David was on the scene that night, "The boy should not have died. The police let him bleed to death instead of calling for the ambulance. They were taking reports." That may well have been true, but Arthur Mixon was likely dead no matter how fast the cops moved. Keywell's bullet had severed an artery, and the seventeen-year old ice peddler quickly bled to death in the arms of his friends.[20]

Six hours after the fatal shooting on Hastings Street, around 1:45 the next morning, radio broadcaster Jerry Buckley was sitting in the lobby of the La-

Salle Hotel reading a newspaper. Later reports said that Buckley was waiting to meet a woman. As he did, three well-dressed members of the Licavoli crew walked inside the lobby, marched up to where Buckley was sitting, and blew the muckraker out of his chair with eleven bullets.[21]

THE FACT THAT Mayor Charles Bowles had been recalled by 31,007 votes was nearly overshadowed by the stunning news of Jerry Buckley's assassination. Every DPD detective was assigned to the case. Michigan Governor Frederick Green threatened to "call out the militia to stop these cold-blooded assassinations." A Wayne County grand jury was convened to look into the Buckley case and turned up evidence that certain members of the Licavoli crew were involved in the shooting. Buckley was rumored to have been waiting in the lobby to see Margie Mansell, known as Pete Licavoli's girlfriend. Licavoli mobsters Angelo Livecchi, Joe Bommarito, and Teddy "The Tiger" Pizzino were indeed charged with Buckley's murder. They would be acquitted some months later, as would West Side gunmen Joe Amico, Joseph Locano, and Benny "The Ape" Sebastiano; who were charged with killing Gaspare Milazzo and Sasa Parrino at the Guastella Fish Market that May.[22]

The so-called "Crosstown War" between the warring Mafia factions would continue into the fall and winter. The end would come in early February 1931, when Chester LaMare was betrayed by a handful of his men and shot to death in the kitchen of his Rosedale Park home.[23]

WHILE THE DETROIT MEDIA had virtually ignored Arthur Mixon's murder, police were making headway in their investigation. Four witnesses positively identified Phil Keywell as the shooter, and he was eventually charged with second-degree murder. Instead of going after Nate Levitt for his role in the killing, police focused on Keywell's sidekick Little Morris Raider (whom the cops probably considered to be the bigger menace.) Both men were released after posting $10,000 bonds. The Mixon shooting showed that the Purples were getting increasingly careless in their crimes. For the rest of the summer and autumn of 1930, various members of the gang traipsed through Detroit courtrooms to answer for their misdeeds.

In the second week of August, Harry "Tim" Kirschenbaum went on trial for shooting construction worker George Barrett, who once again demonstrated exceptional courage by positively identifying the rogue Purple gangster as his assailant. Joe Burnstein was subpoenaed to testify and made his courtroom appearance to a host of camera flashbulbs and scribbling reporters. In fact, Burnstein's "sartorially immaculate" demeanor turned out to be the most noteworthy aspect of the whole trial. An anonymous *News* reporter thought there was something "Hollywoodish" about the Purple Gang boss, "He is of small stature, round of face, smiling, low-voiced and gives the impression of having a kindly feeling toward all mankind. That he should be an associate of gangsters, racketeers, or similar gentlemen of get-it-easy tendencies seems highly improbable – from outward appearances."

Clad in a brown sport jacket, orange-hued necktie, and green-striped white flannel pants, the debonair gang boss claimed that he had merely gone over to the Kirschenbaum house to help resolve a domestic dispute. Joey added, "I had straightened them out once before." Burnstein had walked into the upstairs den and was suddenly hit over the head. He remembered nothing else of the incident. When told that Kirschenbaum had shot him, Joey professed surprise and refused to believe it. They were too good of friends, Burnstein said.

It was left to the *News* to editorialize Joey's predictably useless testimony, "Mr. Bernstein (*sic*) was willing to talk on any subject, prohibition, art, the political situation – national – hot weather dieting, anything at all, in fact, except those subjects which he might have been, had the spirit moved, interesting and instructive. But then a court room isn't just the place to discuss rackets and racketeering." The sarcastic tone accurately captured the feeling of futility amongst law-and-order types when dealing with Detroit organized crime.[24]

Despite Barrett's positive ID of him, Harry Kirschenbaum was acquitted of the shooting. He wasn't out of the woods by a long shot, however, as the feds came right after him for the large stash of opium found in his den. Kirschenbaum drew a brief stretch in federal prison for violation of the Harrison Narcotics Act. George Barrett eventually sued Joe Burnstein in order to pay off the medical bills incurred by his injuries. Both Joe and Abe Burnstein settled out of court with the gutsy laborer.[25]

Morris Raider and Phil Keywell were arraigned for Arthur Mixon's murder on September 10, 1930. The main witnesses against them, William Adams and Hessie and Thomas Miller, had been held in jail for their own safety. On Friday, September 19, a curious incident occurred when two Purple Gang-connected bondsmen attempted to post the $2,000 bonds for the Miller brothers. Max "The Barber" Lefkovitz and Jacob Pearlstein said they were acting on behalf of the Millers' sister, who immediately claimed to have made no such request. The state believed that the Purples were trying to get the boys out of jail in order to permanently silence them.[26]

Assistant Prosecutor Duncan C. McCrea voluntarily placed himself in contempt in order to keep the Millers incarcerated for their own safety. He said, "I believe this was a deliberate attempt by gangsters to get these witnesses out of jail and prevent them from testifying. I purposely placed myself in contempt of court to keep gangsters from tampering with State witnesses." McCrea succeeded in having the Miller brothers' bail raised to $50,000 each plus two sureties.[27]

Keywell went on trial for the murder of Arthur Mixon on October 6. William Adams and the Miller brothers told their stories and positively identified Phil as the man who killed their friend. Four underworld associates of Keywell acted as defense witnesses; all of them would later be charged with perjury. Two days later, the jury deliberated 25 hours without reaching a verdict. Judge Thomas Cotter dismissed them and brought in a new jury. After an hour and a half of deliberation on the evening of Thursday, October 16, Philip Keywell earned the distinction of being the first member of the Purple Gang to be convicted of murder. He was sentenced to life imprisonment in the penitentiary at Jackson.[28] A month later, Little Morris Raider would be convicted of manslaughter in the same case; after fleeing the state while free on an appeal bond, Raider would be captured and begin serving his sentence as well.

Many media commentators spoke of the cowardly nature of the Mixon murder. It also proved to be something of a turning point. No longer were the citizens of Detroit, as a whole, afraid of the Purple Gang. Indeed, the dual murder convictions of Keywell and Raider proved to be something of a harbinger for the Purples.

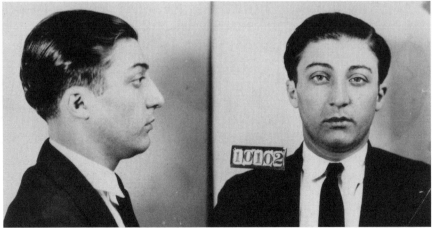

Isadore "Izzy" Burnstein was the youngest of the four Burnstein brothers. Pictured here as a young man, he would later settle in a posh Beverly Hills mansion. *Walter Reuther Library.*

William "Black Bill" Tocco, second from left, and Joe Zerilli second from right glare at Assistant Wayne County Prosecutor William Schemanske after being brought in for questioning regarding the February 1931 murder of rival mobster Chester LaMare. Best friends and brothers-in-law, Tocco and Zerilli would collectively head the city's Mafia family for more than forty years. Detective Sergeant William DeLisle stands between them. *Walter Reuther Library.*

Three top Purples are on trial in February 1930 for carrying concealed weapons in December 1927 in front of the Addison Hotel. Pictured are attorney Edward H. Kennedy, Jr., with glasses, Ray Burnstein to the right of him, Izzy Burnstein holding his chin, Joe "Honey" Miller behind Izzy, and Detective Sergeant William DeLisle in the left foreground. *Walter Reuther Library.*

In the summer of 1930, the East Side and West Side factions of the Detroit Mafia family went to war with each other and turned the city into a shooting gallery. The month of July, known as "Bloody July," saw ten gangland rubouts in twelve days. Angelo Meli, pictured here, led the East Side to victory over the Chester LaMare-led West Side. *Walter Reuther Library.*

WRATH

Change was in the wind for the Detroit underworld in 1931. After Chester LaMare's February 6 murder ended the city's Mafia civil war, the family once again reorganized their structure. Wartime East Side leader Angelo Meli voluntarily relinquished his claim to leadership of the family to fast-rising *caporegime* Black Bill Tocco and took on the role of top advisor, or *consigliere*. Tocco's life-long best friend/brother-in-law Joseph Zerilli became his new underboss. These three men, along with new East Side *caporegime* Peter Corrado, sought to continue the panel-style leadership originally set up by Ignazio Caruso in the wake of the Giannola-Vitale War. As such, the four men would consult each other on all major family business matters. The family was thus rechristened "The Partnership."[1]

The primarily New York-based "Castellammarese War" would end with Joe Masseria's murder in April and Salvatore Maranzano's killing later that year in September. The new boss of the Masseria family, Charles "Lucky" Luciano, took control of the so-called "Grand Council" and opened the door for working with other Mafia families around the country as well as non-Sicilian gangsters. The Detroit Partnership was an integral cog in this operation.

These new developments proved to be somewhat ominous for the Purple Gang. As tough as the North End boys were, for all their flash and newspaper copy, the bottom line was that they were still just a local mob that could not possibly go up against the national crime consortium that the Partnership now belonged to. Nevertheless, rank-and-file Purples continued to sneer about the "Dago Mob", as they crudely referred to the local Mafia. "They did not like Italians," one associate remembered in 1983, "They would go into an Italian bar and tear the place up."[2] Due to the good relations the Purple hierarchy had with the Sicilian leadership, however, the two groups never came into direct conflict. Indeed, both the Purples and the Mafia often worked together on various endeavors throughout the latter years of Prohibition.

THE PURPLES' STRING of bad luck continued right into the New Year of 1931. At 10:30 on Sunday morning, January 4, firemen were called to a blaze at the former Leonard Detroit Storage Company at 8037 Woodward Avenue. Parishioners of the Metropolitan Methodist Episcopal Church across the street watched as firefighters bashed through reinforced steel doors and battled the blaze. It turned out that the building housed one of the Purple Gang's largest whiskey distilleries. The firemen had to don their gas masks going in. Fortunately, the building's ventilation system helped extinguish the fire before a potentially catastrophic explosion occurred.

The distillery had been professionally camouflaged from the surrounding neighborhood and housed more than a dozen gigantic cooking vats of whiskey. At their optimum output, it was estimated they could produce roughly 15,000 gallons of whiskey a day for a value of $50,000. The firemen also seized nearly $250,000 worth of equipment, a large gross of corn sugar, mash, and other booze making ingredients. It was conservatively estimated that the distillery was worth, all told, over one million dollars, making it one of the largest discovered in the United States up to that time. Federal investigators followed the building's paper trial right to the front door of the Sugar House at 8634 Oakland Avenue. A total of twelve men were ultimately indicted, including Henry Shorr and Harry Fleisher.[3]

Southwest Side bootlegger Frank Kaier had to have been living on the edge since his brother Charles, a Downriver rumrunner of some note, had been kidnapped and ransomed for $10,000 in late 1930. It was almost certainly with this successful caper in mind that five members of the Purple Gang approached Frank's home at 10261 W. Fort Street around 8 o'clock on the evening of January 14.

Sam "Fats" Burnstein (the crew's nominal leader), Harry Keywell, Harry Altman, Harry Millman, and Jacob Wellman all forced their way inside and brandished pistols at the frightened Kaier. The boys said they had come to rob Frank of his liquor stash. Kaier pleaded that he was no longer in the whiskey business. Fats Burnstein cursed and bashed the bootlegger over the head with his gun. Kaier peeled himself off the floor and made a break for his bedroom, where he had a shotgun stashed. The boys caught him before he made it there and were administering a severe pistol-whipping when a passing patrolman, Ross Salyer, heard the commotion through the still-ajar front door. Salyer entered the house and got the drop on the Purples before they beat Kaier to death. All five were charged with carrying concealed weapons, assault with intent to do great bodily harm, transporting concealed weapons in an automobile, and possession of guns with defaced serial numbers.[4]

When the Purples' trial came around in early February, they were found not guilty on all charges. Judge W. McKay Stillman termed it a "miscarriage of justice." Prosecutor Harry S. Toy openly speculated about whether the jury had been tampered with, saying it was "peculiar" that they could not reach a verdict of guilty on the "undisputed, unimpeached, and unrefutable evidence" that was presented.[5] Abe "Angel Face" Kaminsky was not quite as lucky when, a week earlier, he had been sentenced to two to four years in Jackson for extortion.

The Purple Gang received some formidable reinforcement on February 10 when Irving Milberg, Abe Axler, Eddie Fletcher, and Harry Sutton were paroled from Leavenworth after serving their Jones Law violation sentences. The boys immediately returned to Detroit and went back to work by attempting to muscle into the Corktown rackets, which had recently been vacated when Irish gang chief Bernard Doherty had been sentenced to a long prison term for armed robbery.

Their probable point man in this operation was twenty-two year old William Bruein, who had served time with them in Leavenworth. Axler moved into a duplex at 1732 Trumbull Avenue that was to serve as a base of operations for the Corktown push. This new venture brought the Purples into conflict with a former crew of theirs who had proved most unpredictable and dangerous since their arrival in Detroit.[6]

JOSEPH "NIGGER JOE" LEBOVITZ, Isadore "Izzy" Sutker, and Hyman "Hymie" Paul were Jewish gangsters who cut their teeth in Chicago's tough underworld during the first half of the Roaring Twenties. The trio operated out of the West Side and began shaking down speakeasy owners for protection money. Those who didn't comply were left in a pool of their own blood. The aggressive yet foolhardy trio began muscling barkeeps that were already protected by the Capone syndicate. Sometime in 1927, a few members of the Capone mob visited the boys and made it clear to them that either their shakedowns or their lives would end. Lebovitz, Sutker, and Paul wisely decided to leave town and hit the road east.[7]

Upon arriving in Detroit, the Chicagoans made a favorable impression on Solomon Levine, a small-time member of the Purple Gang and close friend of Ray Burnstein. Levine introduced the newcomers to Burnstein, who found a place for them in the fabled Third Street Navy crew.[8]

Izzy Sutker was a first-rate *shtarker* who acted as the leader of the trio. With the exception of a six-month stretch in Cook County Jail for burglary, Sutker managed to beat most raps.[9] Nigger Joe Lebovitz, who got his odious nickname from his exceptionally swarthy complexion, was a violent psychopath who had a reputation for shooting first and not bothering to ask questions later. After winning parole from Joliet Prison on a ten-year armed robbery sentence, Lebovitz became known as the trigger-puller of the crew.[10] Although the reserved Hymie Paul was not quite as violent as his pals, only the foolish dared to underestimate him. Sam Solomon tasked Paul with handling bookie action for the Third Street Navy.[11]

The trio proved most efficient at smuggling loads of beer and liquor across the river but found their true calling as high-risk hijackers willing to hit anyone at anytime. They gained a reputation for being extraordinarily treacherous, killing when they were only supposed to maim, and victimizing their own associates. DPD Inspector Frank Fraley was absolutely right when he referred to them as "the terrors of the Third Street district."[12] After tightened federal security on the Detroit River caused the Purples to scuttle the Third Street Navy in early 1930, the so-called "Third Street Terrors" remained in that part of town and went to work for themselves. Their main racket was hijacking booze and re-selling it for a profit, usually to their Chicago underworld associates. They also began passing large quantities of counterfeit $10 and $20 dollar bills.

Perhaps the Terrors' most infamous beef was with the Doherty mob from Corktown. During the summer of 1930, the trio hijacked a truckload of whiskey from the Irish crew and stashed it in a warehouse at 1222 Selden Avenue. In the early morning hours of August 22, Bernard Doherty led a handful of his boys to reclaim their stolen merchandise. The Irish gangsters managed to load down two coupes with their whiskey and beat it from the scene. The Terrors, who had either been waylaid or unaware of the theft, quickly hopped in one of their trucks and gave chase.

The Chicago trio picked up one of the Corktown coupes heading south on Brooklyn Street just north of Grand River Avenue. A high-speed chase of over a dozen blocks ensued as the Terrors tried to force the speeding coupe to the curb. All the while, Joe Lebovitz leaned out the truck's passenger side window and fired on the Dohertys' coupe with a submachine gun. One of his shots crashed into the head of twenty-one year old hijacker William Butler. While the Irish gangsters managed to escape the Terrors, their coupe full of liquor was crippled by the truck's ramming and abandoned not far from their home base. Butler's pals had dumped his dead body out near the corner of

Eighth and Porter streets. When Bernie Doherty went up on his armed robbery conviction a short time later, he told police that "Nigger Joe" had killed his friend Billy Butler. Lebovitz managed to beat the rap when Doherty later recanted his testimony.[13]

It just so happened that the late Butler's best friend was the recently released William Bruein. After their leader was imprisoned, the Doherty crew had disintegrated, leaving the Corktown territory wide open for distribution. The only sticking point was the Third Street Terrors, who were still in the area. Since the Chicagoans were officially on their own now, the Purples began making preliminary forays into the neighborhood in February 1931.

Around 2 o'clock on the morning of February 26, the dark and deserted form of Navin Field loomed over the squat brick homes of Corktown. The crack of baseball bats, calls of vendors, and cheers of fans were replaced by a wintry silence that was punctuated only by the purring of William Bruein's Packard coupe as he guided it past the empty stadium. Riding shotgun was Purple Gang mobster Sam "The Gorilla" Davis. Their exact mission that night was never determined; perhaps they were looking to hijack from the Terrors or were simply spying on them. Either way, the violent trio became alerted to the pair's presence in the neighborhood.

As Bruein slowly drove north into the deserted intersection of Sixth and Elizabeth streets, the Terrors' large coupe suddenly materialized out of the darkness and tried to crowd them to the curb. While the Packard's front bumper had been ripped loose in the collision, Bruein floored the gas pedal and zoomed past the Terrors in an attempt to escape. Two blocks to the north, the Packard made a sharp turn west onto Cherry Street. The Terrors caught up and opened up with pistol and submachine gun fire. William Bruein had the back of his head blown away and Sam Davis was grazed in the shoulder. The now out-of-control Packard smashed into a telephone pole at Brooklyn Street. The Gorilla then lumbered out of the shot-up car and went to find a payphone in order to transmit the bad news to his partners.

Within the next forty-eight hours, federal authorities briefly questioned Lebovitz and Sutker about their counterfeiting operation. After being cut loose, they fled back to Chicago to let the heat cool a bit over the Bruein murder. While they were gone, the Purples effortlessly took over liquor distribution for the Irish neighborhood. Abe Axler and Honey Miller were questioned over the shooting but nothing came of the police inquiries. While the Terrors had proven to be a rather dangerous nuisance, they had not killed any members of the Purple Gang or stolen directly from them. As a result, Ray Burnstein was willing to look the other way.[14]

THE VIOLENT ANTICS of the Third Street Terrors were a microcosm of what was happening to the Purple Gang in general. The gang's loose overall structure gradually began to work against it. While the Purples had certainly banded together and worked as one during the Cleaners and Dyers War, by the early 1930s they were essentially a loose confederation of Jewish hoodlums who were increasingly doing their own thing. Abe Burnstein was frequently absent from Detroit, and Joey Burnstein had gone largely legit since his near-murder in May 1930; according to one story, Joe's wife Marguerite had told him after the shooting that it was either *her* or the gang.[15] Meanwhile, young violent punks continued to gravitate to the Purples, and their sloppy crimes often brought unwanted heat on the crew.

Nevertheless, the Purple Gang was at the height of its infamy in 1931. The well-dressed gangsters were familiar sights at the city's nightclubs and sporting events. The boys held frequent conferences at the newly opened Oakland Avenue Bath House at 8295 Oakland. Over time, the Purples would nickname the place "The Shvitz." One of the neighborhood's denizens remembered encountering the gangsters there when he repaired there for his weekly bath,[16]

"It was a Damon Runyon situation. It wasn't unusual to see federal judges, prosecutors, and the boys make deals. It used to be neutral, and when you left here you never said anything.

"Every now and then, these guys went away (to prison) for 20 or 25 years, and finally it was decided to clean out their lockers. We had to call the Bomb Squad. There was this dynamite that had turned to jelly..."

The boys could be seen loitering in any number of pool halls on Oakland, Woodward, or 12th Street. Many Purples liked to eat at the Cream of Michigan Restaurant on 12th Street, where they would snarf lemon meringue pie and casually build pyramids of sugar cubes while sipping their coffee. So many gangsters went to the place that wisecrackers dubbed the eatery the "Crime of Michigan."[17]

Mass media was also helping the Purple Gang out on the notoriety scale in 1931. The release of two major motion pictures that year, *Little Caesar* in January and *The Public Enemy* in April, helped make the bootlegger a permanent part of U.S. pop culture. Later that fall, the *Detroit Daily Mirror* would introduce the wildly popular comic strip *Dick Tracy*, which featured a superhero-like detective doing battle against colorful gangsters.

The well-dressed mobsters, however, did not captivate everyone in the city. Many people in Detroit's Jewish community saw the boys as a *shande*, or a shame. Certainly the residents of the North End who had been victimized by the Purples, especially those who worked in the cleaning and dyeing industry, would have viewed the gangsters less than favorably. Underneath the glitz of diamond jewelry, the expensive suits and tricked out cars, the iconic movie performances of Edward G. Robinson and James Cagney, the heart of the Purple Gang's power resided in a Seventh Circle-like ring of blunt force and pitiless brutality. Far from being the daring rogues that Hollywood made them out to be, the Purples were fundamentally violent thugs who would kill anyone unfortunate enough to cross them or get in their way.

Enter Ben Bronston. A low-level member of the Sugar House Gang, he had originally caught on with the crew as a young man in the early 1920s. After serving a term in the Ionia Reformatory for uttering and publishing (forgery), Bronston wandered through the underworlds of Toronto, Buffalo, and New York City. The black sheep of a well-to-do Jewish family, Bronston seemed like he was never able to make it big as a professional gangster. One incident on the night of February 1, 1931 underscored his hapless reputation. While leaving Manhattan's Club Calais, Bronston tripped over the feet of performing comic singer Beatrice Lillie. After she playfully commented on his inebriated state, Ben cut loose with a string of obscenities. The ugly scene ended with Bronston being violently ejected from the club by the bouncers.

After returning to Detroit in the spring of 1931, Bronston began bootlegging on a small scale with his pal Meyer "Jew Max" Cohen. Like his friend, Cohen had a checkered reputation in the city's underworld. A year earlier, Cohen had been involved in the robbery of the First National Bank at Glendale and Woodrow Wilson streets. Ex-Detroit cop Henry Borco was the mastermind, and he had dispatched Cohen to buy two submachine guns to be used in the robbery. Cohen allegedly pocketed the money and snitched on his partners, who were all caught.

Nevertheless, the Purples sold a few loads of liquor to the pair, which they then resold to Chicago buyers that Cohen lined up. Bronston and Cohen sought to supplement this by hijacking from other bootleggers (Cohen got a bullet in his leg during one of these attempts.) Ben Bronston eventually pressed his luck a bit too far by stealing a load of booze from the Purples and was taken for the quintessential "one way ride" in the early morning hours of June 21. When his bullet-riddled body was found in the street in front of 3318 Sturtevant Street, Bronston was still incongruously sporting a pair of sunglasses.[18]

Within a month, yet another member of the Purple Gang had fallen victim to his comrades. Like many young members of the so-called "Junior Purple Gang," twenty-year old Earl Pasman passed through adolescence looking up to the Sugar House Boys and wanting to emulate the older gangsters. Although primarily a truck driver and all-purpose gofer, Pasman had just happened to be hanging around an Oakland Avenue poolroom when police went there looking for suspects in the wake of Vivian Welch's January 1928 murder. He was also one of the last people to see Irving Shapiro alive back in July 1929. As a result, the cops had Pasman's name right up there with much more dangerous members of the mob.

During the summer of 1931, Harry "The Indian" Altman was running a beer-selling operation out of his flat at 355 Owen Street.[19] Around 8 o'clock on the evening of July 22, Altman was sitting in the living room of the flat drinking with Earl Pasman and Harry Pont. In the kitchen, a few goons worked the telephones and took orders for beer. At 8:30, Altman got up to leave but, in his drunkenness, walked into an open closet rather than through the front door. Pasman, seizing the opportunity to play a joke on his friend, ran up and held the closet door closed with his body. Pont jumped up to help him as Altman tried to force his way free. The merry pranksters heard Altman say that this wasn't funny and if they didn't let him out he'd shoot his way out. The pair thought he was kidding until a single bullet punched through the door and crashed into Pasman's abdomen.

Pasman fell to the floor and let out a strangled scream. Just then, one of their drivers arrived for a load of beer. Pont and Altman carried their wounded friend to the car while Pont got behind the wheel. He sped to the nearest hospital while his horribly wounded friend hollered in pain from the backseat. To Pont's shock, he discovered that the coupe had faulty brakes and nearly crashed into a garage at Woodward and Seward streets. Earl Pasman died of his wound within an hour.

At first, Harry Pont attempted to shield Harry Altman by telling police that Pasman had been shot by two men named "Crazy Ike" and "Little Lou" in the alley behind the flat. After two days on the hot seat, he broke down and told the cops what *really* happened. While on the stand, Pont changed his story yet again and was hit with a thirty-day sentence for contempt of court. As a result, Altman skated for Earl Pasman's murder.[20]

BY THE SUMMER OF 1931, the Third Street Terrors had hit the skids. While they had been able to earn in the aftermath of the Third Street Navy's break-up the previous year, the loss of the Corktown neighborhood had hit them hard. Due to their financial straits, the trio was forced to sell off their trucks and high-powered sedans. Izzy Sutker and his family had even been evicted from their Merrick Avenue apartment for non-payment of rent. Pretty much the only thing keeping them afloat was the handbook they ran with Solly Levine at 706 Selden Avenue. The betting parlor also served as a front for their drastically reduced bootlegging operation. Most of their business meets were held at Joe Lebovitz's room in the Orlando Hotel at 660 Brainard Street.

Around mid-July, members of the Sicilian mob's East Side crew hit the Terrors' handbook hard in what turned out to be a fixed horse race. The trio was unable to pay off those huge betting losses. In desperation, the Terrors sought to purchase pure alcohol from the Purple Gang. After assuring the Purples they only wanted the alcohol for cutting whiskey, the trio received 50 gallons on credit. Instead, the Terrors secretly undersold the Purples on the market and used the proceeds to pay off the Sicilian bettors.

A few weeks later, the same scenario replayed itself when more East Side mobsters cleaned up on another horse race. Once again, the Terrors bought alcohol on credit from the Purples in order to pay off the Mafiosi. In addition, the Terrors went to both the Downriver crew headed by Joe Tocco and the Islandview crew headed by Pete Licavoli. The trio purchased alcohol on credit from both these groups. By the latter half of August, the Third Street Terrors owed their various creditors in the neighborhood of $15,000 dollars.

The dangerously overextended trio managed to buy a little time by saying they intended to sell booze at the upcoming 13th annual American Legion national convention and pay off their debts. The convention/parade was scheduled for September 21-24 and expected to draw 500,000 to 750,000 thirsty Legionnaires from around the country to Detroit. Despite their dire situation, a wonderful *deus ex machina* appeared for the Terrors in early September when they got word that Purple Gang boss Ray Burnstein wanted a meeting with them. The word was that Burnstein was going to take the trio on as partners in the whiskey business as soon as they squared away their $3,000 debt for the alcohol.

The Third Street Terrors were overjoyed at the news and anxious to formally sign onto the Purple payroll. On September 14, Solly Levine ran into Ray Burnstein at a delicatessen at Woodward and Temple. The Purple boss explained to Levine, "We've got everything straightened out and we're going to let you boys handle the horsebets and alcohol when you straighten out that bill." Solly then attempted to reassure Ray that the Terrors fully intended to recoup their losses at the upcoming American Legion convention and pay off their debt. Burnstein closed the brief conversation by telling Levine that he would call him on the sixteenth with the info as to when and where the meet would be held.[21]

It seems that the idea that the powerful Purple mob was viewing them as equals had the Third Street Terrors in high spirits. The night before their big day, Izzy Sutker sent for his mistress, an eighteen-year old Port Huron girl named Virginia White. The couple spent the evening having several drinks at a cabaret and listening to a jazz combo. Joe Lebovitz, the wild man, went out on the town and got hell-roaring drunk. The more docile Hymie Paul had a couple of drinks alone and retired early, as he was wont do to.

Wednesday, September 16 was a cloudy yet dry day in Detroit; the temperature would peak at seventy-seven degrees that afternoon. Solly Levine got to the Selden Avenue handbook early that morning and quickly got to work administering to the business. Sometime around 10 o'clock, Levine received the phone call from Ray Burnstein that he had been waiting for. Solly wrote down on a pink betting slip that he and his three pals were to be at Apartment 211 at 1740 Collingwood Avenue at 3 o'clock sharp that afternoon.

Joe Lebovitz, Izzy Sutker, and Hymie Paul arrived at the handbook soon after. Visibly giddy about their upcoming meeting, the boys were in good spirits and joking around. Sutker complained good-naturedly that he needed a shave before sitting down with the big shots. Although Lebovitz was fighting a soul-crushing hangover due to his bout with Old Granddad the night before, he called girlfriend Beulah Schwartz around 2 o'clock to let her he would pick her up after she finished work. About a half-hour later, the four men left in Sutker's DeSoto sedan.

Just before 3 o'clock, the Third Street quartet pulled to a stop in front of 1740 Collingwood. After buzzing them inside the building, Ray Burnstein greeted the four men on the second floor and led the way to Apartment 211. Entering the flat, the Terrors initially walked down a hallway that dead-ended at a closet. Another hallway led them inside past the dining room, which featured doors on either side that opened to the bedroom and kitchen. The main feature of the living room was a davenport set against the west wall. A dual picture window overlooked Collingwood Avenue and the building's courtyard. A small hallway connected the living room to the bathroom, which was linked to the bedroom by an open doorway.

The Terrors shook hands with Harry Fleisher, Irving Milberg, and Harry Keywell. Levine was surprised to see Fleisher there, as he knew the feds were after him for the Leonard Storage Company distillery case. Paul, Lebovitz, and Levine plopped down on the couch while Sutker casually sat on the right arm of the sofa. Burnstein offered cigars to the four Terrors, who did not seem to notice how odd it was that they were all bunched together on the couch while the Purples were spaced quite evenly throughout the living room.

After about twenty minutes of conversation, Burnstein piped up, "Where's Scotty with the books?" He then left, ostensibly to telephone Purple bookkeeper Jacob "Scotty" Silverstein. In reality, the gang boss went to the back alley and started his black Buick coupe. Burnstein revved the engine so high that it began to backfire. He then tooted the car's horn. At that sound, Fleisher stood up, drew a .38 caliber revolver, and shot Lebovitz in the head. The bullet zipped so close to Solly Levine's nose that he felt its passage. Milberg and Keywell instantly pulled guns and opened fire on Paul and Sutker, respectively, who were jerked off the sofa by the shock of the attack.

The trapped Terrors blindly staggered toward the bathroom hallway in an effort to flee the relentless hail of .38 caliber slugs that were tearing into their bodies. Joe Lebovitz collapsed in the hallway while Hymie Paul fell critically wounded next to the sofa. Izzy Sutker, hit four times, actually made it into the bedroom and spent the last moments of his life trying to crawl under the bed in a futile attempt to escape. Milberg stood over Paul and emptied his pistol into the dying mobster's head while Keywell darted into the bedroom and pumped a final shot into Sutker.

Those few fatal seconds were a horrific blur to Solly Levine, who sat bolt upright and catatonic on the couch. Harry Fleisher suddenly yanked Solly to his feet and felt his chest, "Come on, come on! Did I hit you? Did I hit you," he asked. All the trembling Levine could manage was, "No, I don't think you did."

The three Purples grabbed the frightened bookmaker by the arm and led him to the door. As they did, each shooter stepped into the kitchen to drop his revolver into an open can of green paint in order to remove fingerprints. The boys thundered down the stairs toward the back alley, where Ray Burnstein was still gunning the Buick's engine. Fleisher abruptly stopped in his tracks and jerked another .38 from his belt. He muttered to his partners, "I don't think I got Nigger Joe…" before dashing back up the stairs to the apartment. Milberg and Keywell shared a nervous glance and dragged Levine out to Burnstein's car, where they heard two clear gunshots ring out from the death roost on the second floor.

Fleisher quickly rejoined his partners and explained to them that he had gone back to finish off the still-breathing Lebovitz. Ray Burnstein floored the Buick's gas pedal and loudly peeled rubber east through the alley toward Woodrow Wilson Avenue. The adrenalized Burnstein was in such a hurry that he nearly struck a little boy who was playing at the mouth of the alley.

After that brief shock had subsided, Burnstein moved into the street and almost hit a passing truck as well. Just a few blocks later, Burnstein jammed on the brakes in order to let Fleisher and Milberg out. As they exited, Fleisher discreetly let his .38 fall to the rear floor of the automobile. The two killers then walked quickly away without looking back.

A short time later, Burnstein stopped once again and gave Levine a few bucks. Ray also instructed his friend to return to the Selden Avenue handbook and to keep his mouth shut. As he stepped out, Levine noticed the revolver on the floor of the car and instinctively picked it up. Keywell told him to place it underneath the backseat cushion. Burnstein actually waved as they pulled out, "I'm your pal, Solly." The visibly shaken Levine caught a taxicab to the handbook.

Solly Levine was only still alive because Ray Burnstein had given his three men strict orders not to harm his friend. His leniency was part of a carefully orchestrated plan to absolve the Purples of any responsibility for the shootings. After letting Solly go, the boys planned to take him on a one-way ride later that night and plant Harry Fleisher's second pistol on the body (the same gun Solly had just inadvertently left his fingerprints on); thus framing Levine for the three murders. Alas, they would never have the chance.

The woman who lived directly below Apartment 211 had heard the loud rattle of gunfire as she was putting her baby to sleep. She later said, "It sounded as if the ceiling were about to come down." She complained to the superintendent, who opened 211's door and discovered the gory crime scene. Large pools of blood had formed underneath the bodies and the smell of cordite still hung in the air.

Police were soon on the scene and they questioned nearby residents. The bullet-pocked walls and positions of the dead bodies were noted. The ambush had happened so quickly that a still-lit cigar was found clenched between Hymie Paul's lips. The three .38's were found in the paint can where they had been dropped; after being cleaned and test-fired, they were confirmed to be the murder weapons. The woman who lived downstairs told what she knew and returned to her apartment to find that blood from the dead men was seeping through her ceiling. A large crowd gathered outside the building to watch while the dead gangsters were loaded into an ambulance.[22]

Police immediately suspected the Purple Gang and began making raids around the city. At 5:30, just two hours after the shootings, the cops raided the Selden Avenue handbook and took Solly Levine into custody. The bookmaker at first told a convoluted story about being kidnapped and being forced to witness the murder of his friends, after which the unknown killers inexplicably let him go unharmed. The hard-boiled detectives didn't buy Levine's tale and booked him a session in the "goldfish bowl", a soundproof basement room that was used for *extreme* interrogation.[23]

Detroit newspapers had a field day and gave the murders front-page coverage. Some observers compared the triple homicide to Chicago's St. Valentine's Day Massacre. While that was too much of a stretch, it was definitely one of the worst mass shootings in the city's history thus far. The killings were soon dubbed "The Collingwood Manor Massacre", after the apartment building where they had taken place.

In the cool recesses of the Wayne County Morgue, far away from the tabloid furor, scenes of pathos played out as the families of the victims claimed their loved ones for burial. Izzy Sutker's wife Dora clutched their young daughter Beverly and moaned, "My baby will never live this down." Hymie Paul's stone-faced older brother Lewis arrived from Chicago to take possession of his remains. As Lewis Paul said, "My family had seen very little of Hymie since he left for Detroit four years ago. We were ashamed of what he was doing and he wrote us very seldom."[24]

Solly Levine clung to his original story for about twenty-four hours or so. Finally, exhausted and frightened out of his mind, Levine broke down and told police the whole story. Solly named the killers and orders were given to bring them in "dead or alive."

Mug shots of Ray Burnstein, Harry Fleisher, Irving Milberg, and Harry Keywell were pasted all over the front pages. By now, the Purples had seen that letting Solly Levine live was a huge blunder and they made plans to get out of town as soon as possible.

Charles Auerbach was known in Purple Gang circles as "The Professor." He had come to Detroit in the early 1920s and quickly rose to the upper echelon of the gang's leadership. At forty-eight years old, Auerbach was a good deal older than just about anyone else in the crew. Standing at above-average height with a large build, receding hairline, and delicate eyeglasses, Auerbach looked like he'd be equally at home on the street or in a classroom. Indeed, Charles had an extensive collection of rare books. As a young Romanian-Jewish immigrant on the streets of Manhattan's Lower East Side in the early 1900s, Auerbach had made a name for himself with his fists and gun. In Detroit, however, Auerbach functioned as an advisor and armorer for the Purple Gang. It was at his flat at 2649 Calvert Avenue that Ray Burnstein and Harry Keywell took refuge in the aftermath of the massacre.[25]

Around noon on Friday, September 18, DPD Chief of Detectives James E. McCarty received an anonymous phone call telling him, "Two of the men you want for the Collingwood murder are at 2649 Calvert. They will be out of town within the hour." Heavily armed police quickly surrounded the Calvert Avenue flat and arrested Burnstein and Keywell without incident. Also taken into custody were Charles Auerbach, his wife Rose, and eighteen-year old Elsie Carroll, said to be Keywell's girlfriend. Police also found four .38 revolvers, a .32 automatic, a .30.30 rifle, several hundred rounds of ammo, a few fountain pens that doubled as James Bond-style tear gas guns, two hundred tear gas shells and nearly $10,000 cash, ostensibly to support the men while they were on the run.

Irving Milberg had gotten little sleep since the massacre. His apprehension no doubt came from the knowledge that they had left an eyewitness to a triple homicide, a witness who could easily send them all away for the rest of their lives. By the late afternoon of the 18th, Milberg and his wife Bertha were holed up at Eddie Fletcher's apartment at 3311 Chicago Boulevard. Irving had his suitcase packed and was going to flee town under the cover of darkness. Abe Axler and Eddie's wife Emma were also crowding the pad. When a breaking news bulletin crackled over the radio about Burnstein and Keywell's arrests, the mood turned even grimmer.

Just as strained as her husband, Bertha Milberg soon called her nearby apartment at 3742 Chicago to check on their two small children. Unbeknownst to her, the police had tapped the Milbergs' phone line and traced the call to the Fletcher apartment on the other side of Dexter Boulevard. At 3:30 the next morning, Milberg, Fletcher, and Axler were playing one final hand of cards before they left. Their wives in the next room were startled awake when the police bashed in the door. Milberg kicked out a window screen in a futile attempt to escape but was caught before he was able to get away.[26]

Harry Fleisher was the only one of the killers who managed to get out of town that night; he, Harry Keywell, Ray Burnstein, and Irving Milberg were specifically charged with murdering Isadore "Izzy" Sutker.[27] The motive was stated that the Purples were furious as being undersold with their own alcohol and took the Third Street Terrors out as a result. On Wednesday, September 30, Solly Levine appeared at the pre-trial examination and named the three defendants as the killers. Levine kept his eyes on Prosecutor Harry Toy at all times to avoid the intense glares of the Purples. Defense attorney Edward H. Kennedy, Jr. made a motion to dismiss the charges, saying that Levine couldn't be believed. The judge denied the motion and ordered the defendants held without bond.[28]

Rumors abounded in the underworld; that the Mafia was looking to rid themselves of their competition and provided the anonymous tip on Burnstein and Keywell; that the Purples put the squeeze on Detroit handbooks in order to contribute to a defense fund for the suspects; that a crazed Purple Gang hitman was ready to sneak into the courtroom as Solly Levine took the stand and gun him down before he could utter a single word. Problems began to multiply for the Purples almost before the jail cell doors clanked shut behind the three suspects.

The Disorderly Persons Act had come into being in the fall of 1931. It was a new law specifically designed by Michigan lawmakers to combat the legions of hoodlums plaguing Detroit and other large areas. The bill made it a crime to be even remotely associated with a business or occupation that could be proven to be illegal. Motor City's gangsters could thus be convicted on their reputation alone. Those found guilty (of a misdemeanor) could be sentenced to 90 days in jail or fined $100. A second conviction under the law meant another $100 fine and six months in the clink. A third bounce meant the fine plus two years imprisonment. Bail bondsmen and defense attorneys were also eligible to be prosecuted as they hung around courthouses, police precincts, and poolrooms while waiting solicit business from the gangsters.

Nicknamed the "Public Enemy Law," the bill was first tried out on the Purples who were arrested with the Collingwood Manor Massacre suspects, Abe Axler, Eddie Fletcher, and Charles "The Professor" Auerbach. Axler's trial began on Monday, October 5. Abe was tried on the common knowledge that he was a member of the Purple Gang. Defense attorney Edward H. Kennedy, Jr. argued that all of Axler's alleged transgressions had occurred before the new law took effect on September 18. After deliberating for less than four hours, the jury came back with a not guilty verdict.

Charles Auerbach was found guilty because of the tear gas bombs found in his house during the raid. The Professor grinned broadly as the verdict was announced. The would-be academic then peeled off a C-note from a fat roll of cash in his pocket and tossed it in front of the judge. Future "Public Enemy" cases against Purples such as Eddie Fletcher, Harry Millman, and Little Morris Raider proved fruitless.[29] The three gangsters imprisoned for the Collingwood shootings would not be so lucky.

All throughout October 1931, Ray Burnstein, Irving Milberg, and Harry Keywell sat in their Wayne County Jail cells and awaited their fate. While the men left no direct record of their thoughts during this period, they could not have been good. Elaborate precautions were taken to protect star witness Solly Levine, who was held in a special cell at DPD headquarters under a $500,000 cash-only bond and guarded 24 hours a day by eight detectives. The upcoming trial promised to be a legal circus. On one side were Wayne

County Prosecutor Harry Toy and his assistant Miles Cullehan, who had been thwarted time and time again in their efforts to prosecute the Purple Gang over the years.

In addition to Solly Levine, the state also planned to call the young boy that Ray Burnstein almost struck while speeding out of the alley behind the Collingwood Manor. Larry Pollack, the driver of the scrap truck Burnstein almost hit seconds later, also identified them. In the worst of all coincidences for the Purples, Pollack just happened to have grown up in Little Jerusalem and knew the suspects by sight. That day "O'Larry", as he was nicknamed, had just been driving his truck down Woodrow Wilson Avenue and found himself embroiled in the city's top murder case. All in all, the state of Michigan planned to call a total of 52 witnesses.

Thirty-one year old Edward H. Kennedy, Junior, one of Detroit's top criminal defense attorneys, headed the defense's legal team. The bespectacled Kennedy was one of the primary architects of the Purples' acquittal during the Cleaners and Dyers trial and known for biting, surgical cross-examinations.

Jury selection for the upcoming trial proved problematic right from the start, as it was no easy task to find twelve veniremen who had no pre-conceived opinions on Prohibition and/or had little to no idea of the bootleggers whose violent exploits regularly dripped from the front pages of the city's newspapers. It ultimately took four days to seat the jury of seven men and five women.[30]

The trial began on Monday morning, November 2 in Detroit's Recorder's Court with Judge Donald Van Zile presiding. The courtroom was jam-packed to capacity at 500 occupants. Relatives of the victims were present, as were a slew of well-dressed Purple gangsters and friends/family of the three defendants. Abe Burnstein was one of many turned away at the door of the standing-room only courtroom. The gang boss, dressed in a dapper symphony of green, was irate and explained how he had rushed back to Detroit from Florida to aid his brother Ray in his time of need.

At 10:30 that morning, a charged silence fell over the courtroom as ten detectives escorted Solomon Levine inside. Despite his numerous bodyguards, it looked as if fear was virtually oozing from Levine's pores. The nervous witness turned his head just once during his walk to the stand and unexpectedly locked eyes with Joe Burnstein, who was giving him a glacial stare. The rumor of the kamikaze hitman was credited, and four armed policeman surrounded Levine as he sat on the witness stand. Solly started off by telling the jury his story; how he got involved in the rackets, how he met the Burnsteins, etcetera. Levine claimed that he thought the meeting was about squaring the alcohol debt between the Purples and the victims. Solly then told in graphic detail about how he saw the defendants shoot down his three pals.[31]

Throughout the rest of the week, Burnstein, Keywell, and Milberg watched helplessly from the defense table as their lives went up in flames. Edward Kennedy and Rodney Baxter did their best on the cross-examinations and tried to focus on Solly Levine's "lack of credibility," but it was evident that the gangsters were in deep trouble. The Collingwood Manor's caretaker proved an especially good witness for the prosecution. Harry McDonald had heard the racing of the getaway car's engine from his open kitchen window. He then heard a slew of gunshots and saw four men dash out to the waiting vehicle. McDonald positively identified the defendants, even going so far as to place his hand on Ray Burnstein's shoulder. McDonald also noted the time of the murders. Even the little boy that Burnstein almost hit identified the gang boss as the man who almost struck him with the car.

The Purples caught a slight break when scrap truck driver Larry "O'Larry" Pollack thought twice about fingering his childhood buds and changed his story on the stand, thereby earning himself a contempt charge. At one point, the jurors were escorted in a bullet resistant police bus to 1740 Collingwood Avenue to view the murder scene for themselves. Several detectives stood guard with submachine guns as the jurors noted the bloodstains, bullet holes, and positions of the victims/killers.[32]

On Monday morning, November 9, Edward Kennedy and Rodney Baxter concluded their defense without calling a single witness. Prosecutor Harry Toy then dramatically aimed his finger at the defendants in his closing argument and accused them of murder, despite vigorous objections from the defense table. Toy stated, "I hold no brief for the victims and their occupation. This is no defense, however. These men checked their books with bullets and marked off their accounts with blood. They lured the victims to the apartment with promises of partnership and killed them when they were unarmed and helpless." The defense's final summation that afternoon hinted that Solly Levine had plotted the murders himself because he "fell heir to the bookmaking and alky business."[33]

At 10:18 the next morning, the jury was given the case for deliberation. Just one hour and thirty-seven minutes later, they returned. Raymond Burnstein, Irving Milberg, and Harry Keywell were all found guilty of murder in the first degree. At the announcement of the verdicts, associates and relatives of the trio broke into loud shouts and curses. Some women screamed and cried hysterically. Several court officers had to climb on top of tables to restore order. DPD Chief of Detectives James McCarty told the media that the convictions "broke the back of the once powerful Purple Gang, writing finis to more than five years of arrogance and terrorism."[34]

In order to avoid a repeat of the courtroom bedlam after the verdicts were announced, Ray Burnstein and Irving Milberg were brought in for sentencing two hours before their scheduled appearance on Tuesday, November 17. Both immaculately dressed Purples stood silently before white-haired Judge Donald Van Zile. "The crime which you have committed was one of the most sensational that has been committed in Detroit for many years. It was, as has been said, a massacre," Van Zile said.

"It was the passing of a sentence by you men, which even the State of Michigan could not impose; that is to say the sentence of death." Van Zile then praised the police for bringing the gangsters to "the end of the trail." The judge then sternly added, "And in traveling this trail, you have established reputations as members of the famous Purple Gang, which has undoubtedly placed you at the peak of racketeer gangs of the City of Detroit and has unfortunately brought an unsavory reputation to this fair city.

"This has all been to me a great tragedy, not only in its results to you, but also by reason of the fact it has demonstrated that such a thing would be done in what we call our enlightened age of civilization.

"I do hereby sentence each of you for murder in the first degree to imprisonment in the branch of Michigan State Prison at Marquette for life."

Harry Keywell was brought in next. Harry, who hadn't even reached voting age yet, remained a loyal Purple to the end and chose to follow his mates to the maximum-security facility in the Upper Peninsula. Judge Van Zile said, "I had intended to separate you three and sentence you to Jackson but I understand you wish to serve your time in Marquette. Is that correct?" Keywell answered, "Yes, sir."[35]

Back at the Wayne County Jail after their sentencing hearing, the trio received family and reporters in the visiting room as they counted down the hours until their departure. An edgy Burnstein chain-smoked cigarettes and occasionally paced as he chatted with those present. Milberg frequently ran a hand across his pomaded hair and talked about "my kid" with attorney Edward H. Kennedy, Jr. Keywell stared, as he had for much of the trial, at the floor and said nothing. He looked like a little boy who knows he's been bad and is anticipating a hell of a spanking. Keywell's father Jonas, who had now lost two sons to the Purple Gang, looked near the point of complete emotional collapse. His son did his best to comfort him.

One of the reporters asked, "How does it feel to be going up for life?"

Burnstein shot the scribe a sour look, "Why ask me that? You know how I feel. How would you expect me to feel? How would *you* feel? Life…" The gang boss lit another cigarette and turned away. Gangster Pete Licavoli, who was being held at the jail while awaiting trial for the still-unsolved Jerry Buckley homicide, passed by the enclosed room in handcuffs and tapped on the glass. All three Purples smiled and waved back. "Swell guy, Pete. Swell guy," Burnstein enthused.

When asked about Solly Levine, all three angrily denounced that he had ever been their friend. The dismal scene was interrupted when Milberg let out an unexpected gust of laughter. People in the room, including the other two Purples, looked at him quizzically. Milberg said, "Funny thing. I went to Leavenworth." A reporter asked what for. "Oh, for selling a bottle of whiskey," Milberg answered somewhat disingenuously. "And they sent poor Harry Sutton along with me. Poor Harry…" He laughed again. "Poor Harry. He was just out of the stir and broke. Started hanging around with us up on Twelfth Street. Gave him a dollar now and then to eat. He made a couple of phone calls. The feds listened in and pinched him with us."[36]

At 9:20 on the evening of November 18, a heavily armed DPD convoy escorted Ray Burnstein, Irving Milberg, and Harry Keywell to Michigan Central Station for their journey to Marquette. A special Pullman car had been specifically added to the train for them. A squad of policemen, all carrying shotguns and submachine guns, escorted the shackled prisoners onto the train. All three prisoners had reasserted their cool gangster demeanor; they chatted and occasionally joked with their guards.

During the fifteen-hour-long ride north, the Purples played pinochle, ate corned beef sandwiches, and read about themselves in the newspapers. Burnstein, still the suave crime boss, whipped out a bankroll and tipped the Pullman car waiter $5 for breakfast. The mood got tense as they neared their destination. Keywell asked Burnstein in a low voice, "I suppose it will be tough at first?" Ray answered, "Yeh. Like everything else, you have to get settled and organized. It will be new and strange at first, but we'll get organized. We always did." Harry nodded in agreement, "Sure we will."[37]

Ray Burnstein and the Purples sped through this back alley while making their escape from the scene of the massacre. Burnstein almost struck a little boy who was playing at the mouth of the alley. *Walter Reuther Library.*

The aftermath of the Collingwood Manor Massacre on September 16, 1931. Izzy Sutker's body is to the left by the bed, while Joe Lebovitz is facedown next to the wall. Hymie Paul is at his feet with blood pooled around his head. Ray Burnstein, Irving Milberg, and Harry Keywell would be convicted of first-degree murder as a result of these shootings. *Walter Reuther Library.*

A crowd gathers outside of the Collingwood Manor Apartments at 1740 Collingwood Avenue just after the massacre. In the center of the picture, Izzy Sutker's DeSoto sedan still sits at the curb where he parked it some two hours earlier. *Walter Reuther Library.*

The bodies of Hymie Paul next to sofa and "Nigger Joe" Lebovitz lay dead inside Apartment 211 of the Collingwood Manor Apartments. They and their associate, Isadore "Izzy" Sutker, had been lured there by the Purple Gang and executed as the result of a bootlegging dispute. *Walter Reuther Library.*

Harry Keywell was one of the convicted Collingwood Massacre shooters. He would ultimately spend the next 34 years in prison. Keywell reformed himself upon his release and passed away in 1997 at the age of 86. *Author's collection.*

DETERIORATION

11

he Purple Gang never totally recovered from the Collingwood Manor Massacre convictions. Three of their top members had gotten life without parole as a result of deliberately leaving an eyewitness to a triple homicide. In the autumn of 1931, the so-called "Junior Purple Gang" began moving to the forefront. While they were no more than the young up-and-coming generation of gangsters that had been present in the Purple ranks dating back to the old days on Hastings Street, the Junior Purples didn't gain widespread notoriety until after the Collingwood convictions. These newer Purples had grown up hearing stories of the Sugar House Gang's exploits and dreaming for the days when they were old enough to emulate their idols. A Detroit union official who grew up with the boys got the pulse of the Junior Purples down in a 1983 interview; [1]

"The brothers who were a few years older or a few years younger seemed to go a different way. Out of those families came judges and doctors and ones (Purples) *who went the other way...*

"Among the young teenagers at the time there was almost a feeling of hero worship. In those days, many people thought the Jews wouldn't fight. Now suddenly out of this came a group of young guys would who were daring in their eyes. And they were very free with their money, you know..."

Harry Millman was one of the dominant members of the newer generation. Born 1911 in Little Jerusalem, he grew up on Winder Street just a block away from the Burnstein brothers. Harry was noted as having disciplinary problems as a boy and grew up trailing after the mostly older Bishop Union kids. Unlike most of his pals, Millman actually made it out of Bishop; he was noted as a star athlete at Northern High School. Harry wasn't there long, however. After a January 1928 arrest, Millman's parents sent him

199

to a military school in Kentucky, from which he would graduate several months later. Millman had the handsome looks of a male model, standing 5-foot 7-inches with a muscular build, clear blue eyes and wavy brown hair. Millman had been an award-winning swimmer during his military school days. Because Harry always attracted plenty of ladies wherever he went, the Purples let him hang around the hot spots along Oakland Avenue and near the Addison Hotel.

Millman was an energetic, pugnacious dude who early in his life developed a taste for alcohol. Like a real life Jekyll and Hyde, Millman was very friendly when sober and near demonic when intoxicated. One Purple associate witnessed his sauce-induced temper when he saw Harry beat his girlfriend in a crowded restaurant, "...you could have heard a pin drop in the place."[2] As Millman's brother Sammy remembered, "Harry wasn't afraid of anyone. He never used guns. He would stand up with any of them with his fists. He liked to drink, and he liked to fight."[3] In addition, Millman was a noted user of both cocaine and heroin. A man of insatiable appetites, stories abound to this day about Harry's prodigious consumption of booze, drugs, and women. Among other things, he was one of five Purples acquitted of assaulting extortion victim Frank Kaier in the winter of 1931 and was questioned in the Collingwood Manor Massacre case.[4]

Sam Drapkin was another prominent member of the "Junior Purple Gang," as police sarcastically dubbed them. At the age of eighteen in July 1927, Drapkin had been shot five times in the Oakland Avenue attack that resulted in the death of his childhood buddy Henry Kaplan. Shortly after that Drapkin went away to the Ionia Reformatory on a charge of grand theft auto. Back in Detroit, he occasionally boasted that he led a "charmed life", having survived five gunshot wounds. Drapkin specialized in pulling high-risk robberies, and he also had a hand in a money counterfeiting business.[5]

Born in Little Jerusalem on November 16, 1912, Myron "Mikey" Selik was another one of the younger guys. The product of a middle-upper class family that had fallen on hard times, Selik began hanging around the same clubs and poolrooms as the Purples, much like Harry Millman. He and three pals stuck up a handbook on October 8, 1931. The take was $225 dollars in cash, as well as assorted jewelry and pistols. One of the hold-up victims managed to get away and summon police, who caught the young bandits red-handed. Selik was sentenced from 6-12 years in the Ionia Reformatory.[6]

It seemed as if everything that the "Junior Purples" did seemed to diminish the overall reputation of the older Purples who were struggling to earn in the wake of the Collingwood Massacre convictions. In December 1931, Harry

Millman, Morris "Butch" Sandler, and "Hunky Sam" Rosenberg were arrested for attempting to extort a man out of $300.[7] With the beginning of the New Year, youthful members of the Purple Gang went on an extended crime spree by holding up handbooks, blind pigs, and private homes with utter abandon. Such garden-variety street crimes were beneath elder Purple gangsters like Abe Burnstein, who was wintering in Florida, and Joe Burnstein, who at this time was more concerned with his oil field investments than penny-ante North End capers.

This crime spree was climaxed in the early hours of February 10, 1932, when Sam Drapkin and Butch Sandler were taken for a "one-way ride." One story was that they were taken prisoner after attempting to hijack a load of booze from the wrong people. Another was that, like so many of their brethren, the two had fallen victim to an intra-gang squabble. Either way, they were driven out to Joy and Beech roads, in what was then considered Dearborn. Drapkin was then shot four times and dumped out of the car. After staggering back to Telegraph and Joy roads, he collapsed. Sam moaned to the truck driver who found him, "Go back and get my partner. I guess he got his too." Sandler never did turn up.

Drapkin's gangster mentality re-asserted itself at the hospital. When police asked the morphine-addled hoodlum who shot him, Sam grinned sleepily at his inquisitors and said, "Santa Claus shot me!" With that exclamation, Drapkin gave himself a nickname that would grace his police file for the rest of his life.[8]

IN EARLY FEBRUARY 1932, *Detroit News* crime reporter Jack Carlisle managed to track down Solly Levine, the sole survivor of the Collingwood Manor Massacre. After the trial, Levine had been smuggled out of the courthouse and onto an ocean liner. He spent several months as a deck ape, traveling around the world, and had now returned to an unspecified location in the Midwest. Shirtless, unshaven, and emaciated, Levine poured out his heart to Carlisle,

"Can't the public forget Solly Levine? I want a chance to live. I am a marked man. You know that. I want to forget Solly Levine and everything he stood for. I want a new name and a new life. The public must forget me and leave me alone. Otherwise, I will be killed. The 'rats' will catch up with me.

"Why should I be made a goat? Must I suffer because I told the truth? Change my story? I couldn't. I told the truth of that killing. I told what I saw. How could I ever forget that? What I saw will always stand out in my mind.

Sometimes yet when I am sitting alone I shudder when I think of how Nigger Joe Lebovitz and Izzy Sutker and Hymie Paul were killed. It's a wonder I haven't gone crazy. I think of it all the time. It never leaves me. I wish I could forget. Am I afraid of death? Every man likes life and happiness. I have lost my happiness. I have only my right to life. Sometimes I wonder if it were not better that I should die. I saw men die. I...haven't a friend in the world."

During the interview, the somber Levine discussed the strain the case put on his family and complained about the harshness of life at sea,

"If I had it to do over again, I don't think I would testify. Why should I? I do what is right and I am the goat. The underworld is after me, and the public won't forget me or leave me alone..."

Levine also had some words for all the aspiring wiseguys out there,

"All this is because of the racket. I wish I had never gone racket. It's no good. I wish I could talk to every young man of 25 who wants to go racket. I'd tell them something. Plenty."

Gazing wistfully out a window, Levine talked rapid-fire about his criminal career, how he started out as an errand boy for the Purples and worked his way up to cabaret owner. However, he blew his fortune by betting the ponies, and "Here I am."

"I thought I was safely hidden. They (the cops) *said they would take care of me. I don't know what happened. Somebody found out where I was. Was I surprised? Certainly. Nervous, too. But it was all for the best, maybe. They'll never find me again. I learned a lesson. This time I stay hid."*

Levine stood up from his chair, smiled, and held out his hand to Carlisle. "So long. Tell the public to forget Solly Levine forever." His final words were a plaintive question, "Why shouldn't I live?"[9]

It was the last public statement Şolomon Levine would ever give.

TWO POWERFUL MEMBERS of the crew still on the streets were the infamous Siamese Twins, Abe Axler and Eddie Fletcher. With Ray Burnstein imprisoned and Harry Fleisher still in hiding, the pair became the go-to men for many street-level Purples. In a move to assert their newfound authority, the Twins planned a crime in mid-February 1932 that would turn out to be one of the most disastrous and embarrassing capers ever perpetrated by the Purple Gang.

Eugene Williams lived on the Chinatown/Corktown border at 2844 Fourth Avenue and operated a small neighborhood speakeasy out of his large house. Short and stocky, with dirty blond hair and a perpetually sleepy expression on his face, Williams was nevertheless a rough customer who was not easily intimidated. Axler and Fletcher had met him years before through the late Johnny Reid, and they knew Williams made excellent engraving plates for phony whiskey bottle labels. Abe and Eddie offered Sam "The Gorilla" Davis $150 to get the plates from Williams. The Siamese Twins followed Davis to the Williams house at about 4 p.m. on February 16. After knocking on the front door, The Gorilla failed to frighten the saloonkeeper and was run off at the point of a shotgun.

The trio of Purples retreated for reinforcements, recruiting eighteen-year old Harry Gold and his buddy Nate Karp. By 9 o'clock they were back in force, while Gene Williams was inside entertaining a party of family and close friends. Axler and Fletcher paused to tie handkerchiefs around their faces, as they were easily the most recognizable of the group. Entering the house, they found that Williams was gone, so they tied up the party guests with neckties and waited for the blustery saloonkeeper. The Purples occasionally took swigs from a bottle of wine they procured from the bar.

Sam Davis had taken young Harry Gold's pistol away from him when they first moved in, as Gold was inexperienced and might misuse the firearm. Abe Axler and Eddie Fletcher grabbed one of the female prisoners, who showed them around the upper floor until they located the engraving plates they wanted. While they were upstairs, Gene Williams walked up to the back door with his wife Irene and sister Frances. The Purples untied Frances's husband Frank Wynne to unlock the rear door. Davis handed Gold his revolver back and told him to run around the house, come up behind Williams, and get the drop on him. Gold hurried out the front door in compliance as Wynne opened the back door for his brother-in-law. As he did, Gold jumped on the back porch and yelled, "Put your hands up!" Williams, who had been expecting trouble after the earlier incident, whipped out a .32 that proceeded to misfire. The youthful Purple instinctively pulled the trigger, missing the saloonkeeper. Williams then rushed Gold, causing the two to tumble into the backyard, where they grappled and traded punches while the women on the porch screamed.

Davis attempted to rush to Gold's aid, but Frances Wynne blocked his path and hemmed the Purple up as the two men continued to fight in the yard. Williams landed some blows while the young Purple Gang apprentice bloodied his mouth and attempted to gouge Gene's eyes out. The Gorilla finally broke loose of Mrs. Wynne and squeezed off two quick shots at the tussling couple. The men broke up instantly, with Gold clutching his side. Davis and Karp hoisted Harry up and dragged him out the front door, trailed by the Siamese Twins. One of the women jotted down the license plate of one of the cars. At Cass and Ledyard, police spotted the same getaway vehicle. They chased it to Woodward and Sproat, where Sam Davis and Nate Karp jumped out, leaving their unconscious friend in the back seat. Harry Gold soon died, a victim of friendly fire.

Before the night was over, Sam "The Gorilla" Davis had left the city he lived in for his entire life. He first took a streetcar through the Southwest Side all the way to Ecorse. Davis then hopped aboard a southbound freight train to Cincinnati. Sam eventually made his way to New Rochelle, New York, where he would open up a gas station.[10]

SIX HUNDRED MILES east of Detroit, on the outskirts of Hopewell, New Jersey, eighteen-month old Charles A. Lindbergh, Jr. was kidnapped from his bedroom crib on the evening of Tuesday, March 1. In the feverish first days after kidnapping of the Lindbergh baby, the FBI seems to have been alerted to the possibility of the Purple Gang's involvement by a Chicago-based tipster named Arthur Candler, who claimed to have done investigative work for the Ford Motor Company in Detroit. Candler pointed the feds initially toward one Scotty Gow, a shifty character who stole auto parts from Ford and sold them to the Purples. Gow's sister Betty just happened to have been young Charles Lindbergh's nurse, and consequently the last one who saw him before his abduction.

According to this line of thinking, the Purples had snatched the baby in order to affect the release from prison either their Chicago ally Al Capone (who had been convicted of income tax evasion the previous October) or Ray Burnstein, Harry Keywell, and Irving Milberg. Suspicion centered on Harry Fleisher, who had disappeared so thoroughly in the aftermath of the Collingwood Manor Massacre that the authorities had not had a confirmed sighting of him in months.

It was later determined that Abe, Joe, and Izzy Burnstein had indeed been in New York City in the latter half of February. In addition, it was revealed that Fleisher and Sam "Lefty" Handel had been arrested by the NYPD back on February 4, 1930 in connection with the kidnapping of a wealthy New Haven, Connecticut real estate developer named Max Price, who had been held captive for nine days after a $30,000 ransom was demanded for his release. Although Price initially identified a mug shot of Fleisher as the man who slugged him and threw him into a car, the Purple mobster was kicked loose when witnesses failed to identify him in person.

With the immense pressure to find the baby, and the Purples past involvement in kidnappings (specifically Harry Fleisher's probable role in the Max Price snatch in the same general area two years earlier), the Purples were investigated closely. Fleisher was wanted for questioning along with New York gangster Abie Wagner. Fleisher's mug shot graced the front page of newspapers from coast to coast, rudely introducing both him and the Purple Gang to the nation at large.

On March 12, at the request of H. Norman Schwarzkopf, Superintendent of the New Jersey State Police, several NYPD detectives raided a Bronx apartment in an unsuccessful attempt to arrest Harry Fleisher. The media suspicion surrounding the North End boys peaked with the March 14 edition of the *New York Daily Mirror*, which featured the headline "PURPLE GANG HOLDS BABY." The paper alleged that two New York mob figures named Salvatore Spitale and Irving Bitz were negotiating with the Purples for a $250,000 ransom, which was to be used as a "defense fund" for the Collingwood Manor Massacre killers. On April 9, two Michigan State Police detectives went across the border into Canada to investigate tips that Fleisher had been seen in either Montreal or Toronto. A week later, Boston-based U.S. Customs and Immigration officials searched for the hunted Purple mobster amongst the passengers of a steamer that had just arrived from Halifax.

The search for Harry Fleisher climaxed when a mysterious message was broadcast to him over a New York City radio station on April 28;

"Harry Fleisher – Dear Harry: Connect with me immediately through my attorney, Henry A. Uterhart, 36 West Forty-Fourth Street. Do it through a third party. No danger of tipoff. I am the party who was the main mug of the Ohio joint where you and Big Mike grifted. Remember the souper you and the Turk gave me?"

The message's author and significance remain unknown to this day. On May 18, six days after young Charles Lindbergh was found dead less than a mile from his New Jersey home (and a month after the ransom had been paid to a mysterious figure in a New York cemetery), fifty lawmen scoured a large Mexico City hotel on a tip that Harry Fleisher was hiding out there. Still, he remained at large.[11]

IN THE FACE OF this federal heat, it is unknown what Abe Burnstein may have thought of the haphazard Eugene Williams caper of February, but he could not have approved. The gulf between the street-level Purples and the upper echelon racketeers was gradually growing wider. This division was especially evident in Abe Axler and Eddie Fletcher. Unlike most of the Purples, they had not grown up in Detroit, and had no close ties to the Burnsteins other than increasingly waning mutual respect. Such attitudes would only continue to fester.

As for Gene Williams, the Purple Gang put an immediate contract out on his life. The blindpigger was so high strung that three months later, on May 14, 1932, he shot and killed a man who was playing a practical joke on him. The victim, Henry J. Montroy, was drinking with Williams in Leah Hubbs's apartment at 711 W. Alexandrine Avenue. As Mrs. Hubbs opened the apartment's front door, Montroy snuck up behind his buddy and suddenly yelled, "Stick em' up!" Williams instinctively jerked his gun and capped Montroy before realizing what was happening. A jury would eventually acquit Gene when he attributed his nervousness to the price the Purple Gang put on his head.[12]

Unnecessary publicity like this hurt the Purples, subjecting them to frequent police round-ups and weakening their reputation amongst the Detroit underworld. More and more members bailed out and/or left the city.

ON THE LAZY MORNING of Thursday, June 9, 1932, Wayne County Prosecutor Harry S. Toy was working at his desk in his office on the fifth floor of the Detroit Police Headquarters at 1300 Beaubien Street. Toy happened to look up from his paperwork and was shocked to see Harry Fleisher standing before him, flanked by his two lawyers, Edward Kennedy, Jr. and William Friedman. The dapper Fleisher was dressed in a blue suit, red tie, and pearl-gray fedora. Harry was tanned, relaxed, and grinning broadly.

In a written statement produced by Kennedy, Fleisher claimed he surrendered on the Collingwood Manor Massacre murder warrant in an effort to exonerate the imprisoned Ray Burnstein, Irving Milberg, and Harry Keywell. As for himself, H.F. said he could not have possibly committed the murders because he was in jail in Reading, Pennsylvania at the time of the massacre.[13] Fleisher had been suspected of crimes ranging from robberies to kidnappings while he was on the lam. Fleisher and Henry Shorr were then questioned thoroughly by members of the FBI, U.S. Treasury Department, New Jersey State Police, and Newark (N.J.) police about the Lindbergh baby kidnapping case. After this Q&A session, Fleisher and the Purple Gang were dropped from suspicion in the Lindbergh case.

Harry Fleisher faced charges of participating in the Collingwood Manor Massacre, but Toy had to ask for a continuance since Solly Levine, the main witness, had vanished. Levine had not been heard from since his February interview with *News* reporter Jack Carlisle. All throughout the summer of 1932, Toy repeatedly asked the Recorder's Court for delays as he frantically searched for his star witness. Judge Thomas Cotter warned the defense team if they were responsible for Levine's disappearance that they would face extreme penalties. Judge Cotter raised possibility of using a transcript of Levine's testimony from the first trial, but Toy said they needed Levine in the flesh; otherwise there would be no case.[14]

On Wednesday, September 7, Harry Fleisher's trial began with Prosecutor Harry S. Toy asking for a motion of *nolle prosequi* on the murder indictment. Toy said, in effect, that the Purple Gang had prevented Solly Levine from testifying. By asking for the *nolle prosequi* motion, Toy assured that the indictment would still be technically open; therefore if Levine was found in the future, Fleisher could still be tried for the Collingwood Manor Massacre. Edward Kennedy argued that his client was entitled to an immediate trial in order to prove his innocence. Both Kennedy and Toy knew full well that without Levine's testimony, Fleisher's acquittal was all but guaranteed, thus making him immune from any further prosecution in the case. Judge Edward Jeffries dismissed the case on the *nolle prosequi* motion.[15]

Fleisher's surrender had been an opening volley in what would become a years-long battle to free Ray Burnstein, Irving Milberg, and Harry Keywell from prison. Almost immediately after the trio was shipped off to Marquette, attorney Edward H. Kennedy, Jr. had filed an appeal with the Michigan Supreme Court. This appeal was still pending in March 1932 when another defense lawyer named Henry Meyers filed a motion with Judge Donald Van Zile for a new trial. This motion rested largely on a purported affidavit from Solomon Levine, which claimed that the Detroit police had tortured him into naming the three Purples as the killers. According to the affidavit, Levine claimed that in the hours after the massacre that the cops had tried to force him to admit that the killers were Abe Axler, Honey Miller, and Izzy Burnstein. After Solly held out, he was then deprived of food and sleep until he named Ray Burnstein, Milberg, and Keywell as the shooters.

In a handwritten letter alleged to be from Levine, Solly claimed that DPD detectives Harold Branton and Earl Switzer took him to Mobile, Alabama after the trial, where he was deposited on a France-bound steamer. After he was refused admittance to that country, he returned to America. Upon his arrival at Norfolk, Virginia, the same two Detroit gumshoes allegedly drove Solly into a nearby swamp and threatened to deep-six him if he didn't give them a statement naming the three imprisoned Purples as the killers before they got to their destination of Oklahoma City. The document said that Levine's statement was "made freely and voluntarily to clear my conscience because I realized a great injustice had been inflicted on the three men." Another affidavit, purported to be from Levine's sister, said she had seen first-hand the bruises on his body from the police beatings.

Judge Donald Van Zile doubted the authenticity of the two affidavits and rejected the motion for a new trial by saying that jurisdiction in the case had passed to the Michigan Supreme Court; they would eventually deny both the appeal and motion for a new trial the following October.[16] Nevertheless, the battle to free the imprisoned Purples was just beginning, as the state Supreme Court threw the Purples a legal bone by authorizing attorney Edward H. Kennedy, Jr. to file a motion for a new trial with Judge Van Zile if additional evidence in the case came to light.

BY THE AUTUMN OF 1932, alcohol had been outlawed in Michigan for fourteen years, yet booze was everywhere, as if it had never been away. Even die hard "drys" that had previously supported Prohibition through thick and thin were now admitting it was a failure. Meanwhile, the Great Depression was growing worse and worse. Banks were closing at a rapid rate, and by 1932 it was a difficult task to find a Detroit financial institution that was still operational. The raucous, carefree attitudes of the Roaring Twenties had given way to a somber populace that saw thousands of unemployed Detroit residents shuffling forward in block-long bread lines. Once wealthy Motor City businessmen now sat in gutters begging for change. As a result of these trying times, more people chose to turn outside the law for income, such as through bootlegging.

By this time, the Purple Gang's decline was painfully obvious. The police had been referring to them as the "former" Purple Gang since late July 1929, when the Siamese Twins and Irving Milberg were sent to Leavenworth and Irving Shapiro was murdered. They were being aced out of a number of rackets, with their racing-wire service being their only stable income. Abe Axler and Eddie Fletcher remained in the booze business, but it was also apparent that Prohibition would not be lasting much longer. Axler had been implicated by an anonymous tipster in the murder of St. Louis gangster Milford Jones in the Stork Club at 47 Rowena Street in the early morning hours of June 15. While two members of the Islandview-based Licavoli crew were said to have pulled the trigger, Abe was believed to have lured the former Egan's Rat into a trap.[17] While they may have been down, it was still a huge mistake for anyone to cross the Purple Gang.

Meyer "Jew Max" Cohen should have known better. He should have been able to calculate the extremely slim chances of being able to successfully steal from the Purples. Cohen had seen first-hand how such foolhardiness had claimed the life of his friend Ben Bronston a year earlier. Perhaps he had become emboldened after the Collingwood Manor Massacre convictions and other Purple setbacks. Or perhaps he was just fatally careless.

Always a bit player on the fringes of the Purple enterprises, Jew Max Cohen had managed to work his way back into the gang's good graces after Ben Bronston's June 1931 one-way ride. As a result, Cohen had continued buying loads of Purple booze to sell to his Chicago partners. In October of 1932, Cohen took a page out of his deceased buddy Bronston's playbook and hijacked a load of Purple liquor in disguise, apparently intending to sell the load of booze back to the gangsters he originally stole it from. The Purple Gang had killed others for far less.

Cohen's reckless scheme backfired in the early morning hours of October 30 when two Purples found him drinking in the Russian Bear Room, located at 25 W. Columbia Street, and said they needed to have a sit-down to discuss these hijacking rumors. At 4:45 a.m. the three men strode up to the front desk of the Angleterre Hotel, an apartment rooming house at 40 Charlotte Street. While the clerk turned and reached for a room key, he heard the largest of the trio growl, "You've double crossed me for the last time." Gunshots then exploded and sent the clerk diving for cover. Four slugs to the chest had ended Meyer Cohen's double-crossing days forever. The two men escaped in a car bearing Illinois plates.

Detroit police rounded up the usual suspects. Abe Axler was picked up and thoroughly questioned, but Abe claimed to have been in Chicago at the time of the murder. Despite the fact that the getaway car's license plate was traced to the same Chicago address Axler gave police, neither he nor anyone else was prosecuted for the Cohen killing.[18]

IN NOVEMBER OF 1932, the tired law that was Prohibition began to shudder in its death throes. New York Governor Franklin D. Roosevelt, an admitted foe of Prohibition, was elected President over the incumbent chief executive Herbert Hoover. Unemployment in Michigan had reached nearly 20 percent, and many people thought the openings of breweries and distilleries would create thousands of much-needed jobs. Arguments against

Prohibition that people ignored years earlier were now being listened to with great interest. Then there were the gangsters. After the St. Valentine's Day Massacre and similar events, much of the public saw bootleggers not as romantic aphrodisiacs but as bloodthirsty criminals. People naively believed that the repeal of the Eighteenth Amendment would drive the gangsters out of business. It was even argued that Prohibition was responsible for the rise of Communism, of all things.

In February of 1933, both the US Congress and Senate voted the necessary two-thirds majority to pass the Twenty-First Amendment, which undid the Eighteenth. Three-quarters of the 48 states needed to ratify the new amendment for it to take hold. On April 10, Michigan's delegates voted 99 to 1 to approve the new amendment. Governor William Comstock set new guidelines for the sale of alcohol. The sale of beer and wine with an alcohol content of 3.2 percent was authorized. Liquor dealers and manufacturers received licenses and charged a tax of $1.25 on each barrel of beer made or sold in the state. New drinking places called "beer gardens" came into existence, where customers could legally buy beer as long as they were sitting at tables in the establishment. These new laws were set to take effect at 6 p.m. on Thursday, May 11.

The night before, the state granted Julius Stroh special permission to serve 3.2 beer to the American Legion Convention that had gathered in Detroit. The event that evening received lots of publicity and was covered live by WJR radio. During the course of the evening, the celebrating Legionnaires drank 300 half-barrels and 500 cases of Stroh's beer. The next day at the appointed hour, Julius Stroh toasted Governor William Comstock with the first glasses of legally produced Michigan beer in fifteen years.[19]

While the American Legion celebration was in full swing, Purple Gang stalwart Joe "Honey" Miller was finally run to ground. He was still active amongst the Purples, working mainly in the illegal lottery (policy) racket. Lately, however, Miller had been showing strange signs, often appearing at a club or at a meet unshaven, smelly, or sloppily dressed. After Miller's May 1933 arrest for carrying a concealed weapon, he appeared largely disconnected during his subsequent courtroom appearance. At one point, Honey suddenly leaned toward the bench and yelled, "I don't want to see a judge! I want to see..." He then proceeded to rattle off the first names of several well-known gangsters. Miller's lawyer said his client was suffering from a nervous breakdown. Honey was thus committed to the Eloise Hospital for the criminally insane.[20]

BY THE TIME THE state of Michigan had Honey Miller fitted with a straitjacket, the problems of Abe Axler and Eddie Fletcher had begun to multiply exponentially. Both men had spent the bulk of the winter of 1933 in Florida with their families. Even before their trip south, the Siamese Twins had seen the handwriting on the wall for Prohibition and took a stab at going legit. Fletcher harkened back to his boxing days and managed a handful of prizefighters.

Often during this period he and Axler could be glimpsed at the Arena Gardens, acting as cornermen for some bruiser during the Monday Night Fights. Many years later one of Fletcher's boxers, Jackie Sherman, spoke fondly of the former featherweight, "Sure, I knew that Eddie and Abe Axler were killers. But they were all right by me. He never had me lay down a fight. He'd tell the tough guys around the gym 'Leave the kid alone. He's a good kid.'"[21] Fletcher soon quit, however, saying, "There's no dough here for me."[22]

More trouble was created by the failure of a Brush Street restaurant named Pete's Barbeque. Axler and Fletcher had entered into a joint venture with several East Side mobsters in the opening of this eatery. The place eventually closed due to lack of business, and the Siamese Twins had a furious falling out with their Sicilian partners in the venture, specifically Joe Bommarito and Pete and Jack Licavoli. Everyone had lost money in the joint and tempers were hot, creating a dangerous rift between the Sicilians and the Twins.[23]

While Axler and Fletcher still commanded the respect of rank-and-file Purples, the rest of the underworld didn't respect them as much. As their track record showed, the Siamese Twins were not businessmen. Their business was being able to effectively jam an ice pick into the other guy's voice box. With Prohibition dying and Detroit's gangsters moving toward more diversified, behind-the-scenes racketeering, the gaudy homicides that Axler and Fletcher specialized in were becoming increasingly rare.

As a result, after the state of Michigan legalized 3.2 beer in May 1933, they were virtually unemployed. The Twins had a piece of a restaurant, of a Woodward Avenue handbook, and of a fruit stand. That was about it. Both men fell into debt, with Axler often borrowing money from close friends. A rumor made rounds in the underworld that Abe had received $30,000 for a "gun job" a few years earlier. He had sat on the money until the heat cooled off. After the winter vacation in Florida and the new booze laws, that money was long gone, and things were not looking good.

With the ever-worsening Great Depression and the impending Repeal of Prohibition creating hard times in the Detroit underworld, Axler and Fletcher had attempted to muscle into the narcotics racket with a handful of Purples during the sweltering summer of 1933. Harry Millman was their point man in the dope racket push, and they began shaking down heroin dealers in the Dexter/Davison neighborhood. The Partnership quickly got wind of this and demanded that the Siamese Twins cease and desist. Abe Burnstein, as well, did not approve of the pair's actions. Burnstein had always been friendly with the Sicilians, and now Axler and Fletcher were needlessly jeopardizing that relationship. Even after federal narcotics agents arrested Fletcher as he entered a notorious dope house on Third Avenue, the Twins persisted.[24]

Abe Burnstein apparently attempted to defuse this situation by loaning Axler and Fletcher a large sum of money to be used for the purchase of a southeastern Michigan brewery. By mid-summer, nearly half of the states needed had ratified the Twenty-First Amendment, and it was widely calculated that Repeal would take effect before the end of the 1933 calendar year. As a result, Burnstein and other high-ranking Purples sought to acquire breweries and distilleries in order to legally manufacture booze after Repeal.

On the surface, it seemed that Burnstein's solution was a win-win for all parties involved; the purchase of the brewery would enable the Twins to make a perpetual flow of cash, which would terminate their need to muscle in on the Partnership's dope racket. However, the deal fell through when Axler and Fletcher were both denied a license to legally manufacture alcohol by the state Liquor Control Commission. Upon their rejection, the Twins began playing with fire by refusing to return their bosses' investment money.[25]

WHILE AXLER AND FLETCHER began making their unwelcome push into Detroit's heroin business, attorney Edward H. Kennedy, Jr. submitted a request to Recorder's Court judge Donald Van Zile to allow New York lawyer Frederick Kaplan to practice law in the state of Michigan. The logic behind this was that Kaplan would join the Collingwood Massacre defense team and pinch-hit for Kennedy if anything happened to him. Kennedy stated he was preparing a second motion for a new trial and getting all his ducks in a row. Van Zile approved his request.[26]

Kaplan's addition to the Purple defense team was not as benign as it seemed. The Big Apple barrister also happened to be on retainer to Joey Burnstein, and Kaplan's partner was well-known defense attorney Isaiah Leebove. The latter had been known for defending such famous underworld clients as Arnold Rothstein, Jack "Legs" Diamond, Owney Madden, and gambler "Dapper Don" Collins. Right around the time Kennedy made his motion, Leebove had sought a private meeting at Marquette with the imprisoned Ray Burnstein, Irving Milberg, and Harry Keywell. It soon came out that he had recently been appointed as a special advisor to Michigan Governor William Comstock. Rumor had it that Fred Kaplan's partner Leebove was going to use his influence with the governor to attempt to get a pardon for the three Purples.

It also turned out that Isaiah Leebove was also a primary investor in the Mammoth Petroleum Corporation, the same oil company that Purple Gang big shots Joe Burnstein and Sam Garfield owned significant shares of. Indeed, not long after Fred Kaplan entered the Collingwood Massacre case fray, Leebove sold a quarter-interest in the company to Garfield. The company was subsequently renamed the Garfield Oil and Gas Corporation. Sam was the president and Joey Burnstein the treasurer. Both Purples now lived in lavish homes in the company's hometown, Mt. Pleasant, Michigan.[27]

On July 16, 1933, Edward Kennedy officially filed his second new trial motion for his convicted clients. From the start, it was evident that the Purple Gang lawyer had brought out the big guns. Thirty affidavits, which comprised one hundred fifty-six pages total, were filed. Three were from the defendants themselves and another from a former Reading, Pennsylvania police officer. They said that Ray Burnstein and Harry Keywell could not have committed the Collingwood murders because they were at home of Ray's sister Jennie taking bets from bookies in New York, Chicago, and Cincinnati on the afternoon of September 16, 1931. Both Irving Milberg and his wife Bertha claimed to have spent that whole day in bed together while Harry Fleisher said he was cooling his heels in a Reading jail cell that day under the alias of Harry Fishman. Another affidavit was from a Detroit handbook operator named Jacob Silverman, who claimed that massacre victim Izzy Sutker had told him on the day of the massacre that he and his partners were due to meet with some unidentified Italian bookies from Toledo.[28]

Abe Burnstein himself testified that he had discovered the phone records that proved the innocence of his brother Raymond and Harry Keywell through a family friend named Lou Bert who happened to work for Michigan Bell, while the arrest slip from the Reading jail of the date of the massacre matched Harry Fleisher's handwriting perfectly. When questioned as to why he hadn't revealed the phone records earlier, Abe claimed that they had been misplaced until April 1932.

Kennedy explained that Lou Bert had died recently and that it had been difficult to obtain duplicate records in the aftermath of his passing. The defense lawyer also claimed that he hadn't used the phone records in the trial because it would have looked poorly if Abe Burnstein said that he had lost records that could have exonerated his brother. When asked why he hadn't included the records in his first appeal in the spring of 1932, Kennedy stumbled.

On Tuesday, August 8, none other than Harry Fleisher was sworn in as an alibi witness. Fred Kaplan hoped that by proving Fleisher's innocence he could do the same for the imprisoned Purples. Kaplan also reiterated the defense's contention that the Detroit police had beaten what they wanted to hear out of the still-missing Solomon Levine. The New York attorney claimed that even forty-eight hours after the shootings that Prosecutor Harry S. Toy was waffling on the identity of the killers and whether or not Solly Levine was even on the scene. Kaplan produced an affidavit from a man who was a prisoner at the Wayne County Jail in the aftermath of the massacre that agreed with the defense's claim that police had beaten Levine until he told them that Burnstein, Keywell, and Milberg were the killers.

After being personally named in Kaplan's charges, Harry Toy gave the defense both barrels from then out. A Michigan Bell employee named Joseph Brett discredited the phone records presented by Abe Burnstein. Brett stated that the lost slips could not have been duplicated, that all records were kept for six months and then automatically destroyed. In addition, Brett and a second employee claimed that they had never met any of the Burnsteins before. Lillian Bates, maid of the Milberg family, blew Irving's alibi by saying he had left early on the morning of September 16, 1931 and returned that evening so nervous that he didn't touch his supper.[29]

The second appeal hearing came to a head over Harry Fleisher's alleged incarceration in Reading, Pennsylvania on the day of the massacre. The seat of Berks County, Reading in the early thirties was a bustling city of 100,000 located about sixty miles northwest of Philadelphia. A manufacturing town primarily centered on railroads (the town lent its name to the Reading Railroad; notable as one of the four railroad properties in the board game Monopoly), Reading was also a notoriously wild berg where illegal booze flowed like water and citizens could place bets at a handbook or jerk "one-armed bandits."

Easily the most powerful gangster in town was thirty-three year old Max Hassel. The Russian-born Hassel had graduated from humble beginnings to become the unchallenged beer baron of Reading during Prohibition. Through his connections with New York gangster Waxey Gordon, Max met many other powerful gangsters from around the country, including Purple Gang boss Abe Burnstein. By the early 1930s, Max was a millionaire racketeer who belonged to a powerful New Jersey-based criminal consortium. His two partners, Waxey Gordon and Max Greenberg, had a controlling interest in up to seventeen illegal breweries up and down the East Coast. Hassel also owned several hotels in Reading; Harry Fleisher was allegedly busted in front of one on the day of the Collingwood massacre. A pink jail ticket with his alias of Harry Fishman supposedly proved it.[30]

Just like the Purples' other alibis, Harry Toy would destroy this one as well. Toy's first witness was the Reading Police Commissioner, J. Stanley Giles, who claimed that prisoners' name were entered onto yellow sheets and then onto pink tickets. Giles stated that the name Fishman did not appear on a yellow sheet for the week of the massacre. Toy had also had affidavits from other Reading jail and police personnel that swore no one named Fleisher or Fishman was locked up there in the latter half of 1931. The Reading jail clerk stated that he had not typed the defense's pink ticket.

Another guard, Samuel Kirchoff, claimed to have worked the jail floor on September 16 and had never seen Harry Fleisher before. Kirchoff told a curious tale of being approached in October 1931, a month after the Detroit shootings, by the acting Chief of Detectives of the Reading Police Department, Detective Lieutenant Charles Dentith, who told him to make out two arrest record tickets for two individuals who had been arrested some time before and to date them September 16. Kirchoff then handed over the tickets after leaving the signature spaces blank; it was the first time in eighteen years of employment at the jail that he had been asked to do such a thing. It was duly noted that Lieutenant Dentith was known as a bodyguard for Abe Burnstein's pal, Reading crime boss Max Hassel.

In desperation, Edward Kennedy arranged for both Charles Dentith and Reading Chief of Detectives Fred Marks to come to Detroit and testify to the veracity of their claims. Neither man was permitted to take the stand. Max Hassel himself had nothing to say on the matter as he was dead by this time; shot dead with Max Greenberg by unidentified gunmen on April 12, 1933 in their Elizabeth, New Jersey hotel. Abe Burnstein's friend had fallen victim to a hostile takeover by Meyer Lansky and Bugsy Siegel.[31]

Detroit Police Department Patrolman Albert Bice claimed in a final affidavit to have seen Harry Fleisher in the North End at the corner Clairmount and Woodward avenues the morning after the Collingwood Manor Massacre, when he was supposedly locked up in Pennsylvania. When Fleisher was named as one of the shooters the next day, Bice reported this to his superior officer. Ironically, Patrolman Bice was then reprimanded for not arresting Fleisher on the spot due to his outstanding warrant in the Leonard Storage Company distillery case.[32]

Looking back in retrospect, Abe Burnstein went to remarkable lengths to free his brother and two associates from prison. Utilizing his friendship with Reading gangster Max Hassel, Burnstein had convinced a corrupt detective to manufacture phony evidence for the Reading jail's records, as well as producing the affidavits from bookies in such diverse cities as New York, Chicago, and Cincinnati. Alas, Abe's efforts came to naught on the afternoon of Friday, October 6, 1933, when the defendants' second motion for a new trial was denied. Barring a legal miracle or an escape, it seemed at the time that Ray Burnstein, Harry Keywell, and Irving Milberg would indeed be spending the rest of their lives in prison.[33]

BY THE END OF THE SUMMER OF 1933, Abe Axler and Eddie Fletcher had finally antagonized the Partnership past the point of no return. It was rumored that on one occasion a Purple (perhaps Fletcher himself) and a Sicilian gangster got into a fistfight in front of a downtown movie theater. The Sicilian hood was badly beaten and ran off swearing vengeance. Shortly thereafter, a carload of torpedoes cruised around the neighborhood looking for the pugilistic Purple gangster, who had wisely left.[34]

On September 11, Wayne County Prosecutor Harry S. Toy had begun a large clean-up campaign to rid the city of organized crime, arresting a group of gangsters and charging them under the Disorderly Persons Act, aka the Public Enemy Law. Among those busted were James Moceri, Joe Bommarito, Jack Licavoli, Sam Drapkin, Abe Axler, and Eddie Fletcher. The newspapers ran large line-up photographs of the gangsters across their front pages, with the men holding handkerchiefs to their faces in true wiseguy fashion.

Axler and Fletcher were then locked in a holding tank with the very same Sicilian gangsters that they had been feuding with for several months. No one will know exactly what was discussed, but as soon as the Twins made bail they fled back to their old neighborhood in New York. They were said to be in hiding after being implicated in a six-year old kidnapping, but their reasons for running were probably far more sinister. By now, they had almost certainly been warned by Abe Burnstein and other high-ranking Purples to return the brewery purchase money they had chiseled.[35]

Meanwhile, Joe Bommarito, Jack Licavoli, Sam Drapkin, Joe Massei, and several others were ultimately convicted on the Public Enemy charges.[36] All were sentenced to a maximum of 90 days in jail. Shortly afterwards, the Disorderly Persons Act was deemed unconstitutional and wiped from the books. Just after serving his sentence, Drapkin was charged by the feds with running a counterfeiting operation with several other Purples out of his apartment at 12th and Blaine.[37]

ONE MORNING IN EARLY NOVEMBER 1933, a well-known North End businessman who lived on Chicago Boulevard had trouble getting his car started. As he walked toward Dexter Boulevard to flag a cab, he was surprised to see Abe Axler pass by him in a brand-new Chrysler sedan. "Hello, Abe, give me a lift?" Axler paused. "All right, but don't ask me again. I don't like to let you drive with me along the street, it might not be so good for you. I wouldn't want anything to happen to you. Anything might happen to me." The friend later remarked, "I thought he was referring to his public enemy trouble."[38]

Axler and Eddie Fletcher had recently returned to Detroit after spending half of September and all of October laying low in New York City. Their friends and families noticed they were extremely nervous and tense upon their return. The Partnership was still after them for the heroin racket kerfuffle. Then there was the fact that the Twins had chiseled their Purple bosses on the brewery deal. The walls were closing in on the pair and they knew it, splitting their time between their apartment building at 3245 Chicago and a rented cottage they kept north of the city near Keego Harbor in Oakland County. While at the latter location, Axler had tried to bribe the local sheriff to lay off his slot machines but was steadfastly refused, a prime example of how much his influence had waned.

While in Detroit proper, Axler and Fletcher rarely left their apartments. When they did, they almost certainly repaired to their favorite Chinatown opium dens. There they would stretch out and toke themselves calm, much as Noodles Aaronson did in the Sergio Leone film *Once Upon A Time In America*. They may have been returning from such an expedition at dawn on November 18 when a vehicle full of gangsters surprised them at the intersection of Chicago and Linwood and riddled their car with bullets. Axler and Fletcher managed to escape unscathed, but the attack unnerved them enough to leave the city for their Keego Harbor cottage.[39]

Exactly one week after the attempt on their lives, the Siamese Twins spent a pleasant autumn day riding horses with their wives Evelyn and Emma in rural Oakland County. Axler had a brief conversation with Charles Stevenson, the owner of the Green Oaks stables, stating to the effect that he was going legit. "I'm through with the racket for keeps. I'll see you Sunday."[40]

Around seven o'clock on the evening of November 25, Abe Axler got a phone call from Harry Millman, who suggested they meet later that evening at a beer garden in the town of Pontiac, twenty miles north of Detroit. Axler then told Eddie Fletcher of the impending conference. By midnight, Abe and Eddie were seen drinking beer in the Pontiac rendezvous as they waited for Millman. After two hours or so, the young Purple gangster still hadn't shown up. The Twins were last seen walking out together at about 1:15. As they made their way to Abe's Chrysler, they were surprised by at least two men.

What exactly happened next is uncertain but it probably became apparent to Abe and Eddie that after so many years of being on the administration end of the infamous "one-way ride" that they were now going to be on the receiving end. Whatever weapons the pair had were taken from them. One man sat in the backseat of the Chrysler with the Twins while another got behind the wheel of Axler's car, chauffeur-style. At least one other man followed in a second vehicle as the grim caravan proceeded south on Telegraph Road through the dark Oakland County landscape. The backseat passenger kept Axler and Fletcher covered with a .38 caliber revolver the whole time.

Perhaps twenty minutes after they started out, the Chrysler's driver swung left onto Quarton Road. About one hundred yards later, he abruptly veered onto the north shoulder and stopped. The second car pulled in behind them, bathing the Chrysler in the harsh glow of its headlights. Abe must have realized what was about to happen and made a desperate grab for the .38 in his captor's fist. The gun discharged a round through his right palm. In the horrible instant of that first shot, Eddie instinctively twisted his head toward Abe's plight and was drilled through the left temple by a .45 ACP slug fired by the Chrysler's driver. The backseat killer then shoved the .38 against the right side of Axler's head and proceeded to splatter his blood and brains with the five remaining bullets. The driver simultaneously pumped two more rounds into Fletcher's chest and broke his right arm with another. In a final macabre gesture, for reasons known only to him, the backseat shooter reached over and clasped Abe's left hand and Eddie's right hand together.

Mere minutes after the shooting, Constable Fred Lincoln was carefully making his rounds along pitch-black Quarton Road when he discovered a brand-new Chrysler sedan parked on the shoulder. Lincoln opened the doors expecting to find amorous teenagers and promptly smelled the sharp odors of blood and cordite. The beam of his flashlight revealed a ghastly *tableau* of two bullet-torn, open-eyed corpses slumped against each other in the back seat. Newspaper photographers later got a close up of the pair's joined hands, which soon ran in the *Detroit News*. A search of the Twins' pockets showed they were down on their luck to the last; Axler had $18.60 while Fletcher carried a mere 60 cents. Evelyn Axler and Emma Fletcher appeared at the Oakland County Morgue to identify the bodies. They broke down in loud hysterics and screamed, "They couldn't do it!!" and "I'll get them dirty rats!!" The wives obviously knew who their husbands had gone to meet, but of course they never told.

After the autopsy, the bodies of the Twins were removed to the Lewis Brothers Undertaking Establishment at 7739 John R Street in Detroit. Like the members and victims of the Purple Gang that had died before them, Abe and Eddie underwent *taharah*, the Jewish ritual of burial preparation at the hands of the local *chevra kadisha*. Both corpses were uncovered and washed thoroughly; their gunshot-punctured skulls miraculously repaired. All dirt and excretions were carefully removed from the skin, as was any jewelry. The men were purified with water, either by being immersed in a *mikveh* or being doused by a steady stream of around three buckets worth. Each body was then dried and wrapped in a *tahrihim*, a white linen shroud. An *avnet* (sash) was wrapped around their waists and tied in the form of the Hebrew letter *shin*, signifying *Shaddai*, one of names of God. The interior of their solid silver caskets were lined with a *sovev* while a *tallit* (prayer shawl) was draped across each body's shoulders.

By the time that the first light of dawn began to illuminate the tin-colored skies over Detroit on the morning of November 27, the open caskets containing the bodies of Abe Axler and Eddie Fletcher had been arranged in a V-shape, with their heads close together. The room that they were resting in was both barren and somber. Not a single flower was present. No one was standing over them, mourning or weeping. There was no light in the room except the candles that encircled the coffins and a large, blue neon Star of David, which hung directly over the deceased and cast an azure glow upon their faces. The only noise was the occasional thumping of the harsh autumn wind against the windows.

The first visitors that morning were three carloads of Purple Gang members and associates. They entered quickly and spent several long moments staring at the bodies of the Twins. One of the Purples muttered the only words said by the group, "They look natural." The men then left quickly, never identifying themselves. Throughout the day, a quiet stream of relatives, friends, and the otherwise curious came to visit the men. Fletcher's younger sister Sophie attempted to remain stoic but soon broke down crying, as did Eddie's uncle, who clutched his nephew's face and pleaded with him to wake up. No flowers or other Purple Gang mobsters appeared over the course of the day, a red flag to the cops that Axler and Fletcher had been killed by their own crew. Despite this knowledge, the police never charged anyone with their murders.[41]

Within a week or so, it would become apparent to police that the Purple Gang's bosses had finally brought the hammer down on Axler and Fletcher in retaliation for their brewery chisel from the previous summer. In the meantime, they investigated the possibility that their murders were connected to another high profile "hit vic" discovered on the northwest outskirts of Detroit on the afternoon of November 29.

The dead man in question was Verne Miller, who was found beaten to death and trussed up with clothesline in a ditch at the corner of Cambridge and Harlow streets, one block north of 7 Mile Road. A South Dakota sheriff-turned-gangster, Miller was badly wanted by the FBI as the lead triggerman in Kansas City's Union Station Massacre, which had occurred the previous June. Detroit police initially speculated that his murder may have been a result of the Axler/Fletcher homicides, but the subsequent investigation determined that Miller was almost certainly whacked by some of his New York criminal associates for a number of reasons rooted in the tremendous amount of law enforcement heat generated by the Kansas City shootings.[42]

While law enforcement and morgue officials examined Verne Miller's corpse in Detroit, Abraham Axler and Edward Fletcher were laid to rest in Beth David Cemetery in Elmont, New York. Even in death, the two were inseparable. Their grieving families watched as their silver coffins were lowered away to the mournful sound of the rabbi chanting *Kaddish*, the Jewish prayer for the dead.

Less than a week later, on December 5, Utah became the thirty-sixth state to ratify the Twenty-First Amendment. The "noble experiment" of Prohibition was finally over.[43]

Detroit Police detectives examine a cache of weapons seized during "Bloody July". The detective on the right holds a Luger P08 identical to the one used by Harry Kirschenbaum to shoot Joe Burnstein. The detective on the left holds a Lugar LP08 used by the one of the killers of radio muckraker Jerry Buckley. *Chriss Lyon Collection*

Harry Fleisher left is standing next to Myron "Mikey" Selik. During his time on the run from murder charges stemming from the Collingwood Manor Massacre, Fleisher was suspected by federal authorities of having a hand in the Lindbergh baby abduction. Fleisher surrendered in June 1932 in what he claimed was an effort to exonerate his imprisoned friends. Due to the disappearance of chief witness Solly Levine, the charges against Fleisher were nolle processed. *Walter Reuther Library.*

Jacob "Scotty" Silverstein was a bookkeeper for the Purple Gang. According to David Levitt, Silverstein's purple sweater might have given the Purple Gang its irresistible name. *Walter Reuther Library.*

Joe Burnstein eventually phased himself out of the day-to-day action of the Purple Gang and invested heavily in a lucrative oil and gas company with childhood friend Sam Garfield. Burnstein retired to California, a millionaire many times over. *Walter Reuther Library.*

DISINTEGRATION

T he Purple Gang business deal that claimed the lives of Abe Axler and Eddie Fletcher was part of a concerted effort by the crew's bosses to acquire breweries and distilleries in order to legally sell alcohol after Repeal. The Purples' inroads into the legitimate booze trade were made possible, in part, through their secret alliance with one of Michigan's most powerful political power brokers.

Frank Donald McKay was born on November 4, 1883 in Grand Rapids. He dropped out of school at an early age to work menial jobs, notably one in a furniture factory. A brilliant, ambitious young man and natural businessman, McKay soon set up a money exchange program for his numerous foreign-born coworkers. Frank also founded a private banking and investment firm for them. The newly prosperous McKay soon bankrolled a local steamship agency and construction companies in the Grand Rapids area. At the age of twenty-three, Frank McKay was elected deputy county clerk and assignment clerk for Grand Rapids' circuit court. Before long he was chairman of the Kent County Republican Party.

By the outbreak of World War I, McKay was a self-made millionaire and serving as an assignment clerk in Detroit. He was also tough and extraordinarily driven. McKay did not hesitate to use intimidation and profanity to enforce his will. In 1919 he was one of 134 people indicted on charges of corruption, fraud, and conspiracy charges in the wake of the political scandal surrounding the election of Republican Senator Truman H. Newberry over Henry Ford. McKay was specifically charged with two instances of bribery. In what would become a pattern in his career, Frank McKay beat the charges. In 1924, he was elected Michigan State Treasurer, a post he would hold for three terms. During this period, McKay "wisened up" by personally campaign across the state of Michigan, even in the oft-neglected Upper Peninsula. McKay also led a successful intra-party revolt in 1926 against liberal incumbent Governor Alex Groesbeck, who was ousted in an election upset by Frederick Green. A grateful Green would appoint McKay as chief legislative lobbyist as well as chairman of the highway and finance committees on the Michigan State Administrative Board. McKay ultimately left the treasurer's office in 1930 under a cloud of suspicion for misappropriating state funds. Nothing came of these charges, either.[1]

Frank McKay first became associated with the Purple Gang in the spring of 1930, during his final term as treasurer. The Oakland Sugar House sold just about all the malt used by beer brewers in the Detroit area in this period and paid federal taxes on only a fraction of it. Charlie Leiter and Henry Shorr managed to get away with this by paying graft to certain members of the IRS. When the state of Michigan attempted to get a piece of this action, Henry Shorr called his main political contact, John Gillespie. A former Detroit police commissioner and current Commissioner of Public Works under then-Mayor Charles Bowles, Gillespie facilitated a meeting between the gangster and state treasurer. With McKay's influence, an unnamed Detroit corporation (that was secretly owned by Henry Shorr) got the contract to produce all of the state's malt tax stamps, which enabled the Purples to make handsome tax-exempt profits in perpetuity. Not long after this deal was put in place, Mayor Bowles was recalled and Gillespie's fortunes turned south. Eventually, Shorr and McKay pushed the former commissioner out of the picture all together.[2]

In return for political favors, Henry Shorr and other Purples acted as McKay's enforcers, often paying intimidating visits to lawmakers and businessmen who failed to bend to the Republican's will. When McKay conducted business in the Detroit area, hulking Sugar House gangster Izzy Schwartz frequently acted as his bodyguard. For prudence sake, Frank himself never personally met with the Purples as a whole. McKay would relay his desires to Leiter, Shorr, and/or Schwartz, either in person or through an emissary. Such insulation was necessary for a politician of McKay's stature.[3]

By the Repeal of Prohibition, Frank McKay, along with fellow GOP heavyweights Edward Barnard (Detroit) and William McKeighan (Flint), virtually controlled Michigan's Republican Party. Their powerful machine would endure for a total of two decades and have a heavy hand in almost every law passed and election conducted. McKay would later accurately boast about these days, "Reporters who covered those conventions had an easy time of it. I would tell them the night before the convention what the ticket was going to be and they could play cards all night."[4]

Using Frank McKay's endorsements, both Charles Leiter and Henry

Shorr acquired several breweries and distilleries throughout Michigan. In addition, Oakland Sugar House co-founder George Goldberg had a sizeable interest in the Grand Rapids Brewing Company. The next order of business was for the bosses to get permits to legitimately produce alcohol in their new properties. However, Frank A. Picard, chairman of the state Liquor Control Commission, turned down Leiter and Shorr. Picard stated that the two "would be barred for life from any legal connection with the liquor business in Michigan." In the aftermath of this, Leiter and Shorr had a fierce quarrel and dissolved their two decades-long business partnership. Shorr then struck out on his own with the Wolverine Distillery.[5]

Leonard Simons, co-head of the fledgling Simons Michelson Company advertising firm, did business with the Purples in the days after Repeal, [6]

"Our young ad agency was struggling. We were hungry for clients, any kind of accounts. When Prohibition died, I heard the Wolverine Distillery was going to hire an ad agency. I was also told it was owned by ex-Purple Gang members who were going legit. They believed their former customers would continue to buy from them. They also owned the Schemm Brewing Company in Saginaw."

Simons figured if the government found suit to issue them a license to sell alcohol, then that was good enough for him. The young executive was directed to the former boss of the Oakland Sugar House, thirty-six year old Henry Shorr.

"Shorr hired us. He said for the present we would be a fairly small account, but said if we were interested in making additional money we could buy some of their supplies for them and bill the company. They would let us make the usual 15-percent advertising agency commission on labels and other purchases. Fifteen percent was 15 percent. I was glad to get it."

Simons saw that although a non-Jewish man owned the company in name, Henry Shorr was actually calling the shots. Leonard also took note of the hardcases hanging around the distillery's office playing cards, and figured them for Purple Gang strong-arms. He nicknamed them "the foyer men." The business got off to a slow start.

"The (pre-Repeal) customers were not buying, using, or selling Wolverine or Schemm products and the business was constantly losing money. When they became slow to pay, I started to worry about it. I knew I wouldn't dare talk

tough with Shorr, so I kept pleading very carefully for some money. He told me they had no cash, only lots of inventory."

If an upper-echelon Purple like Henry Shorr was having trouble earning in the aftermath of Repeal, the street-level hoods that did his bidding were even worse off. With the Partnership controlling just about all of Detroit's major rackets, the Purples continued to be iced out of a number of lucrative ventures. In addition, the gang's loose knit structure continued to unravel like a worn quilt as members left town or quarreled with each other. Indeed, intra-gang sniping had been pecking away at the Purple Gang's ranks since the end of the now long-ago Cleaners and Dyers War. With Repeal and its aftermath, the Purples' self-destruction train gained an increasing head of steam.

In the early morning hours of June 13, 1934, a handful of Purples were drinking in an unlicensed blind pig called Eddie's Hideaway, located to the rear of 480 W. Willis Avenue. The bar, a dilapidated one-story frame dwelling set back far from the street, was essentially a hold-over from an era that had ended forever just six months earlier. George "Eddie" Doran, a former lounge singer, had opened the place just two weeks before. Earlier in the day, detectives questioned Doran concerning the recent North End murder of a Chicago gambler named Edward Pearl, as one of his cards had been found in the victim's pocket. Harry Sutton, the Purple hanger-on who had gone to Leavenworth with Irving Milberg, Abe Axler, and Eddie Fletcher, was now working as a bartender in Eddie Doran's new joint. Also sitting in that evening was a Purple gangster later identified as Harry Millman, who got progressively drunker as the evening wore on. Such a situation was often a recipe for disaster, as the youthful Millman had a hair-trigger temper when intoxicated.

Exactly what set Millman off this night was never satisfactorily determined. Whatever the cause, around 4 o'clock that morning, Doran and Millman apparently got into a nasty fistfight near the piano while a stunned crowd of a dozen customers watched. The one-time lounge singer was having quite a hard time handling the ferocious gangster; Doran's expensive silk shirt was badly torn in the melee. Harry Sutton rushed over to break up the donnybrook and discovered the hard way that discretion is the better part of valor. Just as the three men came together in a tangle of arms and curses, Millman jerked out a .38 caliber automatic and squeezed off two quick shots.

Sutton went down clutching his hip while Doran lurched against the wall, blood gushing from a wound in his side. Screams and shouts filled the room as Doran staggered to the rear of his blind pig in a desperate attempt to escape. Millman gave chase, pumping bullets at him all the while. The dangerously wounded Doran weaved unsteadily through the kitchen, leaving the floor littered with a trail of broken glass and blood. Doran actually made it out the back door and was mere feet from rounding the corner of the yard to safety when Harry Millman stopped on the back porch, took careful aim, and fatally shot him in the back with his last bullet.

The sharpshooting Purple gangster made a point of wiping his .38 clean of fingerprints before leaving it behind. Millman then joined the others in making a quick exit from Eddie's Hideaway. The corpse of the bar's name-sake was soon found by police in the back alley. Visible in the dim glow of a nearby street lamp was the large tattoo on Eddie Doran's outstretched right forearm; a nude woman and the words "Death Before Dishonor."

Harry Sutton showed up at Providence Hospital several hours later mimicking the line of fellow Purple Gang mobster Sam Drapkin, "Santa Claus shot me." Harry Millman fled to Chicago immediately after the shooting; after he was arrested in the Illinois city seven months later, the cops couldn't make their case against him stick.[7]

"YOUSE GUYS, UNDERSTAND, I am going to talk. I'm licked," Sam "The Gorilla" Davis elaborated in his gravelly voice. The fugitive Purple had finally been run to ground in August 1934 after being arrested for carrying a concealed weapon in New Rochelle, New York. After his extradition back to Detroit to face charges for the murder of his friend Harry Gold during the botched robbery of saloonkeeper Eugene Williams, Davis wasted no time in spilling his guts. "Well, on the afternoon of Feb. 16, 1932 - I even got the date down pat - I meet up with the late Mr. Axler and Mr. Fletcher, who got a business proposal for me. It sure was too bad them boys had to get shooted up in a car last fall."[8]

Davis told of his first attempt to gain entry into Gene Williams' house, "... this Williams man comes to the door and, for some reason, gets mad at me and comes back with a big shotgun and so I leave," and of recruiting Harry Gold and Nate Karp, the latter already having been tried and acquitted of Gold's murder.

"When we go through the house I takes Gold's gun from him. He is liable to shoot somebody, you know. Then we finds the plates and there is a rap rap at the back door and Mr. Williams comes home. So I gives Gold back his gun and there is some shooting and we run. Then Gold gets in the driver's seat and he made a funny noise and said, 'I can't drive. I'm shooted.' Then he tells us we better leave him there because there is going to be some trouble about it. So we

*does and I figure there's trouble and so I hitch-hike to Cincinnati and New York
and New Jersey and work like an automobile repair man."*

After a month-long psychiatric evaluation, Sam Davis was convicted of
Gold's murder on Monday, October 1 and immediately committed to Ionia
State Mental Hospital for the Criminally Insane.[9]

ON WEDNESDAY, NOVEMBER 21, 1934, Louis Fleisher walked out of
Leavenworth Federal Penitentiary after serving six years for the Flat Rock
tire truck hijacking. Detroit was a whole lot different from when he left in
February 1928. The Purple Gang had shrunk drastically, with many of his
old friends either dead or in jail. The Mafia had gotten even stronger and
now pretty much ran the city, while the Purples scraped by on a handful of
enterprises. While visiting his older brother Harry upon his return, Fleisher
learned that his old crew was now in the midst of a deadly intra-gang squabble involving his onetime mentor.

Since Charlie Leiter and Henry Shorr had split up earlier in the year, relations between the two men had grown even worse. Republican Secretary of
State Frank Fitzgerald resigned from his post to run for governor in the 1934
election. A close ally of Republican boss Frank McKay, Fitzgerald's chances
looked good despite the corruption taint that hung over McKay's patronage.

According to a confidential FBI memorandum, former Detroit politician
John Gillespie wrote a letter to the editor of a Lansing newspaper claiming
that Fitzgerald must not be allowed to become governor due to his ties to
the notorious McKay. Gillespie had fallen on hard times and was launch-
ing a vindictive campaign against the Republican boss, whom he blamed
for his misfortune. The former commissioner was also worried about being
implicated in the malt tax stamp scheme of 1930, which the new gubernatorial candidate had intimate knowledge of. As a result, Henry Shorr was dispatched to intimidate Gillespie into silence on the matter. In actuality, Shorr
double-crossed McKay and re-forged a secret alliance with Gillespie; most
probably a move designed to cement his newfound independence. In return
for Gillespie keeping quiet about Fitzgerald, Shorr would use his influence
with the new governor to secretly obtain favors for the downtrodden former
commissioner.

Frank McKay, in the dark about Shorr's machinations, did indeed reward
the gangster with future privileges in the governor's mansion once Fitzgerald won the November 6 election. Shorr was playing an increasingly dangerous game by not only making competition against his old Purple pals in the

booze business but also by double-dealing their powerful benefactor.

Two weeks after Frank Fitzgerald was elected governor of Michigan, John Gillespie asked his new ally Henry Shorr for a political favor, which he then relayed to Republican boss Frank McKay. Unfortunately, McKay had by now smelled out Shorr's duplicity. While he had initially agreed to the gangster's request, McKay did not come through as promised.

On Saturday afternoon, December 1, Henry Shorr harkened back to his rough-and-tumble Eastern Market days and rounded up John Gillespie. The gang boss then had the former commissioner drive him from Detroit to Grand Rapids in order to confront Frank McKay. Gillespie waited in the car while Shorr stomped inside the Republican boss's mansion and angrily demanded that McKay come through with his promises. According to one source, Shorr threatened to spill the beans about McKay's collusion with the Purple Gang. After returning to the car, Shorr confidently proclaimed to Gillespie that McKay would now do whatever he told him to. Unfortunately, the former Sugar House boss's fate was probably already sealed by the time Gillespie dropped him off at his North End duplex several hours later.[10]

Henry Shorr lived with his family in an elegant flat at 3239 Fullerton Avenue. Forty-eight hours after his confrontation with Frank McKay, Shorr left his home after telling his wife Mary that he was going to collect money for a needy old man who was well known around the neighborhood. It was later learned that he kept a 9 p.m. meeting with Charles Leiter at a popular delicatessen at the corner of 12th and Pingree streets. The two men were seen leaving this rendezvous together a short time later, destination unknown.

A series of baffling events took place over the next few days. The afternoon after Shorr's family last saw him, Oscar Shorr called the police to report his brother Henry missing. Less than an hour later, the Shorrs received a cryptic phone call hinting that Henry had been kidnapped and that money was trying to be obtained for his release. They were specifically warned to stay quiet on the matter and to stay away from the police. Oscar then re-telephoned the cops and told them that they knew where Henry was and that he was alright. Later that same night, police found Henry's car parked just a few blocks from his home. The ignition key was in the ON position and the gasoline tank was empty, indicating that the engine had been left running. There were no other clues inside.[11]

The next day, December 5, Harry Fleisher was pulled over while driving his Buick coupe in another part of Detroit. It was noted that the back seat upholstery was stained with blood. Additional blood splatter was found on the ceiling of the car above the passenger seat. Fleisher explained the stains away by saying he had slapped one of his girlfriends and bloodied her nose. Between that story and the Shorr family's insistence that Henry was safe, the police were compelled to let Fleisher leave with his vehicle. The following morning, Mary Shorr got yet another phone call telling her that Henry would be home soon and that she should not tell the cops a thing.

Henry Shorr's non-Jewish front man for the Wolverine Distillery called his youthful client, advertising executive Leonard Simons, and asked him to come to the distillery's office right away. As Simons related six decades later, "When I got there he grabbed me and rushed me into a private room. He was scared out of his wits. He told me that Henry Shorr had disappeared. His bloodstained car was found, but not Henry. He believed that Henry Shorr had been murdered and that they might find some excuse to kill him, too. As quickly as I could, I ran from the plant to my office and never went back."

Several days later, one of Shorr's "foyer men" paid Simons a visit in order to close out his account. Leonard grew angry when he saw the goon was only going to pay him $1,000 instead of the $6,000 he was owed. After bickering with the hoodlum for several moments, Leonard reminded himself whom he was dealing with. "All of a sudden, I woke up and said to myself, 'Simons, you idiot! Why are you arguing about money with these gangsters? Wake up, calm down, behave yourself and keep your big mouth shut. Do you want to be found at the bottom of the Detroit River? Be glad you're alive.'"

In a more respectful tone of voice, Simons claimed that he no longer even wanted the $1,000. Everything was square. "But he said, 'No. We have to pay our creditors something.' I kept insisting I didn't want it. Then he looked at me sternly and said, 'Take it!' I took it. I also said my prayers that everything was going to be all right from this point on." It was, as Leonard Simons' advertising agency would go on to become a highly lucrative business. The young executive ended up much better off than most that associated with the Purple Gang.[12]

Shorr's family had initially told police that they thought he had been kidnapped, which brought the FBI into the case. Nothing was heard from Henry or his supposed abductors, however, after the December 6 phone call to Mary Shorr. Henry's fate grew even darker when his mother passed away on December 10 with nary a peep from the missing Sugar House boss. The feds then backed out of the case as it became obvious that Henry had been "taken for a ride."

Detroit police did not notify the media of Shorr's disappearance until over a month after the fact, and then were forced to scramble for leads that were not there. Charlie Leiter admitted to having met Henry on the night of December 3 but did not know what happened to him. Harry Fleisher and Charles "The Professor" Auerbach appeared downtown at the DPD Headquarters for voluntary questioning. Like Leiter, both men confessed to seeing Shorr just before he vanished but, no, they were just as puzzled as police as to their friend's fate. Fleisher's Buick had since been reupholstered, thus eliminating the bloodstains that had been seen in the backseat.

Henry Shorr's body was never found; police believed that it had been disposed of in an industrial incinerator. Several years later, Shorr's widow Mary visited Harry Fleisher in prison and begged him to help prove Henry was dead so she could receive her husband's life insurance money. She did not have any luck.[13]

THE YEAR 1935 saw the city of Detroit with a population of almost 1.6 million residents and nearly another million living in the surrounding area. While unemployment remained high, the town's economy was beginning to show signs of life as the demand for manufactured goods began to slowly climb skyward. Frank Couzens, former City Council Chairman and son of former Detroit mayor James Couzens, now held his father's old job. The city's sports fans had good reason to cheer as Detroit's teams dominated the country's major sports in that year; the Red Wings got off to a red-hot start that would end with them hoisting their first Stanley Cup the following spring while the Lions claimed the NFL championship. In the aftermath of a hard-fought loss to the St. Louis Cardinals a year earlier, the Tigers bested the Chicago Cubs to earn the first World Series title in franchise history.

Over the course of the prior year, the FBI had won the nationwide "War on Crime" by defeating the numerous headline-grabbing motorized bandits of the era, including men like John Dillinger, Pretty Boy Floyd, and Baby Face Nelson. The newly empowered FBI was riding a wave of popularity; unlike the days of Prohibition when bootleggers were romanticized, law-and-order types were now idolized by the masses. Indeed, one of the most popular films that year was James Cagney's *G-Men*.

At the Mafia's ideal level of operation, the general public had little to no idea that they even existed. Avoiding law enforcement and the media, Detroit's "Partnership" continued to flourish with rackets such as illegal gambling, narcotics trafficking, protection racketeering, bookmaking, prostitution, loansharking and increasingly, labor racketeering. The Purple Gang, by contrast, was essentially on life support by 1935. While the bosses had numerous legitimate business interests and ownership of breweries/distilleries, others continued to eke out a meager living in the Detroit underworld. Like their Sicilian counterparts, the Purples dabbled in the above rackets but the returns were often far less than those of their rivals. For all their misfortune, the Purple Gang was still the most identifiable Detroit gang, a factor which probably hastened their overall decline.

On April 11, 1935, agents of the Federal Alcohol Tax Division raided Harry Fleisher's distillery at 5620 Federal Avenue. The distillery boasted eight 6,000-gallon wooden mash vats, four 500-gallon iron vats, 10,500 pounds of brown sugar, 2,000-gallon mixing and receiving vats, and 1,000 gallons of pure alcohol. The Purples had rigged a steel door into the floor, which opened into an underground tunnel that led to the building next door. The idea was that they would duck into this passageway in the event of a raid. When the feds broke the door down they did just that, but the law was waiting for them at the other end. Fleisher and his men were charged with violating the Internal Revenue Law by operating the distillery without a license and not paying federal taxes on the alcohol they produced.[14]

SOMETIME IN 1935, according to underworld scuttlebutt, Abe Burnstein was summoned before the Partnership's bosses and informed that they were taking over the racing-wire service for Detroit. The Burnstein-controlled Consolidated News Service was bumped in favor of the Partnership-allied Nationwide News Service. While the Sicilians had always liked Burnstein, they firmly let him know that he could accept this or he could choose to fight it. Abe could still operate his handbooks, but the wire service itself was now theirs. Burnstein agreed to their terms, and in return received a monthly share of the profits, sort of a pension. It was the final stake in the heart of the organization known as the Purple Gang. They now were little more than a small group of Jewish racketeers running handbooks and penny-ante extortion in Detroit's North End.[15]

Despite the loss of the wire-service, Abe Burnstein himself was still sitting pretty, and his legitimate businesses and high-stakes gambling provided a handsome stake to begin what would be his continuing quest to get younger brother Raymond out of prison. Joe Burnstein had thousands of dollars coming in from his oil company investments. Joey was the treasurer of what was now called the Garfield Oil and Gas Corporation, named after its president, Sam Garfield. Joey Burnstein admitted in an interview that the corporation was a closed company, meaning that no stock would be sold to the public. The one and only stockholder was Joe's younger brother Izzy.[16] Original Purple gangster "One-Arm Mike" Gelfand now owned and operated the popular Famous Graceland Ballroom in Ogemaw County.

Those Purples who didn't have lucrative legitimate business interests were forced to scuffle on the streets of Detroit for the criminal scraps left behind by the Partnership, and the results weren't pretty. Abe Burnstein's old chauffeur Jack Budd, for example, received a life sentence in prison after being convicted of killing an innocent bystander during a botched stick-up in September 1935.[17]

While awaiting trial for violating federal tax laws, Harry Fleisher and his two brothers moved west to Albion, Michigan, ostensibly to help their father in his scrap yard business (and to give themselves an air of respectability for when their trial came around the following spring.) Louis Fleisher, however, had different ideas.

With the Purples dropping like flies in Detroit proper, Lou decided that the bigger money lay in far-flung central Michigan. Smaller towns such as Albion and Jackson had never dealt with anyone quite like the Purple Gang. Beginning in the late summer of 1935, Lou Fleisher pulled off a series of spectacular burglaries and safe-crackings in central Michigan. In addition to his brother-in-law Sam "Fats" Burnstein, Fleisher was assisted by three members of the Hamtramck-based "Lizard Gang"; John Godlewski, Chester Tutha, and Robert Deptla. The Lizards were a primarily Polish crew that specialized in bank robbery and safe-cracking.

Fleisher used his father's Albion junkyard as a base of operations; it was here that he utilized his considerable automotive expertise to customize a 1935 Graham-Paige sedan into a supreme criminal vehicle. The car's V8 engine was fitted with a supercharger in order to outrun any possible pursuers. The back seat and center post had been removed to make room for large safes, which could be easily loaded into the rear of the car by a small ramp that was pulled out from underneath the vehicle. The safes could then be wheeled aboard with a hand truck. The rear window could be taken out and replaced with a solid steel shield, which was thoughtfully equipped with gun ports. Steel tire guards, extending to just above the street, protected the wheels from being shot out by police bullets. The car was also equipped with double rotating license plates that could be turned by hand.[18]

Despite their efforts to remain inconspicuous, the Fleishers and their associates stood out in small-town Albion like a pod of whales in a trout pond. Quite a bit of whispering circulated in the Fleishers' neighborhood that members of the Purple Gang were in town; after years of reading about big city gangsters in the newspapers and watching them on the silver screen, the citizens of Albion now got to see them in living color. The Purples were known to, among other places, frequent the Streetcar Tavern on Austin Avenue and repair to the Bohm Theatre every Sunday to catch a movie (and possibly plot new capers.)[19]

For several months, everything went smoothly for the gang (they shrewdly refrained from hitting targets in their home base of Albion.) The Jackson Police Department, meanwhile, would later suspect them of around fifty burglaries in their area during this period. On April 15, 1936, however, the law finally caught up with Harry Fleisher. He, his brother Sam, Jack Stein, and Jack Selbin (the late Ziggie's stepfather) were convicted of violating the Internal Revenue Law and sentenced to serve eight years in federal prison. In addition, each man was fined $20,000.[20]

Almost a month after his brothers were convicted, on the night of May 11, Lou Fleisher and his crew were pulling a job at the Isabell Seed Company in Jackson when a night clerk saw them rolling a safe into the Graham Paige and interrupted them. When the clerk tried to investigate, Lou ran him off with a sawed-off shotgun. Two weeks after that, on May 30, witnesses spotted them hitting the Riverside Packing Company in Jackson. The Fleisher crew had made off with a safe and a mere $1,500. A day or so later, the Graham Paige was found along the Kalamazoo River. It was duly noted that Lou Fleisher's garage was right across the street. Raiding that place and Fleisher's home as well, police found burglary tools and a large weapons cache.

Lou Fleisher, Fats Burnstein, and the wives of both were arrested in Albion in the early morning hours of June 3. Burnstein was turned loose when witnesses failed to identify him, but he was taken to Detroit and charged with the August 1935 hijacking of a truck loaded with pharmaceuticals. Fleisher eventually made bail, and the State Police offered him leniency if he would return to Detroit and convince Chester Tutha, John Godlewski, and Robert Deptla to surrender. After somewhat agreeing to the deal, Fleisher eventually reported back that he had been unsuccessful.

By September, the charges against Lou Fleisher in the Riverside Packing Company safecracking case had been dropped due to a lack of evidence. The Jackson County Prosecutor then convinced the Albion authorities to charge Fleisher with possessing unregistered firearms, burglary tools, and receiving and aiding the concealment of a stolen car. The prosecutor offered Lou immunity if he would roll over on his pals. The Purple mobster's response was firm, "I have nothing to say. I'd rather be in jail than in a coffin." When Lou appeared in court on September 14, his lawyer managed to get the stolen car charge dropped and the judge allowed him to post $5000 bail. Fleisher promptly disappeared into Detroit and, not surprisingly, failed to appear in court the following May.[21]

BY THE SUMMER OF 1936, perhaps the most notorious remaining street-level Purple gangster was twenty-five year old Harry Millman. Believed by police to have been one of the killers of Abe Axler and Eddie Fletcher, Millman had seen his star rise in the Detroit underworld since their gruesome one-way ride three years earlier. Far from being a low-profile criminal, Harry and his small crew of gangsters fought the Partnership at every turn.

Millman was noted for violently invading Mafia protected-prostitution houses on a weekly basis. He and his pals would beat up the customers while stealing money from both them and the proprietors. Millman's high-octane visits were akin to a hurricane tearing through a peaceful fishing village every week, and caused business at the brothels to drop off to near nothing. Time and time again the Partnership complained to Abe Burnstein about Millman's antics, and Burnstein promised repeatedly that he could control the upstart mobster. And because of the Partnership's inaction on his forays, he became even bolder. Harry Millman was a throwback to the Purple Gang's heyday of the late 1920s; swaggering around with his chin out, dressing in expensive suits and club hopping around the city.[22]

Around the time Lou Fleisher returned to the city, Millman began a well-publicized feud with Sicilian mobster Joe Bommarito, who was the Partnership's unofficial liaison to the Purple Gang. A native of St. Louis, Bommarito had cut his teeth in that city's Russo Gang and fled to Detroit in the wake of a violent gang war. Although he stood only 5'6", Bommarito was tough-as-nails and had a reputation as a ruthless killer. Sometime in his youth he had sustained knife scars on his right cheek, which damaged the facial muscles and resulted in a drooping right eyelid. In the years since, Bommarito had been acquitted of killing radio muckraker Jerry Buckley and now assisted the Purples in a number of labor rackets. He also ran Local 299 of the Teamsters and Truck Driver's Union, of which youthful labor organizer and future Teamsters president James R. Hoffa was a member.

One night in the autumn of 1936, Bommarito and some of his crew were in Sam Finazzo's saloon, located at the corner of Eighth and West Fort streets. In walked Harry Millman and a few of his pals. Millman was already drunk, and soon began snarling at Bommarito. It wasn't long before the two squared off for a fistfight. While their two respective groups watched, Millman and Bommarito punched, kicked, and pummeled each other mercilessly, laying waste to Finazzo's bar in the process. Nearly a half-hour later, both men were bloodied but Millman was still standing, with Bommarito unconscious at his feet. Millman gave him a final kick in the ribs and then stumbled out of the place, silently followed by his crew.[23]

It was considered a fatal sin to hit or disrespect a "made man" like Joe Bommarito. Millman, however, seemed unconcerned and continued to instigate his nemesis. Not long after the barfight, Bommarito was reclining in an East Side barber's chair with a hot towel over his face. Millman quietly entered, lifted the towel, and spat in Bommarito's face. He then beat a quick retreat before the Sicilian gangster could recover. After this latest humiliation, Harry Millman was officially on his own, as Abe Burnstein cut him loose and disavowed any responsibility for the foolhardy mobster.[24]

By this time, Millman and his crew had thrown themselves into labor racketeering, hiring their services to the side that paid highest. He was suspected of taking part in the Newton Packing Company strike in March 1937. A labor dispute had resulted in the union's going on strike, and Millman, Louis Fleisher, and their goons stormed the plant when the company-appointed "scabs" reported for work. During the vicious melee, many were injured by baseball bats, bricks, and two-by-four boards. In the end, the company signed the new contract.

Millman's beatdown of Joe Bommarito during the Finazzo bar fight had signed his death warrant. Harry's repeated shakedowns of Partnership-controlled brothels, handbooks, and clubs were icing on the cake. He was also rumored to be muscling in on the numbers games in both Detroit and Hamtramck along with Simon Axler, cousin of the late Abe Axler.

On the evening of August 28, 1937, Harry Millman had dinner and danced with Harry Fleisher's wife Hattie at the Ten Forty Club, located downtown at 1040 Wayne Street. The Ten Forty was owned by Purple mobster Max Silk and was a favorite hangout of the boys. Not long after midnight, Millman saw Mrs. Fleisher into a cab, while he stayed on to have a few more drinks.

At 3 o'clock in the morning, Millman stepped out the front door and waited for the doorman, thirty-nine year old William W. Holmes, to retrieve his LaSalle coupe. As Holmes slid into the driver's seat and turned the ignition key, the LaSalle exploded with such force that most of downtown Detroit felt the blast. The doorman, his legs nearly severed, was blown into the car's rear windshield and wedged there. Holmes was miraculously still alive when the fire department arrived, but died just as he got to Receiving Hospital. The poor man had the dubious distinction of being the first Detroiter to lose his life to a mob-related car bombing. DPD forensic expert William Cavers later determined that ten sticks of dynamite had been placed under the hood and wired to a spark plug. The explosion was so powerful that windows of the adjoining buildings were shattered by the concussion; the hood of Millman's LaSalle was later found on the *roof* of the five-story building that housed the nightclub.

At the sight of his flaming car, Millman immediately hightailed it up to Hamtramck. After a few more drinks to calm his nerves, he turned himself in to police. Millman nervously tore off and twisted little pieces of paper as smirking detectives showed him pieces of his demolished vehicle. Harry feigned perplexity to cover up his obvious fear. "I can't understand this. I haven't any enemies left over from the old days and I'm not doing anything now that would make anybody want to get me. If they wanted to get me they could get me easy enough. I'm on the streets all the time and I never carry a gun." Millman elaborated, "I'm as legitimate as the next guy. All I do is run a few handbooks on 12th Street, but the police keep raiding them. They're making a goat out of me, kicking me around like a football. It's getting to be a nightmare."

Detective Sergeant Harold Branton remarked about Millman, "His number is up and it's only a question of time. He has kept himself on the streets with his gun and his fists. He is going to die one of these days and die violently."[25]

Soon after the failed bomb attempt Harry Millman, stoked on a dangerous combination of rye whiskey and irrational rage, sprayed a Partnership-protected brothel with gunfire and sent its occupants running for their lives. After he sobered up, Harry fled first to Cincinnati and then to the East Coast. Upon his return a month or so later, Millman began keeping a much lower profile and stopped club hopping around the city's nightspots. Millman now spent most evenings drinking very heavily at Boesky's, a combination restaurant, bar, and delicatessen located at the northeast corner of 12th and Hazelwood streets. In addition to the booze, Millman was using even more heroin than usual. Most hotels in the city would not accept the hunted gangster, for fear of him being gunned down on the premises. At those few that did, Harry often just left his bags in his car because he knew he would have to leave first thing in the morning.[26]

Sometime in the third week of November, ace *Detroit News* crime reporter Jack Carlisle conducted an off-the-record interview with Millman. After a review of Harry's career and the car bombing, the talk turned fatalistic. Carlisle asked Harry if he would write out an affidavit that named his killers, which would only be opened in the event of his murder. Millman just laughed, clapped Carlisle on the back, and called him "a real kibitzer."[27]

Mere days later, on the afternoon of November 24, Harry Millman prepared for his evening by dressing in an impressive brown ensemble before visiting a neighborhood barbershop for a shave and a haircut. By 8 o'clock that evening, Harry was at his usual post inside Boesky's with Hymie Cooper and Sam Gross. A little over an hour later, Cooper and Gross left to go see a movie. Millman stayed on and sipped at his favorite drink, rye whiskey and Coca-Cola.

Looking around Boesky's, Harry saw quite a few people in the bar indulging in some pre-holiday cheer. The restaurant section of Boesky's was connected to the bar by a small archway and had a modest crowd of about 40 to 50 customers. The bar's door opened onto 12th Street while the restaurant's door faced out into the corner. From his table, Harry could see everyone entering and leaving the place. Cooper and Gross returned around midnight and joined Millman at his table. Harry had two good-looking ladies at his side, and the group settled in for some partying.

At one o'clock, Millman got up and weaved his way through the crowded barroom in order to get fresh drinks for the party at the table. As he stood at the far end of the bar waiting for the bartender to refill the drinks, Harry drained the last of his rye-and-Coke and idly chatted with twenty-four year old Harry Shulak, a Toledo furrier who was in town for the holidays.

Two men, clad in expensive overcoats and wide-brimmed fedoras, walked in the 12th Street door and moved through the crowd toward where Millman and Shulak were standing at the bar. His mind hindered by too much alcohol and distracted by the young furrier, Harry's warning system appears to have failed him as he either didn't recognize the newcomers or failed to notice them at all. The well-dressed pair sidled up to the bar behind Shulak and ordered straight shots of whiskey. After downing their shots, the two men stepped back from the bar and whipped out pistols; a .38 caliber revolver and a pair of .45 caliber automatics. Millman may have had just enough time to recognize the danger before a bullet punched into his forehead and scattered his thoughts forever.

As Millman collapsed to the floor and the crowd around him panicked, he was quickly struck by a fusillade of nine more rounds that ripped whatever life remained from his body. Harry Shulak crumpled as well, having been wounded by stray shots. The killers then zeroed their guns on Millman's table, wounding both Sam Gross and Hymie Cooper as they dove for cover. Forty-two year old bystander Abe Betensky got a slug in his back after wandering into the line of fire on his way back from the bathroom. The loud gunshots sent the customers stampeding for the doors. The two shooters melted into the fleeing masses and jumped into a waiting maroon Ford sedan, which sped them east on Hazelwood Street to a clean getaway.

Police admitted that there were so many potential motives for Harry Millman's murder that they did not know where to begin. The shootings had happened so quickly that only the most meager descriptions of the suspects were obtained. One was described as "about 28 or 29 years old. Five feet seven inches tall. Weighs about 150 pounds. Dark complexion. Wore dark clothes. Had a mustache." The other killer was said to be about three inches taller and twenty pounds heavier. Inspector Paul Wencel opined that the shooters were local gangsters, as they obviously knew Millman and his two pals by sight. The description of the mustachioed gunman jibed very closely with Jack Licavoli, who had fled to Ohio some time before with the most of his fellow River Gang mobsters. Nevertheless, Licavoli was not charged.[28]

Police eventually found out that the Michigan license plate number of the getaway car was issued to a man who gave his name as "Joseph Cohen" and what turned out to be a non-existent New York City address. There the trail ended. Two days after the attack, Harry Millman was buried in Workmen's Circle Cemetery at Gratiot and 14 Mile roads. He was only 26 years old at the time of his death. On December 11, police discovered the maroon Ford sedan used by the killers parked along the 3700 block of Richton Street. Two finger-prints were found on the driver's side door, which were then "accidentally" obliterated after the door was removed for evidence. Blood stains were also found in the rear seat; police guessed that one of the gunmen had been injured. On December 16, Sam Gross died of the gunshot wounds he had received in Boesky's. All the other injured bystanders eventually recovered.[29]

While the double homicide remains officially unsolved, the consensus of Detroit police and newsmen at the time was that the Partnership brought in two out-of-town gangsters to kill Harry Millman, either from the old Licavoli crew in Ohio or from New York. Fourteen years later, a new twist on the Mill-man case came out of Brooklyn. Burton Turkus, Assistant District Attorney of Kings County, would hint in a book that the killers were two members of Murder, Incorporated whom he had successfully prosecuted; Harry "Happy" Maione and Harry "Pep" Strauss. Both men would have been presumably selected because of their reputations as two of Murder, Inc.'s most prolific hitmen, and because as out-of-towners, they wouldn't be recognized by the victim or potential witnesses. Neither Maione nor Strauss was charged with the Millman/Gross homicides; both men were convicted of other murders and executed.[30]

It was left to one of Harry Millman's friends to eulogize him thusly in a 1983 interview;[31]

"It was very simple. He was a big, handsome Jewish guy - God, he was a good-looking bastard, big and handsome and well-dressed - and he was knocking off whorehouses and he didn't know that the whorehouses at that period were protected by the Dago Mob...I forget the name, but there was a very fancy blind pig on 12th Street, and he was at the bar having a good time with some people and in walked two Dagos and shot the shit out of him."

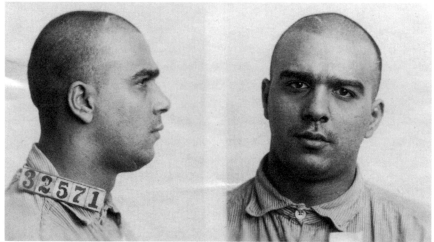

James "Jack" Licavoli, with his cousins Pete and Yonnie, smuggled liquor across the Detroit River. In November 1937, Licavoli would be suspected by police of participating in the Millman/Gross homicides at Boesky's. He is pictured here in 1929 upon his arrival at Leavenworth. *NARA.*

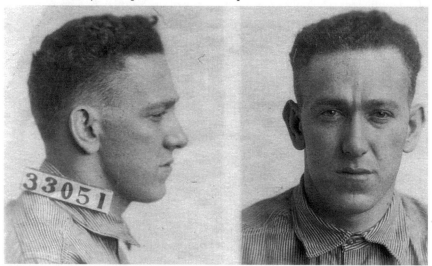

Harry Sutton was a so-called "Yorkie" and joined the Purple Gang in the late 1920s. He served prison time in Leavenworth with Abe Axler, Eddie Fletcher, and Irving Milberg. In June 1934, he was shot and wounded by Purple Gang mobster Harry Millman while unsuccessfully trying to break up a fight between him and bar owner George "Eddie" Doran. *NARA.*

Harry Millman's bombed-out LaSalle as it appeared on the morning of August 29, 1937 in front of the Ten Forty Club in downtown Detroit. Millman's enemies had wired dynamite to the starter, and the bomb killed 39-year old doorman Willie Holmes when he turned the car's ignition. *Chriss Lyon Collection*

The scene outside Boesky's at 12th and Hazelwood streets after Harry Millman's murder on Thanksgiving Eve 1937. Sam Gross was also fatally wounded, and three other bystanders received lesser wounds. *Walter Reuther Library.*

Frank McKay was a wealthy, powerful politician who virtually controlled Michigan's Republican Party for two decades. McKay colluded with a handful of senior Purple mobsters to allow them to produce alcohol legally after Repeal, while they in turn watched his back and helped to enforce his will. *Author's collection.*

ATONEMENT

he police and press declared that the Purple Gang was officially defunct with the November 1937 murder of Harry Millman. "BULLETS WRITE GANG'S LONG OVERDUE OBITUARY" was the headline for *News* crime reporter Jack Carlisle's article on the incident.[1] Individual Purples were still around, but they had no real organizational presence after Millman's murder. Ironically, they may have even worked together with the Mafia to eliminate Millman, who was jeopardizing their long peaceful relations. While Harry had been blazing a self-destructive trail across Detroit's underworld in 1937, four prominent members of the Purple Gang were serving some of the hardest prison time imaginable.

THE ISLAND IN THE San Francisco Bay was initially named *La Isla de los Alcatraces* (Island of the Pelicans) by the Spaniards who discovered it in the 18th century. Alcatraz Island was located a mile off the coast of the city of San Francisco and was home to a series of military barracks for much of the 19th century. By the end of Prohibition, the place had been converted in a super-penitentiary for the most violent, dangerous federal criminals. Those few Public Enemy bandits who survived the so-called "War on Crime" were among the first inmates incarcerated there. In August 1936, after brief sentences at Leavenworth, Harry Fleisher, Sam Fleisher, Jack Stein and Jack Selbin arrived on the island to finish their terms resulting from the Federal Avenue distillery case. Unlike Michigan prisons like Jackson and Marquette, or even the federal hellhole at Leavenworth, life at Alcatraz was exceptionally hard. The prison's operators did not pretend to be in the business of rehabilitation, as Alcatraz was specifically designed to break its prisoners, if they could be broken.[2]

After being searched inside-and-out, the four Purples were assigned clothes and single-man cells in the main cell house. The only amenities in their nine foot-by-five foot cells were a drop-down cot, table, washbasin, and toilet.

For nearly ten hours each day, from the 4:50 p.m. lockdown to the 6:30 a.m. bell, the four Purples saw no one but passing guards. After the morning head count, the prisoners marched to the mess hall and ate breakfast in silence. Since Alcatraz Penitentiary had first opened in 1934, Warden James A. Johnston had implemented a strict policy of silence. Inmates were forbidden from speaking to anyone but prison personnel. Prisoners worked in silence over the course of their day, but were permitted to talk and smoke during their mid-morning and mid-afternoon breaks. After supper at 4:25 p.m., the prisoners were locked down for the night. A total of thirteen head counts were taken over the course of an average day. On weekends, the rules were relaxed a bit. Inmates could congregate and socialize for two hours in the afternoon as they exercised in the yard or worked at their chosen hobbies.[3]

Any violation of the rules, such as talking out of turn or not reacting in a split second to an order from a guard, resulted in the prisoner being dragged to "The Hole", the pitch-black isolation cells in D Block.[4] In addition, D Block housed slightly larger cells for those prisoners who had broken the rules in an especially egregious fashion. If the prisoner resisted, the guards clubbed him silly with their "gas billies," metal batons that doubled as tear gas guns. One prisoner who had the temerity to attack Warden Johnston was left a "drooling wreck" by these multi-purpose truncheons.

In a move specifically designed to ensure that no inmate was able to use money to gain advantage over other inmates, Warden Johnston banned commissaries. Cigarettes, a classic medium of exchange in most prisons, were provided to each inmate free-of-charge from tobacco dispensers strategically placed around the cell house. Prisoners shaved three times a week in their cells, from blades that were passed through the bars to them and then recollected by the guards. Shower water was deliberately run hot, to keep any escape-minded inmates from acclimatizing to the cold waters that surrounded the island. Prisoners did enjoy better-than-average fare in the mess hall; their three meals averaged 3,100-3,600 calories per day compared to the standard 2,100 in other prisons. This was mainly to alleviate food rioting and also to add extra pounds to prisoners so they would be less apt to outrun the guards.[5]

Some of the more famous prisoners at Alcatraz in 1937 included Chicago crime boss Al Capone, Machine Gun Kelly, and bank robbers like Dock Barker, Roy Gardner, and Alvin "Creepy" Karpis (the latter had arrived on Alcatraz at the same time as the Purples.) One familiar face to the Purples was Detroit gangster Elmer Macklin, who was doing time for counterfeiting. Macklin was a former member of the late Chester LaMare's Hamtramck crew; in fact, he had been tried and acquitted of LaMare's murder in 1932.[6]

Any news that Selbin, Stein, and the Fleisher brothers got of the outside world was controlled with an iron fist. Newspapers were forbidden. All magazines were a minimum of seven months old. All their mail, incoming and outgoing, was meticulously censored; even the most off-handed reference to fellow criminals or criminal business was removed. Most outside news that the Purples were able to glean came from arriving prisoners. The only visitors allowed were immediate family members, and they had to write Warden Johnston for permission. Convicted felons were prohibited, which ruled out Lou Fleisher, among others.[7]

In addition to the rigid prison regulations, the four Purples had to deal with the usual hazards of prison life amongst their fellow criminals. The threat of violence lurked around every corner. Just eight weeks before the Purples arrived on Alcatraz, a Texas bank robber named James Lucas unsuccessfully tried to stab Al Capone to death with a pair of scissors in the prison barber shop.[8] The four Detroit gangsters handled the pressure cooker-like atmosphere in their own way. Some prisoners could not deal with the strain of "The Rock" and genuinely lost it. One inmate, while chopping old tires in the prison's Navy mat shop, suddenly hacked off the fingers of his left hand. He then calmly handed the hatchet to the shocked man next to him and asked him to do his right hand in kind. After some time in both the infirmary and the Hole, the disturbed prisoner was returned to the general population after being ruled not quite insane enough for transfer elsewhere.[9]

Suicides were not uncommon. Others tried to escape, but most either died in the process or wished they had. The freezing waters of the bay and the submachine gun wielding guards proved formidable opponents. One potential escapee, Joe Bowers, scaled a fence in clear view of a guard tower. Bowers ignored two warning shots and was killed by a third, causing some observers to wonder if the man had deliberately committed suicide-by-guard. One inmate, who had spent a mere sixteen months on Alcatraz, when asked by a reporter what it was like to serve time there said only, "It's hell."[10]

It was in this environment that Harry Fleisher, Sam Fleisher, Jack Selbin, and Jack Stein existed while what was left of their gang struggled to survive back in Detroit.

AFTER LOSING CONTROL of the racing wire service for Detroit back in 1935, the two dozen or so remaining Jewish gangsters who fell under the banner of the Purple Gang found that it was best to work hand-in-hand with the Mafia rather than fight them. Harry Millman had been the only significant

Purple to buck this trend. With money trickling in from the numbers, dope, and extortion rackets, the old Purple Gang began to get more involved in labor racketeering in the late 1930s. As one of the chief world centers for manufactured goods, Detroit was also a hotbed of organized labor. As in other American cities, organized crime soon found their way into the trade unions.

After infiltrating the unions, the gangsters would disguise themselves under euphemistic titles such as "delegates", "organizers", or "overseers." Not only did the mob get a piece of the union's dues, they received kickbacks from individual workers (payoffs in exchange for good job placement and/or promotions), as well as extortion payments from business/factory owners themselves. This latter operation basically said that unless you pay and/or scratch my back in some way, our guys are not showing up for work. Such extortion could often be carried out over the telephone. A conversation such as this may ensue;

> *Boss: Hello.*
> *Gangster: Got some news for you. You may not like it, but you gotta do it. We're sending over some new people to help you out.*
> *Boss: No thanks. I got more than enough men right now.*
> *Gangster: Don't try to be a hard guy, pally. Ask your rep about us. We mean business. You're taking those two guys on.*
> *Boss: Look, I understand that Hesh and Meyer are very good barbers, but I just don't have room for them. I'll run my own business.*
> *Gangster: Look here asshole. We'll run your business for you. Those two guys don't start work tomorrow; you're a dead man. Got it?"*

There was little the law-abiding business owner could do; he had to either obey or see his life's work ruined and/or have some form of violent physical harm visited upon him.

Upon his September 1936 return to Detroit from Albion, Michigan, Louis Fleisher entered labor racketeering with an old associate of the Purples, Jack Ekelman. The thirty-five year old Ekelman had been a youthful apprentice of Saw Still Gang alky cookers Jake Trager and Sam Abramson back in the early 1920s, and had even been present when Trager was bumped off on Hastings Street in March 1923. Since then, Ekelman had been operating largely behind the scenes as a labor racketeer. In 1933, Jack was instrumental in organizing the Jewish Barbers Association and acted as its business manager. The union was ostensibly created to provide benefits for Jewish barbers in the North End of Detroit.

Ekelman's new organization soon came into conflict with the larger Master Barbers Association. Jack saw an opportunity to forcibly muscle into a legitimate trade union and recruited a handful of Purples to help him do it. Due to vast depletion in the Purple Gang's ranks, Ekelman called upon East Side mobster Joe Bommarito for assistance. Jack pitched his plan by explaining that if they muscled in on the Master Barbers they would gain control over most, if not all, major barbershops in Detroit. Once the takeover was complete, Ekelman would become the new reconstituted union's president while Bommarito received healthy share of the monthly dues. It sounded good to the Sicilian gangster, who gave the Purple racketeer the go-ahead to get started.

In tactics very similar to those used by the Purples a decade earlier in the Cleaners and Dyers War, Ekelman and several of Bommarito's thugs stormed the next meeting of the Master Barbers and explained to them that they would now be combined with the Jewish Barbers Association. The union officers knew the drill and, with an air of weary resignation, handed over virtually everything to Ekelman that night. The Master Barbers Association was even forced to terminate its membership in the American Federation of Labor (AFL).

Frank X. Martel, longtime president of the Detroit Federation of Labor, exhorted the city's barbers not be coerced into Jack Ekelman's union. Like the cleaners and dyers of old, the barbers were unable to resist. Those that did were subjected to the usual litany of terror tactics such as stink bombs, bricks through windows, severe beatings, etc. For a few years, this arrangement proved highly lucrative to all parties involved. By 1936, however, Ekelman decided that the Mafia had "served their purpose" and stopped paying Joe Bommarito his monthly share of the dues. Bommarito was the wrong man to cheat. Almost immediately, Jack got word of a plot against his life and fled town for an extended vacation.

Upon his return to Detroit, Ekelman figured to become a sudden dead man unless he found a powerful friend. The overextended labor racketeer found his would-be savior in Louis Fleisher. By early 1937, Fleisher was making his own inroads into the city's meat unions. Lou specifically gained a foothold in the Kosher Meat Bosses Union, Kosher Meat Cutters Union, and Kosher Barbers Union. Ekelman, for his part, sought to reorganize the Master Barbers Association that he had left behind months earlier.

This newfound alliance was a problem from the start. Ekelman actually hated Fleisher, and the feeling was mutual. The pair thought they could put their differences aside in order to work together fleecing the meat cutting and barbers' unions. Police later estimated that Fleisher was making $2400 a month from his various labor rackets. In May 1937, Fleisher jumped the bond in his pending weapons and burglary tools charges. On his way out of town, Lou borrowed $500 from Joe Bommarito and promised to pay him back when he got a chance; the money was to be used to retain a lawyer for his Albion criminal cases. Fleisher also arranged for Ekelman to send his $50 a week union salary to his New York City hideout.

Under normal circumstances, the desk-bound union delegate Jack Ekelman would not have said "Boo!" to a hardened killer like Lou Fleisher, but once he was out of town, Ekelman promptly began to undermine his partner. Lou never received his salary. Even more serious, Ekelman told Bommarito that he would repay Fleisher's $500 loan. Jack probably offered this in order to regain the East Side mobster's confidence. When he did not turn up with the cash, Ekelman was threatened by the East Sider to pay up or else. Backed by Sam Millman and Hymie Cooper, Jack Ekelman then went to Joe Bommarito's office and lit into him, loudly berating the gangster. Bommarito sat through his tirade, and then quietly asked Millman and Cooper to wait outside the office. Ekelman's bravado left the room with his bodyguards, and he made frantic apologies and offered to pay Bommarito the money he owed him immediately.

In an effort to raise this cash, Ekelman went to Dave Krause, one of Louis Fleisher's collectors. Jack told Krause to give his collections directly to him and not Fleisher. The collector eventually told his boss of Ekelman's scheming. Despite the warrants out for his arrest, Fleisher returned to Detroit in late March 1938 to confront his troublesome former partner. Ekelman made an excuse about being drunk and not remembering what he had said. After sitting down with Joe Bommarito and finding out the truth, Fleisher decided that the duplicitous Ekelman was going to die.[11]

In the late afternoon of April 19, 1938, Jack Ekelman told his wife he was going to meet Louis Fleisher. After picking up Charles Leiter at his home at 2694 Cortland Street, the two started for the town of Mt. Clemens, where the meet was supposed to take place. Sometime that night, the labor racketeer eventually did meet up with Fleisher, but not the way he would have liked to. Ekelman permanently vanished, never to be heard from again. Jack's mud-splattered car was found the next day parked in front of 7 Sibley Street in Detroit.

When interviewed by Detective Sergeant Roy Pendergrass, Charlie Leiter stated that he did not know they were going to meet Fleisher. He and Ekelman had intended to meet with the owners of several area slaughterhouses that day in order to organize them into a union, Charlie claimed. Only four had shown up, however, and Leiter said that the two of them then spent the evening drowning their disappointment in booze. Leiter claimed to have passed out in the car and awoken while being driven south on Gratiot Avenue. Ekelman let him out, and that was the last time he saw him.

Police recalled the similar disappearance, four years previous, of Henry Shorr. And like the Shorr case, the police came up against a brick wall in searching for the missing Ekelman. Molly Ekelman kept a tearful, futile vigil for her husband Jack at their home at 3763 W. Grand Boulevard, "We had been married 16 years. Always I have known where Jack was. Every hour of the day he kept me posted. He called me at 4 o'clock, April 19th. He said he was going to Mt. Clemens on some business and would be home about 9 o'clock. That's the last I heard of him." [12]

Late on the evening of Wednesday, April 27, the Highland Park Police Department got a tip that Louis Fleisher was in the immediate vicinity. Three detectives pulled Fleisher's car over at the intersection of Second and Highland avenues. As detectives approached the vehicle, Lou's wife Nellie jumped out and darted into a nearby tailor shop. The cops saw her toss a large gun behind the counter. The weapon she attempted to hide was a Colt .38 Super automatic that had not only been modified to fire fully automatic but also featured a specially devised 30-round magazine. Essentially, Lou Fleisher was packing a weapon that would not be available to his fellow gangsters for many years; a pistol that spat bullets like a machine gun.

Lou and Nellie Fleisher were promptly taken into custody, as was a young passenger who gave his name as Jack Sherwood. The three were thoroughly questioned about the disappearance of Jack Ekelman a week earlier. When the Fleishers' Highland Park apartment was searched, the police discovered an arsenal that would have made the Wild Bunch blanch. Neatly stacked in a trunk in the Fleisher apartment were a Luger P08 automatic fitted with a 32-round drum magazine and a long-barreled Luger LP08 that was also fitted with a 32-round drum; both Lugers had been modified to fire fully automatic. Also discovered were a silencer-fitted Mauser C96 automatic pistol, a silencer-fitted Colt .22 automatic, a S&W .32 revolver, four more custom-made silencers for automatic pistols in calibers ranging from .22 to .45, brass knuckles, a tear gas gun and shells, five hundred rounds of ammunition and extra magazines for the automatics. An FBI spokesman estimated that it was "the biggest gangster arsenal ever found in the Middle West." Detroit Police forensic technician James Payne later described the pistols as the "most deadly weapons known to man."

Police also found a pair of muddy boots in the apartment. Remembering Jack Ekelman's mud-slathered car when it was found, they braced Lou

Fleisher about the footwear. Fleisher explained he got the boots dirty at his father-in-law's place out in the country. Lou sounded eerily like his brother Harry saying that the bloodstains found in his Buick after Henry Shorr's disappearance were from a bloody nose.

While incarcerated at the Highland Park jail, Nellie Fleisher vehemently complained that she and her husband were being served non-Kosher meals and threatened to set fire to the place in protest. Forty-eight hours after her arrest, she tried to do just that. During the ruckus, her husband and Sherwood had quickly loosened the screws around their windows in what turned out to be a futile attempt to escape. The cops believed Mrs. Fleisher set the fire to cover for an attempted jailbreak.

Police intensively grilled Lou Fleisher and Jack Sherwood. The latter claimed to have lived in Detroit for 10 years, but he did not know basic streets or neighborhoods. A fingerprint check soon revealed that Jack Sherwood was really Sidney Markman, a 21-year old New York gangster on the run for murdering a Brooklyn poultry dealer named Isadore Frank some months previous. Markman was a friend of Lou's brother-in-law, and he had asked Fleisher to keep an eye on the kid and give him a job. When pressed with this new information, Markman blurted, "Yeah, I killed him. So what?"

Fleisher tried to get his young accomplice to take the rap for the trunk full of guns, so he would avoid extradition to New York and the electric chair, not to mention taking Fleisher himself off ground zero. The police were not fooled, as they charged both Fleishers and Markman with violating the National Firearms Act (NFA) by possessing unregistered/untaxed machine guns and firearm silencers.[13]

When the trio finally went to trial a year later, they were nailed on all counts. Sidney Markman, who had been convicted of the Isadore Frank murder two months before, returned to death row at New York's Sing Sing Prison. He would die in the electric chair on January 18, 1940. Nellie Fleisher got 10 years in a federal detention house. Lou Fleisher got the book thrown at him in the form of a 30-year sentence in federal prison; five years for each pistol and the silencers plus a $3,000 fine for each count. After a two-year stay at Leavenworth, Lou would become inmate #574 at Alcatraz Federal Penitentiary.[14]

FOR NEARLY SEVEN YEARS, Purple Gang mobster Irving Milberg had toiled away in Marquette Prison with Ray Burnstein and Harry Keywell. With all their appeals maxed out, it seemed that the trio would be spending the rest of their lives inside for the Collingwood Manor Massacre. In September 1938, Milberg underwent an operation to remove a painful intestinal obstruction. During the operation, the obstruction burst and peritonitis set in. Irving Milberg died at the age of thirty-five on September 29, a week after the botched operation. He was interred in Ferndale's Machpelah Cemetery, just two graves over from Charles "The Professor" Auerbach, who had succumbed to pneumonia on May 19, 1935.[15]

BY THE TIME Lou Fleisher was sent to prison in the spring of 1939, both Joseph and Isadore Burnstein had left Michigan for warmer climes. Joe landed in a huge house in suburban Miami while Izzy went west and moved into a fancy Beverly Hills mansion. Both men continued to rake in huge profits from gambling and legitimate investments. Like his younger brothers, forty-eight year old Abe Burnstein was now a millionaire many times over. Abe lived in a luxury suite on the top floor of the Book-Cadillac Hotel in downtown Detroit when he wasn't traveling the Western Hemisphere on business and gambling ventures. The Burnsteins had come an extremely long way from their meager beginnings in Russia's Pale of Settlement some four decades earlier. One of Abe's deals, however, began unraveling that summer as the result of two seemingly unrelated incidents.

One of the many illegal handbooks in Detroit was the Great Lakes Mutual House, which operated out of an office in the Boulevard Building at 234 State Street in downtown Detroit. The bookie that ran the place was fifty-six year old Dr. Martin C. Robinson. The good doctor had used the Burnstein-controlled Consolidated News Service in years past and had remained connected to various Purples in the meantime. Jacob "Scotty" Silverstein, the bookkeeper whose purple sweater may well have given the Purple Gang their irresistible name, occasionally managed the books at the Great Lakes. Dr. Robinson was also a degenerate gambler whose heavy losses had accrued a sizeable debit to the Purples by the summer of 1939.

Robinson soon concocted a scheme to pay off his debt and make himself some nice change as well. The bookie convinced four low-ranking Purples, Sidney Cooper, Irving Feldman, Joe Holtzman, and Louis Jacobs, to rob his handbook. Ostensibly, everyone would benefit from the plan; the Purples would get the money they were owed and Dr. Robinson would collect on his anti-theft insurance policy. Around noon on Saturday, July 8, the Purple quartet made their move and stuck up Robinson for $2600 cash. As they exited the building into pedestrian traffic, the heisters attracted the attention of DPD Inspector Perry W. Meyers, who had just happened to be passing by on his lunch break. The inspector got the drop on the robbers and arrested them.

The four Purples were booked at the Ninth Precinct, located at the corner of Bethune and John R streets. For two decades, the Ninth had been ground zero in the Detroit Police Department's battles against the Purple Gang. Members of the gang had often been booked, questioned, and held there for varying degrees of time until they made bail. Almost exactly sixteen years earlier, Oakland Sugar House founder Isadore Cantor surrendered to police there after killing Frank Speed on Hastings Street. Six years after that, Irving Shapiro gouged out the eye of one of his fellow prisoners in one of the station's holding cells. After its central role in the Purple Gang's history, it was only fitting that one of the death blows of that organization would originate within the Ninth Precinct's walls.

Even though they had been caught red-handed, Dr. Robinson did not identify Cooper, Feldman, Holtzman, and Jacobs as the men who robbed him. Detectives Byron Farrish and Wilfred Brouillet were assigned to the case. After the line-up with the bandits, Scotty Silverstein appeared at the station and offered the two detectives $300 to reduce the charges of armed robbery to carrying concealed weapons. Farrish and Brouillet got in even deeper when their boss, Inspector Raymond Boettcher, instructed them to return the seized $2600 to Dr. Robinson. According to later testimony, Boettcher received a $1000 bribe to make this happen. Robinson, grateful for getting his money back under-the-table and still being able to collect on his robbery insurance, gave the detectives some of the cash as gratitude.

Word of these not-so-subtle shenanigans soon filtered out and triggered an Internal Affairs investigation of the DPD officers involved. Someone higher up the department's chain-of-command decided there were some things here that IA could not be allowed to find out and the investigation was abruptly terminated within just a week or so.[16] An even bigger boulder was about to fall on organized corruption in Detroit; it was teetering on an emotionally fragile secretary who worked for Dr. Robinson at his downtown handbook.

Janet MacDonald was a thirty-two year old Scottish émigré who lived an apparently happy domestic life with her electrician husband Emmett and eleven-year old daughter Pearl. In the mid-1930s, Janet had taken a job with the Great Lakes Mutual House handbook as an adding machine operator. Before long, she had entered into an extramarital affair with one of the handbook's runners. By the summer of 1939, Janet had been jilted by her lover and was edging closer to an emotional breakdown. Mrs. MacDonald's anguish culminated with deadly consequences a month after the botched robbery.

On Saturday, August 5, MacDonald sent lengthy letters to the editors of all three Detroit newspapers that detailed the inner workings of a massive city-wide gambling graft scheme. Janet's letters fingered numerous city and state officials as to how much and how often they were paid off. Her allegations reached right into the office of Detroit Mayor Richard W. Reading. After the letters were mailed and some time spent in an interior hell due her fragile emotional state, Janet MacDonald took not only her own life but the life of her 11-year-old daughter, Pearl.[17]

From a journalist's standpoint, Mrs. MacDonald's letters represented the investigative equivalent of an H-bomb blast. All three papers printed exposes and the public outrage over such blatant institutionalized corruption was tremendous. It was duly noted that MacDonald worked at the same handbook where the suspicious robbery had taken place in July. The bribe machinations in the aftermath of those busts were re-examined. A one-man grand jury was convened to look into corruption within the Detroit Police Department. It actually consisted of two men; fifty-nine year old Judge S. Homer Ferguson and Special Prosecutor Chester P. O'Hara. The Ferguson grand jury investigations cut a wide swath into the longtime graft relations between Detroit police, politicians, and gamblers.

The grand jury started with DPD Detectives Byron Farrish and Wilfred Brouillet. After being granted immunity for their testimony, the pair declared it was Inspector Raymond Boettcher who returned the robbery money to Dr. Martin Robinson. It eventually came out that Inspector Boettcher was responsible for distributing bribes to numerous police officials, including DPD Superintendent of Police Fred Frahm, who received a sizeable amount of cash every month in a clandestine meeting in the men's room of the DPD headquarters at 1300 Beaubien Street. Elmer "Buff" Ryan, longtime bagman for Detroit's illegal gaming community, was accused of supplying payoffs to the various politicians in the Detroit area.[18]

JUST AS THE Ferguson grand jury was gaining a good head of steam, the Purple Gang was forced to conduct some grisly intra-gang discipline.

In the five years since he had been convicted of Harry Gold's murder, Sam "The Gorilla" Davis had been uneventfully confined at the Ionia State Mental Hospital for the Criminally Insane. On October 30, 1939, Davis and two other inmates escaped from the hospital. The simian-like Purple gangster would never be heard from again.

Police later determined that after his successful break, The Gorilla went back to his old pals in Detroit for help. The Purples, currently being burnt by the heat generated by the grand jury investigation, were in no mood to be troubled by this noisome relic of the past. Nor was it forgotten that in the wake of his 1934 arrest that Davis had sung like the proverbial canary. It is believed that Sam Davis was murdered soon after his escape and his body discreetly disposed of, just like Henry Shorr and Jack Ekelman had been before him.[19]

JUDGE HOMER FERGUSON was relentless in his pursuit of the defendants. One Purple, years later, would refer to him merely as a "sonofabitch."[20] All throughout 1940, the corruption scandal dominated Detroit newspapers along with increasingly ominous wartime news from Europe and the Pacific. By August 1940, Judge Ferguson's charges named 156 participants in the conspiracy, including now former Detroit Mayor Richard Reading, his son/secretary Richard Jr., Abe and Joe Burnstein, Elmer Ryan, Pete Driscoll, T.J. Ryan, 74 police officers, Wayne County Prosecutor Duncan McCrea and his chief investigator Harry Colburn were all accused of splitting nearly $1,000,000 in profits from the handbooks every year.

That same month, the Burnstein brothers responded to their subpoenas to testify before the grand jury. Joey and Izzy Burnstein, deeply tanned and well-rested, were apprehended and extradited to Detroit. All three brothers told nothing of substance on the stand. Luck was with the Purple bosses as they once again escaped the law. Others were not as lucky. A total of 137 police, gambling, and political figures were indicted on charges of conspiracy to obstruct justice. Both Mayor Reading and his son would be convicted of taking $4000 monthly bribes in the scandal. Among many others, Superintendent of Police Fred Frahm would also be convicted of obstruction of justice. The Detroit Police Department underwent a major shakeup as police officials were fired, retired, or transferred. The trials resulting from the Ferguson grand jury would continue well into the 1950s.[21]

IN THE SPRING OF 1940, both Harry and Sam Fleisher had been transferred from Alcatraz Penitentiary to Leavenworth for a short stretch pending their release. After a brief jailhouse reunion with their brother Louis, both Fleishers were cut loose and sent back to the North End of Detroit. Harry became the so-called "street boss" of what was left of the old Purple Gang. Harry's new right hand man was Myron "Mike" Selik, who had been released from Jackson in 1938 after serving six years for the $200 handbook stick-up he had committed as an eighteen-year old kid. Perhaps the most competent of the so-called "Junior Purples" who came to the fore after the Collingwood Manor Massacre, the twenty-eight year old Selik was now a mature, hardened criminal who had "stood up" and shown he could earn with the best of them.

The newly freed Purples set up headquarters at O'Larry's Bar, located at the southwestern corner of Boston and Dexter boulevards in the North End. The tavern, owned by Mikey Selik's older brother Charles, was named after none other than the same Larry "O'Larry" Pollack who had perjured himself during the Collingwood Massacre trial rather than testify against his childhood pals. Unlike the late Harry Millman, Fleisher was well respected by the city's Mafiosi and frequently worked with them in various rackets. In addition to reviving their old fiefdom (albeit on a drastically reduced scale), Harry made many trips west to the State Prison of Southern Michigan at Jackson to visit the imprisoned Purples there. In fact, it became apparent that while Fleisher may have been the street boss of the Purple Gang, he was receiving his marching orders from Raymond Burnstein.

In the summer of 1940, Ray Burnstein and Harry Keywell managed to finagle transfers from Marquette Prison to Jackson Prison. There they reunited with Harry's brother Philip and Little Morris Raider, who were still serving time for the murder of Arthur Mixon. Through their sizable commissaries, and from Charlie Leiter's connection to the Republican Party head Frank McKay, the Purples enjoyed extremely comfortable conditions. Warden Harry Jackson and Deputy Warden D.C. Pettit (who was a frequent visitor to O'Larry's Bar) were fitted snugly in their pockets.

Under that pair's understanding gaze, the imprisoned Purples had the choicest prison jobs and had frequent access to the bar in the basement of Pettit's house. They were allowed to use the warden's office for conjugal visits. Mike Selik, for example, had met his future wife Naomi while serving as the warden's houseboy during the latter half of his term. Naomi became acquainted with Mike while visiting her already imprisoned husband. The two became lovers and thereafter met for a tryst in Jackson's office after Naomi had finished visiting with her unsuspecting spouse. In addition, Ray Burnstein ran the biggest betting operation within the prison's walls. Loansharking and contraband operations were overseen by them, as was drug trafficking, in the form of pilfering nutmeg from the prison mess hall in order to manufacture homemade "speedballs." The profits from these rackets added untold profits to the already large commissaries of the Purples.

In their biggest perk of all, Burnstein, the Keywell brothers, and other convicts within their prestigious clique were essentially able to leave the prison whenever they felt like it. After being provided with civilian clothing and either the warden's or assistant warden's personal vehicle, the boys would visit brothels in Jackson or Detroit, attend Tiger baseball games in the city, or throw weekend parties/picnics at rural cottages owned by Jackson and Pettit.

All these furloughs would take place while the convicts were still officially listed as "on count" within the walls.

Upon their return, the prisoners would always bring in a load of liquor from O'Larry's Bar to restock Deputy Warden Pettit's bar. Burnstein and the others would often meet with Harry Fleisher and the now released Mike Selik in Pettit's basement bar, guzzle booze, and tend to their Detroit rackets long-distance. It would not be a stretch to say that by the time the Japanese attacked Pearl Harbor in December 1941, the imprisoned Purples virtually controlled the largest walled penitentiary in the United States.[22]

REPUBLICAN PARTY power broker Frank McKay had remained untouched over the years despite long standing allegations of corruption and collusion with the Purple Gang. McKay was the target of three separate grand jury investigations in the early 1940s. He was specifically charged with receiving graft from Michigan distillers in exchange for widespread distribution of their products; using the U.S. Mail to defraud the city of Grand Rapids with fraudulent bids on municipal bonds; and extorting a total of $9,918 from Ford Motor Company chairman Edsel Ford under the guise of paying off Republican Party campaign debts. McKay's lawyers successfully argued (probably with some justification) that the chairman was the target of a personal vendetta of U.S. Attorney General Frank Murphy, whose failure to win re-election as Michigan's governor in 1938 was believed to have been engineered by McKay.[23]

Frank McKay once again beat the charges, although his reputation now lay in tatters. He managed to hold on as Michigan's Republican National Committeeman until 1944, when a reform movement led by Governor Harry F. Kelly ousted McKay; incidentally, Kelly had gotten his start under McKay. While the sixty-one year old multi-millionaire financier was now out of political office, he was widely viewed in Michigan as a brilliant, cunning genius. As such, he became the target of an ambitious prosecutor named Kimber "Kim" Sigler.

The son of a wealthy Nebraska cattle rancher, Kim Sigler tried out a number of different professions before deciding on a legal career. A loquacious, flamboyant litigator, Sigler was noted as an extremely dapper dresser (he possessed forty-seven custom made suits) as well as a voracious worker. On December 14, 1943, the forty-nine year old Sigler was appointed special prosecutor of an Ingham County grand jury by Judge Leland W. Carr, whose ostensible purpose was to look into the suspicious destruction of a 1941 anti-chain bank bill that would have protected smaller bank branches from being gobbled up by their corporate brethren.[24]

Even from the start, Sigler suspected that his investigative trail would lead him to Frank McKay. When a friend warned the Republican Sigler not to antagonize McKay if he wished to advance in the party, Kim Sigler replied, "You spoke of Frank McKay and some other big shots. Don't worry, Old Top. I have my heavy artillery constantly trained on them, and one of these days I expect to blow them out of the water. It may take some time and there may be a number of other indictments in the meantime, but you can rest assured that I'm going to give them all I've got, and the funny thing about it, Bill, is that they all know it."[25]

During the course of his 1944 investigation, Sigler turned a major witness in the form of 9th District State Senator Warren G. Hooper. A fourth generation descendant of William Hooper, one of the original signers of the Declaration of Independence, Warren was a forty-year old California native who had attended both the University of California and DePauw University without graduating. Hooper soon married a schoolteacher and took a job with the California Stock Exchange. After his job disappeared along with so many others at the onset of the Great Depression, Hooper deserted his wife and became editor of a Tacoma, Washington newspaper.

By 1935, Hooper had turned up in Albion, Michigan and became the advertising manager of the *Albion Evening Recorder*. Hooper soon enrolled at Albion College, married a local co-ed named Callienetta Cobb, and traveled to Berlin to cover the 1936 Olympic Games. Utilizing his business acquaintances, Warren Hooper successfully ran for the state legislature. After three terms he was elected to the state senate. Hooper's critics sneered that he had been elected primarily because many voters believed he was related to a popular senator from a neighboring district that had the same surname. The Hoopers soon became parents to two children and moved into a nice Albion home. Hooper was appointed as chairman of the Public Health Committee. The senator also, despite the conflict of interest, served as the executive secretary of the Michigan Association of Osteopathic Physicians and Surgeons. In between his legislative duties, Warren indulged in his hobby of collecting rare antiques.[26]

In retrospect, it seems as if Warren Hooper was not quite cut out for the rough-and-tumble, frequently corrupt world of 1940s era Michigan state politics. The inexperienced Republican senator soon succumbed to temptation and fell under the thumb of "The Boss." While being in Frank McKay's pocket had its perks (a seemingly endless flow of cash bribes in exchange for legislative back scratches, comped vacations, etc.), Hooper found himself making difficult decisions that seemed to occasionally work against his constituents. Hooper's home life began to decay around this time as well, as his wife Callienetta often nagged him for new clothes and homemaking items. Warren started flirting with other women and soon began an affair with Vita Rosenberg, wife of (prophetically) former Purple Gang mobster Abe "Buffalo Harry" Rosenberg.[27]

While in this fragile state of mind, Senator Warren Hooper took the stand in front of the Ingham County grand jury. Hooper eventually wilted under Kim Sigler's relentless questioning and admitted taking bribes from Frank McKay. The senator specifically charged that McKay, State Representative William Green, and Benton Harbor sports promoter Floyd Fitzsimmons had requested his assistance a year earlier to defeat a racetrack bill that would require the Detroit Racing Association to set up totalizers at each ticket window of Detroit-area racetracks. The totalizers served to instantaneously compute legitimate odds and ensure that the state got their fair share of tax revenue from each wager. According to Hooper's testimony, McKay said, "Green, Fitzsimmons, and I don't want that pending horse racing bill out of committee. You get busy on it. Bill or Fitz were supposed to see you on it. They have some money for you. You keep the bill in committee and don't worry about the money. You'll get it when the bill is killed." Left unsaid was the fact that the so-called "Totalizer Bill" would prove disastrous to McKay's Purple Gang allies, who made thousands of dollars each year by fixing racehorse odds.

Armed with Senator Hooper's testimony, Kim Sigler saw that he now had a very good chance to do what had never been done before; send Frank McKay to prison. After offering the senator immunity for his testimony, Sigler guided Hooper through three sessions of testimony in late November 1944. In a tactic that would later be questioned in many quarters, Sigler brought Senator Hooper face to face with McKay, Representative William Green, and Floyd Fitzsimmons at his final court appearance. The visibly unnerved senator reluctantly admitted that he had received a $500 bribe from the defendants to kill the horse racing bill. Later that night, after his tense confrontation with McKay, an agitated Warren Hooper confided to his wife that his life was no longer "worth a penny." Mere days later, on December 2, McKay, Fitzsimmons, and Representative Green were indicted on conspiracy charges. Once again, Frank McKay prepared to fight to preserve not only his political career but also his freedom.[28]

It was a fight that he would take to unfathomable limits.

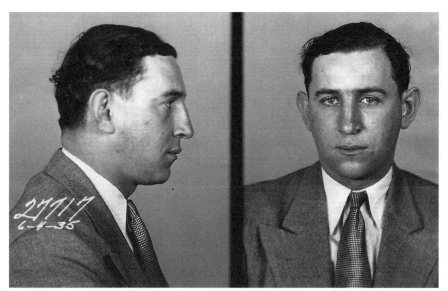

Louis Fleisher was one of three brothers in the Purple Gang. Lou spent a good portion of Prohibition in prison as the result of a 1927 truck hijacking. He was released in November 1934 and resumed his place in the crew. In the mid-1930s, Fleisher began running a burglary and safe-cracking ring based out of the central Michigan town of Albion. *Author's collection.*

Members of the so-called Junior Purple gang under arrest in March 1935. From left to right are Charles Harris, Sylvan Bernstein, Sam Goldfarb, Harry "The Hat" Sosnick, and Sidney Broad. *Walter Reuther Library.*

The staggering weapons cache found inside Louis Fleisher's Highland Park apartment on April 27, 1938. Fleisher, his wife Nellie, and fugitive gunman Sidney Markman were busted during a traffic stop. All were convicted on all counts of possessing untaxed machine guns and silencers. Lou Fleisher got a total of 30 years in prison; with the exception of a six-month stretch in 1957-58, he would spend the rest of his life behind bars. *Walter Reuther Library.*

Louis Fleisher standing at right and looking downward shuffles his feet at Michigan State Police confront him with an arsenal of weapons found in his Albion hideout. Fleisher's customized Graham-Paige sedan is visible on the left. *Author's Collection.*

ASSASSINATION

14 n early December 1944, just days after the Hooper/McKay courtroom showdown, the prominent Jackson prison crew headed by Ray Burnstein and the Keywell brothers assembled in the exercise yard to hear a fellow convict propose an astounding job. The Purple Gang clique, consisting of perhaps a dozen Jewish and Black convicts, listened as the emissary explained that there was a $15,000 "open contract" to whoever killed a prominent yet unnamed politician. Harry Keywell immediately rejected the $15,000 bounty as "too light," and Burnstein agreed.

A week later, the Purples were summoned before Deputy Warden D.C. Pettit, who privately suggested that the fee would indeed be raised. Another few days passed before Pettit introduced to the Purples "a Jew from Flint," who identified himself as Sam Wake. The well-dressed emissary provided a photograph of Senator Warren Hooper and assured the Purple convicts that they would be paid $25,000 for the murder. Wake stressed that the killing had to be committed before January 15, when Hooper was scheduled to testify before a grand jury. When Harry Keywell reiterated concerns about the money, Wake promised to return in a few days with proof of payment. Deputy Warden Pettit, meanwhile, assured the convicts that he would furnish whatever they needed; weapons, transportation, phony license plates, and safe passage to and from the prison.

Four days later, Sam Wake returned with $10,000 cash for the inmates. The money was then given to Pettit to be deposited into the Purples' commissaries. As a show of good faith, Warden Harry Jackson appeared with a silent, well-dressed sixty-something man whom he introduced as Frank McKay. Burnstein and the Keywells appeared to be reassured by the cash and the presence of McKay, who left the meeting after a few minutes without saying a word. Wake said once again that the job needed to be done by the specified deadline. He also hinted that McKay would be extraordinarily grateful and be willing to lend them a helping hand in the future if they so needed.

Prison records duly noted that within three days of this meeting, Ray Burnstein was visited by his brother Abe, Harry Fleisher, and Mike Selik. The four Purples retreated to Deputy Warden Pettit's basement bar for a private conference. What exactly was discussed no one will ever know, but it almost certainly pertained to the stunning offer that was now on the table.[1]

AT FORTY-ONE YEARS OF AGE, Harry "H.F." Fleisher was something of a rarity in the ranks of the Purple Gang. Other than the four years he spent on Alcatraz, he had mostly escaped serious punishment for the misdeeds of a criminal career that spanned parts of four decades. He was now living with his second wife Hattie in a new house at 18616 Roselawn Street in Northwest Detroit. In addition, Fleisher's nineteen-year old son was currently serving in the Pacific with the Marine Corps; young Private Henry Fleish would soon fight with distinction on Iwo Jima and be awarded the Purple Heart after being wounded in action. The Purple Gang that his father now helmed was a far cry from its late 1920s heyday. Nevertheless, H.F. was a professional gangster who was determined to accomplish the sinister mission he had now been tasked with.

In mid-December 1944, as Hanukkah decorations began appearing in the windows of Jewish homes in the North End, Harry Fleisher and Mike Selik began huddling in O'Larry's Bar to plot the murder of Senator Warren Hooper. In order to insulate themselves from getting their hands too dirty, the pair turned a small handful of associates to carry out the deed itself. First and foremost was H.F.'s younger brother Sam. Another was a lower-level Purple associate named Samuel Abramowitz. Thirty-five years old, Abramowitz had been an errand boy for the Sugar House crew in the late 1920s and had not progressed much farther up the criminal ladder. Classified by police as having "dull normal intelligence with an IQ of 90," Sam had spent the vast majority of the 1930s serving various jail terms. By his own admission, "I've been to prison twice, on probation once, and have probably been arrested a hundred times." While Sam was incarcerated at Jackson, he had become a close associate of Mike Selik. After his 1943 parole, Abramowitz took a stab at going straight by opening a barber shop in Flint. Before long, Sam's business went bust and he gradually gravitated to his old pals at O'Larry's Bar.[2]

Another was twenty-eight year old Henry "Heinie" Luks, an armed robber and safecracking specialist who, despite his relative youth, had already served three prison terms. Luks had been a part of the Purples' Jackson prison clique before his early 1940s parole. Around eleven-thirty on the evening of Saturday, December 23, Luks was drinking heavily at O'Larry's Bar when he was summoned to the tavern's private office. There Harry Fleisher and Mike Selik offered Luks $5,000 to wire a dynamite bomb to someone's car. Luks was presumably asked to kill the target this way due to his familiarity with explosives as a "box man." The intoxicated safecracker tentatively agreed but reported back a couple days later that he had been unable to procure dynamite. Fleisher then asked Luks, "Would you be interested in taking care of this fellow some other way?" At this point, Sam Abramowitz was brought into the plotting. Luks's $5,000 share would be divided equally with Abramowitz.

The morning after Christmas, Harry Fleisher, Mike Selik, Heinie Luks, and Sam Abramowitz piled into Fleisher's black Cadillac sedan and sped west toward Albion. On the drive out, they cranked up the Caddy's heater and talked about normal subjects; women, sports, fellow crooks, etc. Once in Albion, the talk turned serious. They soon stopped in front a nondescript white frame house that was pointed out to Abramowitz and Luks as Warren Hooper's home. The senator's car was also identified. The Purples discussed their target's habits while they cruised through the snowy streets of Albion and cased the area around the senator's home and office. The gangsters idly mulled over the best way to kill their quarry. Methods such as explosions, gunfire, strangulation, and bludgeoning were proposed as casually as if they were trying to decide what to order for lunch. By the time they left town later that afternoon, Heinie Luks had had enough. While a thief and all-around shady character, Luks was just not capable of committing premeditated murder. Later that night, the apprehensive safecracker fed Selik a story about the job being "too hot" and bailed on the plot.[3]

With Heinie Luks out of the mix, Sam Abramowitz was given full responsibility for the actual commission of the hit. Sam chose twenty-three year old armed robber Al Kurner to replace Luks. On December 28, however, Abramowitz told his new partner that the job had suddenly been postponed. It was said that the bosses were trying to bribe the senator into silence. That very day, horse racing bill conspiracy case defendant Floyd Fitzsimmons did indeed visit Warren Hooper at his Lansing office. Fitzsimmons offered an unknown sum of cash from "Frank" to cover any "legal expenses" he may have had after keeping his mouth shut.

After hearing the job was off, Al Kurner appropriated a nickel-plated .38 revolver from the secret arsenal at O'Larry's. Kurner would later use this pistol to commit a downtown Detroit stick-up that netted a grand total of $18.

Kurner soon fled for Los Angeles. The next morning, word came down that Senator Hooper had refused their last-ditch bribe offer and was still dead set on testifying against McKay and company.

Later that day, December 29, Sam Abramowitz returned to Albion with Harry Fleisher's brother Sam. The younger Fleisher had brought along a snub-nosed .38 revolver for the job. The pair drove around Hooper's block "ten or twelve times" in Fleisher's black Pontiac. After seeing no sign of the senator for almost two hours, the two beat a retreat back to Detroit. That afternoon at O'Larry's, the pair sheepishly admitted that they missed the senator. Harry Fleisher shook his head, "Jesus, he's a tough guy to get. We'll have to try again."

On Tuesday morning, January 2, Abramowitz and Sam Fleisher returned to Albion to kill Hooper. While scoping out the senator's office, the pair saw their quarry inside. Abramowitz, armed with Sam's .38, had a clear shot at the back of Hooper's head through the window but held off when he saw the senator's wife and two sons inside the office. The two cruised around a while in the vain hope that the senator's family would leave him alone, but they eventually headed back east with their mission unaccomplished.

On the drive to Detroit, Sam Abramowitz's survival instincts began to kick in. While he had had a golden opportunity to kill the senator back in Albion, Sam Fleisher was armed as well. If Abramowitz had gone through the murder, what was to stop Fleisher from shooting *him* on the way back to the city and dumping him into some snow bank? After all, he was now the only expendable one left in the murder plot. A dead senator and a dead crook found with the murder weapon on him would have equaled a closed case. Back at O'Larry's, when Harry Fleisher learned of this latest failure, he cut Abramowitz loose. As the now relieved gangster left the bar, he heard H.F. grumbling that he and Mike Selik would now have to do the job themselves.[4]

Within just a day or so, Harry Fleisher drove out alone to visit Ray Burnstein at Jackson. The two men spoke tensely in private, almost certainly about the murder plot. Both men knew that their deadline was only days away.[5]

THURSDAY, JANUARY 11 found Senator Warren Hooper at his office inside the Michigan state capitol building at Lansing. Those that saw him that day found the senator to be extremely edgy, chain-smoking cigarettes and frequently pacing around his office. No doubt that Hooper's tense demeanor came from the knowledge that his grand jury testimony date was a mere seventy-two hours away. Senator Hooper was planning on skipping that weekend's Republican State Convention in Grand Rapids, which just happened to be the hometown of his new nemesis. The senator probably did not want to pour gasoline on the fire and figured that facing Frank McKay down the following Monday would be more than enough.

Around 2:30 that afternoon, Senator Hooper walked outside into the cold winter air. After picking up his green 1939 Mercury sedan, Hooper drove over to the McLaughlin Osteopathic Hospital. The senator often lodged there while conducting business in Lansing and he wanted to pick up some literature he left behind. He then proceeded to the Porter Hotel to make reservations for eight osteopathic surgeons who were soon coming to Lansing. After having an animated conversation with two young men in the parking lot of the hotel, Senator Hooper steered his Mercury south on M-99 toward his hometown of Albion around 4 o'clock.

The forty mile run south to Albion would normally have taken Senator Hooper around 45 minutes or so, but the senator took his time due to the treacherous patches of road ice. While the day was clear and sunny, the temperatures were still quite chilly; most of the state had been in the grip of a prolonged single-digit cold snap. Whatever thoughts Hooper had during his solitary drive through the snow-covered Michigan countryside will never be known. By five o'clock that afternoon, darkness was rapidly coming on as the senator crossed the Jackson County line just northeast of the town of Springport. At that moment, a red sedan blew past Senator Hooper's Mercury and quickly outdistanced it. Warren apparently then lit a cigarette, possibly to calm his nerves. A minute or so later, the senator passed through the intersection with Harshay Road. Senator Hooper did not see the maroon vehicle until it was almost too late. This car inexplicably moved crossways into the highway, causing the senator to slam on the brakes of his green Mercury. Hooper's car entered a 24-foot skid that left it facing southbound on the shoulder of the northbound lane.

Stunned and groggy from the skid, the senator blinked with bemusement as the driver of the maroon car blocked off his Mercury in a T-shape. Hooper then felt a rush of frigid air as his driver's side door was suddenly opened. A strong, gloved hand grabbed Hooper's overcoat and yanked him toward the open door. The panicked senator instinctively jerked to his right across the passenger seat in a futile attempt to escape, only to be pulled back toward the door. This action jammed Hooper's fedora down over his eyes and caused the cigarette to slip from his now shaking fingers. In the grip of stark terror and blinded by his hat, Warren Hooper could not see the face of the man who had him. Hooper did not know that this man was the polar opposite of himself. A man who had learned violence at a young age on the streets of Detroit's Little

Jerusalem; a man who was able to make truly dangerous criminals do his bidding through the sheer force of his will; a man who had killed and ordered killings throughout the years. He was also a man that could not be bargained or reasoned with, as Senator Hooper discovered when three .38 caliber bullets were triggered into his head at point-blank range.[6]

The loud sounds of gunfire had barely rolled away from the two cars when Harry Snyder rounded the corner into the crime scene. A forty-eight year old Jackson grocery salesman, Snyder had been driving northbound from Springport when he saw the green Mercury parked on the wrong side of the road and the maroon sedan blocking it off crosswise. The salesman cruised slowly toward the strange scene. The driver of the maroon car quickly backed up to let Snyder pass and slightly nicked the front fender of the Mercury as he did (minute chips of maroon paint would later be found imbedded in the fender.) The salesman took note of a man standing at the driver's side door of the green Mercury. Snyder later said, "…he had on a light overcoat, sort of grayish – salt and pepper color – and a soft gray hat. He was very white, light-complected [sic]. He was a pretty good looking fellow. Well dressed. Weighed, from what I could see of him sitting in the car there, about 150 pounds. He looked right at me, and I looked at him."[7]

Snyder thought that perhaps an accident of some kind had occurred and that these men were helping the possibly drunk driver. The salesman accelerated on while simultaneously wondering if he should have stopped and rendered some assistance. Snyder looked in his rearview mirror and saw the well-dressed man at the Mercury sprint over to the maroon sedan, which now sped toward him in an effort to catch up. A suddenly nervous Snyder watched with increasing alarm as the two men in the maroon sedan quickly overtook him and zoomed past on the left. The vehicle rounded a sharp right turn and vanished from view. Unbeknownst to the now-relieved Snyder, the maroon car had veered right onto M-50 and headed southeast in the direction of Jackson.

By 5:30 two other motorists, Floyd Modjeska and Kyle Van Auker, had discovered the now smoking green Mercury parked on the side of the highway. Both men stared at the burning car with nervous uncertainty. The appearance of a third witness spurred them to action, and they tossed handfuls of snow on the flames licking at the dead body now sprawled across the passenger seat. Three women from a nearby house called the Springport Fire Department. The shot-up and slightly charred body found inside was soon identified as that of Senator Warren Hooper.[8]

Newspapers across the state headlined the senator's stunning murder. Special Prosecutor Kim Sigler disclosed to the media that Hooper was the "finger-man" in the upcoming McKay graft trial. Frank McKay, for his part, appears to have had no doubt that Sigler would immediately try to link him to the killing. Frank denounced the murder as "a terrible thing" and asserted that all "law enforcement agencies should be relentless in their search for those responsible."[9] Governor Harry F. Kelly announced that a $25,000 reward had been posted toward the apprehension of the killers. The following Monday afternoon (the very same day he had been scheduled to testify before the grand jury), Senator Warren Hooper was laid to rest after a sparsely attended ceremony in Albion's Riverside Cemetery. The epitaph on his tombstone would read, "With Honesty He Lived, For Honesty He Was Taken."

The Michigan State Police quickly deduced that the murder had all the earmarks of a professional hit. It was initially speculated that someone riding in the car with senator had done the killing. The cops questioned the three motorists who encountered the senator and his Mercury that afternoon; little was learned other than Harry Snyder's descriptions of the man standing by Hooper's car and the man who was driving the maroon sedan. Snyder vaguely described them as "a small man and a large man", the small one being the one he saw by the Mercury. Several size 8 footprints, the killers', were found in the snow near the driver's side door. Another witness, William Bracey, saw the two killers about an hour before the shooting took place. They were parked in a maroon sedan in the same area where Senator Hooper would soon be shot to death. Bracey added that a passing snowplow had forced the car to move and that its two occupants appeared to be screwing on or changing a license plate in the brief moments he had seen them.[10]

The investigation at first proceeded on the assumption that one of Senator Hooper's extramarital affairs turned deadly. His alleged liaison with Vita Rosenberg was duly recalled, and her husband Abe, aka Buffalo Harry, was questioned more than once.[11] During the first months of 1945, the investigation stalled somewhat as the Michigan State Police sifted through thousands of anonymous tips and suggestions. Kim Sigler managed to convict Floyd Fitzsimmons on the conspiracy charges and secure him three years in prison, but main target Frank McKay remained out of reach when the original charges against him were dismissed. While Sigler never told the media flatout that McKay was complicit in the demise of the senator, he continued to drop subtle hints in his frequent interviews.

The trail of the assassins had grown cold by March 22, when the police got a significant break when Sam Abramowitz was brought in for questioning as the result of a tip from the now-imprisoned Al Kurner. The Purple

Gang associate held out for nearly a month before confessing to his role in the conspiracy. Sam passed a polygraph test and named all the other players from O'Larry's Bar. Two weeks later, Henry Luks was picked up and eventually corroborated Abramowitz's story.[12] Warrants were served for the others on April 20; Harry and Sam Fleisher, Mike and Naomi Selik were all arrested. Also picked up was Peter Apostolpoulos aka Pete Mahoney, a gambler friend of Harry Fleisher's who had no criminal record and was something of a gangster groupie.[13]

Rumors began to publicly circulate that Fleisher and company actually took their orders from the imprisoned Ray Burnstein. Indeed, when longtime Purple attorney Edward H. Kennedy, Jr. appeared with a writ of *habeas corpus* for H.F., the gangster declined it by saying he would "get out when I'm good and ready." When brought before Judge Leland Carr in Lansing, Fleisher refused to answer questions and was sentenced to thirty days for contempt. It became obvious to those involved in the prosecution that Harry Fleisher preferred the relative safety of a jail cell to being on the street.[14] On May 3, almost four months after Senator Hooper's assassination, Mike Selik, Pete Mahoney, and the two Fleisher brothers were charged with conspiracy to commit murder. All four men pled not guilty and were held on $25,000 bonds.[15]

The pre-trial examination that began in Battle Creek on May 11 featured witnesses, including armed robber Al Kurner, who discussed seeing/hearing the defendants discuss the proposed murder of Warren Hooper in various locations. By far the most damaging testimony was from Sam Abramowitz and Henry Luks, who went into detail about the failed attempts to ambush the senator in Albion in the days before his actual murder.[16] Two weeks after the examination, the defendants won their freedom on a reduced bail of $15,000.

On Sunday, June 10, Kim Sigler made an unexpected move by seeking warrants against Harry Fleisher, Mike Selik, William "Candy" Davidson, Pete Mahoney, and Samuel Chivas for the December 1 armed robbery of the Aristocrat Club in Pontiac, Michigan. The Aristocrat was an illegal gambling joint whose owner had reportedly rebuffed Fleisher's efforts to muscle in for a percentage. Sigler had learned about the heist (which had not been reported to the police) through his questioning of Sam Abramowitz. While the move seemed to be a non sequitur on the surface, it was part of a calculated move by Kim Sigler to get the defendants to confess that Frank McKay had bankrolled Warren Hooper's murder. While the original murder conspiracy charges carried a maximum sentence of five years, an armed robbery conviction may have netted the gangsters a life sentence. Faced with this potentially severe penalty, Sigler was confident that at least one of the Purples would roll over.[17]

Six days later, with all this in his mind, Kim Sigler announced that a warrant had been issued charging Frank McKay and seven other men (including Purple mobsters Charles Leiter and Isadore Schwartz) with violating the state liquor laws in the years 1939 and 1940.[18] As the summer of 1945 began, the debonair special prosecutor seemed certain that he finally had his man. The Hooper murder conspiracy case was extended to July 16 at the request of Kim Sigler, who did not want an overlapping workload when dealing with the McKay liquor conspiracy case, which had been scheduled to start in the same timeframe. Sam Fleisher, in the meantime, unsuccessfully filed for a severance.

While Harry Fleisher, Mike Selik, Sam Fleisher, and Pete Mahoney were charged with conspiracy to kill Senator Warren Hooper, both they and the deceased senator would be frequently crowded offstage by the real stars of the drama, Kim Sigler and Frank McKay. Flamboyant special prosecutor Sigler already had his eyes on running for governor in the 1946 election. It was obvious to most observers that Sigler saw his ticket to the governor's mansion being punched by a conviction against McKay who, for his part, continued to insist that he was the target of a well-financed political vendetta. The tabloid-style newspaper articles reported all the bombastic sound bites while reducing the once-proud Purple gangster Harry Fleisher and his men to mere pawns in a vast political chess-game. Left unsaid by most was the fact that in the hullabaloo over the murder conspiracy, the search for the *actual killers* of the senator had virtually ground to a halt.

On July 17, a jury of predominately rural southern Michigan citizens over retirement age sat in a broiling Battle Creek courtroom to hear the murder conspiracy charges. At the defense table sat the four defendants and their attorneys; Max Klayman for Harry Fleisher and Mike Selik; Robert G. Leitch for Sam Fleisher, and Theodore I. Rodgers for Pete Mahoney. Also sitting in as a "special consultant" was the omnipresent Edward H. Kennedy, Jr. They watched as the always-dapper Kim Sigler explained to the jury that the state would prove that Harry Fleisher and Mike Selik had received $15,000 to arrange Senator Warren Hooper's murder. Sigler also said that he would prove the involvement of Henry Luks, Sam Abramowitz, and Sam Fleisher as well. Pete Mahoney was accused of being sighted in an Albion tavern with Harry Fleisher on the day of the murder. Sigler ended his opening statement with the subtle hint that Harry and Mike Selik had committed the murder themselves, based on the overheard remark from Sam Abramowitz.[19]

Henry "Heinie" Luks testified as to his role in the Hooper conspiracy while the defense attorneys tried unsuccessfully to portray him as an unreliable drunk who was willing to say anything to save his own neck. Armed robber Al Kurner took the stand with similar results.[20] The widowed Callienetta Hooper sat mutely in court with her small children, as did family and friends of the defendants. Kim Sigler then announced his intention to call her as a witness the next day. Edward Kennedy vehemently objected by saying her mere presence in the courtroom was prejudicial to his clients and that this could be the "last straw" for the jurors. Although Mrs. Hooper was only on the stand a mere five minutes, her testimony had the intended emotional impact.[21]

Sam Abramowitz took the stand next and testified in great detail about making at least two trips to Albion in order to murder Senator Hooper at the behest of Harry Fleisher and Mike Selik. He ended his testimony by stating his fear of being murdered by Sam Fleisher on the return trip from the second attempt. Abramowitz also added that he overheard Harry saying that he and Selik would probably have to do the job themselves after the botched second attempt. Defense attorneys, however, savaged the Purple associate on cross-examination. Holes were poked in parts of his statements about his trips to Albion with Sam Fleisher and Abramowitz was successfully painted as a misanthropic alcoholic who showed absolutely no remorse for either his life of crime or the murder he was tasked to commit. It was pointed out that he lied to Michigan State Police investigators for nearly a month before finally confessing to his role. Kim Sigler attempted to salvage Abramowitz's testimony with a series of witnesses to vouch for his and Sam Fleisher's presence in Albion on the dates in question, but the damage had been done.[22]

Ace defense lawyer Edward Kennedy, Jr. destroyed Kim Sigler's next witness, Albion tavern owner Evelyn Iris Brown, who claimed to have seen Pete Mahoney in her place on the afternoon of Senator Hooper's murder. Kennedy's cross-examination left her in so many shreds that Brown admitted on the stand she had been mistaken in her identification of Mahoney and now claimed to have seen Sam Abramowitz, instead.[23] Defense attorneys unsuccessfully moved for a mistrial after the next witness referred to Sam Fleisher's term served in Alcatraz.

A huge bombshell dropped on July 24 when Michigan Attorney General John R. Dethmers released to the Detroit media a four-part installment that detailed the long history of institutional corruption at the State Prison of Southern Michigan at Jackson. Dethmers claimed in an interview to have "tore the lid from the world's largest walled prison." He made public the very comfortable conditions that major criminals such as Ray Burnstein, Phil and Harry Keywell, Mike Selik, and others enjoyed. The various gambling, extortion, and drug trafficking rackets were probed in detail. The prominent roles of Warden Harry Jackson and Deputy Warden D.C. Pettit were thoroughly exposed (both men would eventually be dismissed in the ensuing shakeup.)[24]

The evidence continued to mount against the charged gangsters, as different witnesses testified to the veracity of the statements of Abramowitz and Luks. Defense counsel led the jury through an endless maze of testimony that hinted that Abramowitz and Luks had committed Senator Hooper's murder on their own. The fact that Sam Abramowitz's shoe size matched the snowy footprints left at the crime scene by the killer was hammered home in Edward Kennedy's closing argument. On the sweltering morning of Tuesday, July 31, the jury retired to deliberate. The wait wasn't very long. Mike Selik, Pete Mahoney, and the two Fleisher brothers were found guilty. All four were sentenced to 4 ½ to 5 years in Jackson.

Harry Fleisher had no comment about the verdict while his brother Sam moaned, "It's all wrong. It's all wrong. I'm not guilty. The jury was prejudiced by the fact that I had a prison record." Mike Selik, who had already spent half his adult life behind bars, merely stared in silent fury. Pete Mahoney, who had no criminal record and whose only crime was being within earshot while the hit was discussed, was incredulous; "I don't know how the jury found me guilty on that evidence. All I know about the case is what I read in the newspapers and what I heard here." When asked if she was happy about the verdict, Callienetta Hooper clutched her two small children and explained in a teary voice, "We are not happy about anything because our Daddy isn't coming home. We need him." While the four men were convicted of conspiring to kill Warren Hooper, they were soon released from custody on $15,000 appeal bonds. The big riddle, as to who the actual trigger pullers were, remained unsolved. As the *Detroit Free Press* editorial page asked, "Who *did* murder Hooper a few days before he was to testify against Boss Frank D. McKay?"[25]

The Oakland County trial for the armed robbery of the Aristocrat Club in Pontiac began in the fall of 1945. The convicted Hooper murder conspirators had already had their motions for a mistrial in that case denied. The main highlight was on Wednesday, November 28 when Harry Fleisher took the stand in his defense for the first time in his life. Reading from note cards prepared for him by his lawyer, Harry stated that his real name was Fleish and emphasized that the "er" had been mistakenly tacked onto his surname after his first arrest in 1921. While he acknowledged growing up with many members of the Purple Gang, Fleisher denied being connected to them, or participating in Warren Hooper's murder or the Aristocrat Club heist.

Once again the testimony of Sam Abramowitz and Henry Luks (who had been granted immunity in this case, as well) did the Purples in. Harry Fleisher, Mike Selik, Pete Mahoney, William "Candy" Davidson, and Samuel Chivas were found guilty and sentenced to 25 to 50 years in prison. On December 10, the five men were led into State Prison at Jackson; Fleisher, Selik, and Mahoney would soon win their freedom on $25,000 appeal bonds. They still had not breathed a word about the "unnamed politician" who had offered $15,000 to have Senator Warren Hooper killed.[26]

The year 1946 saw Kim Sigler win election as the governor of the state of Michigan but lose his final battle against Frank McKay. Despite that fact that old Purples Charles Leiter and Isadore Schwartz had pleaded guilty and testified against him, McKay was found not guilty on February 11. The ecstatic McKay stated afterward, "I hope this is the end of my political persecution. I regard my acquittal as more than a vindication of myself. It is a reflection of the judicial integrity and courage of Judge Simpson, and should be reassuring to all people to know our courts can still dispense justice unhampered by the subtle influences that were aligned against me."[27]

The question as to who Senator Warren Hooper's actual killers were remained unanswered until the fall of 1946, when the solution finally began to take shape. Almost since the investigation first began nearly two years earlier, it had been whispered that the senator's killers had been inmates at Jackson Prison. One of the chief proponents of this theory was Michigan State Police Lieutenant Joseph Sheridan, who, at one point, was working sixteen and eighteen hours a day on the Hooper case. His informants immediately alerted him to the fact that the old Purple Gang mobsters who hung around O'Larry's Bar had plotted the murder. While Sam Abramowitz and Henry Luks slightly fit Harry Snyder's vague description of the assassins and Abramowitz's shoe size did indeed match the snowy footprints left behind by the killer, there was nothing else in the evidence or the suspects' personalities to contradict their sworn testimony that they were involved only in the plotting of Hooper's murder.

Another theory Sheridan considered was the same one that Kim Sigler had hinted to in the conspiracy trial, that Harry Fleisher and Mike Selik had committed the killing themselves once their men came up short. Selik's wife Naomi endorsed this story but her credibility, addled by heavy alcohol and drug abuse, was suspect. While both Fleisher and Selik were fully capable of committing premeditated murder and fit Snyder's eyewitness description, it seemed illogical for them to have done the actual slaying. If Harry and Mike were pinched and convicted of murder, the imprisoned Purples in Jackson would have lost their primary connections to the outside world. As such,

Fleisher and Selik would not have endangered their valuable underworld intermediary status by acting as garden-variety triggermen. H.F. himself said it best when one of his girlfriends asked him on the sly if he and Selik had offed the senator, "Why would we get involved with something like that?"[28]

There *were* two suspects who had nothing to lose, however; two suspects who were already serving life sentences for first-degree murder in Jackson, thus making them virtually immune from prosecution; two suspects who not only had motive but also the opportunity and ability to successfully commit the murder of Warren Hooper.

Two Black parolees from Jackson named Louis Brown and Ernest Henry, former members of the Purple prison clique, filled in all the rest of the missing pieces for Lieutenant Joe Sheridan. Brown and Henry explained how the plot had originated within prison walls and even added the tidbit that none other than Frank McKay had put in a personal appearance at the prison to reassure the Purples. The two men also claimed that on the afternoon that Warren Hooper was murdered, January 11, 1945, both Ray Burnstein and Harry Keywell were summoned over the loudspeaker to Warden Harry Jackson's office. The warden then ordered Louis Brown to the "dress-out shop" to procure civilian clothing for Burnstein and Keywell. The pair was then provided with leather gloves and a nickel-plated .38 caliber revolver.

With Senator Hooper's Lansing movements being closely monitored, Burnstein and Keywell drove away from the prison at the sound of the afternoon dinner bugle at 3:30 in Deputy Warden D.C. Pettit's maroon convertible. A red sedan containing at least two accomplices followed the pair. The two Purples parked on the highway they knew Hooper would be traveling and screwed on a fake license plate while they waited.

Along the route, the accomplices in the red sedan tailed the senator and eventually zoomed past Hooper in order to signal the waiting Purples, most probably by flashing their headlights. Keywell moved the maroon vehicle to the senator's path, causing the Mercury to violently skid to a halt. Burnstein then jumped out of the car, ran over the senator's Mercury, and pumped three bullets into Hooper's head at close range. Just seconds later, Harry Snyder cruised into the scene and locked eyes with Ray Burnstein (who bore a resemblance to Mike Selik) before glancing over at the maroon car's driver, Harry Keywell (who, by 1945, could easily have been mistaken for Harry Fleisher.) Burnstein trotted back to Pettit's car and zoomed after Snyder. Instead of following the witness, they swerved right onto M-50 and sped back to the penitentiary, a mere eighteen miles away.

Back at the prison, Burnstein and Keywell re-donned their jailhouse garb and destroyed evidence of the crime in the prison incinerator; the gloves, license plate, and murder weapon (their accomplices had already returned to the prison sometime before them.) Later on, after the adrenaline had worn off, both men excitedly boasted to their friends how smoothly the hit had gone down and about the great riches that would soon be theirs.[29]

Both Louis Brown and Ernest Henry took and passed polygraph tests. Nothing in their statements contradicted the known facts of the case, and neither man was clever enough to fabricate so detailed a story. Their tale was later backed up to a certain extent by Al Kurner, who claimed to have delivered the same .38 revolver he appropriated from O'Larry's Bar in late December 1944 to a Purple clique convict named Harold Johnson; this weapon was believed to have been the murder weapon.[30] Brown even pinpointed the identity of the mysterious "John Wake" who had brokered the deal; he turned out to be a Flint jeweler named Max Davis. Many other "kites" (letters) from Jackson convicts claiming to have details about Senator Hooper's murder would surface in the late 1940s, but none had the credibility of Brown and Henry's affidavits. After then-Governor Kim Sigler learned of Brown and Henry's statements, he privately confided to Michigan State Police Commissioner Donald S. Leonard that he believed them to be the truth.[31]

Amazingly, no indictments were ever handed down. Ray Burnstein and Harry Keywell were never questioned; even though they fit the physical descriptions of the killers to a T. Nor was Deputy Warden D.C. Pettit's maroon convertible ever examined for forensic evidence. These astounding facts were never revealed to the general public. Given the available evidence, the question isn't so much as *who* killed Hooper but *why* they were never prosecuted. The only man who could have provided an answer, Kim Sigler, never told. As a result, to this day, the murder of Senator Warren G. Hooper has remained officially unsolved.[32]

ON JUNE 14, 1948, the Michigan Supreme Court upheld the murder conspiracy convictions for the two Fleisher brothers and Mike Selik while overturning Pete Mahoney's.[33] Harry Fleisher, Selik, and Mahoney remained free on their appeal of the Aristocrat Club robbery case until October 4 of that year. Pete Mahoney was promptly shipped off to prison while Fleisher and Selik went on the run.[34]

Harry Fleisher managed to elude capture until January 18, 1950, when FBI agents captured the forty-six year-old gangster on the beach at Pompano Beach, Florida. H.F. was lying shirtless on the sand as his girlfriend Bernice Jackson rubbed suntan lotion on his back. During his time on the lam, Fleisher claimed to have been a traveling salesman. On the plane back to Detroit, H.F. was bound with body chains and his face was swathed in bandages to conceal his identity from photographers. Standing before Judge Theodore Levin, the defeated Fleisher explained why he jumped bail, "I was forced to do what I done, that's all. I've been given a bad deal in my other cases and I felt this was a logical thing to do. Not that I wanted to do it. I was forced to do it, as I got a bad deal and I thought I would do what I done." After thirty-plus years, the criminal career of Harry Fleisher was at an end. He was shipped off to prison to begin serving his time.[35]

Mike Selik finally surfaced on February 2, 1951, when the New York Police Department arrested him in connection with a Bronx jewel heist. He, too, was returned to serve his time in Michigan state prisons.

THE BIG NOISE that had been the Purple Gang in their Roaring Twenties heyday had gradually dwindled to discordant static over the course of the Dirty Thirties. Upon Mikey Selik's anti-climatic 1951 capture, that ineffectually anachronistic clamor was switched off permanently.[36]

Sam Fleisher, center holding hat, was the youngest of the three Fleisher brothers. Sam
had served time in Alcatraz with his brother Harry in the late 1930s. Fleisher was tried
and convicted of conspiring to kill Senator Warren Hooper. Standing behind him in the
doorway is Ingham County special prosecutor and future Michigan governor Kim Sigler.
Walter Reuther Library.

Original Purple Gang member "Little Morris" Raider not long after his release from prison in 1944. Raider had served thirteen years in connection with the 1930 killing of ice peddler Arthur Mixon. In later years, Raider became a wealthy real estate figure in Southern California. *Author's Collection.*

Senator Warren G. Hooper was scheduled to testify in January 1945 before an Ingham County grand jury regarding corruption involving Republican boss Frank McKay. Senator Hooper was shot to death on a lonely Michigan highway before he could take the stand. The subsequent investigation revealed that some of the few remaining members of the Purple Gang had conspired to kill him. *Author's Collection.*

SUBSEQUENCE

By the time Dwight D. Eisenhower was sworn in for his first term as America's 34th president, the Purple Gang was largely a memory in Detroit. They were often brought up when individuals reminisced about the wild days of Prohibition. Even as the facts surrounding the Purples' deeds grew hazier with each passing year, the colorful gangsters from the North End still captivated the city's imagination. Most of their number were dead, locked up, or had gone legit. Unlike their Sicilian crime counterparts in the Partnership, there was no subsequent generation of Jewish gangsters to pick up the Purple torch. The vast majority of the immigrant families who had once peopled Little Jerusalem had found prosperity and success in America, and far fewer of them needed to turn to crime.

Many in the city's Jewish community tried hard to forget the Purple Gang. They saw the boys as a great shame, a *shande*, to their neighbors and families. Their descendents caught the collateral damage of that shame. A tragic case in point was that of George Keywell, younger brother to Phil and Harry Keywell. One day in the winter of 1932, after his two siblings had been sent to prison for life, George was sitting in Hebrew school class when his teacher suddenly began to harangue him. The teacher yelled things like, "Your family is shaming the Jewish people!" Young George burst into tears and bolted from the room, never returning to Hebrew school. When he became older, George changed his surname to Kent, was decorated for bravery in World War II, and became a successful attorney and eventually a federal judge.[1]

The families of the Purples and their victims also had to endure years without their fathers, husbands, sons, and/or brothers; whether they had been removed from their homes by murder or prison sentences. For example, Moses Shorr was just eight years old on the December 1934 evening that his father Henry left their Fullerton Avenue flat for an errand that he would never return from. As the sole support for his mother Mary, Moses (or

Mickey, as he was usually referred to) went to work for a local radio station at the age of fifteen. Over the ensuing years, Mickey Shorr would overcome his childhood adversity and go on to a distinguished career as a Detroit radio personality. Shorr would also be noted as the founder of a chain of mobile electronics stores that still bears his name to this day.[2]

THROUGHOUT THE ENSUING YEARS, the members of the Purple Gang met a variety of different fates. Some did not last very long after the Hooper conspiracy convictions. **Willie Laks**, who handled the dope rackets for the Purples in the 1920s, died at the age of sixty-four on September 5, 1945. Oakland Sugar House clerk/mechanic **Jacob Levites** followed him in death some six months later.

By the late 1940s, **Charles Leiter** was running a bar in Detroit. He had given up the gangster life and put in long hours at his place. As he said, "I work fifteen to eighteen hours a day in this joint. I never go anywhere else. I never see anybody. I'm content to be a beer glass guy, a schmuck, selling beer by the glass." The former owner of the Oakland Sugar House died of natural causes in Redford Township, Michigan on December 25, 1977, his 84th birthday.[3]

Leiter's predecessor, **George Goldberg**, eventually went into the real estate business. Goldberg was completely out of the gangster life when he passed away in the old North End neighborhood on New Year's Eve, 1967; the day before his 72nd birthday.[4]

Joe "Honey" Miller was last heard from in March 1950, when the FBI found him living in Hollywood, Florida under the name Harry Harbus. The feds briefly questioned the retired Miller about Joe Burnstein. Contrary to what he told the Detroit media back in 1929, Honey claimed to the feds that the original Purple Gang had consisted of himself, Abe Axler, Eddie Fletcher, Irving Milberg and the Burnstein brothers.[5]

Harry "The Indian" Altman died in prison of cirrhosis on August 29, 1950 while **Jack Selbin** stayed on the West Coast after his release from Alcatraz and turned up dead in Los Angeles on Halloween night, 1952. **Abe Zussman** survived on the streets of Detroit until at least the mid-1950s, still criminally inclined and visibly down on his luck.

Sam Solomon, boss of the infamous Third Street Navy, eventually lost his eyesight due to a case of untreated syphilis. Despite his disability, Solomon later ran a profitable concession stand in the main Detroit Post Office on Fort Street.[6]

By the time of his 1928 acquittal in the Cleaners and Dyers War extortion case, **George Cordell** had begun rum-running on a large scale out of the

Downriver suburb of Ecorse. He was convicted of violating the Volstead Act and shipped off to Leavenworth in February 1931 to serve a fifteen-month term.

On the night of April 16, 1933, Cordell and his wife Ruth hosted a dinner party for several friends at their Detroit home, located at 3903 Courville Avenue. Cordell was drinking very heavily; at one point during the meal, he pulled a gun and offered to shoot out all the lights in the room to demonstrate his marksmanship. Later that evening after the guests left, George staggered off to bed, only to pass out on the staircase. Ruth Cordell then got one of her husband's pistols and fired three bullets into his head and neck. She then fatally shot herself through the heart. Amazingly, Cordell then got up and moved unsteadily to the telephone to call for help. Despite wounds so severe that Rev. Fr. John Kaufman of St. Mary's Catholic Church administered the Last Rites to him, George Cordell survived his injuries. The attempted murder-suicide was said to be the culmination of a long-term abusive relationship.

Although the hearing in his left ear was permanently damaged as a result of the shooting, Cordell spent his later years working as a bookie for the local Mafia.[7]

Max Silk, Purple Gang associate who owned the Ten Forty Club, spent his later years operating a popular delicatessen that was located directly across the street from Tiger Stadium at the corner of Michigan and Trumbull avenues.[8]

Abe "Angel Face" Kaminsky returned to the Pittsburgh area circa 1934 and lived the rest of his life in the town of McKeesport, Pennsylvania with his family. A career criminal that could never quite make it on the straight and narrow, Angel Face was charged and convicted of participating in a counterfeit gasoline ration coupon scheme during World War II. Kaminsky died in 1960 at the age of sixty-five.[9]

After being paroled on the Hooper murder conspiracy charge, **Sam Fleisher** relocated to the Miami area and became a model citizen, passing away on January 17, 1960, at the age of fifty-one. Fleisher's obituary noted that he was president of his local Lions Club.[10]

Louis Fleisher was paroled from prison on November 4, 1957, after having spent a total of sixteen years on Alcatraz. His criminal background made him one of the most respected inmates in the prison. Lou was a compulsive gambler, and his infractions of the prison rules often landed him in D Block, the isolation cells where prisoners were locked down twenty-four hours a day; they were let out only once a week for a shower.

Fleisher had seen it all on the island, including the infamous "Battle of Alcatraz" escape attempt and gunfight in May 1946. Fleisher was a trusty in D Block and witnessed the beginnings of the fracas while he was mopping the floors. The plotters asked him if he wished to go along, but Fleisher declined. Later, six convicts shot it out with prison officials and a battalion of US Marines. The Leathernecks, fresh from the Pacific theater of World War II, fired thousands of bullets, grenades, and tear gas shells into the cell house in a successful attempt to dislodge the escapees. Fleisher and the rest of D Block's inmates huddled in their cells as plaster, cement, and raw sewage showered down upon them as a result of the intense barrage. The gun battle claimed the lives of two guards and three of the escapees; perhaps a dozen others were injured. Lou even briefly left the island on a day trip to San Francisco later that year to testify on behalf of the three surviving mutineers; Clarence Carnes, Sam Shockley, and Miran "Buddy" Thompson. Fleisher's testimony did them little good as Carnes got a life sentence while the other two were sentenced to death.[11]

After he returned to Detroit, Fleisher began extorting local cleaning businesses. Those that resisted had their shops torched. A mere six months after his release, on May 23, 1958, Lou and an accomplice named Joey Aneliak were busted on the roof of the Dorsey Cleaners at 1348 E. 7 Mile Road. They drilled holes in the roof and poured gasoline inside in full view of a DPD surveillance team across the street.[12] Both men pleaded guilty, and Fleisher was initially sent to the federal prison at Milan, Michigan for violating his parole. After a brief transfer to Leavenworth in the early 1960s, Lou filed for the vacation of his original sentence. Fleisher's motion was successful, and he was shipped back to Milan pending the end of his term. Unfortunately, Louis Fleisher never made it home. Just two weeks before his scheduled release, Fleisher was found dead in his cell on the morning of April 3, 1964. The autopsy revealed that he had suffered a fatal heart attack during the night.[13] All told, Lou had spent more than half of his life in prison.

Sam Drapkin, member of the "Junior Purples," died on August 22, 1965, at the age of fifty-six. **Sam Millman**, Harry's brother, served a brief prison term after being found guilty of obstruction of justice during the Ferguson grand jury investigation. After his release, Sam operated on the fringes of gambling and labor rackets for years. He retired to the quiet life and died on March 20, 1969. Sam was laid to rest in Workmen's Circle Cemetery next to his father, mother, and brother Harry.

Prison psychologists diagnosed **Philip Keywell** as being "hostile with a big shot complex." Nevertheless, Keywell was promoted to trustee in 1950; he spent most of his time working on the prison's farm. A couple years later, Phil was transferred from Jackson to the minimum-security Maybury Sanitarium in Northville, Michigan, where he acted as the foreman of the chicken ranch. A media firestorm was touched off when it was alleged that under-the-table payoffs had gotten Phil his cushy job at the sanitarium. The newly formed Michigan Corrections Committee then shipped Keywell back to Jackson.

By late 1962, Phil Keywell was a candidate for release. At the subsequent hearing, it became apparent that the wanton 1930 murder of teenaged Arthur Mixon was still a sensitive issue. Susie Mixon, Arthur's now-elderly mother, pleaded for justice for her son and that Keywell should remain in prison. Phil's father, Jonas Keywell, made a tearful plea of his own on behalf of his son, "Please give my son back to me…I'll set him up. I know he'll make up for the past." Phil himself told the board, "I've regretted the incident my whole life. I was twenty-one, naïve, ignorant, and no doubt, a little bit stupid." When asked if he carried a gun back in 1930, Keywell answered, "I always carried a gun. During the Prohibition era…it was the accepted thing, like wearing an overcoat. Everybody carried a gun." Outgoing Michigan Governor John Swainson commuted Phil Keywell's sentence in December 1962 and he was released from prison. Phil then married, found legitimate employment, and eventually died, presumably of natural causes, sometime before 1993.[14]

Simon Axler ended up working as a minor figure in gambling operations in both Florida and Nevada. Axler died of natural causes in Las Vegas in January 1979 at the age of seventy-seven. **Harry Pont**, the Purple hanger-on who had tried to drive the mortally wounded Earl Pasman to safety back in 1931, passed away in Alameda, California in 1979.[15]

Solomon "Solly" Levine, the terrified survivor and witness of the Collingwood Manor Massacre, disappeared shortly after his 1932 interview with *News* reporter Jack Carlisle. He was reportedly living in Kansas City under an assumed name in the early 1960s.

Abe Burnstein, now a dapper, semi-retired gambling figure in the Motor City, spent many years trying to free his brother Ray from prison. After the 1945 revelations of the corrupt conditions at Jackson Prison, both **Ray Burnstein** and Harry Keywell were returned to the maximum security facility at Marquette, where they enjoyed no special privileges and were reintroduced to the stark realities of prison life; bars, walls, and someone else telling them what to do. Ray conducted education classes in prison; teaching fellow convicts how to read. One of his hobbies was birds. He trained two canaries in his cell. They would come to him when he called, perch on his shoulder, sing. Burnstein eventually sent the canaries as a gift to a close friend.[16]

One of the highlights of Burnstein and Keywell's second tour of duty at Marquette resulted in an off-beat pro sports anecdote for the ages. During a visit from Detroit Red Wings manager Jack Adams, the two mobsters persuaded him to arrange for an outdoor exhibition between the Wings and a team of convict players. Equipment was donated so the inmates could practice and a neat patch of regulation-sized ice was cultivated on the prison grounds. On the chilly afternoon of February 2, 1954, the best hockey players the Northern Michigan State Penitentiary had to offer faced off against the cream of the National Hockey League. The game wasn't even close (the Red Wings were leading 18-0 at the end of the first period) but it provided a welcome break from the grind of prison life for the two Purples and their fellow convicts.[17]

Many appeals for the pair followed through the years, but they were rejected with machine-gun regularity. One 1961 affidavit was allegedly from Solly Levine, who had been supposedly tracked down in Kansas City by attorney John Babcock and the chaplain from Jackson Prison. Levine's affidavit said, concerning the Collingwood Manor Massacre, "I wasn't there. I never went there. I never saw those guys that day." No dice. Their only hope was to get their sentences commuted down to second-degree murder, so they would be eligible for parole.[18]

In the spring of 1963, Ray Burnstein suffered a severe stroke that left him wheelchair-bound and paralyzed on the left side. His speech was badly impaired when orderlies wheeled him before the parole board on October 31, 1963. Ray managed to deny any involvement in the Purple Gang or the Collingwood Manor Massacre, but he also stated, "I needed correction and I got it. I learned that crime certainly does not pay."

On January 16, 1964, after 32 years in prison, Raymond Burnstein was granted a mercy parole and immediately admitted to the University of Michigan Medical Center in Ann Arbor, where he would eventually die at the age of sixty-three on July 9, 1966.[19]

Aberham Burnstein survived his brother Raymond by only two years. The seventy-seven year old leader of the Purple Gang was found dead of natural causes in his long-time suite at the Book-Cadillac Hotel in downtown Detroit on March 7, 1968.[20]

Joseph Burnstein joined his younger brother **Isadore** in California in the late 1940s and settled in San Mateo. Both men lived wealthy lifestyles untouched by police or media scrutiny. Among other things, the Burnsteins owned Mexican casinos and thoroughbred racehorses. They also acted as consultants to the burgeoning West Coast criminal syndicate. Joe and Izzy Burnstein would both die of natural causes; Izzy in November 1978 and Joey in February 1984.[21]

SAM ABRAMOWITZ was last heard from shortly after Harry Fleisher was arrested in Florida in January 1950. In a vaguely ominous development, attorney Edward H. Kennedy, Jr. suddenly produced an affidavit from Abramowitz alleging that Kim Sigler had promised him "a check with figures a mile long" if he would implicate Fleisher, Mike Selik, and Pete Mahoney in the Aristocrat Club robbery case. Sigler angrily responded with, "Oh, nuts! Who's been scaring Sammy? The thing is absolutely silly and false." Indeed, it was a near carbon copy of the affidavits purported to be from Solomon Levine in the aftermath of the Collingwood Manor Massacre convictions. And like Levine before him, after allegedly producing a statement that exonerated the Purples he snitched on, Sam Abramowitz vanished without a trace and was never heard from again.[22]

Henry "Heinie" Luks eventually moved to Bay City, Michigan, changed his name to Henry Pruss, and began working for the Dow Chemical Company. For all intents and purposes, he had gone straight. Luks eventually retired to Lakeland, Florida, where he died on September 19, 1981 at the age of 65.

Pete Mahoney suffered what turned out to be a fatal heart attack in prison and died on June 26, 1959. While not actually involved in the conspiracy to kill Senator Warren Hooper, it was widely believed that the relatively innocent Mahoney knew the truth but never snitched on his friends. Indeed, both Harry Fleisher and Mike Selik sent a wreath to his funeral that remembered him as a "swell little guy who kept his mouth shut."[23]

Special prosecutor **Kim Sigler** served as Michigan's governor for just two years. After being defeated for re-election in 1948, he returned to private law practice. Sigler died on November 30, 1953 when the airplane he was riding in crashed into a television transmission tower in Battle Creek.[24]

Republican Boss **Frank D. McKay** eventually retired to Florida, but not before masterminding the gubernatorial defeat of Kim Sigler in 1948 by convincing key Republicans to stay away from the polls. McKay passed away in Miami Beach at the age of eighty-one on January 12, 1965, a millionaire many times over. In his will, McKay founded an annuity trust at the University of Michigan for the creation of the Frank D. and Agnes C. McKay Medical Research Foundation. In McKay's obituary, Kenneth McCormick recalled, "He always went out of his way to tell you the good things he had done for the underprivileged and to insist on his straight-laced conduct." If Frank McKay ever had any regrets about the bad things, he never voiced them.[25]

Harry Fleisher was released from prison on October 18, 1965. Fleisher had served a total of fifteen years on the murder conspiracy and armed robbery charges. H.F. was a model prisoner and a trusty who worked as clerk of the food department. Fleisher even helped to supervise a successful blood drive, "Operation Leaky Arm," in which he contributed several pints. After his parole expired in 1969, Harry faded into obscurity. Some said he went to Las Vegas, where he supposedly worked for the Licavoli family in some capacity. Another source says Fleisher worked as a warehouse manager for the Ewald Steel Company before dying in May 1978 at the age of seventy-five.[26]

Original Purple **"Little" Morris Raider** was released from prison in the spring of 1944. Raider would eventually settle in Southern California, where he became a successful builder and realtor. He passed away in San Diego in December 1994 at the ripe old age of ninety-three.[27]

Myron "Mikey" Selik was paroled from prison in August 1965. Unlike his pals, Selik returned to crime once his parole expired in 1969 and handled some gambling action for the Partnership. While not technically on the straight-and-narrow, Mikey lived a mostly quiet existence. By the late 1980s, Selik had been admitted to a Southfield, Michigan nursing home. Not long after his arrival, two authors approached the aged gangster for an interview on the Warren Hooper murder case. No help was forthcoming though, as Mikey snarled, "I didn't rat on my pals forty years ago, and I ain't gonna rat on 'em now!" Selik remained at the nursing home, where he died on August 7, 1996 at the age of eighty-three.[28]

Harry Keywell was transferred back to Jackson Prison along with Ray Burnstein when the latter suffered his stroke in 1963. Within two years, Harry's sentence was commuted to second-degree murder, thereby making him eligible for parole. After thirty-four years of incarceration Keywell, still a relatively young man at fifty-four, walked out of prison on October 21, 1965. Harry's family greeted him at the gate. After his parole expired four years later, Keywell married and found a permanent job; he lived out his remaining days as a model citizen of Oakland County, Michigan. Harry ultimately outlived his two brothers, Philip and George, and almost all his old friends. In Keywell's later years, he would often gather at Max Silk's deli at Michigan and Trumbull with other aged Purples to have a cup of coffee and spend time with his old friends. The last surviving core member of the Purple Gang, Harry passed away from Alzheimer's disease in Boca Raton, Florida on August 30, 1997 at the age of eighty-six.[29]

Just about all of the Purples paid for their lives of crime, whether by death, long years in prison, or shame from their families and communities. A very small minority (the Burnstein brothers, Sam Garfield, Mike Gelfand) managed to survive and succeed, but most did not. Yet their name was too colorful to die off completely, and for years afterwards, just about any tough guy that came out of Detroit was automatically labeled a member of the Purple Gang, regardless of whether he actually was or not. Other gangsters around the country took note of the Detroit gang's mystique; in the late 1970s, a particularly violent crew of Italian mobsters based out of East Harlem dubbed themselves "The Purple Gang."

The Purple Gang had an effect on pop culture, as well, and eventually found their way into (of all things) an Elvis Presley song, "Jailhouse Rock";

"Spider Murphy played the tenor sax-o-phone.
Little Joe was blowin' on the slide trombone.
The drummer boy from Illinois went crash, boom, bang.
The whole rhythm section was the Purple Gang."

United Artists released a motion picture entitled *The Purple Gang* in 1960. Robert Blake starred as the psychotic William "Honeyboy" Willard, who leads the teenaged Purple Gang punks (the Burnstein brothers are disguised as the Olsen brothers) into organized crime with the older crooks, presumably the old Sugar House bosses. They take over the Detroit rackets and become embroiled with both the Mafia and the heroic Detective Bill Harley, who has the thankless job of cleaning up the town. The Cleaners and Dyers War is in full swing and the embattled cleaners turn to the Sicilians for protection from the Purples.

Honeyboy starts to get a little carried away with murder when his best friend Hank Smith tries to tip Detective Hanley off to the Mafia leaders' whereabouts. Hank's merely trying to help out the gang, but Honeyboy has Killer Burke seal his buddy alive inside a coffin and drop him into the Detroit River. In a scene reminiscent of both the Miraflores and Collingwood massacres, Blake and two of his goons storm the Mafia's apartment headquarters and machine gun the three leaders, Licovetti, Castiglione, and Ricco. Eventually Blake gets his comeuppance and the film ends.

Later that same year, the Detroit gang was featured in an episode of the ABC crime show *The Untouchables*. Eddie Fletcher was played by B-movie kingpin Steve Cochran.

In more modern times, the Purples served as a plot device for an episode of the short-lived ABC police drama *Detroit 1-8-7*. In addition, a Detroit rap group led by the late Proof appropriated the Purple Gang name in the early 2000s. In the ultimate irony (given how much *illegal* beer the Purples pushed during Prohibition), the Rivertown-based Atwater Brewery currently markets a "Purple Gang Pilsner."

PERHAPS THE MOST FITTING EPITAPH for the Purple Gang was uttered by one of its former associates during a 1983 interview with *Detroit Free Press* reporter Tim Belknap;[30]

"They ruined their lives - for what? A couple of years out there swingin'."

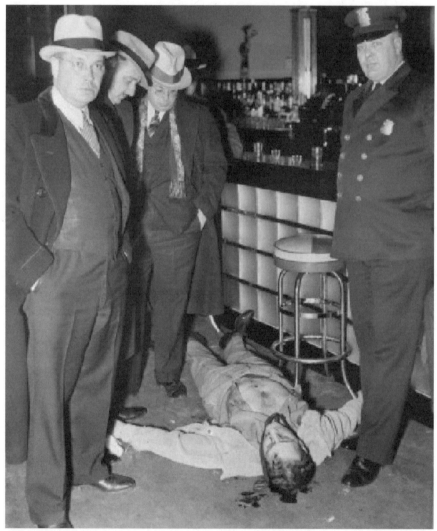

Purple Gang mobster Harry Millman lays dead on the floor of Boesky's in the early morning hours of November 25, 1937. His killers were never positively identified. *Author's Collection.*

APPENDIX

Deep in the Federal Bureau of Prisons file of Purple Gang mobster Eddie Fletcher is a letter from his old friend, Jack Schaeffer, who grew up with him and the Axlers on the Lower East Side of New York. Schaeffer was an associate of gangsters in both that city and Detroit. Jack's letter to his imprisoned pal Fletcher, written in the summer of 1930, is a remarkable document. In it, Schaeffer blissfully discusses moving illegal booze and opening a new policy racket; all the while either unaware or uncaring that Leavenworth Federal Penitentiary mail censors would read about all this malfeasance. Schaeffer tries to boost Fletcher's spirits and makes passing mention of Purples like "Simey" (Simon Axler), "Honey" (Honey Miller), "Abie" (Abe Axler), and Irving Milberg. All in all, the letter is a wonderful time capsule-like look into the personal friendships and everyday life of one of the Purple Gang's most notorious members. Reprinted here in its unedited entirety, for the first time, is Jack Schaeffer's letter to Eddie Fletcher;

July 31, 1930
Dear Pal Eddie:

Words cannot express my feeling upon receiving your letter upon opening same as I started to read I tried to guess beforehand what it might contain. You know, trying anxiously to read the whole letter in one glance. Ideas came to my mind that the Lord knows what a tough picture you were going to describe and what a hard time you were all having. But thank God I was greatly mistaken about that and you can beleive me after reading the letter I felt so happy I wanted to go out and hold up that P.O. so that I could join you in your good time. I hope what you wrote is all true & even better, altho I was told in Detroit last year that you were getting taken care of.

Speaking of Detroit reminds me that I'm going there a week from to-day. And from there to Mt. Clemens to bail out the old "dog." Will be there about 3 weeks & expect to stop at the Olympia Hotel. Will drop you a line from there. I heard from Simey, by letter. He writes that he opened a speak on Hasting St. (5119) under the name of Harry Blum. I'll stop in to see him, altho I think he is a big F--K. Do you remember big Barney Feintuch – the guy from Brooklyn who helped me & Sammy Schiff & Abie when we had the trouble with a dame? Well, he and I hooked up last winter in the whisky racket. He went down to Miami & shipped in stuff from Bimini to NY where I received it. It was the McCoy I had people begging me for it as there was a shortage here. Well, Simey, got the word & wrote Barney down south about hooking up a connection for shipping into Detroit, which Barney agreed to do, but can you imagine Simey wanted us to bankroll a carload to Detroit & when he sold it he would give us back our money (Big hearted.) So we dropped that proposition.

We got along pretty nice in this businen till the agent spotted us & knocked us off for about 100 cases & pinched Barney. His case is still pending but we had it fixed so it will be pigeonholed. He & I are booking a game now. (Clearing house numbers) & making a few. We started June 10 with a G note & went broke about four times but kept on booking & the angels must be with us because we came back each time and are now out of the red. Our book worked up from $50 a day play to the present $550 a day & if we keep going at this rate we will have a book of a G a day in a short while, and you know buddy, that is money, even if you only handle it.

Here is the dirt.

Sammy Schiff got married a few months ago. He hooked up with a dame that is working in Rose's Corner store on Clinton & Rivington. You may know her. Her name is Evelyn and I think she is an old flame of Doc Derdiger. Charlie Axler has another son. And boy this will knock you up. (I hope.)

You remember that redheaded dame that I used to run around with? She worked in Luigi's in Detroit & you wrote me about Honey spotting her in some spot with a fat bootlegger. She is my partner, Barney's, sister & her name is Rae Raymond. A couple of months ago she returned from the South and was trying to get started in a night club in NY. But some manager told her to bob her schnozzle so I took her to a friend of mine, a famous plastic surgeon (Dr. Pratt on West End Avenue) for whom I do publicity & he operated on her nose, an operation for which he gets from 3 to 5 C's but he did it for me free. At that time I cracked to this broad that she is now so good looking that I'll probably lose her. A couple of nights later we were stepping out. I took her to a spot in Greenwich Village, a hole in the wall night club, a clip joint. And who do you think was working there as a waiter. Yes sir, you guessed it. It was Rusty, the guy Abie, you & I met in Oscar's on 51 St. Well I intro-duced the bim to Rusty & since he is a friend of ours I asked him to pull up a chair & drink with us. It was a slow night so he did. He got pretty tight & we went to another joint on 54 St. and after that Rusty was so drunk that I took him to a hotel & the gal drove in her car home. I did not see either of them since, but last night the bim calls me up & tells me she and Rusty got spliced in Bklyn Marriage license Bureau, and a Jewish ceremony will be a week from Sunday & she wants me to be present. But I'm going to Detroit so I'll have to miss it. Now, will you beleive in Santa Claus? I feel like calling up May Slater & propose marriage to her just to get even.

I want you to give my best regards to Abie, Irving, & the rest of the gang & keep some yourself, buddy – Will write a soon as the cramp leaves me. Till then. Good night.

-The same old Jack

If you enjoyed *Off Color,* consider reading *A Killing in Capone's Playground.*

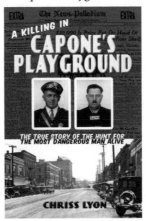

The never before published details of the killing of Officer Charles Skelley and the apprehension of Fred "Killer" Burke that led to revelations about the St. Valentine's Day Massacre.

END NOTES

Chapter 1

1   *Detroit News*, April 1, 1928. This is the most commonly referred to story as to the origin of the *nom de guerre* of "Purple Gang." Both the shopkeeper's remarks and this story itself were almost certainly an invention of the author of the article.

2   Robert A. Rockaway, *But – He Was Good To his Mother: The Lives and Crimes of Jewish Gangsters*. New York, Jerusalem, Gefen Books, 1993, pg. 69.

3   FBI File, *The Purple Gang*, Vol. 2b, pg. 37.

4   Tim Belknap, *Detroit's Purple Gang, Detroit Free Press*, Sunday Magazine, June 26, 1983, pg. 2.

5   Rockaway, pg.69.

Chapter 2

1   http://www.jewishvirtuallibrary.org/jsource/History/pale.html

2   *New York Times*, April 28, 1903.

3   Irving Howe, *World Of Our Fathers: The Journey of the East European Jews To America And The Life They Found And Made*, New York, Galahad Books, 1976, pgs. 1-25.

4   Howe, pg. 10

5   Rich Cohen, *Tough Jews: Fathers, Sons, and Gangster Dreams*, New York, Simon & Schuster, pg. 42.

6   Shvitz is a corruption of the Yiddish term *shvitsn*, meaning sweat. Since heated water was scarce in the Pale, many villagers relied on bath houses for cleanliness. While there, the heated rooms provided the *shvitsbod* (steam bath) which opened their pores and cleansed their skin. The Purple Gang mobsters of the future almost always referred to taking a steam bath as "taking a shvitz."

7   Nathalie Babel (ed.), *The Collected Stories of Issak Babel; The Odessa Stories; How Things Were Done In Odessa*; New York, London, W.W Norton & Co., 2002, pg. 148.

8   Howe, pg. 27.

9   Social Security Death Index. Although Abe Burnstein would routinely shave two years off of his age throughout his adult life, Abe's death certificate and tombstone indicate that he was born in Russia on January 5, 1891. Abe's and his brothers' surname is regularly (then and now) misspelled as "Bernstein."

10 Social Security Death Index. Like his brothers, Joe Burnstein's age fluctuated on public documents. Joey's death certificate shows that he was born in Russia on December 20, 1899.

11 Howe, pgs. 40-41.

12 Howe, pgs. 27-63. The exact date of the Burnstein family's immigration is unknown. The 1910 U.S. Census was used to recreate the approximate dates of their relocation, as well as their ages at the time of the journey.

13 Richard Bak, *Detroit Across Three Centuries*, Farmington Hills, MI, Thomson Gale, 2001.

14 Rockaway, pg. 61.

15 Rockaway, pg. 63.

16 Paul R. Kavieff, *The Purple Gang: Organized Crime In Detroit, 1910-1945*, New York, Barricade Books, 2000, pg. 1.

17 Social Security Death Index. Raymond Burnstein's Beth El Memorial Park tombstone gives his birthdate as January 7, 1903, while Isadore Burnstein's death certificate gives his birth date as March 15, 1909.

18 1910 U.S. Census.

19 Kavieff (2000), pg. 2.

20 Kavieff (2000), pgs. 3-4.

21 Harry Fleish was born to Louis and Mollie Fleish on April 16, 1903, most probably in or around Panevėžys, Russia (present-day Lithuania), and brought to America as a young boy. The 1910 census has the Fleishs living at 291 Alfred Street in Little Jerusalem.

22 Kavieff (2000), pgs. 10, 20.

23 Kavieff (2000), pg. 4. Samuel Purple was born circa 1903 in New York to Russian-Jewish immigrants Louis and Eva Purple and brought to Detroit around age six. The 1910 Census recorded him living with his family at 305 E. Montcalm Street. By WWI, the Purples had moved to 1751 Russell Street. Sammy Purple is sometimes suspected of bequeathing his last name to the gang he belonged to as an adolescent. His younger brother Benny was also a member of the juvenile Burnstein Gang. Sam Purple's "real" name is often incorrectly said to be "Samuel Cohen."

24 Born in Boston on December 24, 1899, Morris "Moe" Dalitz would move to Detroit with his family as a young boy. He lived in Little Jerusalem at 305 Alfred Street and attended the ungraded Bishop School with the Burnsteins. Moe and his brother Louis went into bootlegging at the start of Prohibition (they transported their hooch in laundry trucks.) Both Dalitzs moved to Cleveland in the mid-1920s. Moe Dalitz would later become a nationally respected Las Vegas-based organized crime figure.

25 Kavieff (2000), pgs. 4-5;

26 Little is known about Abe Burnstein's early years in the downtown gaming halls. His employment at the Dresden Café is mentioned obliquely in the September 12, 1933 issue of the *Detroit News*.

27 Kavieff (2000), pgs. 2, 22; *Detroit News*, March 8, 1919. His real name may have been Isadore Cohen, and under the alias of "Joe Murphy," he may have formerly worked for New York gang boss "Dopey Benny" Fein, who inherited leadership of what was left of the old Eastman Gang after the 1912 murder of "Big Jack" Zelig. Murphy may have arrived in Detroit after beating the charges in the 1914 killing of an innocent bystander named Frederick Strauss in a labor sluggers' feud. Murphy's probable connection to the Lower East Side underworld would do well to explain the future presence of many New York hoods in the gang's ranks.

28 Louis Fleish was born on September 15, 1905, most probably in or around Panevėžys, Russia (present-day Lithuania), and brought to America as an infant. By World War I, he and his family had moved from 291 Alfred Street to 165 Division Street. Louis Fleish, Sr.'s junkyard was located at 120 Hastings Street.

29 Kavieff, pgs. 19-20. The 1920 U.S. Census has Abe living with his family at 318 Leland Street.

30 According to his World War I draft card, Samuel Abramson was born in 1887 in Vilnius, Russia (present-day Lithuania) and immigrated to America around the age of eighteen. The 1910 U.S. Census has Abramson living with his cousin at 100 Monroe Street in Manhattan. *Detroit Times*, July 27-29, 1929 provides some background on the Circle Restaurant.

31 Kavieff (2000), pgs. 4-6.

32 Abe Burnstein's Detroit Police Department record shows he was arrested for speeding on May 17, 1918; the case was dismissed. Joe Burnstein was busted on July 2, 1919 for armed robbery. After pleading guilty, Joey was sentenced to probation.

33 Born in Detroit's Little Jerusalem on March 17, 1901, Morris Raider was convicted of armed robbery in 1919 and was being housed in Jackson Prison at the time of the 1920 U.S. Census. Raider's DOB is found at the SSDI (Social Security Death Index.)

34 Raymond Burnstein's DPD record notes that he was arrested for armed robbery on January 26, 1917 and sentenced to ninety days in jail.

Chapter 3

1 For a good overview of Prohibition in and out of Detroit, as well as the methods of making illegal booze, the author recommends, Philip. P. Mason, *Rumrunning and the Roaring Twenties: Prohibition on the Michigan-Ontario Waterway*, Detroit, Wayne State University Press, 1995; John Kobler, *Ardent Spirits: The Rise and Fall of Prohibition*, New York, Da Capo Press, 1993 re-issue. Stroh's syrup quote at Mason, pg. 79.

2 Kobler, pg. 239-241.

3 Mason, pgs. 72-78.

4 Kavieff (2000), pg. 9; Jack Selbin was born on February 17, 1896 in Kiev, Russia (modern-day Ukraine.) Selbin allegedly served for three years as an infantry private in the Argentine Republic before immigrating to America. At the start of World War I, he was living at 497 Gratiot Avenue. Soon after he married Anna Wutkowska, mother of Zygmund aka Ziggie.

5 The 1920 U.S. Census has Jake and William Trager living in a crowded boarding house at 109 Watson Street. Jake Trager was a brother-in-law of Brooklyn gangster Anthony "Little Augie" Carfano. *Detroit News*, March 12, 1923, September 10, 1923; *Detroit Times*, March 12-13, 1923.

6 Description of Oakland Avenue businesses taken from Belknap, pg. 1.

7 According to the 1910 U.S. Census, Kantrowitz most probably immigrated to America in 1906. The same census had him living with his cousin Meyer Mordetzky in an overcrowded tenement at 177 Monroe Street in Manhattan. This address was only a block or so from where Sam Abramson was then living; given later events, it's reasonable to assume that both men met each other in this time frame.

8 George Gerson Goldberg was born in Canada on January 1, 1896. Brought across the border into America as a small child, Goldberg was recorded as living at 324 E. Ferry Avenue in the 1920 U.S. Census. Goldberg was charged with assaulting a John Driscoll over a $200 debt on May 10, 1922. He was also charged, along with George Cordell, with obstruction of justice when they attempted to bribe Assistant Wayne County Prosecutor Seward Nichols into laying off the statutory rape case of one Ray Patton. Goldberg was eventually convicted of stealing the 300 cases of oleo from the Universal Carloading and Distributing Company on January 14, 1923. George settled the matter out of court. FBI File, *The Purple Gang*, Vol. 2c, pgs. 20-21.

9 Charles Leiter's birth date and birthplace can be found on the SSDI and his World War I draft card.

10 By his own admission, Henry Shorr was born in Kiev, Russia (modern-day Ukraine) in 1898. His age and physical specs were reconstructed from the 1930 U.S. Census and an October 1932 Detroit Police Department memorandum found in FBI File, *The Purple Gang*, Vol. 2a, pg. 44. *Detroit News*, December 1, 1935 offers some brief notes on Shorr's background.

11 Much of what is known about the early years of the Detroit Mafia family is marred by inaccuracies and speculation. The Detroit family is often said to have been "founded"

by Vito Adamo circa 1908. In fact, Vito Adamo and his brother Salvatore were Sicilian merchants who were ruthlessly extorted by a pre-existent Mafia crew headed by Tony Giannola. After killing their main tormentor, Carlo Callego, in August 1913, the Adamo brothers were then officially "made" into the rival Mirabile crew. The Callego murder touched off a violent Little Italy vendetta referred to by Detroit's media as the "Shotgun War." Both Adamo brothers would lose their lives in a Mullett Street ambush. The war eventually ended when Mirabile supporters tried unsuccessfully to kill Tony Giannola with a mail-order bomb in April 1914. A generally accurate overview of the root causes of this vendetta can be found in *Detroit Free Press*, November 25-28, 1913.

12   LaMare's birth date and birth place are taken from his Mt. Olivet Cemetery tombstone and his World War I draft card.

13   *Detroit Free Press*, January 4, 1919.

14   *Detroit News*, February 27, 1919.

15   *Detroit News, Detroit Free Press*, March 7, 1919.

16   Marty Steele's birthdate and birthplace were obtained from his World War I draft card. Details of his violent death can be found at *Detroit News* and *Detroit Times*, November 12-13, 1920. Although Abe Burnstein was dressed to the nines and on a first-name basis with the arresting homicide detective, he was referred to as a "shoe clerk" in contemporary newspaper accounts, showing that Abe and his cohorts were still largely anonymous to the Detroit populace. Over the course of his career, Abe Burnstein proved adept at evading the law. He had only two slip-ups; after a August 15, 1921 arrest for being a disorderly person, he was fined $10 or 10 days in jail; Abe was busted on May 21, 1922 for maintaining and operating a gambling place and given 90 days in jail. These dual convictions turned out to be the only jail time Abe Burnstein would ever serve.

17   Samuel Fleish was born on April 28, 1908 in Detroit to Louis and Mollie Fleish.

18   Harry, Louis, and Sam Fleish were (and still are) referred to as "Fleisher" in most sources. After Harry's first arrest on June 9, 1921 for receiving stolen property, the booking sergeant misspelled his name with an "er." Police, newspapers, and fellow gangsters consistently used this moniker. While all three brothers were occasionally referred to by their given name, they more-or-less adopted Fleisher as a family-shielding alias. As a result, for simplicity's sake, I've chosen to refer to the brothers by this widely known name.

19   Kavieff (2000), pg. 19; The 1920 U.S. Census has the Romanian-born Altman living his parents, Joe and Anna, at 171 Delmar Street.

20   Kavieff (2000), pgs. 18-19, Belknap, pg.4; Sam Davis was born circa 1908 in Detroit's Little Jerusalem to Romanian-Jewish immigrants Louie and Gusty Davis, according to his Michigan State Police wanted posters and the 1930 U.S. Census. The 1910 U.S. Census has Sam and his family living at 268 Winder Street, just a block or two away from both the Burnstein family and the Bishop Union School.

21   1920 U.S. Census. Their family name of Keywell may have been an "Americanized" version of Kivelovitz (Jonas Keywell's naturalization record spells his birth name as 'Keywellevitz'.) Philip (born 1909) and Harry (born December 8, 1910) were born in New York City to Russian-Jewish immigrants Jonas and Lena Keywell. The Keywell family moved to Detroit's Little Jerusalem circa 1913 and settled at 683 Cameron Avenue. Philip and Harry's father Jonas initially went into the junk business with a few of his brothers (the Hastings Street junkyard of the Keywell Bros. was catty-corner to that of Louis Fleish, Sr.) before opening a Milwaukee Avenue candy shop. Phil Keywell's first arrest, at the age of 17, was for stealing a car at gunpoint from a Woodward Avenue dealership on August 10, 1926. Keywell gave his occupation as a "salesman" for the Levine Tobacco Company; coincidentally, this was the same Oakland Avenue smoke

shop that George Goldberg was patronizing at the time of the Venice Café Gang's drive-by on September 5, 1923.

22 Irving Shapiro's age is from his Machpelah Cemetery tombstone and the July 27-29, 1929 issues of the *Detroit Times* have biographical data of him.

23 Frank Bari with Mark C. Gribben, *Under the Williamsburg Bridge: The Story of an American Family*, Victoria, BC, Canada, Trafford, 2009, pg. 11.

24 According to his WWI draft card, Isadore Schwartz was born on October 18, 1893 in Warsaw, Russia (modern-day Poland). In 1918, he was living at 153 Superior Street.

25 Abraham Kaminsky's immigration records and tombstone state that he was born in the *shtetl* of Mokra Kaligorka, Russia (modern-day Mokra Kalyhirka, Ukraine) on September 26, 1894 and arrived at Ellis Island with his father Wolf on July 3, 1906. Kaminsky was recorded as living in Duquesne, Pennsylvania at the outbreak of WWI. The 1920 U.S. Census has Abe and his new wife Helen rooming at 301 Melbourne Avenue in Detroit's North End.

26 Paul R. Kavieff, *Detroit's Infamous Purple Gang*, Chicago, Arcadia Publishing, 2008, pg. 23. Wolfe's WWI draft card lists August 13, 1894 as his birth date and Kiev, Russia (modern-day Ukraine) as his birthplace. Jack gave his occupation as "jewelry salesman" and was living with his parents at 555 Rivard Street.

27 One of the older members of the Sugar House crew, Jacob Levites was born on June 22, 1886 in Odessa, Russia (modern-day Ukraine).

28 According to his Hebrew Memorial Park tombstone, William Laks was born in Russia in 1881. He was recorded as living at 55 Adelaide Street in 1918.

29 Born Samuel J. Marcovitz in 1893, Morton was a larger-than-life figure in his lifetime, due to his success on both the battlefield and the underworld. E. Barnett, a booze truck driver for Morton ally Dean O'Banion, told author Rose Keefe in 1988 that Morton began running a "stolen car exchange" with the Detroit-based "Little Jewish Navy" in 1919. Barnett seemed to be under the mistaken impression that the "Navy" was a separate crew from what would later be called the Purple Gang. In retrospect, Morton was almost certainly doing business with the older, more experienced mobsters of the Oakland Sugar House; many young members of the future Purple Gang were arrested repeatedly for automobile theft-related incidents during this time period (Little Morris Raider's first prison term, for example, was for stealing a car.) The Detroit boys appear to have begun shipping genuine Canadian whiskey west to Morton after Chicago went dry in 1920. As a nod to his rep, Samuel "Nails" Morton would later be the inspiration for character "Nails Nathan" in the 1931 James Cagney gangster movie *The Public Enemy*. Rose Keefe, *The Man Who Got Away: The Bugs Moran Story*, Nashville, Cumberland House, 2005, pg. 82-83.

30 Patrick Downey, *Gangster City: The History of the New York Underworld 1900-1935*, Fort Lee, NJ, Barricade Books, 2004, pgs. 99-110. Like Nails Morton, the evidence of Waxey Gordon's partnership with the Purple Gang is limited yet compelling. Born on January 19, 1888 in New York City, Irving Wexler allegedly got his nickname of "Waxey" because he could slip his hand into a mark's pocket as quickly as if it was coated with wax. Author Patrick Downey and Gordon's arrests of pick-pocketing cast doubt on this version. In actuality, his friends dubbed him "Wexey" (a play on his birth name), which eventually evolved into "Waxey." Gordon's membership in Dopey Benny Fein's Lower East Side crew would have been the prime place for him to make contact with the older, New York-originated members of the Purple Gang. Gordon was one of the bigger rum-runners on the East Coast, and his partnership with the Purples seems to have revolved around the sale of narcotics.

31 As previously noted, much that is known about the Detroit Mafia family is clouded by

inaccurate information. A careful perusal of contemporary newspapers, FBI reports and U.S. Secret Service documents had led the author to the conclusions stated above. Ignazio Caruso and Salvatore Catalanotte were the recognized bosses of the family throughout the 1920s. Caruso had originally inherited leadership of the old Downriver Giannola faction after Sam Giannola's October 1919 murder while an old-line Vitale soldier named Joseph DeStefano was dubbed boss of the so-called East Side crew. Chester LaMare's crew was unique in that it consisted largely of gangsters that were not Sicilian but from Southern Italy (as was LaMare himself.) Indeed, they emerged as a third-party during the latter stages of the Giannola-Vitale War and were nicknamed "The Romans," because of their non-Sicilian ancestry. LaMare's crew also featured a number of non-Italians, such as Austrian mobster Henry Tupancy.

32   *Detroit Free Press*, December 1, 1922.

33   *Detroit News*, September 11, 1923.

34   Bari, Gribben, pg. 13.

35   *Detroit News, Detroit Times*, March 12-14, 1923.

36   Bari, Gribben, pg. 14.

37   *Detroit News*, March 26, 1923. This article stated that since New Year's Day, 1922, Joe Murphy's gambling house had been raided by police a staggering 171 times, an average of once every two days.

38   *Chicago Tribune*, May 14, 1923; Keefe, pg. 126. On May 13, 1923, Samuel "Nails" Morton, accompanied by gang boss Dean O'Banion and his wife, along with another friend, went horseback riding at Chicago's Lincoln Park. Morton chose a horse that was later described as particularly nettlesome and high-strung. While riding out in the street, the horse suddenly spooked and sprinted down North Clark Street. Morton stood in the saddle to regain control when his stirrup broke, spilling him to the pavement. The still startled horse then kicked out with its hind leg, striking Nails Morton square in the head and accomplishing what the Imperial German Army and rival Chicago mobsters could not. Morton was given a hero's burial with full military honors. Legend has it that one of Morton's grief-stricken friends, madcap triggerman Louis "Two-Gun" Alterie, led the offending animal out of the Lincoln Park stables, took it to a location outside of city limits, and executed the poor beast with a bullet to the brain. Alterie then telephoned the stable owner and growled, "We taught that ------- horse of yours a lesson. You want the saddle, go and get it." Whether or not this is actually happened is unknown. Regardless of its veracity, the tale made for a notable scene in the James Cagney gangster flick *The Public Enemy*.

chapter 4

1   The most accurate account of this meeting (drawn from Isadore Cantor himself) is in the July 12, 1923 issue of the *Detroit News*. Speed was born Francesco Spede in New York City on March 27, 1895 and cut his teeth in Buffalo's Italian underworld before arriving in Detroit in early 1917. Speed was known as a fast shooter (hence his nickname) and was convicted of the June 29, 1917 armed robbery of the manager of the Temple Theater. Although sentenced to serve seven years in prison, Speed was paroled in January 1921 after serving just three. Although not Sicilian, Frank found a welcome home in Chester LaMare's ethnically diverse Hamtramck crew of the Detroit Mafia family.

2   The Speed shooting is covered in the July 12, 1923 issues of the *Detroit News* and *Detroit Free Press*. Supplemental material in *Detroit Times*, July 12-13, 1923.

3   *Detroit News*, July 22, 1923.

4   Kavieff (2000), pg. 13.

5   The basic details of the shooting are in the September 6, 1923 issues of the *Detroit Free Press, Detroit News*, and *Detroit Times*.

6   The text of Isadore Cantor's interview is in the September 6, 1923 issue of the *Detroit News*.

7   George Cordell would not be arrested until October 1, 1924; the charges against him were dropped. John Bush seems to have been an alias of a member of Chester LaMare's crew; his true identity is unknown.

8   A writ that a prisoner can be released from unlawful detention and/or brought before a judge.

9   *Detroit Free Press*, September 7, 1923.

10   Destined to be the most noteworthy of the Oakland Sugar House Gang's 1923 reinforcements, Irving Milberg was born in New York City on January 16, 1903 to Samuel and Lois Milberg, according to his Federal and Michigan state prison records. His first Detroit arrest was on December 21, 1923, for violation of the Prohibition law. The charges were dismissed. Irving and his wife Bertha would eventually have a boy and a girl, George and Lois.

11   Details of Rothman's murder in *Detroit News*, November 9-10; 13, 1923; *Detroit Times*, November 9, 1923. The story of Joe Rothman's bribe attempt is in *Detroit News*, February 16, 1924.

12   *Detroit Free Press*, *Detroit News*, December 5, 1923. Reporting a car stolen either just after or before it was used in a murder was a common alibi tactic used by Detroit's gangsters during Prohibition.

13   *Detroit Free Press*, December 8, 1923.

14   The circumstances of Isadore Cantor's disappearance are covered thoroughly in the following articles; *Detroit News*, *Detroit Free Press*, *New York Times*, April 19, 1924.

15   The exact date of Cantor's murder is uncertain. The best guess (postulated by the NYC Coroner) is the night of February 7-8, 1924; just hours after he was last seen by his family. *Detroit News*, April 19, 1924.

16   *Detroit News*, February 16, 1924.

17   *Detroit News*, February 19, 1924.

18   *Detroit News*, April 14, 1924.

19   Sam Jacobs's murder and his subsequent funeral; *Detroit News*, April 13-15, 1924.

20   *Detroit News*, *Detroit Free Press*, *New York Times*, April 19, 1924.

21   Kavieff (2000), pgs. 16-17. Henry Shorr quote is on pg. 155 of the same work. Kavieff asserts that Cantor and Goldberg themselves were front men for Leiter and Shorr, while contemporary sources and the events of 1923-24 suggest that Cantor and Goldberg were indeed the rightful owners of the Oakland Sugar House and only relinquished full control when Cantor died and Goldberg remained in perpetual hiding. In addition, an informant known in official paperwork only as "Confidential Informant C" told the FBI in 1945 that George Goldberg was one of the "charter members" of the Oakland Sugar House Gang; it seems highly unlikely that he would make this comment about a mere "front-man." The same informant stated that Goldberg had "pulled out" of the Oakland Sugar House in 1924 when it moved to a new address. FBI File, *The Purple Gang*, Vol. 2c, pgs. 19,25.

22   His real name was William Beriloff and was born in Russia on November 30, 1893 according to his WWI draft card. The same card has him living on Bushwick Avenue in Brooklyn with his wife and child. Beriloff/Weiss was convicted of burglary and larceny (stemming from a fur heist) in 1919 and given a brief prison sentence. Weiss ultimately gained his freedom by turning state's evidence against his partner. He may have been the same William Weiss who (as a member of the Kid Dropper mob) was shot and wounded in a Lower East Side gunfight with rival gangster Jacob "Gurrah" Shapiro (who was also severely wounded) on August 1, 1923. *Daily Long Island Farmer*, May 19, 1920; *New York Times*, August 2, 1923.

23   *Detroit News*, July 28, 1924.

24   *Detroit News*, September 7, 1924.

25   *Detroit Free Press, Detroit News, Detroit Times*, September 15-16, 1924.

26   *Detroit News, Detroit Times*, October 25, 1924.

27   Downey, pgs. 274-277. Born Henry Shapiro, he and his brother Charles (known as Chink) cut their teeth in the Lower East Side underworld like many of their ilk. Chink Sherman was known as a bootlegging specialist and a partner in a fancy Broadway nightclub called the Club Rendezvous. Henry Sherman was a noted narcotics smuggler in addition to acting as Waxey Gordon's emissary and personal hatchet man. *News* crime reporter Jack Carlisle once referred to Chink Sherman as the "ace in the hole" of the Purple Gang and said he could be counted on to show up in Detroit with "20 or 30 guys" anytime the Purples had a beef. *Detroit News*, November 28, 1933.

28   The November 2, 3, and 6, 1924 issues of the *Detroit Free Press* and *Detroit News* were used. Just who Henry Sherman's companions were that night was never determined, most probably at least one of the Burnstein brothers and one of their top men. The owner of the Woodward Avenue nightclub is also unknown, but given his forceful reaction to the brawlers, he obviously pulled a lot of weight in Detroit's underworld.

29   Lonnie Athens, *The Creation of Dangerous Violent Criminals*, Champaign, IL, University of Illinois Press, 1992.

Chapter 5

1   Kavieff (2000), pg. 11.

2   Belknap, pg. 5.

3   Joseph Tallman was born in Detroit on February 13, 1899 and worked as a steamfitter in the years before Prohibition. He eventually got into a violent feud with the Licavoli crew that resulted in his murder on July 13, 1928. A good review of his career can be found in the July 13, 1928 issues of the *Detroit News* and *Detroit Times*.

4   The June 28, 1928 issues of the *Detroit News* and *Detroit Times* have a detailed, illustrated breakdown of Gus Nykiel's colorful career.

5   The Beck brothers had their business forcibly seized by the Downriver Sicilian mob during the winter of 1928 when they were both shot to death while escorting a fresh truckload of beer along West Jefferson Avenue. *Detroit News*, February 8, 1928.

6   An overview of Detroit's 1920s-era policy racket can be found in the December 9, 1928 issue of the *Detroit News*. In later years, John Roxborough would become noted as heavyweight champion boxer Joe Louis's first manager. Frank Loftis was seldom mentioned by Detroit's white press, but there is little doubt of his clout in the city's underworld. Loftis was mentioned quite a few times by the plotters of the 1930 attack on Inspector Henry Garvin. Details of a raid on the Idle Hour can be found in the August 5, 1929 issue of the *Detroit Free Press*.

7   Often incorrectly said have grown up in the "Jewish slums" of St. Louis, the Licavolis were born and raised in the heart of what was then St. Louis's downtown Little Italy neighborhood; most of them lived in a family owned tenement at 1006 North Seventh Street. Both Pete and Yonnie (the latter's nickname was derived from his birth name of Damiano) Licavoli arrived in Detroit in the early 1920s. Yonnie served a brief hitch in the Navy before being dishonorably discharged.

8   Belknap, pg. 5.

9   While there was confusion, then and now, as to the nature of these different Mafia liquor smuggling factions, it is obvious that the Licavolis and Moceris, while blood kin, were two different crews, with the former moving booze across the river in Detroit proper and the latter taking the upper river and Lake St. Clair. Members of the Moceri aka Lake St. Clair crew would later be linked to the June 1930 murders of Grosse Pointe

Park patrolmen Claude Lanstra and Erhardt Meyer.

10   *Detroit News*, May 7, 1930.

11   Kavieff (2008), pg.10.

12   Belknap, pg. 4.

13   Kavieff (2000), pg. 18.

14   The name of "Third Street Navy" comes from a contemporary account in the September 17, 1931 issue of the *Detroit Times*. By 1932, one Detroit newspaper referred to this crew as the "Little Navy." Rival bootleggers, reminiscing decades later, talked of the "Jew Navy." Latter-day accounts mash the various monikers into the "Little Jewish Navy", and it would frequently be mistaken for a rival gang of the Purples. While most modern sources refer to this group as the "Little Jewish Navy", I have yet to find a contemporary source that uses this specific name. Thus, I have chosen to use "Third Street Navy" when referring to them.

15   Info on Sam Abramson's career can be found in the July 29, 1929 issue of the *Detroit Times*.

16   *Detroit Times*, May 17, 1929. The Federal Narcotics Bureau (FNB) was the predecessor of the modern Drug Enforcement Agency (DEA).

17   Milton "Mezz" Mezzrow's interactions with the Purples can be found in his excellent autobiography; Mezz Mezzrow and Bernard Wolfe, *Really The Blues*, New York, Citadel Underground, 2001 re-issue, pgs. 90-103.

18   These gamblers are often inaccurately described as being "members" of the Purple Gang; while they enjoyed protection from the Purples, men like Lincoln Fitzgerald and Danny Sullivan did not hijack whiskey, extort blind pig owners, or gun down rivals in the streets.

19   FBI File, *The Purple Gang*, Vol. 1, pg. 34.

20   FBI File, *The Purple Gang*, Vol. 1, pg. 14.

21   George Goldberg opened a similar business named the Radio Corporation at the same address within several months. During a 1930 bankruptcy case, Goldberg was accused of selling stolen auto parts from this store; specifically spark plugs pilfered from the Oakland Motor Company and resold at cost. These charges, predictably, came to nothing. Around the same time (late summer 1929) Goldberg, along with his successor Henry Shorr, would be involved in a similar insurance scam in Chicago. The two Purple gangsters co-owned the Shorr Salvage and Towing Company at Wabash and 22nd streets in the Windy City. Like Credit Sam's before it, the building was mysteriously firebombed and destroyed one night, after which George Goldberg made out like a bandit on his insurance claims. The former Sugar House boss quickly fled back to Detroit before Chicago police could bring the hammer down on him for fraud. FBI File, *The Purple Gang*, Vol. 2c, pgs. 20-25.

22   William "Two-Gun Willie" Glanzrock's brief, violent stay in Detroit is described in the July 21, 1926 issues of the *Detroit Free Press*, *Detroit News*, and *Detroit Times*. Supplemental material can be found in the July 22, 1927 issue of the *Detroit Times*. Surprisingly, no serious suspicion was thrown Chester LaMare's way in the Glanzrock homicide. The violent Hamtramck confrontation between the two had occurred just a few weeks earlier, and it seems inconceivable that the violent LaMare would let such an act of insolence go unpunished. It is quite plausible that he commissioned the Sugar House Boys, specifically Lou Fleisher, to exact retribution on Willie Glanzrock.

23   According to his WWI draft card, Harry Kirschenbaum was born on July 4, 1893 in Ostrowiec Świętokrzyski, Russia (present-day Poland) and was brought to America as a small boy. In addition to Yiddish, Kirschenbaum spoke fluent Polish. Despite his chronic incarceration, Kirschenbaum was something of an escape artist; in September 1915, while being led across the infamous "Bridge of Sighs" spanning the NYC Criminal

Courts Building and the notorious "Tombs" jail, Harry managed to slip out of his cuff and bolt away before his warders could react. Harry sought refuge at his parents' Brooklyn home. It was a bad idea, as a shamed and enraged Herman Kirschenbaum physically dragged his son back to the jail and turned him over to police. Background info can be found in the May 7, 1930 issues of the *Detroit Free Press*, *Detroit News*, and *Detroit Times*. Kirschenbaum's brief jailbreak is detailed in the September 30, 1915 issue of the *New York Evening Telegram*.

24   According to immigration records and the 1910 U.S. Census, Giuseppe Miragliotta, aka Joseph "Honey" Miller, was most probably born in Sant'Agata di Militello, Sicily in 1899 and brought to the U.S. at the age of six with his family aboard the *Napolitan Prince*. While in Cleveland's Big Italy, the Miragliottas lived in a cramped rooming house at 2012 Woodland Avenue. Few details survive of the Kent, Ohio cop killing Miller was allegedly involved in have survived (for example, there is no entry on the ODMP website for such a killing.) The exact origin of his nickname is uncertain. While Detroit police and media occasionally referred to Miller as "Honey Boy," his friends almost always just called him "Honey." The author has followed their lead in this work.

25   Johnny Reid's birth date is on file at the Evergreen Cemetery office in Detroit, Michigan. His near-murder at the hands of Dapper Don Collins is covered in the May 16, 1921 issue of the *New York Times*.

26   *Detroit News*, January 10, 1925. Additional info at Daniel Waugh, *Egan's Rats: The Untold Story of the Gang the ruled Prohibition-era St. Louis*, Nashville, Cumberland House, 2007, pg. 229.

27   Detailed analysis of Johnny Reid and his gang's crimes can be found in Waugh, pgs. 227-241.

28   Samuel Simon Axler was born in New York City on June 23, 1901 to William and Mollie Axler; he added nine months to his age on his WWI draft card, possibly in an effort to get into the service. If so, it was unsuccessful, as Simon did not serve in the military.

29   Like many members of the Purple Gang, Eddie Fletcher's age fluctuated on public documents. He gave his birthdate as September 12, 1898 on his WWI draft card; it appears that Eddie padded his age by two years when he began boxing professionally at the mere age of fifteen. Newspapers at the time of his 1933 murder reported him as 35 years old. However, Fletcher's federal prison records, Beth David Cemetery tombstone, and last two U.S. Censuses of his life indicate a birth date of May or June 1900. Thus, I favor this year as the correct birth year. Although he often told people he was born in Hoboken, New Jersey, immigration records clearly show that Samuel Fleischacker (Eddie Fletcher) and his family departed Hamburg, Germany on May 23, 1906 aboard the *Amerika* and arrived at Ellis Island almost two weeks later on June 4. His address changes can be found in the 1910 and 1920 U.S. Census.

30   Immigration records show that Abraham Axler and his family left Hamburg aboard the *Amerika* on April 11, 1907 and arrived at Ellis Island almost two weeks later on April 23. The 1910 and 1920 U.S. Census for his address on Clinton Street.

31   In later years, Charles "The Professor" Auerbach would move to Detroit and function as an advisor and armorer for the Purple Gang.

32   *New York Evening Telegram*, November 30, 1920.

33   *New York Evening Telegram*, March 9, 1921.

34   *Detroit News*, April 1, 1928. According to New York prison records, Abe Axler was only at Sing Sing for about a month. On January 23, 1922, Abe was transferred to Auburn State Prison, where he would remain until December 10, 1924, when he was shipped north to Clinton State Prison (colloquially known as Dannemora), where he

would stay until his parole on August 15 of the following year.

35   *New York Evening Telegram*, June 21, 1922.

36   *New York Evening Telegram*, July 3, 1922. The article does not specify which of the boxers fell ill. It was probably Dandy Dick Griffin, as Fletcher returned to New York and immediately fought again, while Griffin was sidelined for nearly a month.

37   Much of Eddie Fletcher's boxing career is on file with http://boxrec.com/list_bouts. php?human_id=51350&cat=boxer. This website lists his record at 6-14-2. A careful review by the author of NYC-area newspapers during WWI bumps Fletcher's win total to 13.

38   *Detroit News*, July 29, 1929.

39   *Detroit Times*, November 27, 1933.

Chapter 6

1   *Detroit News*, October 26-27, 1925.

2   The root causes of the Cleaners and Dyers War are examined in the 1928 trial transcript (People of the City of Detroit vs. Charles Jacoby, Abe Bernstein, Raymond Bernstein, et. al., Detroit Recorders Court, Docket No. 80627), and in the March 30, 1928 issue of the *Detroit News*. Additional background found in Kavieff (2000), pgs. 53-59.

3   Waugh, pg. 231.

4   Mike Dipisa's age and birthplace were acquired from immigration records and his WWI draft card. The murder of Andrew Walk and Dipisa's role in it at October 19, 23, and 24, 1924 issues of the *Detroit News*. Police officials explained away Mike's bruises by saying that he "encountered a heavy door on the way out." Dipisa's killing of Earl Maher at the March 26-30, 1925 issues of the *Detroit Free Press*, *Detroit News*, and *Detroit Times*. His subsequent acquittal on the grounds of self-defense is detailed at *Detroit News*, January 29, 1927.

5   The June 28, 1928 issues of the *Detroit News* and *Detroit Times* were used in addition to Kavieff (2000), pg. 35.

6   *Detroit News*, June 28, 1928.

7   The August 12, 1926 issues of the *Detroit News* and *Detroit Times*.

8   The restaurant, located at 2968 Brush Street, was run by "Papa Leo" Giorlando, a local Mafia figure. Dead in the shooting were Joseph Guastella and Cecil Genovese, the part-owner and chef respectively. Wounded were waitress Marion LeBeis and two hoodlums named Louis Ross (a probable alias) and Mariano Milito (a Mafia associate who was once questioned in the 1918 murder of Giannola *capo* Peter Bosco.) Papa Leo Giorlando and the enigmatic "Jimmy the Dog" were said to have barely escaped the attack. The August 13, 1926 issues of the *Detroit News* and *Detroit Times*.

9   The August 26-27, 1926 and June 28, 1928 issues of the *Detroit News* were used, as well as the August 26-27, 1926 issues of the *Detroit Free Press* and *Detroit Times*.

10   *Detroit News*, March 29, 1927; *Detroit Times*, November 27, 1933 for Abe Axler's criminal record. New York State chauffeur's licenses made out to Abe and Simon Axler found in Apartment 308 at the Miraflores Apartments were dated June 22, 1926, indicating that they didn't arrive in Detroit until after this date. Abe and Simon Axler most probably moved in organized crime circles during this year-long interlude between prison and Detroit; their probable employers include Burnstein ally Waxey Gordon and Jacob "Little Augie" Orgen, a Russian-Jewish gangster who had inherited the Lower East Side crime mantle formerly held by such men as Monk Eastman, Kid Twist Zweifach, Big Jack Zelig, and Nathan "Kid Dropper" Kaplan. Orgen himself would be murdered in October 1927 at the behest of his top underling, Louis "Lepke" Buchalter.

11   Additional info on Axler's appearance in Richard Bak, *Detroitland: A Collection of Movers, Shakers, Lost Souls, and History Makers from Detroit's Past*, Detroit, Wayne State

University Press, 2011, pg.287. Jack Carlisle's reference to Axler is in the November 27, 1937 issue of the *Detroit News*.

12   *Detroit News*, September 20, 1926.

13   The October 30, 1926 issues of the *Detroit News* and *Detroit Free Press*; Waugh, pgs, 235, 266-267. Mentioned by the alias of Abe Woods in the articles, Abe Axler's DPD record confirms his arrest on the date in question. Ironically, Axler had first arrived in Detroit from New York a mere three days before his arrest. Charles "Tennessee Slim" Hurley eventually wound up back in St. Louis. He lasted almost exactly a year longer before he was taken for a "one-way ride." Hurley's dead body was found floating in Horseshoe Lake, located in St. Clair County, Illinois, in October 1927.

14   *Detroit News*, November 10, 1926; the DPD records of all four Purples show they were arrested on the date in question on a charge of robbery armed (the usual charge given when a member of the Purple Gang was held for general questioning.)

15   George Cordell's real name was Cordelli. He was apparently born circa 1893 in Italy and brought to America as a boy. He was charged along with George Goldberg in June 1922 with attempting to bribe the father of a girl who had filed a statutory suit against a friend of theirs. Cordell appears to have defected from the Sugar House mob to the LaMare crew in 1923 (Isadore Cantor identified him as being in the maroon murder car in the September 1923 drive-by.) All appears to have been forgiven during the Cleaners and Dyers War, however.

16   Primary details of Samuel Sigman's murder are found in the December 10-12, 1926 issues of the *Detroit Times*, *Detroit News* and *Detroit Free Press*.

17   Johnny Reid's violent demise was covered thoroughly in the December 27-29, 1926 issues of the *Detroit News*. Supplemental material is found in the November 27, 1933 issue of the *Detroit News*. Leo Dipisa's death at the Fair Haven roadhouse is covered in the November 24-25, 1926 issues of the *Detroit Free Press* and *Detroit News*. Whether or not the Canadian hijackers had anything to do with Johnny Reid is uncertain.

18   The consensus of all sources, then and now, was that Frank Wright was hired by Mike Dipisa to finish the job he started the previous summer. *Detroit News*, March 29-31, 1927; Kavieff (2000), pgs. 37, 42-43. Frank Wright appears to have been a pseudonym for a Chicago-based Polish-American hoodlum; Wright was known in some circles as "Frankie the Polack"; his true name is unknown to the author. Sometime after Prohibition began in 1920, Wright drifted west; he was arrested in both Santa Monica, California and Ogden, Utah for larceny. In 1923, under the alias of Edward O'Brien, Wright escaped from the Utah prison detail as described here. Frank Wright had great connections in the Chicago underworld (as did Mike Dipisa) and was noted as a close friend of gangster Eugene "Red" McLaughlin. The latter would eventually meet a violent end as well; his decomposing body, chained to a 75 pound metal block, surfaced in a Chicago drainage canal in June 1930. Four days earlier, upon hearing of Red McLaughlin's disappearance/murder, Verne Miller sprayed a Lake County, Illinois roadhouse with submachine gun fire in retaliation. Three men were killed and two others wounded in the "Fox Lake Massacre." Miller, incidentally, would be found murdered in Detroit in November 1933 just three days after two of Frank Wright's alleged killers, Abe Axler and Eddie Fletcher, were discovered dead in Oakland County. All in all, the underworld is truly a small world.

19   Fellow Purple mobsters Abe "Angel Face" Kaminsky and Joe "Honey" Miller were living in the same Leicester Court apartment building at the time.

20   The February 4-5, 1927 issues of the *Detroit Free Press*, *Detroit News* and *Detroit Times* were used in addition to Waugh, pg. 236.

21   The real names of Joseph Bloom and George Cohen were Isaac Riesfeld and William

Harrison, respectively. The author mistakenly transposed the names on pg. 302 of *Egan's Rats*. A George Cohen appeared at Detroit police headquarters after the Miraflores Massacre and inquired if "George Cohen" was really his long-missing brother Reuben. He was not, but George Cohen is still incorrectly referred to as "Reuben Cohen" in some sources as a result. Both men were originally from New York City; Cohen/Harrison was dodging a 1925 murder indictment while Bloom/Riesfeld was wanted for a $75,000 jewel robbery and a statutory offense. The duo turned up in Chicago circa in early 1926, which is probably where they fell in with Frank Wright, an association that would prove fatal to both. The March 29-April 2, 1927 issues of the *Detroit News* and *Detroit Times* were used.

22   The name of the apartment building, Miraflores, is a Spanish expression that translates to "watch flowers" or "flower's view." Contemporary sources frequently misspelled it as "Milaflores."

23   The main details of the Miraflores Massacre can be found in the March 28-April 2, 1927 issues of the *Detroit Free Press*, *Detroit News*, and *Detroit Times*. Many accounts say that 110 bullet holes were found in the walls of the third-floor hallway; this seems to have been an exaggeration. According to DPD ballistic expert William Cavers, the following weapons were fired at the victims; a Thompson submachine gun fitted with a 50-round capacity drum magazine; a .45 caliber automatic pistol; a .45 caliber revolver; a .38 caliber revolver. With each weapon emptying once, it would appear that 70 shots were fired in the ambush. Initial accounts had a total of four men doing the shooting; later accounts amend it to three. The basic mechanics of the Miraflores Massacre (luring the victims to a private location and machine-gunning them without warning) would serve as a virtual blueprint for Chicago's St. Valentine's Day Massacre two years later; the common denominator in both cases, St. Louis gunman Fred "Killer" Burke.

24   A quote from true crime author/historian William J. Helmer.

25   For a wonderful look at the American legend that is the Thompson submachine gun, the author highly recommends William J. Helmer, *The Gun That Made The Twenties Roar*, Garland Park, NJ: Gun Room Press, 1969. Also used were Robert J. Schoenberg, *Mr. Capone*, New York: William Morrow, 1992, pgs, 140-141; The Unofficial Tommy Gun Homepage at http://www.nfatoys.com/tsmg/, and Auto-Ordnance's home website at http://www.auto-ordnance.com/.

Chapter 7

1   Like Fred Burke and the others, Ted Werner was a fringe member of the St. Louis-based Egan's Rats gang during their early 1920s heyday. Werner initially fled St. Louis after being implicated in a late 1923 messenger robbery. Details of his murder can be found in the following newspapers; *New Orleans Times-Picayune*, April 17-18, 1927; *St. Louis Post-Dispatch*, April 18, 1927; *Detroit News*, May 8, 1930.

2   Lou Fleisher's physical specs are in the FBI File, *The Purple Gang*, Vol. 2a, pg. 45. Details on Fleisher's personality and quotes from his acquaintances are in Rockaway, pg. 81.

3   Kavieff (2000), pgs, 161-163.

4   This violent shooting was covered in the July 22-23, 1927 issues of the *Detroit Free Press* and *Detroit Times*. While no evidence of exact responsibility ever materialized, police assumed that New York friends of the murdered William Glanzrock had done the shooting, while subsequent events indicate that the Egan's Rats refugees, specifically Miraflores Massacre shooter Fred "Killer" Burke, had conducted the attack in retaliation for the Ted Werner killing in New Orleans. The relationship between the Rats and the Sugar House Boys would only continue to deteriorate.

5   The violent demise of Godfrey Qualls and Hobart Harris at the hands of Abe Axler and

Irving Milberg is curiously absent from most histories of the Purple Gang. Those few that do discuss it uniformly (with no evidence whatsoever) dismiss Qualls and Harris as hoodlums. Primary details of the double shooting are found in the August 13-16, 1927 issues of the *Detroit News* and the *Detroit Times*. While the actions of the mostly Black crowd that night made it seem that Milberg overreacted, his lawyers successfully argued in his second trial in early 1928 (the jury had hung in the first trial) that Qualls and Harris had instigated the confrontation. Axler would soon marry the woman who accompanied him that night, Evelyn Burkley. Milberg had a pregnant wife and baby daughter at home on the night of the shooting.

6   William J. Helmer and Arthur Bilek, *The St. Valentine's Day Massacre: The Untold Story of the Gangland Bloodbath That Brought Down Al Capone*, Nashville, Cumberland House, 2004, pgs. 80-85. Georgette Winkeler mistakenly identified the kidnapped man as Henry Wertheimer, who didn't exist. Fred "Killer" Burke had already snatched Mert Wertheimer for a $50,000 ransom a year earlier. Just which Wertheimer brother Gus Winkeler and company grabbed in 1927 remains uncertain.

7   Eddie Fletcher and Abe Axler were the two Purples who had gotten closest to Fred Burke and the other Rats and, by September 1927, were the only two that the St. Louisans even remotely trusted.

8   Main events surrounding the botched attempt on Raymond Shocker's life are covered in the September 7-8, 1927 issues of the *Detroit News*, *Detroit Times*, and *Detroit Free Press*. Detroit Police believed that his attackers were Abe Axler and Eddie Fletcher, as said in the November 27, 1933 issue of the *Detroit News*. The author initially speculated that the attackers were Irving Shapiro and David Banks on pages 241-242 of *Egan's Rats*. Raymond Shocker also went by the alias of Schulte, but his real name was Charles Maginness. Like his pals, Shocker/Maginness was a graduate of both the Egan's Rats and Cuckoo gangs of St. Louis. A behind-the-scenes type, Shocker would be named by FBI informant Byron Bolton as one of three men who dismantled the Cadillac detective sedan used by Chicago's St. Valentine's Day Massacre killers in February 1929. One of the last survivors of the old Johnny Reid crew, Charles Maginness aka Raymond Shocker would be shot to death by unknown killers in St. Louis on May 28, 1936.

9   The career of Henry Garvin and the history of the Crime and Bomb Squad are covered thoroughly in Detroit newspapers almost daily during the early months of 1930 during the corruption trials that emerged from the January 2, 1930 attempt on Garvin's life. Additional info found in Kavieff, pgs. 84-88.

10   *Detroit Times*, September 8, 1927.

11   Details of this chase are found in the December 8, 1927 issues of the *Detroit Free Press* and *Detroit News*. The DPD records of both Jack Budd and Irving Shapiro list their sentences for the crime.

12   The full details of these behind-the-scenes machinations wouldn't could to light until February 1930, when the gangsters were finally brought to trial for carrying concealed weapons. The February 25-27, 1930 issues of the *Detroit News* were used, as well as Kavieff (2000), pgs. 86-88.

13   *Detroit News*, December 21, 1927. This episode showed that while 24-year old Ray Burnstein may have been a gang boss, he had no qualms about getting his hands dirty with heavy work.

14   Vivian G. Welch was born in rural Montgomery County, Mississippi on March 20, 1906 to Calvin and Virgie Welch. Background information on him was drawn from his WWI draft registration card and the 1910 and 1920 Census, as well as from his tombstone at Crape Creek Cemetery in Choctaw County, Mississippi. Welch's life, career, and death in Detroit are covered extensively in the February 1-4, 1928 issues of the *Detroit Free Press*,

Detroit News, and *Detroit Times*. Additional info used from Kavieff (2000), pgs. 47-52. Welch's name is occasionally misspelled as "Welsh" in contemporary sources.

15   This noteworthy quote is from the February 1, 1928 issue of the *Detroit Times*. It lends a bit of credence to the later claim of *Detroit News* crime reporter Jack Carlisle that the name "Purple Gang" was actually coined by an inventive Detroit police inspector; Crime and Bomb Squad head Henry Garvin makes a handsome suspect.

16   Police line-ups were more commonly called "show-ups" in Prohibition-era Detroit.

17   *Detroit Free Press*, February 9, 1928. Police believed that Fletcher's bulletproof vest was the first of its kind ever seized in Detroit.

18   *Detroit News*, June 8, 1928.

19   *Detroit Free Press*, June 27, 1928.

20   The final months of the Purple Gang's reign of terror on the cleaning industry were detailed by Harry Rosman during the trial. His testimony is in both the trial transcript and the June 8, 1928 issue of the *Detroit News*.

21   Details of Sam Polakoff's murder are found in the March 22, 1928 issues of the *Detroit Free Press*, *Detroit News*, and *Detroit Times*.

22   The best overall sources for the Purple Gang busts are the March 30-April 1, 1928 issues of the *Detroit News*.

23   Zygmund Wutkowska (or Wutkowski) was born in 1908 in Aleksandrów, Russia (modern-day Aleksandrów Łódzki, Poland.) Zygmund's biological father died when he was at a young age; he and his remaining family members immigrated to America in April 1914 aboard the *Graf Waldersee*. Not long after arriving in America, Zygmund's mother Anna married Jack Selbin. "Ziggie", as he was called by his family, took his stepfather's last name. He also occasionally used the alias of John Selbin, but he is better known to history as Ziggie Selbin. The 1920 Census found the Selbins living at 234 E. Alexandrine Avenue. Info about the diamond ring incident found in Kavieff (2000), pg. 83. Ziggie's shooting of brother-in-law Joseph Sykes in the April 18, 1928 issue of the *Detroit News*.

24   *Detroit News*, April 20-21, 1928.

25   Kavieff (2000), pg. 28.

26   The text of Sam Lerner's testimony can be found in the April 24, 1928 issue of the *Detroit News*. Kavieff (2000), pgs. 21-31 has a detailed description of the case. Further information can be found in the April 25-26, 1928 issues of the *Detroit News*.

27   *Detroit News*, June 5, 1928.

28   Primary details for the opening phases of the trial and be found in the court transcript and the June 4-July 11, 1928 issues of the *Detroit Free Press*, *Detroit News*, and *Detroit Times*.

29   On the night of June 27, 1928, Mike Dipisa sent one of his henchmen, James Zanetti, to Gus Nykiel's saloon at 8824 W. Jefferson Avenue to extort money from the owner. One account said that Nykiel nicked Zanetti's fender as he parked his car. Another said he refused Dipisa's goon, just as Johnny Reid had. Either way, Nykiel knocked Zanetti sprawling with his fists; the humiliated extortionist ran off in defeat. Twenty minutes later, James Zanetti returned with his boss. Gus Nykiel ignored a warning from his brother William and walked outside to talk to the two Sicilian gangsters. They hadn't been outside two minutes when the pair pulled guns and shot Nykiel dead. Constable Edward McPherson ran outside and fatally shot Mike Dipisa as he fled. Zanetti and his getaway driver managed to escape, wounding McPherson in the jaw as they did. The constable survived his wound and was decorated for bravery. James Zanetti would be acquitted of Gus Nykiel's murder in September of that year after his lawyers successfully put the blame on the dead Dipisa. *Detroit Free Press*, *Detroit News*, *Detroit Times*, June

28, 1928. Zanetti's acquittal in the September 11, 1928 issue of the *Detroit News*.

30   *Detroit Free Press, Detroit News*, June 29, 1928.

31   *Detroit Free Press, Detroit News, Detroit Times*, September 13-14, 1928.

Chapter 8

1   Marty Gervais, *The Rumrunners: A Prohibition Scrapbook*, Emeryville, Canada, Biblioasis, 1980,2009; pg. 146.

2   The premier resources on America's most famous gangster are still the oldest; Fred D. Pasley, *Al Capone: The Biography of a Self Made Man*, New York, Ives Washburn, 1930 and John Kobler, *Capone: The Life and World of Al Capone*, New York, Putnam, 1971. The best modern biography is the aforementioned *Mr. Capone* by Robert Schoenberg. These three works speak extensively of the business alliance between the Chicago mob boss and the Purple Gang.

3   For an excellent look at the oft-misunderstood Chicago gang boss George "Bugs" Moran, this author recommends the following work; Rose Keefe, *The Man Who Got Away: The Bugs Moran Story*, Nashville, Cumberland House, 2005.

4   Keefe, pg. 257.

5   An unfired .38 caliber revolver belonging to Frank Gusenberg was later found on the floor near the wall, suggesting that the frisker either dropped it in his rush or missed it entirely.

6   Forensic info on the massacre was obtained from the original Chicago Police Department reports and the Cook County Coroner's autopsy notes. John May's gruesome head wound is often mistakenly said to have been caused by a shotgun blast; the .45 ACP slug that caused the wound was removed from his skull during the autopsy. Ultimately, the autopsy notes clearly show that the only victim hit by shotgun fire that morning was Reinhart Schwimmer. Pete Gusenberg, standing second from the left in the line, had slumped sideways across a chair after being fatally shot in the opening barrage, hence the wound to his posterior. Gusenberg's brother Frank was miraculously still alive when police first arrived on the scene; he died three hours later, never breathing a word about who shot him.

7   *Detroit Free Press, Detroit News, Detroit Times*, February 16, 1929.

8   *Detroit News*, February 21-23, 1929. Some sources inaccurately say that Harry Keywell was picked up and questioned, as well. After clearing Phil Keywell and Eddie Fletcher, Chicago police apparently decided not to bother with 18-year old Harry, further evidence that they had no reason to think that the Purples had anything to do with the shootings. The massacre investigation then decidedly shifted away from Detroit and towards numerous leads pointing at St. Louis-based gunmen.

9   The best available resources on the St. Valentine's Day Massacre are William J. Helmer and Arthur Bilek, *The St. Valentine's Day Massacre: the Untold Story of the Gangland Bloodbath That Brought down Al Capone*, Nashville, Cumberland House, 2004; William J. Helmer, *Al Capone and his American Boys*, Bloomington, IN, Indiana University Press, 2011. Both books are sourced by the surviving Chicago Police Department reports (on file with the Chicago Crime Commission) as well as the testimony of Byron Bolton (one of the lookouts) and Georgette Winkeler (wife of one of the gunmen.) These sources (which were source material for the preceding pages dealing with the massacre) indicate that the Purple Gang had nothing to do with the massacre, and that the actual shooters were none other than Fred "Killer" Burke and the remnants of Johnny Reid's old St. Louis crew, who had established an autonomous relationship with the Capone mob similar to the one they formerly had with the Purples. Capone, who dubbed them his "American Boys," used the St. Louisans for high-risk jobs (in addition to the massacre, they also journeyed to Brooklyn in July 1928 and murdered gangster Frankie Yale.)

After being convicted of the December 1929 murder of St. Joseph, MI Police Officer Charles Skelly, Fred Burke was sentenced to life imprisonment at Marquette. He would die there of heart disease at age 47 on July 10, 1940, never having breathed a word about his action-packed life of crime.

10   Belknap, pg. 3

11   Several anecdotes to the Purples' recreational habits can be found in Bak (2011), pg. 288. Abe Axler and Eddie Fletcher's love of boxing is detailed in the November 27, 1933 issues of the *Detroit News* and *Detroit Times*.

12   This quote first appeared in the May 22, 1929 issue of the *Detroit News*. The article discussed about how Capone had been rebuffed during a gangland conference in Windsor, most probably by the Catalanotte-allied Pascuzzi Combine. The Chicago boss prudently retreated, as Capone had no desire to get into a protracted shooting war with Sicilian Mafiosi on both sides of the border. Over the years, however, this tale was twisted to make it sound as if it was the *Purples* who gave Capone this ultimatum, and not Sam Catalanotte and Roy Pascuzzi. This has been repeated *ad infinitum* in numerous sources with some occasional variations, i.e. "Stay the hell out of Detroit!" to become one of the core myths of the Purple Gang; that Al Capone was so afraid of them that he chose to "deputize" the Purples as his liquor agents rather than anger them. This author finds such an idea patently ridiculous. In a straight-up gang war, there is little doubt that the monolithic Capone organization would have crushed the Purple Gang in a matter of weeks, a fact that the Burnstein brothers were undoubtedly aware of. For that matter, why would the shrewd Abe Burnstein deliberately antagonize the notoriously violent Capone with tough guy rhetoric like "That is our river!" or "Stay the hell out of Detroit!"? Even if he had, would Capone have allowed Burnstein to turn him down so contemptuously? What most likely happened is after being respectfully yet firmly denied a whiskey franchise by Sam Catalanotte and Roy Pascuzzi, Capone peacefully entered into a mutual agreement with the Purples to purchase shipments of Old Log Cabin whiskey. Abe and Joey Burnstein had known Al Capone and his predecessor, Johnny Torrio, for a number of years. Both Capone and Burnstein were articulate, charming men who genuinely liked each other, and both saw that there were great riches to be had by working together. Their relationship was one of reciprocal respect, and there was no need for either man to attempt to intimidate the other. Thus, the idea that Al Capone (who had personally dispatched an estimated dozen men and ordered the deaths of scores more) was actually afraid of a Detroit gang that was a mere fraction of the size of his own is absurd. It is this author's opinion that the whole "That is our river!" story is just as fictional as the "Those boys are tainted...off-color!" story put out by the same newspaper a year earlier.

13   According to Isadore Shiller's WWI draft card, he was born in Russia on July 20, 1887. Shiller was noted as a burglar, safe-cracker, and thief. He was serving time in the Ohio State Penitentiary when America entered WWI in 1917. Shiller had been free for roughly a year when he was busted in Scranton, Pennsylvania in January 1922 for a burglary spree; he ended up serving four years in Eastern Penitentiary. Details about his criminal career were taken from the April 24, 1929 issues of the *Cleveland Plain Dealer* and *Detroit News*.

14   According to the 1920 Census, Morris Ferstman was born on September 23, 1901 in Russia and brought to America at the age of five (he added two years to his age and a native-born status to his WWI draft card.) Ferstman's record dated to 1922 and held a veritable smorgasbord of charges. He served 10 months in the Atlanta Federal Penitentiary for violating the Dyer Act (transporting a stolen car across state lines.) His most notable caper before his trip to Detroit was being arrested in Cincinnati during the

summer of 1928 on suspicion of kidnapping local bookmakers for ransom. *Cleveland News*, April 24, 1929.

15   Sam Abramson's troubles with the Cleveland hijackers are discussed in the April 24, 1929 issue of the *Detroit News* and the July 28, 1929 issue of the *Detroit Times*.

16   The specifics of Abramson's murder are in the April 18, 1929 issues of the *Detroit Free Press*, *Detroit News*, and *Detroit Times*. Supplemental material found in the July 28, 1929 issue of the *Detroit Times*. Despite being worth nearly a half-million dollars during his mid-1920s heyday, Sam Abramson left an estate of less than $50,000, which was inherited by his widow Lena and his mother, who still lived in Russia.

17   *Detroit Times*, July 27-28, 1929.

18   Details for the gruesome demise of Izzy Shiller and Skinny Ferstman can be found in the April 24-25, 1929 issues of the *Cleveland News*, *Cleveland Plain Dealer*, *Cleveland Press*, and *Detroit News*. Supplemental material can be found in the July 28, 1929 issue of the *Detroit Times*.

19   The May 15, 1929 issues of the *Detroit Free Press*, *Detroit News*, and *Detroit Times*. Additional information on the Purples' liquor losses can be found in the May 22, 1929 issue of the *Detroit News*.

20   The May 2, 1929 issues of the *Detroit Free Press*, *Detroit News*, and *Detroit Times*.

21   *Detroit News*, May 13, 1929. The charges against Kaminsky, as could have been predicted, came to nothing.

22   Born in New York City in 1899, Harry Sutton was a minor hanger-on of the Purple Gang who had served jail time at Blackwell's Island in 1924 for receiving stolen property. He got along best with fellow "Yorkies" like Abe Axler, Eddie Fletcher, and Irving Milberg.

23   This sting operation had its genesis with a February 19, 1929 DPD raid on the offices at 8679 12th Street. The cops were ostensibly looking for concealed weapons and other bootlegging evidence. Booze delivery slips were noted amongst the paperwork. These were confiscated, as were telephone and bank records (the latter made out to Eddie Fletcher and Irving Stein.) Upon their return to the Thirteenth Precinct, the raiders contacted the SAC of the Detroit office of the U.S. Treasury Department (the TD had assumed Prohibition enforcement duties within the last couple years.) Agents of the Treasury Department then placed a tap on one of the Hart Novelty Company telephone lines (the feds deliberately left the Detroit police in the dark about the tap, most probably for fear of corrupt cops leaking word to the Purples). The tap remained in place until May 4, when it was switched to another line at the same address. Ten days later, the agents made their arrests. The next day, May 15, the feds seized Purple Gang-distributed liquor at the following addresses; 112 Alfred Street, 914 Montcalm Street, 2644 and 2971 John R Street, and 2304 Hastings Street.

24   The May 15-16, 1929 issues of the *Detroit Free Press*, *Detroit News*, and *Detroit Times*.

25   The text of these interviews can be found in the May 18, 1929 issue of the *Detroit News*.

26   *Detroit News*, *Detroit Times*, May 17-18, 1929.

27   The Atlantic City meet of May 1929 is a mythical event in American organized crime history, with no two sources agreeing on who was there. Meyer Lansky's quote on the Purple Gang is in Rockaway, pg. 86.

28   *Detroit Free Press*, *Detroit News*, *Detroit Times*, August 4, 1929.

29   *Detroit Times*, July 23-24, 1929. Coincidentally, Treasury Agent Sam McKee would soon join the FBI (then still officially named the Bureau of Investigation) and distinguish himself under Chicago-based SAC Melvin Purvis during the so-called 1933-34 "War on Crime" against the Public Enemy bandits.

30   Although not officially named in the court papers or news accounts, "Earl from

Wyandotte" was almost certainly Wyandotte bootlegger Earl Begeman.

31 The trial and sentencing of the four Purples was covered by the July 22-28, 1929 issues of *the Detroit News* and *Detroit Times.*

32 The immediate details of Irving Shapiro's murder are covered extensively in the July 27-29, 1929 issues of the *Detroit Free Press, Detroit News,* and *Detroit Times.*

33 *Detroit Free Press,* July 31, 1929. This article, while a tad melodramatic, accurately reflects the apprehension the Purples felt on their way to Leavenworth.

34 The detail of the investigation of the Rapaports is covered in detail in the August 3-7, 1929 issues of the *Detroit Free Press, Detroit News,* and *Detroit Times.* DPD Police Commissioner Harold Emmons would testify during the Van Coppenolle corruption trial in February 1930 that the department's specific information was that Simon Friedman drove the gray touring car and that David Rappaport fired the fatal bullets into Irving Shapiro from the back seat. *Detroit News,* February 12, 1930.

35 This crucial incident in the history of the Purple Gang went unreported at the time, only coming out during the Ferguson grand jury investigations of 1940. *Detroit News,* August 21, 1940.

36 Jack Isenberg was an associate of both Irving Shapiro and Ziggie Selbin. He was shot to death in an automobile in the alley behind 2288 Euclid Avenue. His murder is covered in the August 27-28, 1929 issues of the *Detroit News* and *Detroit Times.* The murder of John Paul, whom police believed had been killed in a botched extortion attempt, is found the September 17, 1929 issue of the *Detroit News.* Ziggie Selbin was questioned in both cases but released.

37 The October 28, 1929 issues of the *Detroit Free Press, Detroit News,* and *Detroit Times.* Selbin's mother Anna said over his coffin; "Ziggie never talked much of his affairs, but this isn't the end of the affair. That's all I can tell you." *Detroit Times,* October 29, 1929.

Chapter 9

1 The attempt on Inspector Henry Garvin's life was covered extensively in the January 2-5, 1930 issues of the *Detroit Free Press, Detroit News,* and *Detroit Times.* The shooting and subsequent trial board would dominate the city's media for the first months of 1930.

2 The February 8-9, 1930 issues of the *Detroit Free Press, Detroit News,* and *Detroit Times* were used for the primary points of Van Coppenolle and Waldfogel's testimony.

3 The February 10, 1930 issues of the *Detroit Free Press, Detroit News,* and *Detroit Times* detailed the Rappaports' testimony.

4 *Detroit Free Press, Detroit News, Detroit Times,* February 11-12, 1930.

5 *Detroit Free Press, Detroit News, Detroit Times,* February 25-28, 1930. Additional information on the Purple Gang concealed weapons case found in Kavieff, pgs. 85-88.

6 Kavieff (2000), pgs. 151-152.

7 *Detroit Times,* May 7, 1930. In an ironic sign of the times that he lived in, young Hyman Lapedus would be arrested several days later and charged with hauling 84 pints of whiskey and 18 quarts of gin in the very same automobile he chased Harry Kirschenbaum in. Lapedus claimed to be getting $3 a load from a wholesaler whom he claimed not to know in order to help pay for his education. The boy was given three years probation. *Detroit News,* October 25, 1930.

8 The details of the Joe Burnstein shooting and the events leading up to it were covered extensively in the May 7-8, 1930 issues of the *Detroit Free Press, Detroit News,* and *Detroit Times.* Although Harry Kirschenbaum's weapon is referred to as a "Mauser" in these accounts, pictures reveal it to be a Luger P08 pistol (the Mauser Company had taken over manufacturing Lugers that same year.) The *Free Press* called it a "submachine gun," probably because of the gun's drum magazine; it is uncertain from contemporary accounts whether Kirschenbaum's Luger had been modified to fire fully automatic. An

additional note, the 1930 Census incorrectly records the Kirschenbaum family living at *4021* Cortland Avenue.

9   *Detroit News, Detroit Times*, July 4, 1930. Frank Foster and the other three hoodlums arrested with Kirschenbaum in the round-up were members of Chicago's infamous North Side Gang, and were believed to be in Los Angeles to set up a beer distribution network for crime boss George "Bugs" Moran (most accounts intimate that 'George Davis' was a long-term member of the Moran mob without realizing that he was fugitive Purple gangster Harry Kirschenbaum.) How and why Harry hooked up with the North Siders is unknown; perhaps it was a simple case of "the enemy of my enemy is my friend", as the Moran crew's arch-rival Al Capone was noted as the number one customer of the Purple Gang that was now hunting Kirschenbaum. Incidentally, Harry's near escape from the LAPD was very similar to his 1915 break from NYC's Tombs.

10   Some brief details of Sam Catalanotte's funeral can be found in the July 13, 1930 issue of the *Detroit News*. His nickname, derived from the traditional spelling of his surname of Catalanotti, was "Singing in the Nighttime."

11   Giuseppe Masseria's Mafia family is today known as the Genovese crime family while Nicola Schiro's Castellammaresi family is the present-day Bonnano crime family.

12   Mob boss Joseph Bonnano, a first-hand participant in the events, gives some behind-the-scenes insight as to what was going on the Detroit underworld during this time period in his autobiography; *A Man of Honor: The Autobiography of Joseph Bonnano*, St. Martin's, 2003, pgs. 93-105. Additional info on these events in David Critchley, *The Origin of Organized Crime in America: The New York City Mafia, 1891-1931*, New York, Routledge, pgs. 176-180.

13   The June 1, 1930 issue of the *Detroit Times* has the best overall coverage of the Milazzo/Parrino homicides. Detroit police and media of the period referred to Gaspare Milazzo by the name of "Scibilia", which was both his wife's maiden name and his most frequent alias. Additional background information can be found in the February 10, 1931 issue of the *Detroit Free Press* and the February 7, 1931 issue of the *Detroit Times*.

14   Bonnano, pgs. 93-97.

15   For the most part, the casualties of "Bloody July" were low-level gangsters; the actual leaders were deep in hiding for fear of assassination. Chester LaMare, for instance, was said to have decamped to New York after the fish market murders of May 31st. The August 11, 1930 issue of *Detroit News* offers mug shots and brief biographies of most of the major players of the "Crosstown War." Elsie Prosky's quote is in Rockaway, pg. 85.

16   The July 16, 1930 issues of the *Detroit Free Press, Detroit News*, and *Detroit Times* were used. While his surname is spelled "Overstein" by police and the media, the true spelling of his name was Ovshtein. The 1930 Census records David Ovshtein living with his family at 9551 Cameron Avenue.

17   Kavieff (2000), pg. 95.

18   Information about Arthur Mixon recreated from the 1920 and 1930 Census. He was recorded as living with his family at 1346 E. Alexandrine Avenue at the time of the shooting.

19   The intersection of Hastings and Hendrie was the same place where, seven years earlier, Oakland Sugar House boss Isadore Cantor shot and fatally wounded LaMare gunman Frank Speed.

20   Initial details on the Mixon shooting were taken from the July 23, 1930 issue of the *Detroit News*. Additional information from the October 17, 1930 issues of the *Detroit News* and *Detroit Times*. David Levitt's eyewitness testimony (including the true identity of Phil Keywell's companion) taken from Rockaway, pgs. 79-80.

21   The July 23, 1930 issues of the *Detroit Free Press, Detroit News*, and *Detroit Times* have

the initial details of Jerry Buckley's assassination.

22   The Buckley grand jury's investigation was covered thoroughly by all of Detroit three major newspapers almost daily throughout the summer and fall of 1930. After Angelo Livecchi, Teddy Pizzino, and Joe Bommarito were acquitted of Jerry Buckley's murder in the spring of 1931, Livecchi and Pizzino were convicted for their roles in the July 1930 double murder of William Cannon and George Collins in front of the LaSalle Hotel. Some years later, it was announced the Buckley's probable murderers were Licavoli crew members John Mirabella, Joe English, and Russell Syracuse. Whoever they were exactly, the radio announcer's killers were never brought to justice. The acquittal of Joe Amico, Joe Locano, and Benny Sebastiano for the murders of Gaspare Milazzo and Sasa Parrino is detailed in the October 23-24, 1930 issues of the *Detroit Free Press* and *Detroit Times*.

23   LaMare's murder was covered in the February 7-10, 1931 issues of the *Detroit News* and *Detroit Times*. Based on fingerprints found at the scene, Joe Amico and Elmer Macklin were charged with his murder. They were both acquitted in the spring of 1932.

24   *Detroit News*, August 15, 1930.

25   Kavieff (2000), pgs. 92-93.

26   *Detroit News*, *Detroit Times*, September 20, 1930.

27   *Detroit News*, September 23, 1930.

28   *Detroit News*, *Detroit Times*, October 16-18, 1930.

Chapter 10

1   Scott M. Burnstein, *Motor City Mafia: A Century of Organized Crime in Detroit*, Chicago, Arcadia Publishing, 2006, pg. 33.

2   Belknap, pg. 4.

3   The January 5, 1931 issues of the *Detroit Free Press*, *Detroit News*, and *Detroit Times* were used. The federal grand jury didn't actually indict Henry Shorr, Harry Fleisher, et.al until June 25, 1931. The Leonard Distillery case would drag on for a total of two years; charges were ultimately dismissed against Shorr and Fleisher.

4   The assault on Frank Kaier is detailed in the January 16 and February 5, 1931 issues of the *Detroit News*.

5   *Detroit News*, February 5, 1931.

6   *Detroit Times*, March 16, 1931. Although the Purple Gang's push into Corktown in early 1931 has never been formally documented, the author believes that a careful examination of the evidence surrounding the February 1931 murder of William Bruein, who served time with the Purples in Leavenworth, Abe Axler's renting of the Trumbull Avenue duplex in the neighborhood, and Sam Davis's presence at the murder scene show a never-before told aspect of the Purple Gang's history. The death of Bruein's friend William Butler at the hands of the Third Street Terrors would have been sufficient reason to hold a grudge, and assisting the Purples in taking over Corktown would have been a way of satisfying it. Bruein was born in December 1909 to John and Emily Bruein at 374 Perry Street in Detroit, mere blocks away from where his life would violently end in February 1931.

7   While most sources say that the trio left Chicago for Detroit in 1926, Hymie Paul's brother Lewis specifically stated that at the time of Hymie's 1931 murder that he hadn't seen his brother in four years, which indicates a Motor City arrival date of 1927. *Detroit Times*, September 18, 1931, Kavieff (2000), pgs.109-110.

8   Solomon Levine, usually referred to as "Sol" or "Solly", was born circa 1901, possibly in Russia. It is often said that he grew up in Little Jerusalem with the original members of the Purple Gang and was especially close with Raymond Burnstein; Solly later claimed to have known Burnstein since 1916. Levine was the black sheep of a well-to-do family who entered the Detroit underworld as a "thrill seeker," even though his

father had allegedly bought him an $85,000 scrap business to run. Levine dabbled in gambling, bookmaking, and liquor smuggling. By his own later admission, Levine was a compulsive gambler who lost just about every cent he ever made betting on horses. On December 13, 1927, Levine was shot through the leg by two Border Patrol inspectors who caught him and two others offloading a load of booze at a river dock along the foot of Parkview Avenue. Solly Levine was also said to have ran a blind pig with Purple Gang associate Max Silk at the corner of Cass and Canfield avenues. The September 17-18, 1931 issues of the *Detroit News* have some background information on Solly Levine.

9   According to immigration records, Isadore Sutker was born circa 1903 in Płock, Russia (present-day Poland) and landed with his family at Ellis Island aboard the *Zeeland* on May 29, 1912. The 1920 Census recorded the Sutkers as living at 1847 S. Homen Avenue in the North Lawndale section of Chicago's West Side. He and his wife Dora had one daughter named Beverly (born 1926.) Sutker frequently used the alias of Joseph Suttlof; many contemporary sources, including the 1930 Census, refer to him as "Joseph" Sutker.

10   Joseph Lebovitz was born in Russia circa 1900 and was brought to America as a small child. Like Sutker and Hymie Paul, he passed through adolescence in Chicago's Jewish ghetto. He was convicted of a Chicago robbery in 1920 and sentenced to ten years in Joliet Prison; he was paroled after serving half his sentence. During their saloon extortion career, Lebovitz and Hymie Paul frequented a Chicago gambling joint run by a Paul Dorfman, son-in-law of Hamtramck crime figure Jacob "Yosher" Kaplan. This connection may have been a deciding factor in their decision to flee to Detroit.

11   According to the 1910 Census, Hyman Paul was born circa 1899 in Russia and immigrated to America with his family at age five. By the beginning of Prohibition, Hymie and his brother Lewis were rooming with Lewis's in-laws at 1239 S. California Avenue in the North Lawndale section of Chicago's West Side. Often inaccurately, then and now, referred to as "Herman" Paul.

12   This quote is from the September 17, 1931 issue of the *Detroit Times*. Many modern accounts describe them simply as the "Little Jewish Navy", as if that group was a rival of the Purples; at any rate, that group had dissolved by the time of their September 1931 murder. Kavieff referred to them as the "Third Avenue Terrors" on pg. 111 of his 2000 work. The first number streets of Detroit (First, Second, Third, and Fourth) are interchangeably referred to as "Street" and "Avenue" on city maps; most commonly the "Street" designation is used in and below downtown Detroit while "Avenue" is more common to the north. Contemporary accounts specifically refer to Third "Street" rather than "Avenue" when dealing with the Purple factions, thus in this work, I have chosen to refer to the Chicago trio as the "Third Street Terrors" for ease of reference.

13   Basic details of the Butler killing are found in the August 22, 1930 issues of the *Detroit News* and *Detroit Times*. Lebovitz's involvement in the September 17-18, 1931 issues of the *Detroit News* and *Detroit Times*. Additional info in the February 26, 1931 issue of the *Detroit News*.

14   I reconstructed the Bruein murder from the February 26, 1931 issues of the *Detroit News* and *Detroit Times*, as well as the March 16, 1931 issue of the *Detroit Times*.

15   Kavieff (2008), pg. 38.

16   Belknap, pg. 2.

17   Bak (2011), pg. 288; *SOULFUL DETROIT: The Schvitz*, http://faac.us/adf/messages/35297/35353.html.

18   According to the 1900, 1910, and 1920 U.S. Census, Benjamin Bronston, Jr. was born circa 1905 in Green Bay, Wisconsin to Benjamin, Sr. and Anna Bronston. His first arrest occurred in 1922 in Brooklyn, New York, where he was charged with forgery.

Arrested on a charge of uttering and publishing in Detroit a year later, Bronston drew a sentence of 3 to 14 years in the Ionia Reformatory. His name is occasionally misspelled as "Bronstein." Basic details of his life and murder are found in the June 22, 1931 issues of the *Detroit Free Press*, *Detroit News*, and *Detroit Times*. Additional info in the October 30, 1932 issues of the *Detroit News* and *Detroit Times*.

19   This was the same flat where Irving Shapiro had formerly lived.

20   According to the 1920 and 1930 U.S. Census, Earl Pasman was born to Nathan and Rose Pasman in 1911 in Sheboygan, Wisconsin. By World War I, Earl and his family were living in Peoria, Illinois. By the time national Prohibition began in 1920, the Pasmans had relocated to Little Jerusalem. The 1930 Census had Earl living with his family at 9653 Cameron Avenue, a mere block away from David Overstein's family. Pasman's name is occasionally misspelled as "Passman." The basics of his murder are found in the July 23, 1931 issues of the *Detroit Free Press*, *Detroit News*, and *Detroit Times*, as well as Kavieff (2000), pgs. 107-108.

21   The events preceding the Collingwood Manor Massacre are agreed upon by virtually all sources. The Purples had apparently begun planning retaliation against the Third Street Terrors as early as mid-August. On August 15, 1931, a tall, well-built blonde-haired man appeared at the Collingwood Manor and asked to rent Apartment 215. This apartment was not available at the time. The blonde man returned on September 1, identified himself as "James Regis," paid one month's rent in advance ($60), and received the keys to the recently vacated Apartment 211. Just who "James Regis" was remains unknown. The September 17-19, 1931 issues of the *Detroit News* and *Detroit Times* were used. As was the September 29-October 1, 1931 issues of the *Detroit News*. Additional info in Kavieff, pgs. 111-113 and Joseph E. Wolff, *Appointment With Death – Purple Gang's Revenge*, Detroit News, Sunday Magazine, September 26, 1971, pg. 1.

22   My account of the massacre was constructed from the following sources; *Detroit Free Press*, September 17-19, 1931; *Detroit News*, September 17-22, 29-30, October 1, 1931; *Detroit Times*, September 17-22, 29-30, October 1, 1931; Kavieff (2000), pgs. 113-115; Wolff, pg.1.

23   Sessions in these rooms, conducted by pre-Miranda Act cops, frequently turned violent.

24   *Detroit Times*, September 18, 1931.

25   Charles Auerbach was born in 1883 in Romania and immigrated to America in the 1890s. As a teenager on the Lower East Side of New York, Auerbach initially worked as a peddler and was an amateur boxer. On the night of August 5, 1901, eighteen year old Charlie Auerbach shot and killed a fellow amateur boxer named Louis Josephs in front of the Café Europe near the corner of Clinton and Houston streets. The shooting was allegedly in revenge for Josephs handing a bad beating to Auerbach in Hamilton Fish Park several hours earlier. Auerbach was convicted of first-degree manslaughter five months later and sentenced to a brief prison term. By the end of the decade, he had returned to New York City and fallen in with local street gangs. Auerbach frequented Segal's Café on Second Avenue and was a contemporary of gang bosses Big Jack Zelig and Dopey Benny Fein. Private investigator Abe Shoenfeld, hired by a group of wealthy Jewish businessmen to investigate the gangs plaguing the Lower East Side, had this to say about Auerbach in his list of the "habitués" of Segal's Cafe, "Charlie Auerbach – mack (*pimp*) - strike breaker – life taker." Charles Auerbach moved west in the late 1910s; the 1920 Census found Auerbach and his wife Rose living at 1800 Cherry Street in Toledo, Ohio. The future Purple Gang mobster was most probably in the North End by the time of the Oakland Sugar House War. Auerbach's position in the Lower East Side underworld makes it reasonable to assume he was well-acquainted with such early

Purples like Jake Trager, Sam Abramson, and Joe Murphy. 1910 and 1920 U.S. Census, Albert Fried, *The Rise and Fall of the Jewish Gangster in America*, New York, Columbia University Press, 1993, pg. 2. Details on Auerbach's killing of Louis Josephs were taken from the August 6-7, 1901 and February 5-7, 1902 issues of the *New York Evening Telegram*.

26   The capture of Ray Burnstein, Harry Keywell, and Irving Milberg is extensively covered in the September 19, 1931 issues of the *Detroit Free Press*, *Detroit News*, and *Detroit Times*.

27   The formal indictment listed Sutker under the alias of "Joseph Sutker."

28   *Detroit Free Press, Detroit News, Detroit Times,* September 29-October 1, 1931.

29   *Detroit News*, October 5-7, 1931; Kavieff (2000), pg. 121.

30   *Detroit News, Detroit Times*, October 28-November 1, 1931; Kavieff (2000), pg. 117.

31   *Detroit Free Press, Detroit News, Detroit Times,* November 3, 1931.

32   Details of the trial were taken from the following sources; *Detroit Free Press, Detroit News, Detroit Times,* November 4-8, 1931; Kavieff (2000), pg.118; Wolff, pg. 1.

33   *Detroit Free Press, Detroit News, Detroit Times,* November 9-10, 1931; Wolff, pg. 1.

34   *Detroit Free Press, Detroit News, Detroit Times,* November 10-11, 1931; Wolff, pg. 1.

35   Wolff, pg. 1.

36   The Purples' last interview before their departure was detailed by Jack Carlisle in the November 18, 1931 issue of the *Detroit News*.

37   Detroit News, November 19, 1931; Wolff, pg. 1.

Chapter 11

1   Belknap, pg.3.

2   Kavieff (2000), pg. 181.

3   *Detroit Times*, November 26, 1937.

4   According to his tombstone, the 1910 and 1920 U.S. Census, Harry Millman was born in 1911 to Joseph and Esther Millman at 228 Winder Street in Detroit's Little Jerusalem. By the mid-1920s, the Millmans had relocated to 510 Josephine Street. More information on his background found in the November 26-27, 1937 issues of the *Detroit Times*, as well as the following books; Kavieff (2000), pgs. 179-181; Bak (2011), pg. 288.

5   Samuel Drapkin was born in 1909 in New York City to Maurice and Roman Drapkin according to the 1920 U.S. Census. That same year, the Drapkins were recorded as living at 302 Frederick Street.

6   Myron "Mikey" Selik was born on the specified date, most probably at 101 Division Street in Detroit's Little Jerusalem to Anna and Bernard W. Selik. Mikey's father was a machinist by trade, and ran a profitable machine shop with his brothers on 24th Street. The Seliks were well-off by the standard of the day. By the time of World War I, they had moved into a nicer house at 200 Medbury Street. By the mid-1920s, the Seliks' marriage was crumbling, largely due to Bernard's infidelity and compulsive gambling. Anna soon filed for divorce. In retrospect, it was probably around this time that Mikey fell in with the Junior Purples. He managed to stay in school until dropping out in the 10th grade. The 1930 Census has Mikey living his mother, stepfather Abe Katz, brother Hyman, and half-siblings at 1663 Gladstone Avenue. His birth date was obtained from the Social Security Death Index (SSDI). Additional info on Selik's upbringing from Kavieff (2000), pgs. 122-23; the 1910, 1930 U.S. Census.

7   Also involved in the plot were Sam Drapkin and Jack Goldman. The proposed victim, Isadore Stern, was lured to a candy store at Oakland and Kenilworth avenues on the morning of December 10, 1931. He was then taken for an auto ride and threatened with death if he didn't cough up $300. Occupants of a passing police car recognized the gangsters and pulled them over; their suspicions confirmed when one of them tossed

a revolver out of the car's window. The frightened Stern claimed not to know the men; indeed, the charges against them came to nothing. *Detroit News*, December 12, 1931.

8   *Detroit Free Press, Detroit News, Detroit Times*, February 10-11, 1932.

9   The text of Jack Carlisle's interview with Solly Levine is in the February 4, 1932 issue of the *Detroit News*.

10   *Detroit News*, February 17, 1932. Sam "The Gorilla" Davis's first-hand account is found in the August 30, 1934 issue of the *Detroit Free Press*.

11   Harry Fleisher's fellow suspect, Abe Wagner, was a member of New York's Waxey Gordon mob. Around this time, Wagner had run afoul of both Meyer Lansky and Bugsy Siegel and moved with his family to St. Paul, Minnesota. Hitmen working for Lansky and Siegel found him there on July 25, 1932 and fatally shot him. Despite a wave of revisionism over the last few decades, the evidence overwhelmingly suggests that young Charles Lindbergh, Jr. was kidnapped and murdered by Bruno Richard Hauptmann. The best books on the market dealing with the case are both by Jim Fisher, a former FBI agent and current Edinboro University professor; *The Lindbergh Case*, New Brunswick, NJ, Rutgers University Press, 1994,; *The Ghosts of Hopewell: Setting the Record Straight in the Lindbergh Case*, Carbondale, IL, Southern Illinois University Press, 2006. For this work, I have used the following; FBI File, *The Purple Gang*, Vol. 2a, pgs. 5-27; Kavieff (2000), pgs. 129-131; *Detroit News, Detroit Times*, June 9-11, 1932; *New York Daily Mirror*, March 14, 1932.

12   *Detroit News*, May 20, 1932.

13   *Detroit News*, June 9-10, 1932; *Detroit Free Press, Detroit Times*, June 10, 1932.

14   *Detroit Free Press, Detroit News, Detroit Times*, June 21-25, 27-30, July 25-26, August 1-2, 1932; Kavieff (2000), pgs. 128-132.

15   In an ominous hindsight, it's obvious that Harry Fleisher only gave himself up when he and his fellow Purples were apparently certain that Solly Levine had been neutralized, one way or another. *Detroit Free Press, Detroit News, Detroit Times*, September 7-8, 1932; Kavieff (2000), pgs. 133-134.

16   *Detroit Free Press, Detroit News, Detroit Times*, March 17-19, 1932; Kavieff (2000), pg. 128.

17   Milford Jones, like his old pals Fred "Killer" Burke and Gus Winkeler, was a former member of the St. Louis-based Egan's Rats and Cuckoo gangs. Jones had a long standing feud with members of that town's Russo Gang, of whom the Licavolis and many of their men were formerly members of. In fact, Milford Jones may have been one of the Cuckoo gangsters responsible for the July 1928 machine gun trap that killed Jimmy Russo, one of five brothers who headed that gang during Prohibition. The subsequent grand jury investigation into Milford Jones's murder concluded, based on eyewitness testimony, that Jones's killers were Pete Licavoli and Joe Massei; Pete Corrado and Joe Bommarito were identified as their two companions. Neither Licavoli nor Massei would be convicted, as the key witness against them mysteriously blew town and never returned. Abe Axler was fingered in the plot by an anonymous tipster, and was believed by some to have actually been inside the Stork Club when Jones was killed. Details on Jones's murder can be found in the June 15-16, 1932 issues of the *Detroit News* and *Detroit Free Press*. Axler's suspected role is covered in the June 25, 1932 issue of the *Detroit News*. Kavieff (2000), pgs. 123-25.

18   Details of Cohen's murder are found in the October 30-31, 1932 issues of the *Detroit Free Press, Detroit News*, and *Detroit Times*.

19   *Detroit Free Press, Detroit News, Detroit Times*, May 11, 1933.

20   *Detroit Free Press*, May 10, 1933. Honey Miller would end up spending a total of four months in the mental hospital.

21 Bak (2011), pg. 290.

22 *Detroit Times*, November 27, 1933; *Detroit News*, November 28, 1933.

23 *Detroit News*, November 28, 1933. Axler (along with Fletcher) may have been rewarded for his role in the Milford Jones hit with a percentage of this restaurant.

24 Axler and Fletcher's increasingly hard times are detailed extensively in the November 27-28, 1933 issues of the *Detroit Free Press*, *Detroit News*, and *Detroit Times*.

25 The brewery embezzlement story is taken from Kavieff (2008), pg. 32. While this claim is unsourced, the author of this work finds it plausible under the circumstances. The police postulated a slightly different version in the November 27, 1933 issue of the *Detroit Times*, saying that the Twins had been entrusted with the operation of a distillery while its rightful owner went on vacation in the summer of 1933. Instead of turning over the profits to the owner, the pair siphoned them off for themselves. Just how Axler and Fletcher expected to get away with taking this money remains unknown. Perhaps they felt it was owed to them after years of such violent yet efficient service. Perhaps it was just the desperate act of two desperate men.

26 Kavieff (2000), pg. 135.

27 Isaiah Leebove's interview request was eventually denied; Kavieff (2000), pgs. 149-153; FBI File, *The Purple Gang*, Vol. 2a, pgs. 62-63. Like more than a few of his clients, Leebove died violently; he was shot to death on May 14, 1938 during an argument with oil promoter Carl Jack Livingston in the Tap Room of the Doherty Hotel of Clare, Michigan. Purple Gang mobster Sam Garfield was on the scene and acted as a material witness. In his subsequent trial, Livingston claimed he killed Isaiah Leebove out of fear the attorney would send his Purple Gang associates after him. Defense lawyers were able to prove that Leebove and Joe Burnstein had business dealings. *Detroit Free Press*, *Detroit News*, and *Detroit Times*, May 14-16, 1938. Additional information on Leebove's background was taken from the June 16, 1933 issue of the *Detroit Free Press*.

28 *Detroit News*, July 16-17, 1933; *Detroit Free Press*, *Detroit News*, July 17, 1933. Kavieff (2000), pgs. 135-136.

29 *Detroit News*, August 8-10, 1933; *Detroit Free Press*, *Detroit Times*, August 9-10, 1933; Kavieff (2000), pgs. 136-137.

30 A fascinating character in his own right, Reading gangster Max Hassel is the subject of his own biography; Edward Taggart, *Bootlegger: Max Hassel, the Millionaire Newsboy*. Lincoln, NE: iUniverse, 2003.

31 Downey, pgs. 104-110, 275-277, 285-287. This hostile takeover, which Mafia turncoat Joe Valachi would refer to as the "Jew War" thirty years later, came about for reasons that remain unclear to this day. Author Patrick Downey lays out a plausible scenario in his work *Gangster City* that says that the crew headed by Meyer Lansky and Bugsy Siegel (The Bug and Meyer mob) had provided security for Waxey Gordon's vast East Coast brewery empire. The legalization of near-beer in April 1933 essentially made Gordon, Max Greenberg, and Max Hassel legitimate businessmen who no longer needed gangsters to guard their interests. Kicking Lansky and Siegel loose turned out to be a fatal mistake. After the April 12th double homicide (which Gordon was said to have escaped by the skin of his teeth), Waxey Gordon's men were cut down all over New York City. Henry Sherman, facing imminent gangland execution, committed suicide at his brother Murray's Bronx home in the early morning hours of October 12, 1933. His other brother, Charles "Chink" Sherman, managed to survive the Bug and Meyer mob purge only to wind up in an upstate New York lime pit in November 1935. Waxey Gordon cheated his enemies by going up on a tax evasion conviction in the fall of 1933; he was sentenced to ten years in Leavenworth Federal Prison. After his release, Gordon went back to selling heroin and committing crimes a far cry from those of his

Prohibition-era heyday. Waxey Gordon was busted for narcotics trafficking in the early 1950s and sentenced to 25 years in prison. While undergoing a physical examination at Alcatraz Federal Penitentiary on June 25, 1952, the 64-year old gangster suffered a fatal heart attack.

32   Kavieff (2000), pgs. 138-142.

33   *Detroit Free Press*, *Detroit News*, *Detroit Times*, October 7, 1933; Kavieff (2000), pgs. 142-143.

34   *Detroit Free Press*, November 27, 1933.

35   *Detroit Free Press*, *Detroit News*, *Detroit Times*, September 11-13, November 27-28, 1933.

36   *Detroit Free Press*, *Detroit News*, September 24, 1933. Incidentally, around this same time period, specifically September 22, 1933, high ranking Purple mobsters Izzy Burnstein and Henry Shorr were arrested in Washington, D.C. by members of the Federal Narcotics Bureau. After "severe" questioning, they were released. Burnstein and Shorr claimed they were in the nation's capital to find out why they had been denied a permit to legally produce alcohol after the coming of Repeal. As a UPI scribe dryly noted, the pair's arrest "was not calculated to aid their quest for a permit."

37   *Detroit Free Press*, *Detroit News*, *Detroit Times*, November 14-15, 1933.

38   *Detroit Times*, December 1, 1933. Axler was driving the very same Chrysler sedan that he and Eddie Fletcher would be murdered in just a few weeks later.

39   The attack on Axler and Fletcher is referenced in November 28, 1933 issues of the *Detroit Free Press* and the *Detroit News*. While the *News* places that attempt a week before the pair was killed, the *Free Press* dates it to two weeks before the current issue. My belief is that the *News*'s date is closer to the truth. Exactly who the assailants were is uncertain; police chalked up it to the Mafia, specifically Yonnie Licavoli (who allegedly came up from Toledo for the specific honor of personally offing the Twins.)

40   Both Abe Axler and Eddie Fletcher were avid horseback riders. At the Green Oaks stables, Axler kept his sorrel mare Waffles. Fletcher had stabled his horse, Vanity, there as well until he had sold it a year earlier. In addition to the reported conversation, Axler told Charles Stevenson that he was planning "a little trip soon to Florida."

41   My reconstruction of Axler and Fletcher's murder is drawn from the November 27-28, 1933 issues of the *Detroit Free Press*, *Detroit News*, and *Detroit Times*. Harry Millman's role in the double homicide wouldn't become public knowledge until his own 1937 murder; *Detroit Times*, November 28, 1937.

42   Verne Miller's homicide was never solved; the November 30-December 1, 1933 issues of the *Detroit Free Press*, *Detroit News*, and *Detroit Times* covered it extensively. For those interested in a closer look at Miller, the author recommends the following rare yet superb biography; Brad Smith, *Lawman to Outlaw: Verne Miller and the Kansas City Massacre*, Bedford, IN, JoNa Books, 2002.

43   While Repeal officially took effect on December 5, 1933, the state of Michigan did not authorize the sale and manufacture of intoxicating liquor, wine, and 5% beer until December 30 of that year.

Chapter 12

1   Frank McKay's career is reviewed extensively in the January 13, 1965 issue of the *Detroit Free Press*.

2   This chain of events was detailed in a confidential FBI memorandum dated May 22, 1939. While the names of Henry Shorr's contacts are blacked out, later accounts and events solidly indicate they were John Gillespie and Frank McKay. FBI File, *The Purple Gang*, Vol. 2b, pgs. 58-60.

3   FBI File, *The Purple Gang*, Vol. 2b, pgs. 59, 64; *Detroit Free Press*, *Detroit Times*, June 17,

1945; Bruce A. Rubenstein and Lawrence E. Ziewacz, *Three Bullets Sealed His Lips*, East Lansing, MI, Michigan State University Press, 1987, pg. 110; Kavieff (2000), pgs. 191-192.

4   *Detroit Free Press*, November 17, 1963.

5   The intricacies of this liquor conspiracy would not come out publicly until 1945, when both Charles Leiter and Izzy Schwartz testified against Frank McKay. The Republican boss was acquitted on all charges. *Detroit News*, January 11, 1935; *Detroit Free Press*, September 1-2, 1945; *Detroit Times*, September 1-3, 1945; FBI File, *The Purple Gang*, Vol. 2c, pgs. 23-24. George Goldberg, among others, was noted in the FBI file as having a controlling interest in the Puritan Wineries of Paw Paw, Michigan, of which Charles Leiter, Izzy Schwartz, and Frank McKay were all stockholders. Coincidentally, in the months before Repeal, George Goldberg narrowly escaped being kidnapped. On July 15, 1933, Goldberg was accosted in front of his apartment building at 1926 Collingwood Avenue. Goldberg grappled with his assailants, who savagely pistol-whipped him before they were scared off by witnesses. Goldberg spent the next couple weeks recuperating at a cottage along Bear Lake, outside of Manistee, Michigan. The identity of George Goldberg's attackers, and their subsequent fate, is unknown; *Detroit Free Press*, July 27, 1933; FBI File, *The Purple Gang*, Vol. 2c, pg. 23.

6   Leonard Simons' reminisces are found in a Neal Shine column entitled "Distilled Memories" in the March 27, 1994 issue of the *Detroit Free Press*.

7   Doran's murder was covered extensively in the June 13-14, 1934 issues of the *Detroit Free Press*, *Detroit News*, and *Detroit Times*. Eddie Doran was noted to have sung for a time at an Ecorse nightclub run by East Side mobster Joe Massei. Harry Millman's almost certain involvement was revealed in the November 28, 1937 issue of the *Detroit Free Press*.

8   The text of Sam "The Gorilla" Davis's confession is found in the August 30, 1934 issue of the *Detroit Free Press*.

9   Sam Davis's official DPD record confirms the date of his sentencing and committal to the Ionia State Mental Hospital as October 1, 1934.

10   Henry Shorr's final blow-up and feud with Frank McKay and his old Purple Gang partners is found in the FBI File, *The Purple Gang*, Vol. 2b, pgs. 58-60. As indicated, while their names are blacked out, it's clear that Frank McKay and John Gillespie are the individuals at the center of this feud. While the specific date of Shorr and Gillespie's visit to Grand Rapids is not listed, the most likely date is Saturday, December 1st, just two days before Shorr's disappearance. This confidential FBI memorandum makes it obvious that Shorr was murdered not only because he was making competition for his former Purple Gang partners, but because he posed a direct threat to Republican Boss Frank McKay.

11   It is interesting to note that immediately after Oscar Shorr called the police to report Henry missing, someone in the Purple Gang got wind of this and promptly made the intimidating phone call to the Shorr house. The Shorr family, no doubt, figured that someone in the DPD had tipped off the Purples. The Internal Affairs division of the DPD later launched a small, off-the-record investigation as to who leaked this info to Shorr's killers. The results of this inquiry were never made public, and no action was taken.

12   *Detroit Free Press*, March 27, 1994.

13   The particulars of Henry Shorr's disappearance/murder weren't revealed to the public until a month after the fact. For my reconstruction of it, the January 11-14, 1935 issues of the *Detroit Free Press*, *Detroit News*, and *Detroit Times* were used. Mary Shorr's visit to Harry Fleisher in prison is detailed in Kavieff (2000), pg. 157. John Gillespie was extremely afraid for his life after Shorr vanished. Gillespie disappeared on April 4, 1935 in a near identical manner to his Purple Gang associate. Gillespie turned up a few days

later, claiming to have been lying low with a close friend in Lansing. Another bizarre incident occurred in October 1935 when John Gillespie and a local cab driver were found, armed and dangerous, lurking outside of Frank McKay's estate. Gillespie claimed to be carrying a gun for his own protection. His family claimed that he had suffered a nervous breakdown. *Detroit News*, April 5-9, 1935.

14 *Detroit Free Press, Detroit News*, April 12, 1935.

15 The September 22, 1940 issue of the *Detroit News* gives a consolidated history of the city's racing wire service; Kavieff (2000), pg. 149.

16 Kavieff (2000), pgs. 151-152.

17 Jack Budd was convicted and sentenced to life in prison for killing a machinist named Frank Olsen during the attempted robbery of a saloon at 747 E. Woodbridge Street on September 27, 1935. Budd and three other masked individuals had stormed into the place and ordered the owner and customers to turn out their money. Olsen, who had come into the bar to cash his weekly paycheck, was pushed when he failed to comply quickly. Olsen grabbed Budd back and was fatally shot in the chest. Budd's handkerchief dropped from his face and, as a result, he was the one robber subsequently identified by witnesses. *Detroit Free Press, Detroit Times*, September 28-30, 1935.

18 Kavieff (2000), pgs. 163-164; *Albion Morning Star*, December 15, 1996.

19 *Albion Morning Star*, December 9, 1996.

20 *Detroit News*, April 15, 1936. In addition to the eight year sentence and $20,000 fine, the IRS hit Harry Fleisher with a tax lien of $14,028 on the Federal Avenue property that housed the distillery.

21 *Detroit News*, June 3-5, 1936; Kavieff (2000), pgs. 163-167.

22 The November 25-27, 1937 issues of the *Detroit News* and *Detroit Times* provide background on Harry Millman's invasion of the Mafia's prostitution racket. Additional info was drawn from Kavieff (2000), pg. 181.

23 *Detroit News*, August 29, 1937; *Detroit Times*, November 25, 1937.

24 Kavieff (2000), pg. 182.

25 The bombing death of Willie Holmes was thoroughly covered in the August 29-30, 1937 issues of the *Detroit Free Press, Detroit News*, and *Detroit Times*.

26 *Detroit Times*, November 27, 1937; Kavieff (2000), pg. 184.

27 Belknap, pg. 5. The exact date of their talk is uncertain. As Jack Carlisle noted in 1983, "I interviewed him on Tuesday and he was killed on a Saturday night." Carlisle's memory may have been playing tricks on him here, as Millman was murdered in the early morning hours of Thanksgiving Day, Thursday, November 25.

28 My account of the Millman/Gross homicides was recreated from the November 25, 1937 issues of the *Detroit Free Press, Detroit News*, and *Detroit Times*. Additional information was drawn from the November 26-28, 1937 issues of the *Detroit Times*.

29 *Detroit News, Detroit Times*, December 16-17, 1937; Kavieff (2000), pg. 185.

30 Burton B. Turkus and Sid Feder, *Murder Inc.; The Story of the Syndicate*; Da Capo Press, Cambridge, MA, Reissued 1992, pg. 9; Kavieff (2000), pgs. 186-187. The consensus of all modern sources is that Happy Maione and Pep Strauss (no one but police and media called Strauss by his better known nickname of 'Pittsburgh Phil') came west from Brooklyn to kill Harry Millman. Most even have it that Murder Inc. informant Abe "Kid Twist" Reles specifically fingered them to Burton Turkus. However, this is not the case. Nowhere in Reles's extensive testimony is the 1937 killing of Harry Millman mentioned. Nor did any of the other half-dozen informants that Turkus utilized in his Murder Inc. prosecution have anything to say about the Millman/Gross homicides in Detroit. Turkus doesn't specifically say that Maione and Strauss killed Millman in his book, he only hints at it (Harry Gross is forgotten in most accounts of the shooting.) In fact,

the *only* clue that New Yorkers may have been involved was the fact that the Michigan license plate was traced to a vehicle that had been purchased by an individual that gave a fictitious New York address. While it is certainly feasible that Maione and Strauss could have done the shooting, the case for their guilt is nowhere near as clear cut as conventional wisdom would have it. In truth, like many other gangland hits of the era, we will probably never for certain just who Harry Millman's killers were.

31   Belknap, pg.5.

Chapter 13

1   Jack Carlisle's piece appeared in the November 27, 1937 issue of the *Detroit News*.

2   These two books are excellent sources for the history of Alcatraz Federal Penitentiary; John Godwin, *Alcatraz: 1868-1963*, Garden City, NY, Doubleday, 1963; James A. Johnston, *Alcatraz Island Prison*, New York, Scribner's, 1949.

3   Schedule from an interview with former prisoner in the September 6, 1936 issue of the *New York Herald Tribune*; Godwin, pgs. 80, 121-122.

4   Godwin, pgs. 78, 122.

5   Godwin, pgs. 84-85; Johnston, pg. 245.

6   Serbian-American gangster Elmer Macklin had been a key member of Chester LaMare's crew back in Detroit and a front-line participant in the Crosstown War of 1930-31. Although he couldn't be officially "made" into the city's Mafia family, Macklin was entrusted with a lucrative counterfeiting ring as a reward for his participation in LaMare's murder. He was convicted of counterfeiting in January 1934 and arrived at Alcatraz early the next year after a brief stay at Leavenworth.

7   Godwin, pg. 80; Johnston, pgs. 31-33.

8   *Chicago Daily Times*, June 23-24, 1936.

9   Godwin, pgs. 123-124. This incident was the basis for a particularly shocking scene in the 1979 Clint Eastwood film *Escape From Alcatraz*.

10   *New York Herald Tribune*, September 6, 1936.

11   Kavieff (2000) pgs. 167-172 has a detailed description on Jack Ekelman and Louis Fleisher's labor racketeering and subsequent feud. Supplemental material found in the April 28-30, 1938 issues of the *Detroit News* and *Detroit Times*.

12   Details behind Jack Ekelman's disappearance/murder were drawn from the April 28-29, 1938 issues of the *Detroit Free Press*, *Detroit News*, and *Detroit Times*.

13   The capture of the Fleishers and Sidney Markman were covered thoroughly by the April 28-May 2, 1938 issues of the *Detroit Free Press*, *Detroit News*, and *Detroit Times*. James Payne's quote at Kavieff (2000), pg. 176.

14   *Detroit News*, April 7, 1939; January 18, 1940.

15   *Detroit News*, September 30, 1938.

16   The initial handbook robbery was covered in the July 8-11, 1939 issues of the *Detroit News*, as well as the July 9-11, 1939 issues of the *Detroit Free Press* and *Detroit Times*. Kavieff (2008), pgs. 103-110 provides photographs and a general summary of the robbery and subsequent scandal.

17   *Detroit Free Press*, *Detroit News*, August 6-10, 1939; *Detroit Times*, August 7-11, 1939.

18   The Ferguson grand jury hearings were intensively covered by the three major Detroit daily newspapers all throughout the remainder of 1939.

19   *Detroit News*, October 31-November 1, 1939; Kavieff (2008), pg. 82.

20   Belknap, pg. 2.

21   The September 22, 1940 issue of the *Detroit News* provides a summary of Judge Homer Ferguson's findings.

22   The vast majority of the imprisoned Purples' privileges were revealed to the Dethmers revelations in the summer of 1945. *Flint Journal*, *Albion Evening Recorder*, July 24, 1945;

Detroit Free Press, July 24-25, 1945.

23   *Detroit Free Press*, January 13, 1965; *New York Times*, November 13, 28, 1940, July 13, 1941; Rubenstein and Ziewacz, pg. 5.

24   *Flint Journal*, December 14, 1943; biographical sketch of Kim Sigler, authored by Carrie Sharlow, is found on pg. 38 of the May 2012 issue of the *Michigan Bar Journal*; Rubenstein and Ziewacz, pg. 7.

25   This quote found in a private letter from Sigler to William R. Cook, dated May 9, 1944, located in the Marshall L. Cook and William R. Cook Papers, on file with the Michigan Historical Collections, Bentley Historical Library, University of Michigan.

26   Testimony of Warren G. Hooper, The People of Michigan vs. William J. Burns, Docket 7723, Ingham County Circuit Court, October 8, 1943, pgs. 13-18; Rubenstein and Ziewacz, pgs. 15-16.

27   *Detroit News*, January 19, 1945; *Detroit Times*, January 20, 1945.

28   Rubenstein and Ziewacz, pgs. 12-14.

Chapter 14

1   The inner workings of these jailhouse interactions were taken from the Statement of Louis Brown, Inmate #48529-J, given on January 27, 1947 to Kim Sigler, Donald S. Leonard, Joseph Sheridan, *et. al* and the Statements of Ernest Henry, Inmate #13172-J, taken on April 1, 22 and May 1, 1947 in the office of Circuit Judge James Breakey, Ypsilanti, Michigan. Both men were part of the Purple Gang clique in Jackson Prison. Both sets of statements are on file in Box 19 of the Donald S. Leonard Papers in the Michigan Historical Collection, Bentley Historical Library, The University of Michigan. Supplemental material was taken from Rubenstein and Ziewacz, pgs. 195-196.

2   According to the 1910 U.S. Census, Sam Abramowitz was born in 1909 in Ohio to Abraham and Yetta Abramowitz. Sam grew up in Little Jerusalem at 294 Adelaide Street. Abramowitz later claimed to have known the Fleishers since childhood. Additional info on Abramowitz taken from Rubenstein and Ziewacz, pg. 97.

3   Henry Luks's background and role in the Hooper murder conspiracy is detailed in the following sources; The April 18, 1945 testimony of Henry Luks, Box 19 of the Leonard Papers; the May 13, 1945 issues of the *Detroit Free Press* and *Detroit Times*; Rubenstein and Ziewacz, pgs. 85-97.

4   Sam Abramowitz himself detailed the events of the murder conspiracy after Henry Luks's removal from the plot during his trial testimony in the summer of 1945; People of the State of Michigan vs. Harry Fleisher, Peter Mahoney, Myron Selik, and Samuel Fleisher, 37th Judicial Court, Calhoun County, Michigan, File 15-64, Docket 42436, pgs. 56-104 (to be referred to as the 'Hooper Murder Conspiracy Trial Transcript' in further citations); Rubenstein and Ziewacz, pgs. 121-123, 197.

5   Rubenstein and Ziewacz, pgs. 197.

6   My account of the last hours of Senator Warren Hooper's life were re-created from the January 12, 1945 issues of the *Albion Evening Recorder, Detroit Free Press, Detroit News, Detroit Times*, and *Lansing State Journal.*; *Detroit News, Detroit Times*, January 13-14, 1945; Rubenstein and Ziewacz, pgs. 15-19, 198-199.

7   Statement of Harry Snyder to Kim Sigler, Murl Aten, Oscar G. Olander, *et. al.*, Box 19 of the Leonard Papers.

8   Rubenstein and Ziewacz, pgs. 21-24.

9   *Detroit Times*, January 13, 1945.

10   Rubenstein and Ziewacz, pgs. 38-40.

11   *Lansing State Journal*, January 19, 1945; *Detroit Free Press, Detroit Times*, January 20, 1945. Abe Rosenberg, a middle-level of the Purple Gang in years past, picked up his nickname of "Buffalo Harry" because he had come to Detroit from the New York city of

the same name.

12 Rubenstein and Ziewacz, pg. 69.

13 *Detroit News*, April 20-21, 1945; *Detroit Free Press, Detroit Times*, April 21-22, 1945.

14 *Detroit Times*, April 24, 1945; *Flint Journal*, April 29, 1945.

15 *Detroit Times*, May 3, 1945.

16 *Albion Evening Recorder, Detroit Free Press, Detroit News, Detroit Times, Flint Journal*, May 11-13, 1945.

17 *Detroit Free Press, Detroit Times*, June 11, 1945; Rubenstein and Ziewacz, pgs. 109-112.

18 *Detroit Free Press, Detroit News, Detroit Times*, June 17, 1945.

19 *Detroit Free Press*, July 18, 1945.

20 Hooper Murder Conspiracy Trial Transcript, pgs. 21-34.

21 Rubenstein and Ziewacz, pg. 120.

22 Hooper Murder Conspiracy Trial Transcript, pgs. 60-116.

23 Ibid., pgs. 117-141.

24 *Detroit Free Press*, July 25-28, 1945.

25 *Detroit Free Press, Detroit News, Detroit Times*, August 1, 1945.

26 *Detroit Free Press, Detroit News, Detroit Times*, November 29-30, December 11, 1945; Rubenstein and Ziewacz, pgs. 156-157.

27 *Lansing State Journal*, February 14, 1946; Rubenstein and Ziewacz, pgs. 157-158.

28 Rubenstein and Ziewacz, pgs. 190-191.

29 This re-creation of Senator Hooper's murder was constructed from the statements of Louis Brown and Ernest Henry, all four of which are on file in Box 19 of the Leonard Papers. Additional material from Rubenstein and Ziewacz, pgs. 198-199.

30 Official report of Michigan State Police Detectives Walter B. Williams and Murray Young, written on April 13, 1948. On file in Box 19 of the Leonard Papers.

31 Rubenstein and Ziewacz, pgs. 200-203.

32 Bruce A. Rubenstein and Lawrence E. Ziewacz conclude persuasively in their definitive book on the Warren Hooper murder case (*Three Bullets Sealed His Lips*) that the key to understanding why Ray Burnstein and Harry Keywell were never prosecuted for the senator's murder is found in then-Governor Kim Sigler's personality. They argue that Sigler was a very driven yet vain man who had extreme political ambitions that may have reached as far as the White House. Sigler understood that a conviction against the bankroller of the senator's assassination (Frank McKay) would serve his career far better than publicly exposing that the senator was killed by two hoodlums who were already serving life sentences for murder. Even with the testimony of Louis Brown and Ernest Henry, Sigler knew that no jury in Michigan would take the word of two minority armed robbers over that of a prominent white multi-millionaire. Thus realizing he was in a no win-situation, Sigler covered up these facts with frightening efficiency; many people involved in the investigation were fired. Those who remained were so beholden to the governor; they would keep their mouths shut. Kim Sigler's last hope at getting McKay died when Harry Fleisher and Mike Selik went on the run in 1948. If he had exposed Burnstein and Keywell at point, Governor Sigler would have had to face an avalanche of questions about why he was engaging in a political vendetta against Frank McKay instead of prosecuting the actual killers of the senator. Undoubtedly seeing that his political career would go down in flames as a result, Sigler remained silent, Ray Burnstein and Harry Keywell remained in prison, and Frank McKay remained a free man.

33 *Detroit News*, June 14, 1948.

34 *Detroit News*, October 7, 1948.

35 *Detroit News*, January 19, 30, 1950; *Detroit Times*, January 30, 1950.

36   *Detroit News*, February 2-4, 1951, February 13, 1952; *Detroit Times*, February 3-4, 1951.

Chapter 15

1   Rockaway, pg. 212 changed the Keywells' name to "Kushner." The August 20, 1993 obituary of George Kent in the *Detroit News* confirms his kinship to Harry Keywell and his judgeship.

2   Bak (2011), pg. 285; 1930 U.S. Census.

3   Social Security Death Index (SSDI); Kavieff (2000), pg. 200.

4   From his tombstone in Clover Hill Cemetery in Birmingham, Michigan.

5   FBI File, *The Purple Gang*, Vol. 2c, pg. 44.

6   Kavieff (2008), pg. 120.

7   *Detroit Free Press, Detroit News, Detroit Times*, April 17-18, 1933; Kavieff (2008), pg. 27.

8   Bak (2011), pgs. 281, 284.

9   Kaminsky's death date is off his North Versailles, Pennsylvania tombstone. Kaminsky was also a prominent spectator at a Hickey Park prizefight in Pittsburgh, according to the July 30, 1935 issue of the *Pittsburgh Press*. The October 27 and November 6, 1943 issues of the *Pittsburgh Post-Gazette* mention Abe's arrest in the black market gas coupon scheme.

10   Rubenstein and Ziewacz, pgs. 206.

11   Louis Fleisher's life on Alcatraz, his role in the Battle of Alcatraz, and its subsequent trial of the mutineers are detailed in Ernest B. Lageson, Jr., *Alcatraz Justice: The Rock's Most Famous Murder Trial*, Berkeley, CA, Creative Arts Book Company, 2002, pgs. 191-193.

12   *Detroit Free Press, Detroit News*, May 24, 1958.

13   *Detroit Free Press*, April 4, 1964.

14   Kavieff (2000), pgs. 202-204.

15   Both Axler's and Pont's dates of death were taken from the SSDI.

16   Belknap, pg. 4.

17   Bill Dow, *The Jailhouse Rocked When The Red Wings Played In Prison*, Detroit Athletic Co. Website, October 13, 2009, http://blog.detroitathletic.com/2009/10/13/the-jailhouse-rocked-when-the-wings-played-in-prison/. After the Wings got out to the 18-0 lead in the first period, the scorekeeper quit keeping score. Gordie Howe remembered the game fondly, "I deked around their goaltender, put it in the far side and their defenseman was laughing. The goalie says to him, 'I'll kill you, you bastard.' The other guy was so damn good natured and I told him it bothers me that you're in here. He says, 'the worse thing I did was run. I was just cleaning my finger nails with my knife when this guy runs around the corner and ran into it five times.'"

18   Kavieff (2000), pg. 201.

19   Wolff, pg. 1.

20   Abe's date of death in from his Beth El Cemetery tombstone; Kavieff (2000), pg. 204.

21   Both Joe and Izzy's death dates are from the SSDI; Kavieff (2008), pg. 125.

22   Rubenstein and Ziewacz, pgs. 205.

23   Ibid., pgs. 206.

24   *Detroit News*, December 1, 1953.

25   *Detroit Free Press*, January 13, 1965.

26   Rubenstein and Ziewacz, pgs. 205-206; Kavieff (2000), pg. 204.

27   Date of death from the SSDI; Kavieff (2008), pg. 112.

28   SSDI; Kavieff (2000), pg. 204.

29   Detroit News, October 21, 1965; Bak (2011), pgs. 281-282; Rubenstein and Ziewacz, pgs. 209; Keywell's date of death taken from his Machpelah Cemetery tombstone.

30   Belknap, pg. 5.

BIBLIOGRAPHY

Athens, Lonnie, *The Creation of Dangerous Violent Criminals*, Champaign, IL, University of Illinois Press, 1992.

Babel, Nathalie (ed.), *The Collected Stories of Issak Babel; The Odessa Stories; How Things Were Done In Odessa*; New York, London, W.W Norton & Co.

Bak, Richard, *Detroit Across Three Centuries*, Farmington Hills, MI, Thomson Gale, 2001.

Bak, Richard, *Detroitland: A Collection of Movers, Shakers, Lost Souls, and History Makers from Detroit's Past, Detroit*, Wayne State University Press, 2011.

Bari, Frank with Mark C. Gribben, *Under the Williamsburg Bridge: The Story of an American Family*, Victoria, BC, Canada, Trafford, 2009.

Bonnano, Joseph, *A Man of Honor: The Autobiography of Joseph Bonnano*, St. Martin's, 2003.

Burnstein, Scott M., *Motor City Mafia: A Century of Organized Crime in Detroit*, Chicago, Arcadia Publishing, 2006

Cohen, Rich, *Tough Jews: Fathers, Sons, and Gangster Dreams*, New York, Simon & Schuster, 1997.

Critchley, David, *The Origin of Organized Crime in America: The New York City Mafia, 1891-1931*, New York, Routledge, 2008.

Downey, Patrick, *Gangster City: The History of the New York Underworld 1900-1935*, Fort Lee, NJ, Barricade Books, 2004.

Fisher, Jim, *The Ghosts of Hopewell: Setting the Record Straight in the Lindbergh Case*, Carbondale, IL, Southern Illinois University Press, 2006.

Fisher, Jim, *The Lindbergh Case*, New Brunswick, NJ, Rutgers University Press, 1994.

Fried, Albert, *The Rise and Fall of the Jewish Gangster in America*, New York, Columbia University Press, 1993.

Godwin, John, *Alcatraz: 1868-1963*, Garden City, NY, Doubleday, 1963.

Helmer, William J., *Al Capone and his American Boys*, Bloomington, IN, Indiana University Press, 2011.

Helmer, William J., *The Gun That Made The Twenties Roar*, Garland Park, NJ: Gun Room Press, 1969.

Helmer, William J. and Arthur Bilek, *The St. Valentine's Day Massacre: The Untold Story of the Gangland Bloodbath That Brought Down Al Capone*, Nashville, Cumberland House, 2004.

Howe, Irving, *World Of Our Fathers: The Journey of the East European Jews To America And The Life They Found And Made*, New York, Galahad Books, 1976.

Johnston, James A., *Alcatraz Island Prison*, New York, Scribner's, 1949.

Kavieff, Paul R., *Detroit's Infamous Purple Gang*, Chicago, Arcadia Publishing, 2008

Kavieff, Paul R., *The Purple Gang: Organized Crime In Detroit, 1910-1945*, New York, Barricade Books, 2000.

Keefe, Rose, *The Man Who Got Away: The Bugs Moran Story*, Nashville, Cumberland House, 2005.

Kobler, John, *Ardent Spirits: The Rise and Fall of Prohibition*, New York, Da Capo Press, 1993 re-issue.

Kobler, John, *Capone: The Life and World of Al Capone*, New York, Putnam, 1971.

Mason, Philip P., *Rumrunning and the Roaring Twenties: Prohibition on the Michigan-Ontario Waterway*, Detroit, Wayne State University Press, 1995.

Mezzrow, Mezz and Bernard Wolfe, *Really The Blues*, New York, Citadel Underground, 2001 re-issue.

Okrent, Daniel, *Last Call: The Rise and Fall of Prohibition*, New York, Scribner, 2011.

Pasley, Fred D., *Al Capone: The Biography of a Self Made Man*, New York, Ives Washburn, 1930.

Rockaway, Robert A., *But – He Was Good To his Mother: The Lives and Crimes of Jewish Gangsters*. New York, Jerusalem, Gefen Books, 1993

Rubenstein, Bruce A. and Lawrence E. Ziewacz, *Three Bullets Sealed His Lips*, East Lansing, MI, Michigan State University Press, 1987.

Schoenberg, Robert J., *Mr. Capone*, New York: William Morrow, 1992,

Smith, Brad, *Lawman to Outlaw: Verne Miller and the Kansas City Massacre*, Bedford, IN, JoNa Books, 2002.

Taggart, Edward, *Bootlegger: Max Hassel, the Millionaire Newsboy*. Lincoln, NE: iUniverse, 2003.

Turkus, Burton B. and Sid Feder, *Murder Inc.; The Story of the Syndicate*; Da Capo Press, Cambridge, MA, Reissued 1992.

Waugh, Daniel, *Egan's Rats: The Untold Story of the Gang the ruled Prohibition-era St. Louis*, Nashville, Cumberland House, 2007.

INDEX

ACCOLADES

"Dan Waugh has written a vivid and compelling chronicle of the life and crimes of Detroit's infamous Purple Gang. *Off Color* follows the rise of the Purples from their evolution as a street gang through their rise to underworld power and ultimate self-destruction. This book transports readers through the unspeakably dark side of Detroit's Prohibition history. *Off Color* reminds us that while Chicago and New York bootleg wars made headlines, Detroit also had a thriving bootleg market during the 1920s that both enriched and destroyed the gangsters who sustained it."
- Rose Keefe, Author of *Guns and Roses*

"Off-Color is a door opener! Detroit's Purple Gang can run, but they can't hide from Daniel Waugh! This is a true crime odyssey with breathtaking research by one of the best authors in this discipline. The Burnstein brothers ran their criminal racketeering empire next door to Chicago's Capone Outfit, and as he illuminated the Gangs of St. Louis and especially Egan's Rats, Waugh has unearthed the toughest Jewish gangsters of all time with alacrity and a microscopic investigation. We've been waiting for this one for 80 years—it's elegantly crafted, exciting, and so under-the-skin that you can taste the Gefilte Fish and smell the gunpowder!"
- Jeffrey Gusfield
Author of *Deadly Valentines*, www.deadlyvalentines.com

"*Off Color* is the 'Bible' on the Purple Gang. Not only does Daniel Waugh deliver the most comprehensive historical profile on the subject, but he does so in a voice that is positively captivating and entertaining."
- Valerie van Heest, author of the award-winning *Fatal Crossing* and other nonfiction books.